# Hold Your Friends Close

# Hold Your Friends Close

*Countering Radicalization in Britain and America*

SARAH LOGAN

OXFORD
UNIVERSITY PRESS

**OXFORD**
UNIVERSITY PRESS

Oxford University Press is a department of the University of Oxford. It furthers
the University's objective of excellence in research, scholarship, and education
by publishing worldwide. Oxford is a registered trade mark of Oxford University
Press in the UK and certain other countries.

Published in the United States of America by Oxford University Press
198 Madison Avenue, New York, NY 10016, United States of America.

© Oxford University Press 2023

All rights reserved. No part of this publication may be reproduced, stored in
a retrieval system, or transmitted, in any form or by any means, without the
prior permission in writing of Oxford University Press, or as expressly permitted
by law, by license, or under terms agreed with the appropriate reproduction
rights organization. Inquiries concerning reproduction outside the scope of the
above should be sent to the Rights Department, Oxford University Press, at the
address above.

You must not circulate this work in any other form
and you must impose this same condition on any acquirer.

Library of Congress Control Number: 2022941724

ISBN 978–0–19–092032–6

DOI: 10.1093/oso/9780190920326.001.0001

1 3 5 7 9 8 6 4 2

Printed by Sheridan Books, Inc., United States of America

*For my parents*

# Contents

| | |
|---|---|
| *Acknowledgments* | ix |
| *Abbreviations* | xiii |
| Softly Softly: Introducing Counterradicalization | 1 |
| 1. Homegrown extremism, jihadi strategic studies, and the symbolic power of political community | 23 |
| 2. Counterradicalization in global context | 44 |
| 3. For Queen and country: Counterradicalization and political community in Britain | 69 |
| 4. Legislating against homegrown extremism in Britain | 82 |
| 5. A suspect community: Countering radicalization in Britain | 101 |
| 6. To form a more perfect union: Political community in America | 127 |
| 7. Legislating against homegrown extremism in America | 144 |
| 8. Civics, rights, and wrongs: Countering radicalization in America | 167 |
| Conclusion | 188 |
| *Appendix* | 201 |
| *Notes* | 203 |
| *References* | 231 |
| *Statutes Index* | 271 |
| *Index* | 273 |

# Acknowledgments

For many International Relations academics of my generation, the discipline is energized not by the end of the Cold War, as it was for our predecessors, but by the events of 9/11. For some of us, that energy was ignited further by the events of 7/7 in London in 2005. For this Australian, 7/7 found its echo in a series of anti-Muslim riots that occurred in a beachside suburb of Sydney later that year. Ideas of community, identity, and belonging that had long seemed resolved, if not solved, raised their heads and wove their way into public discourse in ways I found shocking—perhaps naively.

The real puzzle began, though, when these ideas found their way explicitly into counterterrorism policy. This book began its life as a conversation with a much valued senior colleague in the corridors of Australia's peak foreign intelligence analysis agency, in 2006. My colleague, Claire Young, had secured a Fulbright scholarship to study counterradicalization programming in the United States. Her deeply informed ideas alerted me to the fact that highly regulated security agencies, tasked with the somber task of managing counterterrorism in the post-9/11 era, were funding measures such as citizenship education classes, sporting teams, and job-seeker programs as ways to counteract the threat of another 7/7. These measures felt very different to existing well-trodden measures, like no-fly lists and deportation and detention, in ways I couldn't yet define. They were also untested and untried, and their success was unmeasurable.

I was intrigued and began my PhD on the topic in the Department of International Relations at the Australian National University (ANU) the following year. My research was generously funded by the ANU, which allowed me a huge amount of freedom to travel for fieldwork and conferences and to collect resources, for which I will always be grateful. I was also supported by an Australian government Endeavour Foundation scholarship, which provided further opportunities to travel, to meet scholars I had always admired, and to spend long months chasing interviews. At the ANU I had the good fortune to be supervised by Dr Jacinta O'Hagan and Dr Ian Hall. Their congenial and knowledgeable support gave me a wonderful basis on which to form the ideas which became this book. In particular, Dr O'Hagan introduced me to Professor James Piscatori, then at ANU's Centre for Arab and Islamic Studies. Professor Piscatori suggested that the root of the puzzle of counterextremism was its conceptualization of political community as both a cause of the problem and its salve. This conversation resonated in ways I didn't appreciate for many years, but certainly do now.

From ANU, I undertook a year of fieldwork. While pursuing interviews with communities and policymakers who were—perhaps unsurprisingly—reluctant to speak on such a sensitive topic, I took up residence in Aberystwyth, New York, and London. I was a visiting scholar at Aberystwyth University in Wales, where I met the incredibly insightful Dr Charlotte Heath-Kelly, whose stellar career I have seen unfold exactly as I expected after our first meeting. I was also a visiting fellow at Columbia University at the Center for Democracy, Toleration and Religion, and at the London School of Economics, where I was lucky enough to take Professor Chandran Kukathas's course on multicultural theory. This course informed my research in important ways by confirming that one of my original approaches, which focused on the puzzle of counterextremism as a function of liberalism, would ultimately be unproductive.

On graduating with my PhD I was introduced by my friend Andrew Zammit, Australia's foremost terrorism researcher, to Dr David Malet. I had admired Dr Malet's work on foreign fighters for some time and gratefully asked his advice on publishing. I also sought advice from my mentor, Professor Toni Erskine, who took the time to talk me through the process. I will be forever grateful for her calm, considered, and extremely effective advice. Professor Madeline Carr also provided consistent inspiration and support throughout, demonstrating the value of collegiality and professionalism in ways which will resonate throughout my career. Professor Lyria Bennett Moses of the Faculty of Law and Justice at the University of New South Wales provided me not only with advice, support, and encouragement, but also with a considerable amount of time to work on the manuscript, funded by the Data to Decisions Cooperative Research Centre. Preparing the manuscript for submission was aided to an enormous extent by the substantial efforts of my colleague, Mary-Louise Hickey, of the Department of International Relations at ANU. Mary-Louise expertly led the manuscript to its final submission, riding elegantly over multiple challenges with editorial skills of which I remain in awe. My erudite friend Gordon Peake also improved the manuscript immensely, engaging with it as both reader and scholar. I also thank my editors at OUP, David McBride and Emily Mackenzie, for their support and consideration. I am particularly grateful for my reviewers, especially reviewer B, whose deep, informed engagement with my work improved it beyond measure.

Worthy of a book rather than a sentence is my husband, Graeme Smith, whom I met during my research. He has brought so many smiles and endless, unwavering support to my work. He continues to do so, though now with the added bonus of the smaller, no less joyful smiles, of our two small sons. I suspect Graeme has already done more childcare than a generation of men before him, all while maintaining his own career, sense of humor, and generosity of spirit.

My siblings have also supported me throughout this process. My brother, John Logan, is a pilot, and has provided flights and endless patience in managing my travel over the years, allowing me to take advantage of many other opportunities I would otherwise have been forced to miss. My sister, Kate Donnelly, knows me better than I know myself and has provided boundless emotional and material support and hours of laughter. For this, but most of all for her absolute unswerving love, I will always be thankful.

My parents, Tony and Wendy Logan, raised me with a deep respect for education and worked hard to provide me with the best they could. They supported me in every endeavor and always believed in my abilities. They are not here to see me complete this book. I imagine them sitting on a verandah somewhere, probably with a small dog nearby, making each other laugh and looking down on me and my siblings, pleased and proud.

# Abbreviations

| | |
|---|---|
| ACLU | American Civil Liberties Union |
| AEDPA | Antiterrorism and Effective Death Penalty Act |
| AQ | Al-Qaeda |
| AQAP | Al-Qaeda in the Arabian Peninsula |
| AQIM | Al-Qaeda in the Islamic Maghreb |
| BCOT | Building Communities of Trust |
| BNPT | Badan Nasional Penanggulangan Terorisme |
| CAB | Community Awareness Briefing |
| CIA | Central Intelligence Agency |
| CREX | Community Resilience Exercise |
| CTITF | Counter-Terrorism Implementation Task Force |
| CTS | critical terrorism studies |
| CVE | countering violent extremism |
| DCLG | Department for Communities and Local Government |
| DHS | Department of Homeland Security |
| DoJ | Department of Justice |
| EPA | Northern Ireland (Emergency Provisions) Act |
| EU | European Union |
| EWIW | Engaging with the Islamic World |
| FBI | Federal Bureau of Investigation |
| FCO | Foreign and Commonwealth Office |
| FISA | Foreign Intelligence Surveillance Act |
| FKPT | Forum Koordinasi Pencegahan Terorisme |
| GEC | Global Engagement Center |
| GSEC | Global Strategic Engagement Center |
| ICE | Islam and Citizenship Education |
| IS | Islamic State |
| MEAP | Muslim Engagement Action Plan |
| MINAB | Mosque and Imams National Advisory Board |
| NATO | North Atlantic Treaty Organization |
| NCTC | National Counterterrorism Center |
| NDAA | National Defense Authorization Act |
| OCRCL | Office for Civil Rights and Civil Liberties |
| OECD | Organisation for Economic Co-operation and Development |
| OSCT | Office for Security and Counter-Terrorism |
| PET | Politiets Efterretningstjeneste |
| PTA | Prevention of Terrorism (Temporary Provisions) Act |
| RICU | Research, Information and Communications Unit |

| | |
|---|---|
| SIP | Strategic Implementation Plan |
| SMSC | spiritual, moral, social, and cultural |
| TPIMs | Terrorism Prevention and Investigation Measures |
| UK | United Kingdom |
| UN | United Nations |
| UNGA | United Nations General Assembly |
| UNSC | United Nations Security Council |
| USA PATRIOT | Uniting and Strengthening America by Providing Appropriate Tools Required to Intercept and Obstruct Terrorism |

# Softly Softly
## Introducing Counterradicalization

In Saudi Arabia, a country not known for being "soft" on security, the state funds programs for young men considered at risk of radicalization as part of its counterterrorism strategy. Somewhat counterintuitively, these measures are less coercive than might be expected. They include religious education, summer holiday camps with four-wheel drive excursions into the desert, and state-approved camp counselors. The state also funds public religious education programs described by Saudi officials as similar to US drug awareness programs or "drink milk" campaigns (Boucek 2008a). Similar so-called soft measures exist elsewhere. In the UK, the Islam and Citizenship Education program, which by 2011 had expanded to two hundred madrassahs, included lessons titled "Good Muslim, Good Citizen" and "Understanding Democracy" (Islam and Citizenship Education 2010: 14; HM Government 2011a: 69). In Germany, the Federal Office for Migration and Refugees runs a "radicalization hotline" for anyone concerned about the radicalization of a relative or acquaintance (BAMF 2013). And in Indonesia, the government's counterterrorism agency initially proposed holding shadow puppet performances to attract attendees back to traditional Javanese culture (IPAC 2014: 5).

Governments progress these measures in a post-9/11 (September 11, 2001) era otherwise dominated by more traditional coercive counterterrorism policies such as restrictions on movement and preemptive detention. Known as counterradicalization measures, these soft approaches exist in states as diverse as Indonesia, Morocco, and the United States. They are designed to address the problem of homegrown extremism, which means acts of violence committed by citizens against their home state, often (but not always) inspired by violent jihadist thought and generally committed on home soil, such as the London bombings of 2005. In this incident, four British citizens, facilitated by Al-Qaeda (AQ), detonated three bombs on the London transport system, killing fifty-two individuals and wounding 700, including many fellow British citizens, and causing widespread fear and panic (see Hoffman 2009 for an overview).

In the post-2001 era, such acts have drawn the attention of policymakers because they form part of an ongoing strategy by global jihadi groups including AQ and Islamic State (IS) which particularly target Western states. Importantly, no conclusive evidence or agreement exists on either the causes of or effective responses to homegrown extremism, especially to the process known by policymakers as radicalization, meaning the process by which citizens are thought to come to engage in acts of homegrown extremism. This means there is little agreement among policymakers working in national security on how to respond effectively to the problem.

But despite a lack of shared understanding of the causes of homegrown extremism and radicalization, and in an environment where these terms are highly contested and where cooperation on counterterrorism policy is generally difficult,[1] counterradicalization strategies across the West and in Muslim majority states share two striking and similar characteristics. First and most clearly, they are integrationist: they aim to make individuals feel more "a part" of the political community—the state—of which they are a member. In doing so, they seek to draw the boundaries of that political community more tightly and to integrate the members of that community more closely, especially those perceived as at risk of radicalization. Second, they are explicitly concerned with persuasion: they seek to persuade individuals who are in danger of radicalization that views about the world held by global jihadists who would seek to recruit them are wrong. They are also concerned with the persuasive capacities of individuals themselves: they target the ability of some already radicalized individuals to persuade others to share their view of the world. These soft measures are in stark contrast to traditional counterterrorism measures, which are concerned more explicitly with coercion.

This study asks why such a diversity of states have responded in such novel and similar ways to a problem on which there is no clear consensus as to its cause, and on an issue—counterterrorism—on which international cooperation is historically problematic (Romaniuk 2010). It seeks to understand how they converge and why this is the case. The study investigates this broad convergence on policy measures initially at a global level, highlighting similarities across jurisdictions. Taking an interpretivist, narrativist approach (Bevir 1999), it offers a deep analysis of counterradicalization policies in two states, the United States and the United Kingdom (UK), in an effort to understand this apparent convergence in practice. The United States and the UK are strong partners in the post-2001 counterterrorism environment. They present a united front on global counterterrorism efforts (Shapiro and Byman 2006; Rees and Aldrich 2005), face similar levels of threat from homegrown extremism, and agree on an ultimate goal of countering the radicalization of individuals toward violent extremism.

In investigating the extent of *convergence* in counterradicalization policy, the study by definition also investigates the extent of *divergence*. Despite their similarities and their history of strong counterterrorism cooperation, US and UK policymakers have approached the problem of homegrown extremism in very different ways. The United States, for example, has very thin counterradicalization policies at the federal level, with little policy detail and comparatively minor attention in the context of counterterrorism. The policies are subject to constitutional constraints and values embedded in those constraints that revolve around concepts of freedom of speech, religion, and association. These policies and associated legislation have been developed in a policy environment where background understandings of citizenship, and of citizen-state relations, are informed by the US history of sedition, immigration and integration policy, and history of domestic terrorism, especially domestic right-wing terrorism.

The UK, by contrast, has very thick counterradicalization policies. These policies have been through successive iterations and have adapted to developments in the recruitment practices of the global jihadi movement and to changes in the local homegrown extremist landscape. They are implemented from the very highest levels of government to local councils, and in schools, hospitals, and doctors' offices. The UK also has a very different post-empire experience of migration and integration, and in the conflict in Northern Ireland, it has experience with domestic terrorism in a way which differs from that of the United States. As in the United States, these experiences form a background for policymakers seeking to understand radicalization and develop policies to counter it. Given the differences between the United States and the UK, this study seeks to understand why and how these states converge and diverge on this policy in important and interesting ways. Building on a small body of work in constructivist terrorism studies (Perliger 2012; Perliger and Milton 2018; Omelicheva 2007; Foley 2009; Katzenstein 2002, 2003), it asks what we can say about patterns in this congruence and divergence on counterradicalization, developing the analysis beyond differences in bureaucratic and governance structures, as per Crenshaw (2001), and into the realm of ideas about citizenship and statehood.

But understanding counterradicalization first requires an analysis of the meaning and power of homegrown extremism, the problem to which such policies respond. As discussed further in the following chapters, the definition of homegrown extremism is highly contested, largely because the definition of terrorism is controversial and difficult. But the strategies of global jihadists are much clearer, and this book argues that homegrown extremism is a conscious formulation of not only material but also symbolic power by global jihadists. Symbolic power refers to an agent's ability to construct a specific perception of reality and that agent's ability to instill the system of meaning associated with that perception in other actors. It means creating an effective set of meanings—often referred to as a "narrative"—of political or social reality and convincing others to accept the validity of these mechanisms (Bourdieu 1991; Perliger 2012).

This book argues that the symbolic power of narratives associated with homegrown extremism rests on ideas about the nature and membership of political community. Using propaganda targeted at potential homegrown extremists, often in the West, global jihadi strategists foster a mismatch between the political community to which homegrown extremists might ordinarily be expected to show allegiance—the state of which they are a citizen—and the political community to which, by their actions, they demonstrate their allegiance—the global jihadi community. This, I argue, explains why homegrown extremists commit acts of violence against their fellow citizens in the name of an organization that is in active conflict with their home state and their fellow citizens.

To understand the impact of this symbolic power, this book unpacks the concept of political community, drawing on literature in citizenship studies and International Relations (Joppke 2010; Gibney 2013; Ruggie 1993). In doing so it emphasizes the distinction drawn in this literature between formal and informal political community. Formal political community is the legal, rights-based political community of which I am a member by definition as a citizen of a particular state. The indicators of membership of a formal political community can include a passport, the right to vote, a social security number, and so on. Informal political community is the values, norms, and ideas that are ideally shared by members of that formal political community, and which mark its members just as formal membership does. Indicators of membership of an informal political community might be a shared language, a shared commitment to "national values," a shared religion, a shared understanding of history, and so on. The boundaries of formal and informal political community are generally congruent—together, they form the basis of the modern nation-state.[2]

The nation-state is by no means the only possible form of political community but has over time evolved to be the dominant form in world politics today and is the chief analytic unit of International Relations scholarship (Ruggie 1993). At its most basic the concept relies on a unity of political authority and territory, which is in itself constitutive of international order (see Phillips 2011: 27; Reus-Smit 2004). The nation-state forms a "system of meaning" shared by all states that participate in international politics (Kratochwil 1989; Katzenstein 2003).

Sociological and historical work on the development of the modern nation-state shows that it combines bounded territory with effective political authority over and for its citizens (Tilly 1992; Spruyt 1994; Skinner 1978; Philpott 2001; Pocock 1975, Wight 2015). This authority is physical, material, and coercive, meaning that a state is defined by the monopolization of force within state boundaries, the ability to effectively project it, and the ability to deliver collective goods to members of that community. However, it is also ideational: this authority is drawn from and legitimized by a "life-world" shared between members. This is Benedict Anderson's "imagined community": the social, moral, and normative bonds providing the basis of the ontological security of the modern nation-state (Anderson 1991) and co-constituting it with material bonds of physical security.[3]

Weber makes this link between the nation and the state clear when he writes of a nation as "a community of sentiment which would adequately manifest itself in a state of its own; hence, a nation is a community which normally tends to produce a state of its own" (Weber 1948: 176).

By political community, then, this study means the grouping of people determined by underlying needs for physical as well as a type of existential security. That is, political communities offer individuals security from physical threats and also provide a "shared life world," which provides for the "creation of shared systems of meaning that articulate and institutionalize a community's most basic moral, social and even spiritual values and ideals" (Phillips 2011: 16). This is the basis of "informal" political community. "Formal" political community is by contrast the material benefits of membership that define a community, such as access to resources and protection and the territorial and legal boundaries that mark the edges of the allocation of those resources.

The congruence of formal and informal political community underpins the system of sovereign states (Kratochwil 1989; Katzenstein 2003). Global jihadism and the homegrown extremism it inspires disrupt this congruence. Here, the affective attachment a citizen might be expected to hold toward his or her political community is missing. Instead, a homegrown extremist demonstrates affective attachment to the global jihadi community and the global Islamic *ummah* framed by that community. This is a different community to that of which they are a citizen, and is definitively a non-state community.[4] In this way, this book argues, global jihadism and the homegrown extremism it inspires institute a disjunct between formal and informal political community. Homegrown extremists belong to an informal political community that is not the same as their formal political community. They do not harbor an affective attachment to the state of which they are a citizen, and indeed seek to act against it.

Homegrown extremism is then by definition a mismatch—a disjunct—between formal and informal political community. Jihadi strategists have developed tools of propaganda to explicitly institute and foster this disjunct, developing and deploying an effective form of symbolic power in the Bourdieusian sense. These tools are employed to recruit homegrown extremists by fostering an attachment to an informal political community—global jihadism—which is at odds with the formal political community of which homegrown extremists are a member by virtue of their citizenship. In making this argument I build substantially on work on transnational Islamism, especially by Mendelsohn (2005, 2012), concerning the tension between the AQ network and the Westphalian system as organizing principles in world politics, applying Mendelsohn's argument to questions of homegrown extremism and counterterrorism policy (see also Wight 2009).

This study argues that even in the absence of conclusive research on the causes of homegrown extremism, states converge in the ways they respond to the problem of radicalization because of the shared threat homegrown extremism poses to a system of meaning they share. This system of meaning concerns the congruence of formal and informal political community, which both defines the nature of the modern state and is challenged by homegrown extremism. Both homegrown extremism and counterradicalization are concerned with a perceived disjunct between formal and informal political community: homegrown extremism seeks to mobilize the symbolic power associated with this disjunct, while counterradicalization intuitively seeks to reinstate it. Counterradicalization policies attempt to embed citizens at risk of radicalization deeper into the informal political community of the state of which they are a citizen—that is, the policies try to realign the boundaries of the formal and informal political community.

Counterradicalization is a "common sense" response to this problem in that it relies on preexisting understandings about the world rather than explicit scientific exploration or consensus.[5] Because there is no consensus on what causes radicalization, or indeed on the solution to it, policymakers fall back on preexisting understandings about the world and "taken for granted" understandings (Schwartz-Shea 2015: 123) or "traditions," meaning the "ideational background" against which individuals, such as policymakers and the audiences they serve, adopt an "initial web of beliefs" about the world (Bevir and Rhodes 2010: 78).

These beliefs about the world inform the intuitive emphasis counterradicalization policies have on ideas, beliefs, and values shared by citizens as they seek to pull individuals more deeply into informal political community shared by citizens. But the ideas and values on which counterradicalization policies focus are not always the same among states. Indeed, by definition they are different. The study argues that despite strong convergence on an overarching push toward integration, states—in this case the United States and the UK—diverge on some aspects of counterradicalization precisely *because* the policy invokes ideas about informal political community: American values are not the same as British values. These values are informed by different histories and different populaces. In particular, the study suggests, they are influenced by their historically informed experiences of citizenship, as embedded in their respective histories of migration and integration policy, and also by their historically informed experiences of citizen violence in each state, including sedition and terrorism. Like counterradicalization policy, these concepts also trade in ideas about national identity and belonging and the beliefs and values that structure these ideas.

## The significance of counterradicalization

Counterradicalization is increasingly prominent in policymaking. States from Canada to Indonesia introduced counterradicalization measures in the years following 2001, and especially following the 2005 London bombings, and the issue draws significant political attention in states across the globe. Multilateral attention is also increasing. Much of the latter has originated in the West, especially the United States, as governments grapple with increasing problems of homegrown extremism, including the newly urgent policy problem of "foreign fighters" fighting under the auspices of IS in Syria and associated battlefields. At the United Nations (UN) in September 2014, President Barack Obama called on member nations to do more to address violent extremism within their regions. In February 2015, the White House convened the first global summit on the problem of violent extremism as a precursor to the UN General Assembly meeting in September of that year. Ministers from nearly seventy countries, the UN secretary general, senior officials from other multilateral bodies, and representatives from civil society and the private sector gathered during the summit to exchange information and work on developing a collective response in the lead-up to the General Assembly.

US-led multilateralism on the issue builds on the creation of the Global Counterterrorism Forum in 2011, supported by the United States and to a lesser extent Turkey. With thirty members (twenty-nine states and the European Union), the forum has at the time of writing five working groups, one of which focuses on countering violent extremism and another that focuses on foreign fighters. The forum has overseen the creation of two independent entities concerned with extremism: the Abu Dhabi-based Hedayah—an international center for relevant training, dialogue, and research—and the Geneva-based Community Engagement and Resilience Fund—the first private multilateral financing mechanism to provide community-based organizations with funding to counter extremism.

Policy attention is not confined to the West. Muslim majority states are also concerned by homegrown extremism, and this extends to the multilateral arena. The Muslim World League organized a three-day anti-extremism conference in Mecca in 2014, and the Organisation of Islamic Cooperation hosted an event on countering radicalization at the UN in late 2014 and has hosted counterradicalization workshops in Niger and jointly with the United Arab Emirates. Chapter 3 also shows that non-liberal Muslim minority states such as China and Russia are active on the issue domestically and internationally.

Despite this increasing policy profile there is a paucity of theoretically informed scholarly research on counterradicalization policy. Conceptually, the issue sits within the broader field of terrorism studies, which is dominated by research and debates concerning the causes of terrorism (Pape 2005; Abrahms 2008; Hoffman 1995; Crenshaw 2011; Wiktorowicz 2004) and definitional debates (Laqueur 1977; Schmid and Jongman 1988) rather than theory-driven work. A notable exception is Colin Wight's 2015 book, which emerges from the field of International Relations and analyses terrorism as a phenomenon in the context of the modern nation-state and political violence (Wight 2015). However, as one of the leaders in the field of terrorism studies notes of his own discipline, it is "an ever expanding intellectual quilt that (has) had a tendency to grow in size but less in layered intellectual depth" (Ranstorp 2007: 14; for overviews of the field to this effect, see Silke 2004; Ranstorp 2007).

A much smaller body of work within the broader field of terrorism studies has focused on counterterrorism, and it is this to which this study contributes. In particular, this study explores factors which shape counterterrorism policy: why do states respond to terrorism in the way they do? An assumption favored in academic, political, and media circles is that counterterrorism policies are shaped by the intensity of terrorist attacks and the material capabilities of states (for brief overviews of this debate, see Katzenstein, Keohane, and Krasner 1998; Fearon and Wendt 2002; Perliger 2012). And most existing scholarship has drawn on rationalist understandings of state interests. These interpretations argue that material interests drive policy adoption, meaning a state adopts a policy if the costs associated with enacting it do not exceed the expected benefits from its implementation. This study interrogates this assumption by delving into the evolution, spread, and underlying structures of counterradicalization policy globally and within two case studies on the United States and the UK.

This study builds on a small body of comparative, historically informed work, which argues that the social and political institutions of counterterrorism policy-making and their social context can also determine a state's response to terrorist violence. It is the first such study of counterradicalization. Crenshaw's (2001) seminal work showed how the bureaucratic history of US counterterrorism policy influenced the government's ability to act on these issues and the nature of the policies it chose to implement (see also Chalk and Rosenau 2004).[6] And the limited body of constructivist scholarship on counterterrorism has examined the role of such factors in more detail and extended the lens of analysis to other social, historical, and political factors. For example, Katzenstein (1996, 2002, 2003) and Leheny (2002) have argued that states' history of conflict determines their counterterrorism responses rather than the nature of the threat they face. In his examination of Germany's and Japan's responses to 9/11, Katzenstein (2002, 2003) shows that their past experiences of the Second World War and of domestic terrorism inform their response to international cooperation in the post-9/11 environment (see also Perliger 2012; Foley 2013; Farrell 2002; Ruggie 1998; Onuf 1989; Kratochwil 1989).

Foley's (2009, 2013) work comparing French and British domestic counterterrorism policies explicitly engages in such an analysis of counterterrorism. He examines substantial differences between British and French responses to domestic counterterrorism and explains these differences as the result of contrasting organizational routines and interinstitutional conventions. In doing so, he outlines the way these factors draw on a rich mix of the history of domestic terrorism in each state, and ideas about state identities and values more broadly. Omelicheva (2007), meanwhile, makes a similar argument concerning the counterterrorism policies of central Asian states. She argues that, as well as material factors, governments' interpretations of the threat are shaped by "ideas about who terrorists are and how much of a threat they pose," which are themselves historically informed (Omelicheva 2007: 376). Arie Perliger's (2012) work is in a similar vein and substantially informs this study. Perliger examines responses to domestic terrorism across a range of liberal states, from weak to strong liberal democracies. Diminishing the importance of the material aspect of the terrorist threat, he finds that the symbolic power of terrorist threats strongly informs state responses.[7] Drawing on Bourdieu, by symbolic power Perliger means the challenge the threat is perceived to pose to the "legitimate" construction or narrative of political reality (Perliger 2012: 506–507, 527).

I use Perliger's work not only to support the argument for the divergence between counterradicalization policies of various jurisdictions, but also to drive the argument that there are also important convergences between counterradicalization policies of different states, specifically the United States and the UK. Following Perliger's work, in Chapter 1, I argue that global jihadi strategists consciously frame homegrown extremism as a type of symbolic power that draws its impact from disrupting the congruence between the formal and informal political community that underlies the modern nation-state. In Chapter 3, I show that despite differences in bureaucratic structures and in the nature of informal political community, broad similarities emerge in the key features of counterradicalization policy globally. I argue that these shared features—a focus on integration and persuasion as counterterrorism measures—are informed by shared experiences and perceptions of the symbolic power inherent in the threat of homegrown extremism, a power cultivated by global jihadi strategists.

Counterradicalization is understudies in the still limited pantheon of academic work on counterterrorism, despite its increasing policy relevance (see Aziz 2014; Kundnani 2014). An important exception is research conducted under the rubric of critical terrorism studies (CTS). Inspired by critical security studies (Krause and Williams 1997; Booth 2004), particularly the Welsh School, CTS seeks to widen the disciplinary base of terrorism studies and counterterrorism studies, working from a set of assumptions that terrorism is "fundamentally a social fact rather than a brute fact" (Jackson, Smyth, and Gunning 2009: 222). CTS is fundamentally normative and approaches the issue of counterradicalization from "an explicit commitment to a set of normative values derived from a broadly defined notion of emancipation" aimed at "ending the use of terrorist tactics (whether by state and non-state actors) and to addressing the conditions that impel actors to resort to terrorist tactics" (Jackson, Smyth, and Gunning 2009: 223, 224; see Jackson 2005; Heath-Kelly 2012; Gunning 2007; Spalek and McDonald 2010 for overviews of the field).

Most, if not all, CTS research has focused on the UK's counterradicalization policy—there are very few studies within CTS on policies outside the UK and no theoretically informed comparative studies.[8] Given its concern with Western liberal states, in the few instances where it has ventured outside the UK, CTS has also by default focused on counterradicalization in liberal, Muslim minority states (see McDonald 2009: 17; Lindekilde 2012; Gutkowski 2011). And CTS largely treats counterradicalization policies ahistorically (see Neal 2012a, 2012b for an elaboration of this critique). There are thus few, if any, attempts to go beyond analysis of initial policy responses to terrorist events.

This study builds on the insights provided by CTS and also those provided by the small and growing body of work on comparative counterterrorism (Perliger 2012; Katzenstein 2002, 2003; Foley 2009, 2013). Adding to existing work on this topic, this study also explicitly centers counterradicalization in a global narrative: as well as the US and UK case studies, it provides an initial global survey of counterradicalization policies including Muslim majority and illiberal states, and focuses on global convergence as well as local divergence. In doing so, it adds a global level of analysis to existing theory-driven analysis, while adding detailed case studies of US and UK counterradicalization policy.

## Definitions

The overriding argument of this study is that counterradicalization policies are similar globally and yet diverge in important ways in the UK and the United States. The terms used to analyze the issue are by nature contentious, and a brief discussion of the definitional issues is useful here.

## Citizenship

Counterradicalization policies often deal in the language and concepts of citizenship, and the two facets of political community outlined in the beginning of this chapter—formal and informal—find their practical expression in the management of membership of the modern nation-state via citizenship. The practice and meaning of citizenship are inherently linked to the nature of political community. Indeed, the "oldest, most basic, and most prevalent meaning [of citizenship] is a certain sort of membership in a political community" (Smith 2001: 1857).

Although terminology varies, key scholars agree that the concept of citizenship has at least three defining characteristics (Joppke 2007: 38). The first is status, meaning *formal* state membership and the rules of access to it. This is essentially a legal characteristic. The second is rights, meaning the formal, legal rights and obligations associated with status. The third is identity, meaning the *informal* beliefs, values, and ideas of individuals acting and conceiving of themselves as members of a collectivity, classically the nation, or the normative aspects of such behavior designated by the state.

"Informal" and "formal" citizenship here refer to the difference between formal markers of membership—citizenship documents, passports, voting practices, and so on—and informal markers such as shared values. Citizenship, then, is both a legal and a normative construct and demarcates both a territorial community and a membership association (Brubaker 1992). Citizenship policies both include and exclude people from such membership and thereby distribute the goods of legal protection, political power, and symbolic recognition.

## Homegrown extremism

There is no commonly accepted definition of homegrown extremism, but a review of literature dealing with this issue highlights two common distinctive features: the idea of individuals being born and raised in the one state—or at least having a strong affective or legal attachment to that state by virtue of residency or heritage—and the idea of individuals or groups acting on their own behalf against the state, often taking orders or inspiration from a group outside that state (Crone and Harrow 2011). Precht (2007) highlights the fact that most examples of homegrown extremism in the post-2001 era are discussed in the context of Muslim minority states in the West, despite the increasing importance of far-right homegrown extremism in many of these states. He suggests that we understand homegrown extremism as "acts of violence against targets primarily, but not always, in Western countries in which the terrorists themselves have been born or raised." He qualifies this suggestion by adding that a "distinctive factor of home grown terrorism is that it is carried out by persons who have had their formative phase, upbringing and cultural influence in the Western world" (Precht 2007: 15). Genkin and Gutfraind (2011: 3), meanwhile, emphasize the importance of citizenship by suggesting that homegrown terrorism should be conceived of as "terrorist acts that are carried out by groups whose membership is composed entirely or predominantly of the native-born citizens of the country that is being attacked."[9] This broader approach allows us to consider acts of homegrown extremism in Muslim majority states which broadens the scope of enquiry beyond the Western world, as in Chapter 3.

Chapter 2 details a spectrum of homegrown extremism in the post-9/11 context, from attacks by citizens of the West wholly organized from a distance by leaders in the global jihadi space, to lone actors operating of their own volition but inspired by global jihadism, to waves of foreign fighters in AQ and IS-defined battlegrounds. Underscoring the delineation of this spectrum is the acknowledgment that homegrown extremism concerns a conceptual disjunct between formal and informal modes of citizenship: between formal membership of a state and an absence of attachment to its normative values and identity. In this book, the term is used to describe acts of political violence committed against the state by its citizens or those who might otherwise be expected to have such an attachment via residency, for example. Such violence can be inspired by ideological frameworks such as animal-rights extremism or far-right extremism and some jurisdictions such as the United States, the UK, and Germany are at pains to emphasize that their counterradicalization programs apply to all types of political violence. However, the fact remains that in most jurisdictions where counterradicalization exists, it focuses almost exclusively on homegrown extremism generated by the broader geopolitical and ideational framework of transnational jihadism, emphasizing the role of political frameworks external to the state in inspiring or directing such action.[10]

Mendelsohn (2012: 590) analyses the role of jihadi visions of world order in promoting visions of political community which challenge the primacy of the state. He refers to radical transnational Islamist groups like AQ as "couriers of systemic challenge," who "interpret religion as a source of global order and act to realise this vision." Homegrown extremism, then, involves a clash between the informal markers of two self-defined political communities: the broader global jihadi political community, and the smaller, more defined political community of the nation-state of which the actor is a member. It refers to violence perpetuated against such a political community by individuals who are formal members of that political community, but who see themselves as members of a larger political community defined in almost wholly "informal" terms.

As Perliger (2012) argues, terrorism is inherently concerned with perpetuating an alternative vision of political community: the violence of terrorism is symbolic of a larger political project (see also Wight 2009, 2015). Terrorist attacks are a form of symbolic power used to communicate a political message aimed at challenging the hegemonic and "legitimate" narrative of political reality (see also Crenshaw 1981: 379; Wight 2015: 120–121). Acts of terrorism by citizens against their own state, then, take on a particular importance. They are claims by citizens about the nature of their own political reality. In liberal democracies in particular, these claims step knowingly outside normal democratic procedures and thus make a claim about the *type* of alternative they propose (Wilkinson 2011).

One of the important debates within discussions by policymakers on homegrown extremism is the difference between homegrown extremism and homegrown violent extremism. The latter refers only to violent acts, while the former includes the holding of ideas which may lead to violent acts. This study uses the former term as a way to encompass policies targeting both violent and nonviolent homegrown extremism, thus encompassing significant differences in two case studies and in the way the issue is discussed globally. "Extremist" views are implicitly understood in most policies as leading to an increased propensity for violence. Points of disagreement concern the nature of the process as well as the meaning of extremism itself. The latter is contentious and undefined in almost all of the jurisdictions in which counterradicalization policies exist. The concept is rarely subject to deep scrutiny and is inherently dependent on context (Neumann 2013: 878).

## Radicalization

There is little consensus on what causes radicalization in the context of homegrown extremism, or even what the term means, given continuing debate about the meaning of extremism and violent extremism (see Schmid 2016 for an overview of the problem of definition). For example, Della Porta and LaFree (2012), in a special issue of the *International Journal of Conflict and Violence*, used and/or quoted seven different definitions alone in their introduction. As Dalgaard-Nielsen (2010: 797) writes, even though the "topic has become 'hot' in policy circles the empirical knowledge base remains weak." This judgment is echoed by one of terrorism studies' leading scholars, who writes that "[d]espite over a decade of government funding and thousands of newcomers to the field of terrorist research, we are no closer to answering the simple question of 'What leads a person to turn to political violence?'" (Sageman 2014: 567). Above all, researchers agree that radicalization is a complex phenomenon which cannot be classified or researched easily (Neumann 2013). There are no prominent studies that use verifiable methodological procedures, for example (for an overview of these issues, see Spaaij and Hamm 2015).

For the purposes of this study, radicalization is a process which may take different forms and meanings depending on how states define the endpoint of homegrown extremism—that is, the underlying basis of the definition is its relationship to homegrown extremism, which is itself a contested term. In all cases, varying definitions share an element of transformation toward a particular state defined by behaviors, and occasionally thoughts and views, which situate individuals under the rubric of homegrown extremism associated with post-9/11 global jihadism. The concepts of process and linear transformation underlie the definition: radicalization is the "process whereby people become extremists" (Neumann 2013: 874).[11]

Although it has existed in policy discourse since at least the 1970s (Schmid and Price 2011), radicalization has received a barrage of policy attention in English-language academia in the years since the Madrid bombings of March 11, 2004 (3/11) and the London bombings of July 7, 2015 (7/7).[12] This has led to the development of various models of radicalization, all of which seek to understand the process by which individuals move to a position where they commit violence against their own state in the name of a value system located outside that state. Models of radicalization are many and varied. They range from the staircase model, which portrays radicalization—including homegrown extremism—as a process of six consecutive steps culminating in terrorism (Moghaddam 2005), to the "pyramid" model (McCauley and Moskalenko 2008), which suggests that the small number of people who turn to terrorist action are at the apex of a much larger group of sympathizers who share their beliefs and feelings, to the "conveyor belt approach," which sees a timeline between nonviolent extremist beliefs and violent homegrown extremism (Baran 2005). Others link radicalization to structural socioeconomic issues while some link it to processes of identity, self-esteem, and belonging (Kepel 2004; Roy 2006).

Empirical evidence is inconclusive. For example, an extensive interview-based study by the US Department of Homeland Security found that the only generalizations which could be made were that homegrown extremists were overwhelmingly male and about two-thirds were under the age of thirty (Schanzer, Kurzman, and Moosa 2010: 10). This is echoed by British government research which also suggests there are no broad socioeconomic trends in homegrown extremism (Travis 2008; see Crone and Harrow 2011; Dalgaard-Nielsen 2010 for an assessment of different models). Other waves of influential scholarship draw on network theory and social movement theory to provide insights into radicalization (Sageman 2008c; Wiktorowicz 2002, 2004; Gunning 2009; Lindekilde 2008; Olesen 2009, 2011). They approach the problem as driven by a jihadi-inspired collective identity that can be usefully thought of as a bottom-up process, whereby recruits self-generate an ongoing narrative of collective persecution and a collective identity defined by contentious politics and rallying against Western oppression, and which militates adherents to act based on a core narrative of grievance and oppression.

These social network scholars argue that the narrative that influences radicalization drives a crudely sketched, amorphous *transnational political community* that is fluid in geographic and "formal" terms but by definition has clear "informal" values-driven boundary lines along which radicalized individuals can arrange themselves and their worldview (Neumann and Rogers 2007). As discussed in Chapter 1, there exists a conscious attempt by AQ-core and, more recently, IS, to create a crude narrative of such a community, which is now to some extent self-perpetuating. Some research has found a strong collective identity framework among radicalized Muslims in the West around a global oppressed "Muslim" identity (Wiktorowicz 2004; Neumann and Rogers 2007).[13] Adamson, Triadafilopoulos, and Zolberg (2011) point out that this identity consciously transcends other ethnic, national, or sectarian identities. In the case of homegrown extremism, this identity transcends membership of the political community defined by membership of the state. Although studies of radicalization rarely agree on the pathway to homegrown extremism, problems of identity and belonging are common to most theories, even those outside the general framework of social movement theory (see, for example, Dalgaard-Nielson 2010).

Radicalization, in this context, is an inherently preemptive and temporal concept, describing a *process* which occurs over time, with an endpoint—extremism—that policymakers seek to avoid and is ill-defined. This, along with the lack of clarity concerning the causes of radicalization, results in a lack of conceptual clarity in counterradicalization policies. Adding to confusion, ideas are regularly recycled. For example, the White House's first major summit on violent extremism focused on the concept of the "root causes" of radicalization, a cause last in vogue in the first decade of the twenty-first century and one which is at odds with recent influential research on social network theory (White House 2015; Kepel 2004). Despite policy innovation, then, the problem of understanding the process of radicalization persists.

## Counterradicalization

Counterradicalization refers to policies that seek to arrest the process of radicalization, despite the absence of research on its causes and the absence of consensus on its meaning. Counterradicalization is a distinctive form of counterterrorism, but differs from other counterterrorism policies in both intent and form. On the former, counterradicalization differs from traditional counterterrorism policies in that it is preemptive and concerned with a process rather than a specific act.[14] In contrast to traditional counterterrorism policies, which address behaviors at the point at which they occur or afterward, counterradicalization is concerned with addressing the "process whereby people become extremists" (Neumann 2013: 874). In enacting these policies, states seek to engage in an intervention in timelines, and they focus on individuals in the context of the risk of those timelines unfolding. Other terms are also used by policymakers to describe these policies. The most prominent of these is countering violent extremism (CVE). The term preventing violent extremism has also emerged. CVE is used most prominently in the United States, and increasingly in the academic literature, although the UK and many European governments continue to use the term counterradicalization. This study uses "counterradicalization" in preference to CVE precisely because the former emphasizes the process-driven and time-dependent goals common to all policies described by these terms.

Importantly, another group of policies outside the scope of this study are called "deradicalization" policies. These policies seek to change the views of an individual who is already radicalized, and often of those who have demonstrated this by committing a violent act. Deradicalization policies are often found in prisons, or in the context of ex-offenders, and the policies are designed to reintegrate those individuals back into society, using similar "soft" reintegrative techniques to those described in counterradicalization policies. Indonesian deradicalization policies, for example, focus on counseling and on finding ex-offenders jobs and wives. Nigerian programs have included vocational education and art therapy (Barkindo and Bryans 2016), and the Saudi deradicalization program has included art therapy, vocational training, and religious counseling (Boucek 2008a). Deradicalization policies, then, target those who have already committed violent acts and seek to reshape their thinking, which has already developed beyond the point of violence. Such policies target a different point in time in the context of the violence of homegrown extremism—they are post hoc rather than precursory. This study treats the two types of policies as analytically separate, although they share important similarities. It uses the term counterradicalization to reflect the process-driven nature of radicalization and to reflect the fact that separate, related, policies exist that also use this terminology.

Counterradicalization policies also differ from traditional counterterrorism in their form. Traditional counterterrorism practices are explicitly coercive. They seek to force limitations on the movement and activities of terrorists. No-fly lists, detention without trial, changes in policing practices, and so on are all classic counterterrorism policies. By contrast, although they are still a subset of policies that are ultimately concerned with coercion, counterradicalization policies are explicitly concerned with persuasion rather than coercion. This is apparent in two ways. First, counterradicalization policies are concerned with integrating members of the community rather than removing them. They seek to make individuals feel a part of their community, focusing on the values and ideals of that community, and realigning the boundaries of informal political community. As a result, the policies focus on the way individuals *feel* about their lives, the world, and their community. Informal political community is driven by ideas about the world, and counterradicalization policies seek to influence these ideas.[15] Second, counterradicalization policies are also concerned with the persuasive capacities of individuals who are *already* radicalized, and who would otherwise have the capacity to inculcate others with their worldviews. This is because it seeks to counter the appeal of the worldview perpetuated by jihadi narratives, as discussed in Chapter 1. This explains why counterradicalization policies can include restrictions on speech, on incitement, and on the publication and sharing of material. These practices are in many ways coercive, in that they restrict individual freedoms, but they are nevertheless explicitly concerned with persuasion.

Unsurprisingly, given the absence of consensus on what causes radicalization, there is no consensus on what counters it. The empirical chapters in this book show that counterradicalization policies traverse a wide range of policy and legislative platforms in an attempt to achieve the goal of stopping people from becoming homegrown extremists. They can include such diverse measures as holiday programs for young men considered at risk of radicalization, as in Saudi Arabia, or changes in migration and integration regimes, the propagation of online counternarratives, and plays about "British Islam" in schools.[16] Such measures echo the fluidity and scope of post-9/11 counterterrorist regimes: their ambit goes beyond specifically labeled legislation and policy measures, and counterterrorism regimes in general shift constantly in response to the evolution of threats and domestic policy concerns (Finn 2010).

Aside from the problems of understanding what causes radicalization itself— and even defining it—measuring the efficacy of counterradicalization measures and thus arriving at consensus on "what works" is methodologically fraught. Most studies lack control groups or counterfactuals to substantiate their findings (Cragin 2014). Indeed, measuring a negative outcome (counterradicalization) in the context of a fraught definition of radicalization is almost impossible.[17] Despite this underlying lack of clarity, at least two trends have emerged in recent years in some counterradicalization policies, especially among Western allies. Analysis focusing on the role of social networks is increasingly prominent in counterradicalization policies (Meleagrou-Hitchens 2011). The concepts of social networks, narratives, and counternarratives appear regularly in policy documents that aim to counter homegrown extremism, suggesting that these concepts are gaining utility as a means of explaining the processes of radicalization (White House 2010, 2011c; HM Government 2011a). Indeed, one of the main proponents of using social movement theory to analyze homegrown extremism, Quintan Wiktorowicz, was the first appointment to the US National Security Council to oversee US engagement with Muslim communities.

This focus on radicalization as a process of social movements, networks, and narratives—as a problem of persuasion—has increased the prominence of the internet in discussions concerning counterradicalization, although debates rage about the utility of the internet as an effective radicalizing agent. These arguments focus, for example, on whether significant numbers of individuals can be radicalized via the internet, or whether offline social structures are key, and the problem of collecting empirical evidence for these claims (see Sageman 2008a: 111; Stevens and Neumann 2009; Conway 2017; Edwards and Gribbon 2013). Despite these debates, policy responses err increasingly on the side of addressing online radicalization. Internet-based initiatives have formed a significant component of counterradicalization initiatives in recent years, with the United States, Saudi Arabia, the UK, and Singapore, among others, each developing specific policies and bodies to address it. The UN has also developed a working group on the issue, and both the European Union and NATO have initiated similar programs in recent years, as has the Global Counterterrorism Forum. However, it is important to note that trends do not indicate consensus. As discussed previously, counterradicalization policies cover a wide range of approaches and can simultaneously include old and new ways of thinking about the problem.

## Convergence and divergence in counterradicalization

In an environment characterized by the absence of conclusive research, and driven in many cases by fear and politicized understandings of the problem, counterradicalization falls back on assumptions and common sense understandings about the nature of the problem and its solution.[18] The empirical chapters of this study, Chapters 3–8, focus on two case studies, the United States and the UK, in the period from the introduction of counterradicalization policies to the 2016 presidential election in the United States and the 2015 general election in the UK.[19] These case studies use the development of counterradicalization policy in the United States and the UK as a lens through which to investigate convergence on counterradicalization policy, but also, by default, to investigate the extent and nature of divergence on these policies. These case studies are chosen as most similar case studies: because they are similar, rather than—as is common in most comparative studies—because they exhibit variation. In this approach the study responds to an important methodological critique of comparative analysis, which holds that an extensive focus on explaining variation is a limitation of the comparative approach (see Caramani 2010; Van Kersbergen 2010). Rather, this study seeks to explain how, and why, two similar cases exhibit differences on important details of the policy.[20]

The United States and the UK exhibit significant general similarities, and also similarities specific to the post-2001 era. They share a conception of the liberal democratic political sphere and important related strains of political culture, including the rule of law, separation of powers, bureaucratic specialization, and the independence of mass media, according to Almond's (1956: 392–393) classic formulation of Anglo-American political culture. They also share a strong embedded conception of the Anglo-American concept of the rule of law (Dicey 1962), with its roots in a shared philosophical tradition of rights-based liberalism drawing on a shared political, intellectual, and cultural heritage. The United States and the UK also exhibit a similar framing of the threat from homegrown extremism, seeing it as both severe and imminent: it has been listed as a high-level threat in both countries' national security policies and each has devoted space in their counterterrorism policies to it and devised standalone policies. This shared framing of the threat level is unsurprising given the close transatlantic security alliance and their close cooperation on the "war on terror" in the post-2001 environment.

But despite these similarities, the United States and the UK exhibit differences in important details of their counterradicalization policies. They have each introduced policies which are integrationist in intent and persuasive in a manner common to other policies globally. But US policies are far less ambitious than their British counterparts in attempting to address the way US citizens think about the world and choose to act upon those thoughts—that is, in directly countering the persuasive power of jihadi narratives. Significant differences exist at the level of policy design and orientation that are not explained only by differences in bureaucratic structures (see Crenshaw 2001). US policies are far thinner, despite the threat from homegrown extremism being framed by policymakers as among the most high-level security threats faced by the United States during the period this study addresses. There has been one wide-ranging, federal-level policy initiative in this period, with minimal funding, and the policies began only some years after the first known attack, despite the threat level having been raised at this point. Such reluctance extends to the failure of the US Congress to pass legislation equivalent to UK legislation addressing certain forms of homegrown extremism via a reduction in citizenship rights for perpetrators.

By contrast, the UK policy is wide-ranging and multiscalar, comprising a suite of extensive policies over several levels of government. UK policies also engage closely with a wide range of individuals, from children to prison detainees and returnees, and with the teachers, nurses, and social workers who interact with them. British legislation has expanded the definition of terrorism to include the expression, and glorification, of certain ideas by British citizens, and has directly addressed the question of the congruence of formal and informal citizenship by linking citizenship rights for dual citizens to radicalization policy. More recently, the UK has publicly targeted US technology companies to take an active role in preventing terrorism, including homegrown extremism (Asthana and Levin 2017). The United States has been reluctant to adopt policies that explicitly target individuals considered at risk, while such policies are increasingly prominent in the UK (see Mastroe 2016; Bjelopera 2013).

Some of these differences are due to important structural differences between these communities—between a federal and a unitary system, for example. But others are due to the values and ideas associated with political community—what citizenship means and what it looks like in practice. These are not explicit differences, but they are reflected in "common sense" understandings that come to the fore in the absence of conclusive research interacting with formal institutions and structures. The notion of "taken for granted" or "common sense" understandings is particularly relevant in the context of counterradicalization given a lack of understanding of the causes of radicalization and the highly politicized environment surrounding counterterrorism policy in the post-2001 era. The task of the empirical chapters, then, is to detail how, and ask why, UK and US counterradicalization policies both converge and diverge, and in doing so help to better understand how UK and US policymakers "make sense of their worlds," and the "intricate, evolving connections between taken for granted understandings and practices" (Schwartz-Shea 2015: 123).

The empirical sections begin with preliminary chapters—Chapter 3 for the UK and Chapter 6 for the United States—that lay out three axes I use to analyze "common sense" understandings of political community, which I argue form the backdrop to counterradicalization policy in each. The first of these axes is the values that define the informal political community in each jurisdiction. These introductory chapters begin by engaging in a short literature review on the nature of "American values" and "British values" respectively. The second axis is the history of migrant citizen and integration policy in each jurisdiction. Migration and integration policy are manifestations of political community: they clearly set out the meaning and practice of membership of a formal political community and link it to ideas about national values and informal political identity. As Smith (1997: 31) argues, these sorts of laws and policies designate the criteria for membership in a political community and the key prerogatives that constitute membership. He writes that they are "among the most fundamental of political creations . . . they proclaim the existence of a political 'people' and designate who those persons are as people." The third axis is the history of measures against and instances of citizen violence against the state in each jurisdiction—of precursors to what we might now call "homegrown extremism." These include a brief outline of the history of sedition in the United States and the UK and of previous domestic terrorism and counterterrorism measures targeted at citizens in each. This shows us what policymakers have done or have not done or at least considered possible in the past, and in some cases indicates what may or may not be possible in the current situation.

I operationalize the case studies by constructing a policy history of counterradicalization in the United States and the UK, taking a narrativist, interpretivist approach to this task (Bevir 1999). I use legislative and policy documents to construct this history and to establish the broader arguments about convergence in counterradicalization policy globally, arguing that they demonstrate the underlying ideas and beliefs that shape and drive this narrative. The two bodies of empirical material—legislative and policy documents—each offer particular value in adding to the study of counterterrorism policy more generally. As Neal (2012a, 2012b) points out, much scholarship focused on post-9/11 counterterrorism has concentrated on the executive branch—often rightly so given the dominance of this branch of government in the post-9/11 environment. Examining policy documents allows access to this thinking in a public form designed to frame the problem and its response for the broadest possible audience, distilling the policymaking process to its desired outputs.

However, this study also examines legislation in the UK and the United States respectively, in Chapters 4 and 7, especially beyond the initial emergency responses to 9/11. Activities of the legislative arm of government serve to "refine and crystallize public debate" and their resultant texts provide a useful body of evidence of this debate (Oleszek 2013: 2). To this end, this study examines all legislation dealing with counterradicalization and the problem of "citizen terrorists" more broadly in the post-9/11 era in the United States and the UK until the 2015 UK general election and the 2016 US presidential election—thirteen pieces of legislation in total. Following Neal (2012a, 2012b), this approach elicits not only a demonstration of executive overreach in rushed emergency legislation, but also evidence of a broader, arguably more considered response in legislation, which encountered resistance or at least further debate in both the UK Parliament and US Congress.[21]

Policy documents were sourced from searches in the national archives in both the United States and the UK for material dealing with homegrown extremism or radicalization. In the United States, this was a simple procedure. Federal counterradicalization policy is relatively recent and comprises few publicly available official documents. In the UK this was a rather more complicated process. Outlines of counterradicalization policy in the UK have emerged from at least three different government departments since 2001, in the context of standalone policies and as part of multiple broader counterterrorism policy reviews. They range from clear policy outlines to policy guidelines and policy reviews. I identified policy statements that resonated across both forms—specific policy outlines and broader counterterrorism documents—as both were clearly linked in the broader policy statements. In doing so I identified policy statements from the UK Home Office, the Department of Communities and Local Government, and the Office for Security and Counter Terrorism that used the same language and were released as part of the same overall counterterrorism policies. These judgments were confirmed by a whole-of-government review of the policy conducted by a new government in 2011, which listed key policy documents. Three reviews of the policy and the issue conducted by committees in the House of Commons in 2009, 2010, and 2012 also assisted in confirming the policy documents selected for analysis.

Aside from primary policy and legislative texts, I also make use of secondary material where relevant. This ranges from congressional hearings, debates in Congress and Parliament, and civil society statements on counterradicalization and homegrown extremism. This material assists in establishing the policy narrative, and broadens the discussion of the policy as a "collective activity" within the narrower analytic focus on policy and legislative texts (Bevir and Rhodes 2010: 100–115; see also Bevir 1999). Twelve interviews with policymakers and civil society representatives were conducted in both the UK and the United States in order to make sense of, and contribute to, this broader narrative undertaking.

The empirical chapters show that, as expected, there is certainly convergence between UK and US counterradicalization policies. Both are integrationist, in that they seek to draw more closely the bounds of informal and formal political community. They are both also concerned with persuasion—they focus on the problem of persuasion and seek to persuade the individuals they target of ideas about the world and their place in it, and they each focus on curtailing the persuasive powers of those who would seek to inspire homegrown extremists. But the two policies are also different, and in important ways. This study argues that differences in understandings of the nature of citizenship and political community, especially informal political community, influence these divergences beyond structural differences. For example, informal political community in the United States is defined by "constitutional patriotism" and clearly defined values, beliefs, and ideas associated with constitutional rights to freedom of speech and association. In contrast, informal political community in the UK is far less defined and is subject to conjecture driven by the ebb and flow of history—particularly the history of empire—in different ways.

# 1
# Homegrown extremism, jihadi strategic studies, and the symbolic power of political community

In 2005, nine Australian men were arrested on a range of terrorism charges associated with plans for large-scale attacks on infrastructure in Australia's largest cities. The men were inspired by AQ, although the network was almost entirely homegrown (Harris-Hogan 2013). In 2010, a forty-two-year-old Singaporean cleric, Muhammad Anwar Jailani, was charged under Singapore's Internal Security Act for distributing extremist material originally produced by AQ propagandist Anwar al-Awlaki (Lee 2016). In 2014, a thirty-year-old Somali-born Dutch national was arrested in the Netherlands as part of an international network providing financing for al-Shabaab operations in Somalia (*DutchNews.Nl* 2014). In 2015, a young Danish citizen was shot dead in Copenhagen after killing a security guard at a synagogue and a filmmaker at a freedom of speech debate associated with a cartoonist who had been targeted by AQ for producing cartoons it deemed blasphemous (Chrisafis 2015). And in 2017 a twenty-two-year-old British citizen, Salman Ramadan Abedi, detonated a bomb at Manchester Stadium in the UK in 2017, killing twenty-two and injuring eight hundred after allegedly becoming radicalized in the UK and traveling to Libya to meet with IS militants (Dearden 2017).

The individuals committing these acts are all described in press and judicial material as homegrown extremists, but what unites such a broad array of acts and levels of violence? What could possibly be equivalent between the dissemination of online propaganda and the murder of twenty-two individuals, or the wiring of funds to a distant conflict? Homegrown extremism can mean many things, but a common thread underlies most uses of the term. The unifying factor here is the citizenship status of the individuals involved. Homegrown extremism is defined by the membership of perpetrators of the political community against which they commit their attacks—attackers are citizens, or permanent residents, or otherwise identifiable as members of that community. Attacks like these are committed by homegrown extremists in the name of *another* political community—in this case, the global Islamic community, as defined by decades of jihadi strategy and propaganda. It is the symbolism of the actor committing violence against members of their own political community in the name of another which unites these otherwise disparate acts. This chapter situates homegrown extremism in the context of jihadi strategy and traces its evolution as a terrorist strategy over time. In doing so it shows how homegrown extremism, like all terrorist acts, is an act imbued with potent symbolic power in the Bourdieusian sense.

## The symbolism of terror

Terrorism is almost impossible to define, but common among most definitions is the move to differentiate terrorism from other forms of violence. Scholars do so by describing terrorism as marked by an emphasis on symbolic communication, driven by a mismatch in physical capability between terrorists and their adversaries. Crenshaw (1981), for example, describes terrorism as "symbolic violence" used to communicate a political message aimed at challenging the "legitimate" construction of political reality or associated narratives. In this view, terrorism is a violent act whose different components such as timing, the actors involved, and the targets selected combine as a communicative act to convey meaning to audiences in order to "impact the perception of reality and one's place in it" (Schmid and Jongman 1988: 7).

In practice, this means that terrorism is associated with the *symbolism* of violence as much as the materiality of violence because it is via the symbolism of targets and methods that material differences can be overcome and messages effectively communicated. It explains why terrorists might target passenger planes, visually spectacular or iconic locations, or civilians or politicians. These targets have symbolic as well as material value: terrorists are unable to meet the material forces of their targets—for example, the military might of the United States—and so adopt symbolic violence in an attempt to even the ledger. The Twin Towers in New York, for example, were centers of financial power as well as physical buildings and workplaces for thousands of individuals. Symbolic value and the symbolic power of an associated attack can also be drawn from a terrorist group's goals. Arie Perliger (2012: 507) finds that revolutionary terrorism, meaning terrorism which has as its goal the overthrowing of modes of political organization, has the most symbolic impact, arguing it is reasonable to assume that "the components of the terrorist acts that are associated with, or symbolize, values and norms that directly challenge the existing socio-political order will elevate the symbolic power of the act."

Acts of terrorism by citizens against their own state, then, take on a particular salience. They are claims by citizens about the nature of their own political reality. In liberal democracies in particular, these claims step deliberately outside normal democratic procedures and thus make a claim about the *type* of alternative they propose (Wilkinson 2011). Because they are citizens, homegrown extremists activate the symbolism of citizenship when they attack, elevating the symbolic power of the attack itself. Citizens are not meant to act violently against other citizens in the name of a political community other than the state. When they do, they are a key component of the attack, and a key component of its message. This message shapes the perception of (political) reality by disrupting the practices of citizenship and political community. Homegrown extremist attacks are a form of symbolic power used to communicate a political message aimed at challenging the hegemonic and "legitimate" narrative of political reality (Perliger 2012). Formal citizenship, or membership of a political community, is defined by congruent membership of a formal and informal political community: jihadi strategy aims to disrupt that congruence via the employment of symbolic power promoting an alternative vision of political community.

In making this argument I draw strongly on Perliger's work on symbolic power and counterterrorism policy. Taking a Bourdieusian approach, he argues that counterterrorism responses to domestic terrorism are shaped by the symbolic power of terrorist attacks, noting that they "take into consideration the sensitive relations between the regime and its citizens in democracies, including the effect on civil liberties, separation of powers, and minority-majority relations" (Perliger 2012: 493). Perliger avoids applying his work to international terrorism, arguing that international counterterrorism brings into play bilateral considerations and international norms and institutions. This book adapts Perliger's work to counterradicalization policy, which bridges the worlds of international and domestic terrorism.

## Bourdieu and symbolic power

The concept of symbolic power is widely used in a range of disciplines, from International Relations to Political Science and Communication Studies. The concept is founded on Bourdieu's set of central "thinking tools" developed to analyze the nature of "taken for granted" or common sense understandings between agents and the lack of commonality between agents from different backgrounds, in an effort to historicize and account for these understandings and changes within them (Samuel 2013: 399). Symbolic power is one of these tools, described by Bourdieu as the power to make people believe and see certain visions of the world rather than others. It is a "power of constituting the given through utterances, of making people see and believe, of confirming or transforming the vision of the world and, thereby, action on the world and thus the world itself" (Bourdieu 1991: 170). Other "thinking tools" fundamental to

Bourdieu's work include the concepts of habitus, field, and capital. It is beyond the scope of this book to analyze their relationship with homegrown extremism, although some scholars of terrorism do adopt them in their work.

For Bourdieu (1989: 20), symbolic power is driven by processes of categorization of the social world. He sees the social world as organized by social actors into a symbolic system—a "legitimate vision of the world" for those social actors who share it. This system draws on, reinforces, and influences the material world by dividing material characteristics via terms which ascribe meaning to difference. In his description of class, for example, Bourdieu shows that the characteristics of social agents—for example membership of certain clubs, certain habits, and certain ways of dress—are signifiers of membership of a certain class and thereby of difference. These characteristics are material, and they have material affects when used as markers of group identity, but they derive their power from the binary relationships they signify via language: between upper class/lower class, elite/non-elite, and so on. One might think here of the group identity marked by a political community and of the difference between citizen and non-citizen, drawing on the "common sense understanding" of sovereignty imbued in the post-Westphalian system of territorial states and implicitly shared by all citizens. One might also think of categories of believer and disbeliever, used to differentiate groups on the grounds of religious affiliation. These categories have material implications and draw on material realities (birthplace, location, markers of religious practice) but are also binary ordering categories in themselves. These categories, and changes in them, in turn have material consequences.

Bourdieu seeks to understand the interplay between agency and structure in the concept of social change, meaning how and why social change occurs, and the role of agents, groups, and structures within that change. Adapting his work to the study of homegrown extremism draws on a larger movement in terrorism studies toward sociological and relational explanations for terrorism. Moving on from studies that emphasize psychological or root causes, work in this vein has emphasized social and relational causes (e.g., Wiktorowicz 2004; Sageman 2008b; Berntzen and Sandberg 2014; Vertigans 2013). Wiktorowicz's (2004) work, for example, explicitly draws on social movement theory to understand radical Islamic activism and mobilization of individuals into what is often a high-risk, high-cost endeavor, especially in Western democracies. This work draws on scholarship on transnational Islam (Roy 2006; Mandaville 2009) and transnational social movements and migration (Adamson, Triadafilopoulos, and Zolberg 2011), which build on similar concepts, and also seeks to understand the impact of Islam, radical Islam, and associated terrorist networks as identity movements.

Although there are few researchers in terrorism studies using a broad Bourdieusian approach, this is in keeping with the discipline's generally atheoretical focus on practical, policy-related research. The concept of symbolic power is certainly implicated in some discussions of policy responses discussed in the empirical chapters, especially discussions of narratives and counternarratives. Some theoretically driven analyses of terrorism and counterterrorism have adopted Bourdieu's work as a way to situate policy responses into broader theoretical literatures. Perliger (2012) is the scholar who has adopted the idea of symbolic power most directly. But Bourdieu's broader work, and other conceptual tools of habitus, field, and capital, outlined briefly below, are also used in Neal (2012a) and Stampnitzky (2013) to explain policymakers' motivations, and in some critical terrorism studies (e.g., Gunning and Jackson 2011) to understand the production of knowledge about counterterrorism policy. Bourdieu's concepts have also found a place in recent work within terrorism studies which analyze processes of radicalization. Ilan and Sandberg (2019), for example, adapt Bourdieu's work on identity formation and habitus to a study of the crime–terror nexus, while Crone (2016) applies the concept of habitus to Sageman's (2008a) "group of guys" theory regarding radicalization, analyzing how ideas flow between social networks.[1]

These later works focus on the way ideas are translated into material action. For Bourdieu, the relationship between symbolic power and the material, objective world is understood via the concept of *fields*. A field is a cluster of practices, like the practices of citizenship, for example, bound together by relatively autonomous internal logics, but which coexist within a broader space recognizable to members of different fields. Examples could include the field of economics, the field of politics, or a particular collective identity. Symbolic power exists whenever the arbitrary nature of a field's structure and rules is forgotten and understood only as natural, meaning it is accepted as the "unthought premises of social interaction" which Bourdieu refers to as the *habitus* (Samuel 2013: 401). Symbolic power is, then, "the power to make the world by imposing instruments for the cognitive construction of the world" (Bourdieu 2002: 170). One might think here about social change such as the idea of a woman's right to work outside the home. Here, the economic field in many contexts has adjusted, and this means the *habitus* of individuals in that space includes an unthought premise that women *do* work outside the home where previously they did not. This change came about via a number of factors, but certainly included the operation of the symbolic power of the state via the enactment of legislation.[2] Such legislation changed the official and everyday definition of work, pay, and implicitly "woman," with material effects. One might also think of the symbolic power of associated public figures, able to implement change by demonstrating or agitating for it themselves.

Bourdieu argues that although they may appear set, distinctions in language and their relationship to the material world are constantly at play. They contain "a degree of indeterminacy and vagueness, and, thereby, a certain degree of semantic elasticity" (Bourdieu 1989: 20). This is not only because language itself is fundamentally subjective but because the material world is also constantly subject to change. Words can mean many different things to different people, and the characteristics they describe may (indeed almost certainly will) change over time and between individuals. We can see this in changing definitions of citizenship over time, for example, in the nature of values applied to informal political communities over time, and the ways they are enforced and materialized. The meaning of what it means to be "American" or "Australian," "European" or "Indonesian" can change over time, then, even if the specific terms used do not. The indeterminacy of social categories and the tension within them helps us to understand the existence of the "plurality of visions of the world" which is itself linked to the "plurality of points of view" (Bourdieu 1989: 20). Just as there is no timeless and stable definition of a word as a social category, there is no timeless and stable meaning of the group or classification it denotes.

This indeterminacy means that determining a "legitimate vision of the world" in a social space is an exercise in symbolic power. As Bourdieu puts it, the necessary and inescapable plurality of viewpoints "provides a base for symbolic struggles over the power to produce and to impose the legitimate vision of the world." This is the struggle for "common sense" understandings of the world and is "the stake par excellence of political struggle" (Bourdieu 1989: 20, 21). In the context of terrorism, this is the "legitimate" construction of political reality which terrorists seek to alter and which states seek to maintain. He writes of such construction: "The power to impose and to inculcate a vision of divisions, that is, the power to make visible and explicit social divisions that are implicit, is political power par excellence. It is the power to make groups, to manipulate the objective structure of society" (Bourdieu 1989: 23). The primary power which drives the successful imposition of "legitimate visions of the world" is symbolic power, which he describes as a power of "world-making," a power of constitution (Bourdieu 1989: 22).

The struggle for this world-making power is essentially one of categorization. Those engaged in the struggle to legitimate their worldview of appropriate divisions of society can employ objective means such as a protest, for example, or an act of violence. But they can also employ subjective elements, such as the manipulation of the schemata of classification and perception via the use of particular vocabularies, or by the construction and reconstruction of historical narratives, or by the selection of targets with specific symbolic meaning. These are symbolic struggles with material impacts.

For Bourdieu, symbolic power is operationalized via battles over schemata of perception—the categorization of the social world. The upper hand in these tussles can be obtained by ordination from those who have existing amounts of what Bourdieu describes as "symbolic capital." This is the "sum of economic or cultural capital" when it is "known and recognized"—that is, evident in material or symbolic fields (Bourdieu 1989: 21). Bourdieu (1989: 22, 1998: 33) notes that states, which produce the "official classification of a common sense understanding of the world," are the "supreme tribunal" of such struggles. This is certainly the case in the context of formal citizenship, where states are the ultimate arbiters of this sort of group membership and its meaning and the associated way it structures perceptions of the world. But people with widely recognized positions of power, for example, may also possess substantial amounts of symbolic capital and denote their approval of others, or of ways of viewing the world, via its exercise. For Bourdieu (1989: 23), symbolic capital is "the power granted to those who have obtained sufficient recognition to be in a position to impose recognition." He is thinking here of official spokespeople, for example, or leaders, or elites. One might think here of *fatwas* issued by clerics, or of authoritative readings of religious texts, or current events shared online by influential media actors. One might also think of national discourses around identity—commentators opining the changing nature of "Britishness," for example, or tracking the impact of migration on "the American dream." Bourdieu (1989: 24) also allows for the fact that this power can be self-proclaimed. He writes that a class, nation, people, or other group may exist if and when there are "agents who can say that they are the class, by the mere fact of speaking publicly, officially, in its place and of being recognized as entitled to do so by the people who thereby recognize themselves as members of the class, people or nation."

Given that constructions of the social world are prone to shift, certain factors contribute to the effectiveness of stability or disruption of such categories. For Bourdieu, the effectiveness of symbolic power—the force with which it can institute the objective and symbolic mechanisms of "group making" and the stability of the common sense understanding it imposes—rests on two conditions. The first is the symbolic capital held by those who seek to engage symbolic power: they must have the social authority to do so. Second, efficient activation of symbolic power depends on its relationship with reality. The construction of social categories—of groups and ways of viewing the world—cannot be constructed as a mere fantasy. As Bourdieu (1989: 23) writes: "Symbolic power is the power to make things with words. It is only if it is true, that is, adequate to things, that description makes things." Important in this context is the interplay between categorization of Muslim identity in state discourses, and in discourses of Muslims themselves, and between actual foreign policy or domestic events, and the way they are perceived and narrated by jihadi actors. As Schmid (2014: 7) notes, "the strength of al Qaeda's single narrative is that much of it is grounded in grievances and perceptions that many Muslims—perhaps even a majority in some countries—actually believe to be true." It also points to the problem of the unintended consequences of counterextremist work reinforcing categories which ground grievances (e.g., see Parker and Davis 2017; Vertigans 2010). Official narratives and counternarratives regarding the problem of homegrown extremism can reinforce the categories and grievances found in terrorist master narratives (see de Graaf and de Graaf 2010; Schmid 2014; Russell and Rafiq 2016: 8).[3]

## Symbolic power and political community in jihadi thought

The role of symbolic power in understanding homegrown extremism derives from the impact of a jihadi "master narrative" on homegrown extremism. Widely recognized by scholars and policymakers alike,[4] this narrative is perpetuated by jihadi actors and is one that frames events, relationships, and goals in terms of a transnational anti-Western identity. It serves to foster a sense of an aggrieved transnational Islamic identity which can serve as a worldview which drives and justifies acts of violence, including by homegrown extremism (Sageman 2008a: 139). A jihadi worldview may be seen as a "world-making" capacity associated with symbolic power as identified by Bourdieu. Broadly put, the jihadi narrative seeks to categorize historical events, current political identities, and the future in terms of a binary believer/non-believer identity. As Schmid (2014: 6, emphasis in original) writes of AQ, "[t]here is a *vision of the good society*: a single political entity—the Caliphate—that replaces corrupt, apostate rulers under Western influence, by rule under *Sharia* (Islamic Law) wherever there are Muslims so that Allah's will be done and order is restored." Halverson, Goodall, and Corman (2011: 20) write that:

> [T]he reason the narratives of al-Qaeda and other Islamist extremists carry such potency is because they possess an internal coherence for their intended audiences that connects them to grand, deeply culturally embedded, views of history—to master narratives—that Muslim audiences, in broad terms, readily understand, identify with, or feel little need to question. As an exercise in transhistorical pattern recognition, those narratives, and their connection to master narratives, contain powerful persuasive messages that not only resonate or "ring true," but also compel a certain level of ideological identification, behavior, and actions.

This approach frames the ummah—a global, informal, political community—as a contrast and a challenge to nation-states and the sovereignty they accrue in the international system.[5]

The roots of modern global jihadism and its narratives lie largely in the anticolonial movement in Egypt and one of its leading thinkers, Sayyid Qutb (see Ryan 2013; Pasha 2019; Al-Barghouti 2008). Qutb's work has a particular perspective on political community that resonates with the master narrative perpetuated today. His work analyzed global politics from the perspective of a binary global crisis of values, solvable only by the active promotion of Islam on a global scale. He saw an underlying conflict between Islam and the values of the nation-state, drawing on the work of an earlier thinker, Abul A'la Maududi, to argue that "Islam is a revolutionary ideology and program which seeks to alter the social order of the whole world and rebuild it in conformity with its own tenets and ideals" (quoted in Ryan 2013: 51).

Such lofty goals draw strongly on the Islamic concept of *hakimiyyah*, broadly translated as sovereignty, and its relationship to the validity of secular state structures in the Islamic world. For Qutb, and those who draw on his work, national sovereignty is at odds with Islam, as it requires Muslims to submit to a secular authority, when the only valid source of such authority is Allah.[6] The attention paid by Qutb and others to this concept draws strongly on the impact of the First World War on the geopolitics in the Middle East. For example, global jihadists continue to draw on the Sykes–Picot agreement, signed in 1916, as a source of grievance. As AQ's second-in-command Ayman al-Zawahiri wrote in 2009, for example, "[s]anctifying national unity is one of the rotten fruits of the Sykes-Picot agreement, which divided the Muslim Ummah into various pieces of booty, in order to plunder the wealth left over from the Ottoman Empire" (quoted in Ryan 2013: 157). And Osama bin Laden referred to it directly in a 2003 communique, naming the George W. Bush–Tony Blair axis as the new Sykes-Picot agreement, and IS have used it as a touchstone in propaganda videos (Hamdan 2016).

References to Sykes-Picot in jihadi communications suggest that secular state structures and the role of great powers in dividing up the Islamic world drive an understanding of modern nation-state sovereignty as problematic in global jihadi struggles, for reasons both theological and historical. Qutb frames what he sees as the problematic status of modern nation-states in terms of *hakimiyyah* by highlighting the fact that sovereignty belongs to Allah alone, and that therefore Muslims must reject all hybrid laws and constitutions. He urges his readers, for example: "Do not permit the sovereignty of Allah to be compromised with mixtures of other legal systems" and predicts that "[u]ltimately, Islam will be the global Islamic ummah which will not be a nation but a community of revolutionary Salafist countries or nations welded together by their adherence to the Sharia and loyalty to the Caliph" (quoted in Ryan 2013: 52). This community, then, is driven by the values of an informal political community, Qutb arguing that "the only bonds we have are the bonds of Islam" (quoted in Ryan 2013: 55).

It is important to note that the actual acquisition of territory has long played a role in jihadi tactics and that sometimes control of this territory looks like a form of state control. The acquisition of territory can provide a base for jihadis to wage war against the United States and the West and provide a population on whom jihadis can impose strict Islamic governance in demonstration of their ideological purity.[7] As Lia (2015: 33) notes, protostates such as the Islamic Emirate of Afghanistan and the Islamic Emirate of Somalia have long been favored by jihadi actors as a way of furthering ideological goals. For Lia, these goals are consistent with the broader narratives of global jihadism. He argues that they are "intensely ideological projects" and inherently internationalist. By this he means they are established in the name of theologically inspired goals and that as a result their commitment to a *particular* territory is relatively low.

The emergence of IS in approximately 2014 is an important development in the long history of protostates in jihadi thought. Although its fortunes are still unfolding at the time of writing, at one point IS controlled territory in Syria and Iraq about the size of the UK, which was in recent times occupied by up to ten million people (Speckhard and Yayla 2015: 96). And like some other protostates but even more intently, IS instituted measures at the height of its control which approximated state bureaucracy, in the form of tax collection, infrastructure maintenance, and even vaccination programs (see Tinnes 2015, 2016, 2017, 2018 for a four-part bibliography on IS). As McCants (2015) argues, however, IS's acquisition of territory is driven by an entirely religious framing, with apocalyptic overtones: it is driven by values which privilege a religious, global form of political community over the state. In this context, attention to the structures of bureaucracy is a mode of population management instituted in response to the group's earlier defeats and as a demonstration of ideological purity rather than an attempt at statehood itself (see McCants 2015: 99–120; Lia 2015: 37). For Winter (2015) and others (Zelin 2015; Mahood and Rane 2017), one of the most consistent themes in IS messaging is the idea of a "utopia caliphate." As McCants (2015) points out, the apocalyptic undertones present in IS messaging means that this theme is inherently concerned with *ontological* security, rather than an attachment to territory. Here, like earlier protostates, the proposed caliphate's political community is defined primarily by informal citizenship—religious belief—rather than the congruence of informal and formal political community which defines the modern nation-state. As Lia (2015: 38) notes, for jihadi strategists, territory represents simply a tactical front in a larger transnational insurgency with multiple focal points and a largely de-territorialized support base.

Mandaville (2009: 499) describes this approach to political community as an underlying "global anti-systemic militancy," meaning that jihadi thought challenges not only the concept of sovereignty but international sovereignty as a whole (Mendelsohn 2005).[8] In one of the few bodies of work theorizing terrorism in the context of International Relations, Mendelsohn (2009b: 666) argues that one of jihadism's most distinctive features is its approach to sovereignty,[9] and that the global jihadi narrative draws heavily on this thinking: "jihadis reject the anchoring of political life in a secular institution such as the state, or the division of the global terrain into independent separate states bounded by rules and norms that are set through practice or man-made (rather than divine) decisions." This "anti-systemic militancy" comprises historical narratives of grievance, the identification of a global struggle against the West and, as a result, a framing of global politics as contentious politics, with adherents to global jihadi ideologies on one side and the West and other infidels on the other, and can be adapted to local or individual grievances with ease.[10] Mendelsohn (2012: 592) notes that unlike many other transnational, religiously motivated actors, global jihadism's master narrative is not embedded within the state-based order but provides an alternative model. This model challenges states' monopoly over the use of coercive means and sovereign political authority as well as the authority and legitimacy of the institutions of international society (see Mendelsohn 2005; Philpott 2002: 83–92).

For Mendelsohn (2012: 593), the challenge is to what he describes as "organizing principles": the "fundamental authority structure of world order," meaning "the source of universal authority, the status of the units comprising it and the order in which they relate." As he points out, the state-based principle of territoriality creates an inside/outside distinction, meaning states have exclusive authority within their own boundaries, but no authority outside those borders. This means that other states are free to choose which good to pursue and the means to achieve it. In this way, the Westphalian system allows for—and indeed depends upon—the capacity for multiple visions of the good. In a religiously inspired order, however, "the source of authority is one, and it demands exclusivity, denying the existence of any other truth but its own" (Mendelsohn 2012: 595). Mendelsohn (2012: 590) coins the term "couriers of systemic challenge" to describe jihadi actors who "interpret religion as a source of global order and act to realize this vision."[11]

In this way, homegrown extremism, particularly in the West, is not only an act of political violence; it is a claim about political community. It says of the perpetrator: "despite the formal markers of my membership I am not a member of this political community and in fact I wish to act against it." This claim is made in the name of a larger, almost wholly "informal" political community. The narrative that establishes such a boundary—for example, between infidels and non-infidels, between observant Muslims and non-observant Muslims— is described by Wiktorowicz (2004: xi) and other social movement theorists as boundary activation: "making one of several previously existing divisions among social locations so salient that it suppresses other divisions and organizes most political interactions around (or across) that division alone." Adamson (2011: 900) describes this process in the context of global Islamic politics as strategically deploying the "category of 'Muslim' as a means of constituting and representing an identity community for political purposes, thereby creating a constructed constituency that transcends other ethnic, national or sectarian identities."[12]

## "Couriers of systemic challenge": Homegrown extremism in jihadi strategy

Global jihadism in the way we understand it today emerged in the mid-1990s in response to Bin Laden's adoption of an anti-US doctrine in 1996, which switched the emphasis of militant Islam from domestic socio-revolutionary action in Arab states to the global stage, reasoning that focusing on the United States and its allies would precede a second, more established goal—political change in apostate states in the Middle East (Hegghammer 2006). This shift was contextualized by scholars[13] who took up the challenge of debating the strategy, tactics, and inspiration of this move—usually described in the literature as the move from a near enemy (apostate states) to a far enemy (the United States and its allies). This move shows how, like all acts of terrorism, homegrown extremism is situated in the context of material mismatch between perpetrator and target and adapts symbolic violence as a way to overcome this disparity. This strategic choice is embedded in larger thinking about political community outlined in the previous section.

Occupying a stream of thought usefully described as "jihadi strategic studies," jihadi texts and debates on strategy provide a useful source on the way homegrown extremism is formulated as a strategic move by leaders within this broader context (Hegghammer 2006: 28–30). The "strategic studies" genre emerged in the early years of the twenty-first century and has as its main purpose identification of best possible approaches to defeating the enemy. This activity draws on a range of thinkers and texts that are described in great detail in important scholarly works such as those by Hegghammer (2006), Lia (2009), McCants (2015), and Ryan (2013). The following paragraphs do not reproduce this scholarly work, but rather draw on it to provide an outline of the thinking of key figures who have contributed to the development of homegrown extremism as a strategic undertaking in the context of global jihadism.[14]

In the post-2001 period, AQ leaders found themselves managing the consequences of a devastating defeat in Afghanistan by US-allied forces. Writing from this period highlights the issue of homegrown extremism more closely, largely in the context of a reassessment of tactics to deal with the post-2001 environment, where AQ's material resources were massively reduced.[15] This led to an increasing focus on the role of individuals in jihad, and of symbolic attacks by Westerners, as a way to overcome material constraints. For example, the book *Knights under the Prophet's Banner* was written by key AQ commander al-Zawahiri in the context of the loss of AQ's safe haven in Afghanistan. In writings similar to those later published by AQ tactician Abu Musab al-Suri, al-Zawahiri focuses on the need for individual jihad "against the client rulers" of regional apostate states and their "masters in Washington," and highlights jihad as an individual obligation for Muslims everywhere. In his description of a "third circle" of jihadi activity, outside regional battlefields, he refers to the utility of what we might call homegrown extremism in the battle against the United States and its allies: "if the spread of battle were to reach into their houses and bodies, would they not exchange charges with their clients concerning who was negligent in their role? . . . Therefore, we must move the battle to the land of the enemy in order to burn the hands of those who light the fires in our lands" (quoted in Ryan 2013: 108).

The writings of influential strategist Ahmad al-Qurashi appear in a series of articles on military strategy between 2002 and 2003 and build on similar themes. Al-Qurashi sees the propaganda aspects of warfare as among the most powerful, as they strike fear into the hearts of rulers (see Ryan 2013: 103–111). He argues that all acts of jihad have a psychological effect and marks every individual act of jihad as an instrument of propaganda. Importantly, while urging physical attacks in the "heart of America," he also highlights the importance of propaganda in the "international" dimension, noting that the manifestation of international discontent in one's enemies, is one of the key components of revolutionary war. Al-Qurashi notes the importance of the internet in delivering such propaganda, and for distributing instructions—for example on bomb-making (Ryan 2013: 124).

One strategist in particular explicitly advocates tactics of homegrown extremism in pursuit of global jihadism's strategic goals. Al-Suri, who released *The Global Islamic Resistance Call* in 2005,[16] led a shift in jihadi thinking which further facilitated the growth of homegrown extremism. Al-Suri argued that the centralized, hierarchical, and regional jihadi organization model, which had hitherto characterized AQ operations, had outlived its role and that a more appropriate model was "the jihad of individual terrorism," practiced by self-contained autonomous cells. Indeed, given the reality of post-9/11 politics, al-Suri argued that individual jihad was the best option for most. Adapting leftist guerrilla thinking to the new AQ context, al-Suri called for individual resistance as a response to the unavoidable might of US-led invasions in Iraq and Afghanistan (Ryan 2013: 227). This could include training or fighting at home—including in the West—using whatever means available (Lia 2008: 536). Al-Suri emphasized the importance of spontaneous attacks by individual jihadists in the United States and its allies, and their importance in creating propaganda,[17] which would draw the support of the global Islamic community to the cause (see Cruickshank and Hage Ali 2006 for a useful view of al-Suri's thought). Indeed, al-Suri emphasized the importance of propagandists in generating the "global Islamic resistance," especially of young Muslim men around the world looking for ways to participate (Brachman and McCants 2006: 314–316). Lia (2009: 537) characterizes this as religious, ideological, and spiritual indoctrination privileged over physical training.

Al-Suri saw these attacks of "individual resistance" not only as a way to exact revenge on the United States, but also as a way to unite the global ummah. It was this which was behind both his thoughts on propaganda and his musings on the power of the internet as a training medium and as a powerful conduit for strategic communication. He saw the creation and sharing of propaganda as a type of jihad—clearly and influentially outlining the role of those who did not want to engage themselves in violent conflict but wanted to participate.[18] Unsurprisingly, al-Suri's writings have been found in properties associated with the 2004 Madrid bombings as well as in premises associated with other bombings in Spain, Italy, and Germany (Lia 2009).

Jihadi media strategies undoubtedly become more important in the years following 9/11, as along with an emphasis on propaganda they compensated for AQ's reduced capability to commit acts of terror. Similarly, an emphasis on individual acts of terrorism as outlined above compensated for the inability of jihadis to plan large-scale attacks or to act in the homelands. As Lynch (2006: 1) argues, in the years following 2001, AQ underwent "a 'constructivist turn,' employing not only violence but also a dizzying array of persuasive rhetoric and public spectacle toward the end of strategic social construction." In 2005, two days after the London bombings, AQ-core's then second-in-command, al-Zawahiri wrote to Abu Musab al-Zarqawi, leader of AQ in Iraq, of the importance of media management, noting: "We are in a battle, and more than half of this battle is taking place in the battlefield of the media . . . we are in a media battle for the hearts and minds of our Ummah" (Al-Zawahiri 2005).

Jihadi organizations developed specific media strategies to operationalize the symbolic power of the master narrative as propaganda. AQ's media wing, As-Sahaab, released its first propaganda video—online and in VHS form—following AQ's successful attack on the US warship *USS Cole* in 2000. At this point, its videos sought to "awaken the Islamic ummah to revolt against America," primarily by attracting recruits to Afghanistan (Kohlmann 2008: 99). Following AQ-core's loss of its Afghan base in 2001, this process turned increasingly to facilitating the globalized "leaderless jihad" Sageman (2008b) identifies, with products influenced increasingly by al-Suri's ideas.

In line with the strategic approach of al-Suri and others like him, global jihadi media operations have involved specific targeting of Western audiences in an attempt to recruit and inspire homegrown extremists (see Ciovacco 2009; Soriano 2007 for further overviews of AQ-core's media strategies). Scholars have traced a shift in media from highly centralized distribution and production to a more dispersed model, with an emphasis on high production values (see, for example, Veilleux-Lepage 2016; Farwell 2014; McCants 2015). These efforts have been enhanced by the development of internet technologies, but also reflect the strategic thinking outlined in the previous section. The most prominent examples of this turn, outlined below, have involved American or European citizens, speaking in English in products distributed online and urging their fellow citizens to act, and English-language products targeted explicitly at Western markets. Although debate rages about the actual radicalizing effect of these efforts (Von Behr et al. 2013; Conway 2017; Lemieux et al. 2014), they are important examples of attempts by AQ-core and other actors to foster the "semblance of unity and purpose" Sageman (2008c: 39) describes, particularly in the context of homegrown extremism.

Perhaps the most important media producer in this regard was Anwar al-Awlaki, a US citizen killed by a targeted drone strike in Yemen in 2011. Al-Awlaki was widely recognized as a key propagandist and an important actor in the Western jihad movement. His activities showed a deliberate attempt by an AQ-core member to inspire homegrown extremists, especially in the West. A lecture, "Constants of Jihad," which he delivered in 2005 and which circulates widely online, is a useful example here. A popular translation of key Islamic texts, and a framing of their messages in the context of global jihad, the sermon called on Western Muslims to act against their own governments, arguing: "Jihad is global. Jihad is not a local phenomenon. Jihad is not stopped by borders or barriers . . . Jihad does not recognize borders that were drawn by some colonial countries in the past, that are drawn by a ruler on a map and then Muslims are supposed to abide by them" (quoted in Meleagrou-Hitchens 2011: 9).[19] He also emphasized the online environment as a valid site of individual jihad, noting in a 2008 publication that:

> Some ways in which the brothers and sisters could be "internet mujahidin" is by contributing in one or more of the following ways: establishing discussion forums that offer a free, uncensored medium for posting information relating to jihad; establishing e-mail lists to share information with interested brothers and sisters; posting or e-mailing jihad literature and news; and establishing websites to cover specific areas of jihad, such as mujahidin news, Muslim prisoners of war, and jihad literature (quoted in Awan 2010: 11).

Prominent English-language publications and online entities facilitated by AQ-core and targeted at inspiring homegrown extremists flourished around this time (Brachman and Levine 2011; Watts 2012). In March 2010, As-Sahaab released an English-language video entitled *A Call to Arms*, featuring a US-born spokesperson, Adam Gadahn. The video, directed at jihadists in the United States, Israel, and the UK, praised an attack by Major Nidal Hasan in glowing terms and held him up as an exemplary figure for having struck at the heart of the United States, and in absolute defiance of his "unbeliever" commanders. Hasan was a US army major who fatally shot thirteen people on a US military base in 2009, having been in contact with al-Awlaki. Gadahn used the example of Hasan to call on other Muslims in the "Crusader West," especially in the United States, UK, and Israel, to undertake lone-actor attacks. He advised his listeners to focus on targets that would do serious economic damage to these countries and pointed to 9/11 to show that such attacks need not necessarily employ conventional firearms. In a June 2011 English-language video message, headlined *Do Not Rely on Others, Take the Task upon Yourself*, Gadahn more clearly emphasized lone-actor operations.

Another prominent English-language production targeted Western Muslims even more clearly. Produced by AQ affiliate Al-Qaeda in the Arabian Peninsula (AQAP), the online magazine *Inspire*, first released in July 2010, had high production values, magazine style content, and was produced entirely in English. It featured a section entitled "Open Source Jihad," encouraging homegrown extremists. Its first issue featured instructions on how to make a bomb from commonly available kitchen materials—instructions which were reportedly used by the Boston marathon bombers in 2013, among others. Later editions praised lone-actor terrorists in Sweden and the UK. In its fourth edition, of Roshanna Choudry, a UK citizen charged with terrorism after she stabbed her local member of parliament, the magazine wrote:

> Through her actions, she proved to the world the power of a borderless loyalty: Islam. The ummah, and specifically its mujahadin, are waiting to see more people of her caliber. We say to the kuffar: the borderless loyalty is a religious sentiment of the people in your midst. As long as the Muslims remain in your focus, you will remain in ours. No matter the security precautions you may take, you cannot kill a borderless idea. (AQAP 2011)

Here, as in other extracts quoted earlier, there is an emphasis on the disjunct between membership of a formal political community and that of a larger transnational informal political community.[20] *Inspire*, as the embodiment of al-Awlaki's vision, marks a key shift in strategy from organizationally led jihad toward "DIY" terrorism, or "open source" jihad (see Lemieux et al. 2014; Rudner 2017).

This emphasis is reinforced by evolutions in jihadi messaging and activity driven by the rise of IS and associated shifts in the global jihadi landscape (see

McCants 2015 for an outline of AQ-IS tensions and their impact on tactics). IS's sophisticated use of messaging to target foreign fighters, for example, has engendered new forms of propaganda (Bodine-Baron et al. 2016; Farwell 2014). Prospective recruits can use social media platforms to learn about what battlefield life is like, and to contact facilitators. For example, in June 2014, just as the Caliphate was declared, IS produced a thirteen-minute English-language video, *There is No Life Without Jihad*, featuring testimonials from self-identified British and Australian foreign fighter citizens, encouraging other Westerners to join. An online magazine, *Dabiq*, produced by IS media group al-Hayat was first released in January 2014 and last published in July 2016. The magazine was striking because of its sleek and sophisticated production, and it was published in a number of languages, including English, French, and German. Like *Inspire*, it included commentary that both congratulated and urged acts of homegrown extremism, especially in the West.[21] Issue 6, for example, released early in 2015, praised lone-actor attacks in Australia, Canada, the United States, and France, noting: "The Muslims will continue to defy the kāfir war machine, flanking the crusaders on their own streets and bringing the war back to their own soil" (quoted in Ubayasiri 2019).

IS has also benefitted from the advent of web 2.0 services, especially the rise of social media.[22] Unlike earlier jihadi content, IS media production is almost entirely decentralized and fast-paced and relies on a two-tiered production line. There are multiple "official" production units, often attached to battlefield groups. Unofficial creators and disseminators of IS-associated content on social media played an important role in propagating IS-associated content, building on the idea of online work as an act of jihad. Disseminators are described in one study as "unaffiliated but . . . broadly sympathetic individuals who are deeply invested in the conflict" (Carter, Maher, and Neumann 2014: 1). This study shows that key "disseminators" are in fact citizens of Western countries states and that many are outside the physical battlefield of IS and associated groups (Carter, Maher, and Neumann 2014).

By allowing the group to project strength and gain visibility, IS-affiliated social media accounts have inspired recruits from all over the world. Indeed, IS propagandists "have openly singled out for recruitment 'he' who 'lives in the West amongst the *kuffar* [disbelievers] for years, spends hours on the internet, reads news and posts on forums'" (quoted in Kohlmann and Alkhouri 2014: 2). Recent research on the narrative frames embedded in IS propaganda show that this material actively engages notions of civilization identity: framing the "West" as an oppositional identity (Ingram 2017; Baele, Boyd, and Coan 2019; Lorenzo-Dus, Kinzel, and Walker 2018) and, like its predecessors, actively lifting notions of political community beyond the state (see Laghmari 2019 on the influence of Qutb's writing on IS civilizational narratives). As Baele et al. (2021: 14) note, this narrative plays a distinct role in radicalization strategy: "When presented to a European or American audience, such a depiction of the West sharpens group differences and erases the possibility of holding multiple identities at once, thereby encouraging Western Muslims who feel disenfranchised by their society to think that they can neither practice their faith nor live happily in a Western country." Although debate rages over the impact of the internet on radicalization, the discursive structures that it enables play an important role in cultivating a "leaderless jihad," providing a "tolerant, virtual environment," and facilitating a "semblance of unity and purpose'" despite geographic dispersal (Sageman 2008c: 38; Conway 2017; Pearson 2018). It plays a role in facilitating the informal aspects of political community outlined earlier in this chapter—values, beliefs, and ideas.[23]

## From money to murder: The spectrum of homegrown extremism

Today, states must respond to homegrown extremism with a range of policies. The policy problem is driven by a threat that is fundamentally symbolic, directly engaging symbols of political community. In addition, as jihadi tactics have changed in response to material pressures, the nature of homegrown extremism has evolved. Within the broader strategic impulses and master narrative outlined here, policymakers must now contend with an increased spectrum of behaviors employed by jihadi strategists but also identified as dangerous behaviors by states themselves. The spectrum of homegrown extremism activity shows that as tactics, strategies, and battlefields changed, so did the nature of homegrown extremism.

There are three broad categories of homegrown extremist acts within this spectrum of behavior: (1) attacks coordinated by core global jihadi leadership, (2) lone-actor attacks, and (3) attacks by foreign fighters. These categories are united by the fact that the acts of violence are committed by citizens against citizens.[24] The spectrum along which they sit is defined by the level of control exhibited by global jihadi organizations and networks over the organization and individuals involved in attacks. Until the emergence of IS onto the international stage in approximately 2010, this core leadership group could usefully be referred to as AQ-core, although now it is far more disparate.

At one end of the spectrum are attacks committed by Western citizens directed by AQ-core members and often the result of years of planning. The arrest in 2001 of British citizen Richard Reid, the so-called "shoe bomber," is a useful example of this sort of plot, involving a citizen specifically targeted for recruitment by AQ-core because he held a British passport. A similar plot involving Umar

Abdulmutallab, to bring down an airliner over Detroit in 2010, is another example of these sorts of attacks: plots that are highly organized, and which recruit citizens of the West to conduct attacks against the West in order to evade security protocols. Britain's 2005 7/7 (July 7) attacks are also part of this end of the spectrum.[25] These attacks involved a cell of volunteers, loosely recruited by AQ-core, with some members training in Pakistan at AQ-run training camps, although not specifically for this event.

The attack by Major Nidal Malik Hasan in the United States in 2009 is a useful example of homegrown extremism slightly further along the spectrum, moving into the category of lone-actor terrorists, who act alone and without specific direction or training, but who are inspired by global jihadist propaganda, often online.[26] A US army psychologist, Hasan killed thirteen people and injured over thirty at Fort Hood, Texas. Hasan viewed AQ propaganda online and exchanged emails with a key AQ propagandist, but acted alone. He was arguably radicalized almost entirely online, and acted without specific direction, although he certainly was in contact with at least one senior AQ figure, who knew and approved of his plans (Pantucci 2011a: 23).

Other examples include the Tsaernev brothers, responsible for attacks in 2013 in Boston, and attacks in Quebec and Ottawa in late 2014. In both the Boston and Canadian examples, the perpetrators did not have any contact with AQ-core and acted without the knowledge of any formal group. Lone actors like these are not recruited directly by central jihadi actors AQ-core or IS and do not act on direct instruction—they act alone, rather than in a group. Although such actors are often mentally disturbed, it is important to note that they justify their actions in political terms (Vidino 2012: 478).[27] Debates continue to rage about the actual threat from lone-actor terrorism (Bjelopera 2013; Neumann 2009: 63; Schuurman et al. 2019), but policymakers in the United States, the UK, Canada, the Netherlands, and Sweden among others, have highlighted the threat of lone actors as increasing and, as discussed below, both AQ-core and IS arguably see the inspiration of lone-actor attacks as an important strategy (see, for example, Olsen 2013: 3). Individuals acting as disseminators of radicalizing material may also be included in the lone-actor category—they are certainly captured under counterterrorism policy in some cases, and as discussed earlier, spreading information, especially online, has been openly framed as a terrorist act by jihadi strategists.

Situated further along this spectrum of homegrown extremism are so-called foreign fighters. Foreign fighters are those who fight in the name of radical Islamist identified struggles in battlegrounds like Afghanistan, Yemen, Somalia, or Iraq, who are not citizens of those states. Ideologically driven fighters have always come together to fight in states which are not their own—this in itself is not new and not specific to global jihadi terrorism (see Malet 2013). As AQ-relevant conflict zones have multiplied, as the very nature of AQ-core has morphed into a "franchise"[28] rather than a "headquarters" model, and as IS has emerged, opportunities for foreign fighters have multiplied. Indeed, one of the most striking features of the post-9/11 environment is the presence in jihadi training camps in northern Pakistan and in IS-associated battlegrounds in Iraq, Syria, and elsewhere of aspirational, self-selected foreign fighters without obvious or long-standing ethnic ties to the region, particularly those from the West. Foreign fighters are a particularly important source of recruitment to IS: most analysts agree it far exceeds any previous foreign fighter migration (Lia 2015: 37). And as outlined previously in this chapter, recruitment of foreign fighters has played an important role in IS messaging.

Such fighters have in the past assumed prominent, long-term organizational roles in AQ affiliates, while others are more opportunistic, and may travel between their home country and battlefields that emerge into global radical Islamist ideology (see Malet 2013 for an overview). They may represent significant diaspora communities in their source country. For example, the Somali diaspora in the United States was the source of its first suicide bomber, who detonated an explosive in Somalia in 2008, and US foreign fighters in Somalia remain a significant concern to US security officials (Folk 2011). The risk posed by the return of such citizens to their home countries is an ongoing concern to policymakers, intensified by recent events in Syria and in other IS-associated battlefields, which have specifically engaged foreign fighters.[29] A 2017 report suggests that over 40,000 fighters from 100 countries have joined IS-associated battlefields, with 5,600 having returned home (see Barrett 2017: 5, 12, also for a discussion of changes in foreign fighter flows).

Hegghammer (2013) finds that such individuals are often more successful in committing acts of homegrown extremism when they return to their home country from a foreign battlefield, given increases in both motivation and skills. As amply demonstrated by attacks in May 2014 by a returned foreign fighter in Brussels and two attacks associated with returnees in Paris in 2015, the worlds of foreign fighters and homegrown extremism often combine. The perpetrator of the Brussels attack was a Belgian citizen who had recently returned from fighting in Syria. Policymakers are unsurprisingly concerned about such developments (Farr 2014; White House 2015; Dawson 2018; Hegghammer 2013).

## Conclusion

As this spectrum indicates, violence borne of global jihadi thought is presently most usefully analyzed as a bottom-up enterprise rather than a core command and control structure, as may have been the case in the past, although the issue has been subject to furious debate (Hoffman 2008; Sageman 2008b). Sageman (2008a: vii) describes this phenomenon as "leaderless jihad," arguing:

> The present threat has evolved from a structured Al Qaeda leadership group, controlling vast resources and issuing commands, to a multitude of informal local groups trying to emulate their predecessors by conceiving and executing operations from the bottom up, to a vast, atomized network of recruits and potential recruits acting on a chaotic battlefield, or self-starting violence at home, particularly in the West: these "homegrown wannabees" form a scattered global network, a leaderless jihad.

He describes this phenomenon as part of a third wave of global terrorism, building on a worldview "characterised by grievance, moral outrage and a transnational anti-Western identity" (Sageman 2008a: 139).

This "worldview" is the jihadi master narrative outlined earlier in this chapter. Like all terrorism, homegrown extremism trades in symbolic power, given material constraints. The narrative propagated by global jihadi strategies, which Sageman argues is increasingly the driving force of terrorist activity, both consciously mobilizes the symbolic power of a disjunct between formal and informal political community and citizenship, and inevitably does so as a response to material constraints. Jihadist master narratives posit a global Islamic identity that is in direct contest with the nation-state. These narratives urge Muslims to choose the former over the latter and suggest they cannot co-exist. They draw on developments in jihadi "strategic studies" that bridge ideas about global Islamic identity with specific tactics and strategies designed to pursue global jihadi goals in the post-9/11 environment, including a spectrum of forms of homegrown extremism to which policymakers must respond.

# 2
# Counterradicalization in global context

One of the chief concerns of this book is to analyze the ways in which the counterradicalization policies of different states converge. Although the empirical chapters examine the United States and the UK in detail, counterradicalization policies exist in a wide range of jurisdictions across the world, from Norway to Saudi Arabia, from Mauritania to Indonesia. Do these states converge in the way they approach the issue of counterradicalization? This chapter shows that counterradicalization policies do indeed converge on two related features: a focus on integration and a concern with discursive approaches that seek to persuade rather than coerce targeted individuals. But why does this convergence take place?

The first section of the chapter addresses why such convergence might take place: the overwhelming influence of powerful actors, especially the United States. I argue that such similarities are unlikely to be the result of policy diffusion on the part of powerful states given the controversial nature of terrorism and the United States' previous inability to engender global cooperation on terrorism. Instead, I propose that these similarities are the result of states responding in similar ways to the symbolic power of global jihadi narratives in the context of homegrown extremism, as discussed in Chapter 1. Here, states seek to reinscribe the boundaries of political community in response to this threat, drawing the boundaries more tightly by focusing on integration.

The second part of the chapter argues that states draw these boundaries closer using policy initiatives that focus on discursive, persuasive methods rather than coercive methods associated with traditional counterterrorism, for two reasons. First, states are responding in kind to the symbolic power embodied in jihadi discourses, using discursive strategies in an attempt to structure the cognitive and material worlds of individuals deemed at risk. Second, states are for the most part limited in the coercive techniques they can employ in response to radicalization. In seeking to draw individuals more closely into the political community, they must act in a way that legitimates that community and the state institutions it entails. Drawing briefly on literature regarding the relationship between consent and political legitimacy, I argue that the absence of overt, explicit coercion found in other counterterrorism policies plays an important role in such legitimation.

Counterradicalization policy is not easy to research. The relevant policies are by their nature inchoate, and analyzing them in a consistent manner is challenging. The concept is a new and emerging development in counterterrorism and is often highly politicized, meaning policies slip away or emerge as new actors and influences arise. Additionally, counterradicalization goals can be pursued by states without a cohesive policy titled as such: they may be pursued via policing or integration policies, for example. Relatedly, even in states with a cohesive policy, counterradicalization goals may be pursued via a variety of agencies: unlike traditional counterterrorism, counterradicalization does not have a natural "home agency." Agencies involved include interior ministries, justice ministries, immigration agencies, police, local council bodies, and faith groups: as the UN definition of counterradicalization outlined in the Introduction to this study suggests, it is a "package of measures."

Counterradicalization may also be pursued at a variety of levels of governance. In the Netherlands, for example, a national program existed at the same time as city-based policies, while in Germany most policies—like other domestic security policies—are progressed via sixteen sub-national administrative units rather than by a federal agency. In the United States, federal attorneys are the main agents of the US counterradicalization program, but many states have also introduced their own policies. This study focuses on national-level policies in all cases, but it is important to note that other levels of policymaking exist. In general, the multiplication of security functions across a variety of agencies is a feature of post–Cold War security that finds particular expression in the post-9/11 environment, especially in counterterrorism (Heng and McDonagh 2011). To make matters even more confusing, preexisting civil society groups and government agencies may receive counterradicalization funding to undertake activities that essentially continue preexisting activity under a different funding banner, making the isolation of their counterradicalization activities almost impossible. And states may undertake activities proclaimed as counterradicalization, which in other contexts have long been categorized as state-building or security measures—as in state control of religion in some Arab states, for example.

To help address the issue of identifying relevant actors and policies, I identify counterradicalization policies as those which have counterradicalization as their goal, stated or unstated. I use state reporting in the first report of the UN Working Group on Addressing Radicalisation and Extremism that Lead to Terrorism (established by UN Security Council resolution 1624) as a starting point to establish the range of states active in this space (CTITF 2008). In the case of Muslim majority states, many of which did not readily report to the UN on this issue, I use US State Department Counterterrorism Country Reports from 2006 to 2016[1] as an alternative list of states active on this issue. Overall, this chapter shows that counterradicalization policies exist in liberal and illiberal states and across a range of Muslim minority and majority states.

## Counterradicalization globally: Policy diffusion or striking convergence?

This chapter identifies similarities between a wide range of states in their approach to counterradicalization. But what if this convergence is simply the result of the activities of policy diffusion via security communities, norm entrepreneurs, or Western hegemony? Western-dominated security communities have certainly acted strongly on counterradicalization (Adler, Barnett, and Smith 1998). For example, the North Atlantic Treaty Organization (NATO) and the Organisation for Economic Co-operation and Development (OECD) have counterradicalization policies, and the European Union (EU) was one of the first bodies to move on counterradicalization: the EU Declaration on Combating Terrorism, adopted on March 25, 2004 following the Madrid bombings, and the EU Plan of Action on Combating Terrorism adopted later that year. The plan of action was the first public EU policy document to refer directly to radicalization and counterradicalization, in Objective 6. The EU counterterrorism policy, adopted in November 2005, built on these earlier initiatives, introducing a pillar of action specifically to address radicalization.

In practice, Western (especially US-led) efforts have seen substantial successes in multilateral counterterrorism more broadly. Such multilateralism generally accords strongly with US goals, driven by material and social incentives associated with US hegemony (Mendelsohn 2009a). Particularly in the years immediately following September 11, 2001, the United States drew on a reserve of support for counterterrorism measures that was unparalleled.[2] This level of support was also prominent in support expressed by UN members for United Nations Security Council (UNSC) resolution 1624, submitted by the UK immediately following the July 2005 London bombings. This resolution was the first time in which the UN addressed preemptive counterterrorism, of which counterradicalization is an exemplary example. It was passed unanimously at an extraordinary heads of government meeting at the UNSC and in the United Nations General Assembly (UNGA). The resolution draws on many of the themes of counterradicalization, and called on all states to:

> continue international efforts to enhance dialogue and broaden understanding among civilizations, in an effort to prevent the indiscriminate targeting of different religions and cultures, and to take all measures as may be necessary and appropriate and in accordance with their obligations under international law

to counter incitement of terrorist acts motivated by extremism and intolerance and to prevent the subversion of educational, cultural, and religious institutions by terrorists and their supporters. (S/RES/1624 (2005): para. 3)[3]

The first United Nations Counter-Terrorism Strategy, adopted in 2006, similarly addressed preemption in a manner reminiscent of counterradicalization, adopting in its plan of action: "Measures to address the conditions conducive to the spread of terrorism" (UNGA 2006).

This success arguably extends beyond multilateralism. For example, Omelicheva's (2009) work on counterterrorism in Estonia shows that implementation of domestic counterterrorism regimes occurred in the absence of a substantive terrorist threat. She argues that Estonia sought to use the implementation as demonstration of its eligibility to join a particular security community (the EU): that is, Estonia implemented this policy, including some elements of counterradicalization, based on socialization incentives rather than because of any real domestic policy concerns, essentially importing a counterterrorism regime.[4]

However, values and policy goals shared within security communities and the influence of hegemons do not explain important differences in the adoption and design of counterradicalization policies between states: national-level concerns and structures also play an important role and the very nature of counterradicalization policy "brings the state back in" in a way other counterterrorism policies may not. Counterradicalization is local by definition: this means that sharing is by definition limited. For example, important differences exist within the EU regarding the extent to which states have implemented its guidelines. Some states, such as the Netherlands, have adopted wide-ranging counterradicalization policies while others, such as Spain, have not. A former key adviser on European Commission-level counterradicalization policy suggested that differences between states in the extent of their adoption of political community within the EU are due to differing experiences in the integration of Muslim diasporas as well as perceptions of the capacity of preexisting counterterrorism institutions to manage radicalization.[5] Similarly, referring to the UK's Prevent program, a senior EU counterterrorism policymaker highlighted the problem of actually defining radicalization given its local implications, noting: "The huge problem with the Prevent work is that radicalization means something different to different people. It means something different in the UK than it means in Germany again. We are not always, EU-wise, on the same page to get the coherence."[6]

This problem is supported by scholarly work on the issue. Foley (2013) finds France's failure to adopt counterradicalization policies in any detail is the result of path-dependent outcomes in the design of local security institutions (see

Lister and Otero-Iglesias 2012 for a similar argument on Spain). And Germany hosted several of the 9/11 bombers and has uncovered several large plots by its citizens, but has a relatively limited counterradicalization program delivered primarily via regional rather than federal authorities and with limited coordination. Germany's limited approach, it has been argued, is largely due to constitutional provisions regarding religious freedom and the monitoring of religious groups dating from the post–Second World War period, while others have argued that the fragmentation of security services embedded in Germany's constitution limits the development of federal programs.[7]

Strong differences on radicalization have also been a feature of otherwise relatively harmonious transatlantic counterterrorism cooperation. Until 2009 the United States saw radicalization in the West as a European problem (Vidino 2009), and arguably saw attention to "soft" measures as a distinctly European response. As one scholar of EU counterterrorism argues: "The EU and its member states have been acutely aware, from a very early stage in the current campaign against terrorism, that victory will not be achieved as long as the circumstances by which individuals turn into terrorists are not addressed—contrary to the American view that speaking of 'root causes' implied condoning terrorist acts" (Coolsaet 2010: 866–867). Similarly, Muslim majority states such as Saudi Arabia and Indonesia have long resisted responding to external pressure to combat radicalization, doing so instead on their own terms and with selective exchange with officials and the broader counterradicalization-focused epistemic community[8] and at least in the Saudi case, beginning their programs before those developed in the United States and elsewhere in the West.

Perhaps more important than the nature of counterradicalization itself in disavowing policy diffusion as an argument for convergence is the fact that global cooperation on counterterrorism has always been controversial and limited due to the political nature of the definition of terrorism. Despite initial shows of unity, cooperation has fallen by the wayside since 9/11, as old controversies surrounding counterterrorism re-emerge, aggravated by the clarity of US hegemony on this issue (Romaniuk 2010: 100). This disjunct is evident on the problem of counterradicalization as addressed specifically at the UN. As noted above, UNSC Resolution 1624 received overwhelming support at the UN and mandated the establishment of issue-based working groups on prevention, under the auspices of the newly established Counter-Terrorism Implementation Task Force (CTITF). Five working groups were established as a result, including Addressing Radicalisation and Extremism That Lead to Terrorism. From the outset, UNGA members expressed "concern that the Task Force was being selective in focusing on those parts of the strategy of particular concern to powerful states" (Romaniuk 2010: 103) but despite initial controversies, all the working groups have persisted (with varying degrees of success) except the working group on addressing radicalization, which was shut down in 2009, following concerns by Arab states that it was biased toward the West given the language of informal values used. These states argued that this language linked counterradicalization to a particular type of political practice, which by definition excluded many non-Western states (Hegemann 2011: 20).

As Romaniuk (2010: 4) notes, at least in the context of multilateralism, it is difficult to imagine a situation in which broad-based cooperation against terrorism (that is, cooperation on all aspects of counterterrorism policy, including counterradicalization) might emerge in the future. Indeed, the Global Counterterrorism Forum initiated by the United States in 2012 is designed to facilitate the sharing of best practice and information on countering violent extremism (among other issues) in an effort to overcome continued divisions on these issues at the UN. A senior member of the UN's CTITF remarked on the difficulties of counterradicalization in particular at a multilateral level, noting: "even within the taskforce there were people who thought this was pretty thin ice to be treading on, certain member states also said: this seems to us to be focused entirely on Islam and Muslim majority states, on terrorism which is being associated with a particular religion."[9]

The CTITF experience suggests that overt and conscious shared understandings about the meaning of radicalization and counterradicalization do not exist and that the absence of shared understandings reflects the broader and similarly contentious issue of cooperation in counterterrorism. It also suggests that counterradicalization engages questions of informal political community which are defined differently in Muslim majority and Muslim minority states. Policy diffusion by powerful actors, then, may have some impact. But it is an insufficient explanation of similarities given the controversial nature of counterterrorism policy and resistance by some governments. As Mendelsohn (2009b: 668) notes:

> states' responses have been conditioned by their inability to reach a common definition of terrorism [and] diverging perceptions of the causes of terrorism . . . divergent opinions on terrorism are not simply a reflection of instrumental considerations. Rather, they often reflect genuine disagreements—expected in a thin international society—that are based on dissimilar cultures, identities, prevailing norms and historical experiences.

## Integration as counterradicalization

Despite difficulties in cooperation, counterradicalization policies globally converge in their attention to integration as a counterterrorism measure. This integration focuses on the boundaries of informal, value-driven political community: counterradicalization programs implicitly and explicitly promote the concept that a cohesive community is a secure community. The policies are fundamentally concerned with the role of Islam within their particular community, and as such the implementation of this integrationist goal differs between Muslim minority and Muslim majority states, although the underlying aspiration remains the same.[10] In Muslim minority countries, policies focus on the failure of Muslim immigrant and diaspora integration as a cause of radicalization and seek to address this failure. These policies are often explicitly directed at global jihadi inspired terrorism: they target Muslim communities and address activities in mosques, by imams, and in religious schools. In Muslim majority countries, the policies focus on reaching agreement around a state-sanctioned version of Islam, either implying or explicitly stating that a previous consensus has been fractured.

In each of these cases, we see states reinscribing the boundaries of the political community with which the state identifies as a counterterrorism measure. The policies use integration into a political community—defined by Islam, or defined by a secular state—as a counterterrorism measure. In doing so, states are responding to the threat of homegrown extremism in a manner that responds to the symbolic nature of the threat. The threat seeks to create a disjunct between informal and formal political community by drawing homegrown extremists into a larger informal political community defined by global jihadism. This underlies the promotion of informal political community—values, beliefs, and ideas associated with a particular nation-state—as an antidote to radicalization.

## Counterradicalization in Muslim minority states

Muslim minority states converge in their focus on Muslim diasporas of immigrant heritage as targets for counterradicalization programs and, in doing so, link broader immigrant integration programs and goals with counterterrorism policies. This link between immigration and counterterrorism in general is not unusual in the overall terms of post-9/11 counterterrorism policy—a key component of many counterterrorism policies is an emphasis on the formal aspects of entry into, and exit from, a formal political community via visa restrictions and increased movement and border restrictions.[11] However, this link is especially significant in counterradicalization policy because it goes beyond the entry and exit restrictions commonly associated with post-9/11 immigration-related counterterrorism measures and focuses instead on integration—on informal political community rather than formal (citizenship). By focusing on integration and failing in all cases to distinguish between citizens and non-citizens, instead focusing on "minority status," such programs emphasize the immigrant heritage of citizens who are targeted, and de-emphasizes their citizen status. In doing so, they inherently destabilize such citizens' membership: citizenship of Muslim minority states is no defense against counterradicalization.

The link between immigration, integration, and counterradicalization is often explicit. For example, the UK government instituted its Commission on Integration and Cohesion in 2006 as a direct response to the 2005 London bombings. The commission was tasked specifically to investigate extremism and radicalization as well as, for example, the training of imams, community security and police relations, and women's issues (Brighton 2007: 1). The UK strategy "coordinates closely" with work in "community cohesion" (HM Government 2009a: 84) and challenges views that "reject and undermine our shared values and jeopardize community cohesion" (HM Government 2009a: 87). US policies are less developed, but aim to achieve "community empowerment," and past statements on the topic by the secretary of the US Department of Homeland Security (DHS) show an underlying rationale to the effect that "successful immigrant integration" can "build a common civic identity" (Napolitano 2009). Associated DHS research focuses on community policing initiatives that prioritize "inclusiveness, promoting integration and, potentially minimize the disaffection that can lead to radicalization, particularly among Muslim youth" (quoted in Bjelopera and Randol 2010: 53, note 254).

Similarly, the European Commission notes that "policies in this field [integration] can have positive effects on preventing violent radicalisation" (Commission of the European Communities 2005: 2). The Norwegian Ministry of Justice and the Police (2011: 23, 31) notes that in pursuit of counterradicalization goals, "significant efforts" have been made in Norway to "ensure integration and social inclusion of immigrants and their children," and a Contact Committee between Immigrants and the Authorities has been established. In Denmark, the security service has established a Division for Cohesion and Prevention of Radicalization (Norwegian Ministry of Justice and the Police 2011: 12). In Germany, the Federal Office for the Protection of the Constitution (2007: 7) argues confidently that "successful integration is a substantial contribution to the prevention of extremism and terrorism." In the Netherlands, the Intelligence Service produced a resilience and resistance report in concert with the "Polarisation and Radicalisation Action Plan 2007–2011" (General Intelligence and Security Service of the Netherlands 2010; Netherlands Ministry of the Interior and Kingdom Relations 2007).

In most cases, counterradicalization policies in Muslim minority states operate in concert with agencies that manage migration or integration—either in terms of policy design or implementation. For example, in the United States, the DHS runs workshops that include teams from its immigration and citizenship branch with local Islamic community representatives (Bjelopera and Randol 2010: 55). In the Netherlands, an early counterradicalization assessment report, "Policies on Integration and Prevention of Radicalisation in the Netherlands: A Progress Report," was produced by the Netherlands Ministry of Immigration and Integration (2006). Similarly, the European Policy Planners Network on Countering Radicalisation and Polarisation brings together policy planners from security and integration ministries, and the Dutch program, ReCora, brings together security, policing, and immigration agencies with local communities. In Denmark, the national security and intelligence service, PET (Politiets Efterretningstjeneste), runs a counterradicalization program through which "voluntary identity mentors" are available for direct dialogue with young migrants (Ranstorp 2010: 12). In Canada, Citizenship and Immigration Canada runs counterradicalization programs (Government of Canada 2013: 28), while in Australia the immigration department plays a key role in delivering counterradicalization programs designed to promote "respect, inclusion and a sense of belonging, in ways which address issues impeding social cohesion" (Australian Department of the Prime Minister and Cabinet 2010: 65).

Programs in Muslim minority countries explicitly focus on informal citizenship: on integration measures and citizenship education measures. For example, many counterradicalization programs include funding for citizenship education programs as a way of progressing integration. By default, this implies that a faulty application or understanding of citizenship may contribute to radicalization. The UK "Prevent" policy, for example, funds the Islam and Citizenship Education program, which includes financing citizenship education in madrassahs (HM Government 2008b: 22). Similarly, in testimony before the Senate Committee on Homeland Security and Governmental Affairs, Secretary Janet Napolitano linked US counterradicalization efforts to the promotion of a "common civic identity" among immigrants, and noted that some programs with counterradicalization benefits were delivered by the US Citizenship and Immigration Service (Napolitano 2009: 5). The Dutch policy pays particular attention to "active citizenship" as a counterradicalization measure, aiming to "promote the knowledge and skills of democratic citizenship" (Netherlands Ministry of the Interior and Kingdom Relations 2007: 58).

These informal national values are laid out explicitly in many senses. The UK "Prevent" strategy, for example, urges local governments to only work with local partners (Muslim community groups) who "uphold our shared values of tolerance, respect and equality" (HM Government 2008a: 14). Other UK policy documents emphasize "the strong and positive relationships between people of different ethnic, faith and cultural backgrounds in this country" (HM Government 2009a: 87). In a similar vein, Council of Europe policy documents state: "Raising awareness and stimulating reflection about the fundamental values the EU must defend and uphold in its fight against terrorism is an essential aspect of the EU's counter-terrorism policy" (Council of the European Union 2007: 9). The same policy documents refer to "core values" of liberty, democracy, respect for human rights, "freedom of religion and belief" (Council of the European Union 2007: 10), while the Canadian National Security Policy suggests that "[t]he deep commitment of Canadians to mutual respect and inclusion helps to mitigate extremism in our society" (Government of Canada 2004: 2).

In the United States, the Office of Civil Rights and Liberties in the DHS has historically been one of the key bodies delivering counterradicalization programs. These programs focus on communicating the way in which the United States protects the rights of all citizens as part of its fundamental values (Bjelopera and Randol 2010: 65; Couch 2010). Former DHS Secretary Napolitano related this concept of security to counterradicalization when she referred in early 2010 to the need to inculcate "American values" in immigrant communities as a way to deter radicalization (Napolitano 2010), and the Chief of the US National Counterterrorism Centre's Global Engagement Group focused on communicating US respect for civil liberties to American Muslims as a key component of counterradicalization (Couch 2010). Similarly, Norwegian counterradicalization policy links counterradicalization to the "fundamental values" of Norwegian democracy: "popular sovereignty, division of powers and human rights," and funds dialogue directly focused on communicating these values (Norwegian Ministry of Justice and the Police 2011: 5, 31).

Ultimately, this attention to integration in Muslim minority countries focuses on Islam, given the role of counterradicalization in post-9/11 counterterrorism policies. It is important to note that in some jurisdictions such as Norway, the Netherlands, and Germany, counterradicalization policy is also ostensibly aimed at terrorism enacted by other types of homegrown extremists such as far-right or animal-rights groups. However, the bulk of funding has historically gone to counterradicalization programs aimed at the Muslim community (see Goodwin, Ramalingam, and Briggs 2012). Indeed, most counterradicalization programs are clear about this distinction and link it to the greater threat posed by AQ-inspired terrorism. Many European programs, for example, highlight interfaith relations as a counterradicalization measure, through activities that take place in mosques and local Muslim youth centers, and engage Muslim clerics and community leaders in the effort. In the United States, the DHS engages Muslim leaders in roundtables as part of its counterradicalization effort (Bjelopera and Randol 2010: 125–126)—no other foreign or religious communities in the United States get the "same type of scrutiny" (Bjelopera and Randol 2010: 55). In France, counterradicalization programs have focused almost entirely on French Muslims (McAuley 2016; Hellmuth 2015). The targeting is even clearer in the first and second versions of the UK's "Prevent" policy, with regional funding allocated based on the number of Muslims per capita (HM Government 2008a, 2011a).

Policy measures that seek to develop a relationship between the state and Islam—or a particular version of Islam—as a counterradicalization measure are common to both Muslim minority and Muslim majority countries. Even France, which has avoided introducing extensive counterradicalization policies as the result of both a determinedly secular identity and pre-9/11 draconian anti-terrorism laws (Foley 2013), has engaged on the issue of interfaith negotiations and dialogue as a concession to religious identity politics linked to the ongoing threat from homegrown extremism (Camilleri 2012; US Department of State 2013; Streiff 2006; Hellmuth 2015). To help curb radicalization, the government announced in 2012 that it would increase the number of Muslim chaplains in French prisons in 2013 (US Department of State 2013: 72), and as of early 2015 there were 182 Muslim chaplains in French prisons—with an extra sixty announced following the *Charlie Hebdo* attacks in January 2015.[12] A law proposed in October 2014 aimed to ban incitement and glorification of terrorism online, as well as to ban French nationals from traveling to IS battlefields (Human Rights Watch 2014). Following the *Charlie Hebdo* attacks, the government decreed new online counternarrative and surveillance measures and created an online campaign to directly target IS propaganda (Haddad 2015). And in 2015, also in response to *Charlie Hebdo*, France introduced a range of counterradicalization measures in schools, to promote secular and republican French values (Davies 2018: 13).

The European Commission funds significant research into the concept of a "European Islam" (Goldirova 2007). And in Spain, the government's most visible "soft" response to the Madrid bombings was an intensive reinvigoration of long-standing attempts to formalize Islamic representative bodies within Spain, while the Ministry for Religious Affairs has produced textbooks for children's religious instruction detailing Spanish values in the context of religion (Alonso 2010: 221; Bravo 2010). As part of a minimal counterradicalization program, the Italian government has created an institute that trains and accredits imams to Italian standards (Vidino 2005), as has Norway (Norwegian Ministry of Justice and Public Security 2010: 31), while the UK has delivered similar funding for both research into British Islam and the training and certification of imams and mosques (HM Government 2007a). Overall, national identity as a synonym for the "safe" practice of Islam is a common theme in counterradicalization programs in Muslim minority states. That these hybrid identities are presented as the peaceful end point of counterradicalization policies is instructive. It suggests that not only are these identities separate to the state but that one, modified identity is more peaceful than the alternative, unmodified version.[13]

The Singaporean program, for example, directly engages with the notion of national incorporation of Islam into a Muslim minority state.[14] The program was introduced in 2003 as a direct response to the arrest of Jemaah Islaamiya operatives in Singapore in 2001 (Hassan 2010; Tan 2008). It promotes public discussion of Islam as a tolerant, pluralist religion and links this to a Singaporean version of Islam that reflects and promotes these features. Public discussion is promulgated by the security agencies and their partnerships. Prominent among these partnerships is the Religious Rehabilitation Group, a group of local Muslim scholars who counsel detainees, offer expert opinion on extremists' misinterpretation of Islam, produce counter-ideological materials on relevant religious matters, and conduct public education for the Muslim community on religious extremism. Singapore's relationship with its Muslim minority is centered on its often-conflicted relationship with Malaysia, and the group undoubtedly draws on this political heritage and on earlier programs designed to promote interfaith understanding as a nation-building measure in light of this history (Tan 2008).[15]

Similarly, the UK's "Prevent" program, promotes a "British Muslim" identity,[16] and funds research and teaching into a "Radical Middle Way" for Islam in the UK (HM Government 2009a: 88), while the European model promotes "European Islam" and the Dutch version promotes "Dutch values" and integrating Islam, as does the Norwegian program. The German Islam Konferenz, meanwhile, is part of a broader dialogue about the link between integration, radicalization, and Islam and is committed to integrating German values and religions (Deutsch Islam Konferenz 2013). This approach characterizes religion as a driving force in radicalization despite research which suggests that most extremists are actually religious novices and that a well-established religious identity actually protects against violent radicalization (Travis 2008). Importantly, underlying informal national values and identities are implicitly treated as separate to the religious identity of "Muslim." By default, such policies in Muslim minority countries portray Islam as a monolithic identity across time and space, which is separate to a national identity and must be moderated so that it can be incorporated.

Some counterradicalization policy statements make explicit the link between counterradicalization and the cohesiveness of the state by including separatist movements in this context. For example, Russia's 2009 National Security Strategy predicts that: "Nationalist sentiments, xenophobia, separatism and violent extremism will grow, including under the banner of religious radicalism" (President of the Russian Federation 2009: 3). According to the Director of the UN's CTITF, Russia was initially a major supporter of counterradicalization initiatives at the UN. He noted of Russia's vigorous support for counterradicalization at the multilateral level that it had to do with repression and management of the more formal, territorial aspects of the Russian political community, suggesting that "it has a lot to do with the threat from Chechnya" and noted that there was also at times a "repressive element... it can be a mechanism to stifle certain types of dissent" which can at the same time be used as an "international basis for domestic action."[17]

An explicit focus on integration as a response to threats to internal unity also arguably informs China's efforts in countering radicalization, noting that the Chinese Communist Party has long linked terrorism, extremism, and separatism as the "three evils" (Clarke 2018: 17–19). The 2016 Xinjiang Anti-Extremism Regulation, for example, calls for counterextremism to "guide religions to become more compatible with socialist society" (Doyon 2019). Indeed, according to the Ministry of Foreign Affairs of the People's Republic of China (2018), counterterrorism policies in Xinjiang, which hosts a substantial Muslim population, are "active efforts" to "prevent terrorism and eliminate extremism with the view to nipping the evil in the bud." The Counter-Terrorism Law 2016 introduced support both counterradicalization and deradicalization policies into Chinese law for the first time. In Xinjiang, these policies include programs to engage civil society, via groups including Islamic Associations and Women's Federations, for example, which are nominally nongovernmental but are in fact government controlled (Zhou 2019).

## Counterradicalization in Muslim majority states

Integrationist initiatives aimed at strengthening the relationship between national identity and Islam also exist in Muslim majority countries, demonstrating convergence with Muslim minority states on this issue. Such programs build on a long tradition of Muslim majority states approaching relationships between the state and religion as a state security and state-building practice. This is particularly true of Arab states in the context of ongoing political debates regarding the influence of Salafist thought in the Muslim world in the post–Cold War period (Wiktorowicz 2001, 2005; Karawan 1992; Barnett 1995; Stemmann 2006). The plethora of programs emerging after 9/11 in Muslim majority states, often in conditions that have been hostile to international policy diffusion on counterterrorism, suggests that old practices have been refashioned for new purposes, or at least that counterradicalization is a new way to describe and justify such habits. Like policies in Muslim minority states, these practices seek to address the problem of state citizens or other members of the political community engaging in activity against the state in the name of AQ-inspired ideology. Although they draw on more established practices of (sometimes repressive) relationships between the state and religion than liberal democracies in particular, in practice these states employ similar tools. These tools include redrawing the boundaries of the informal values, beliefs, and identity of the state (in this case symbolized by Islamic values and identities) in the name of security against a similar threat, in extremism perpetuated by citizens.[18]

For example, Indonesia's counterradicalization program, initiated in 2010, is the government's first attempt to manage broad-based domestic radicalization: a prison-based deradicalization program has been in place since 2004 (ICG 2007). The counterradicalization program began with the inauguration by presidential decree of the BNPT (Badan Nasional Penanggulangan Terorisme) or National Anti-Terrorism Agency in 2010, which was divided into three units, the first of which is Prevention, Protection, and De-Radicalization (Sumpter 2017). Indonesia's experience is interesting as for many years it resisted introducing broad-based counterradicalization programs despite intense pressure from the United States and Australia to do so, and despite accepting support on "hard" counterterrorism issues. Despite the 2002 and 2005 Bali bombings, Indonesian security agencies and civil society groups persisted in seeing radical Salafism as a threat targeted at foreigners and emanating from outside Indonesia. However, a series of events in 2009–2010 motivated the government to act, especially the 2010 assassination plot against the president and a shift in local jihadi discourse from a focus on the "far enemy" to a focus on the "near enemy" (Solahudin 2013). According to one analyst, the assassination plot against the president in particular "made it clear this was now a threat to the security of the state," whereas in the past it had been seen as a foreign issue. This galvanized the state's security apparatus into action despite longstanding discomfort in engaging in discussions about terrorism, Islam, and Indonesia.[19]

The BNPT produced its first strategic plan in January 2011. This detailed the causes of domestic terrorism in Indonesia as "the problem of a weak sense of nationhood; a narrow-fanatic understanding of religious teachings; the weakness of citizenship education; the erosion of local values by a wave of negative modernisation; and lack of coordination and integration of efforts to prevent terrorism" (IPAC 2014: 4). The plan set four goals to be largely achieved by the end of 2014: "raising awareness and vigilance," "protecting 'vital objects,' residential areas and public spaces," "reducing radical ideology and propaganda; and preventing communities from being influenced by radical ideologies and persuading convicted terrorists, their families and networks to disengage from terrorism" (IPAC 2014: 4). Responsibility for delivering the plan was shared across twenty-four government agencies.

Like many counterradicalization programs, the BNPT program was designed without reference to extensive research. Many proposals were not designed with the support of religious community representatives: proposals to certify clerics and speakers and to subject Friday sermons to government review were opposed by all sides of the religious spectrum (IPAC 2014: 5). The Coordination Forum for the Prevention of Terrorism (Forum Koordinasi Pencegahan Terorisme, or

FKPT) is one of the most concrete initiatives to come out of the plan. Initiated in 2012, it was tasked with preventing the "propagation of radical ideas closely associated with terrorism" (Erviani 2013). On introducing the program, the governor of Aceh described it thus: "The FKPT is expected to foster togetherness and harmony among the people of Aceh to make them understand that terrorists are our common enemies" (AntaraNews 2012). By mid-2015, community forums sponsored by the FKPT existed in thirty-two of Indonesia's thirty-four provinces (US Department of State 2017). The forums liaise with the local government via the Office of Political Affairs and National Unity. Each FKPT hosts "Terrorism Prevention Dialogues" designed to encourage discussion and debate on a range of issues determined centrally by a "syllabus" designed and delivered by BNPT. The syllabus has five topics, including Religion and the State, which discusses the concept of the state in Islam, the relationship between Islam and the state in Indonesia, and the "value of heterogeneity in building a strong nation" (IPAC 2014: 6).

The National Terrorism Prevention Program, instituted in 2013, built on BNPT's strategic plan. Headed by the deputy minister for religion, the program's taskforce has a strong focus on deradicalization, but also includes support for counterradicalization measures. Its activities include strengthening the capacity of mosques, religious schools, high schools, and universities to resist violent jihadism. A new curriculum, implemented in 2013, introduced new emphases on religious education and character development. Curriculum documents refer to the need to "form an Indonesian 'humankind' which is capable of balancing the needs of the individual and society to progress their identity as part of the Indonesian nation and the need to integrate as one entity, the nation of Indonesia" (Mendikbud 2012: 7–8). To that end, religious education and social skills form two of four core competencies in the new high school curriculum, a satiation seemingly at odds with government goals to increase international standing in core competencies such as mathematics and English (Parker 2017: 1253), although it should be noted that the link between national identity, cohesion, and curriculum design is long-standing in Indonesia.

Introduced in 2004, Saudi Arabia's whole-of-government Prevention, Rehabilitation, and Aftercare strategy was also initiated in the context of a threat to the fabric of the state; one of the first counterradicalization programs in the world, it provided inspiration for Western counterradicalization programs in many ways.[20] Saudi Arabia had traditionally been reluctant to act on counterradicalization, even following 9/11, and the issue remains sensitive. However, the 2003 Riyadh bombings, which saw militants drive car bombs into compounds close to the city, killing twenty-six people and marking the start of a concerted AQ attack, galvanized the state into action. One analyst retells the story of then CIA director George Tenet relaying intelligence to

Crown Prince Abdullah that AQ was planning to attack the royal family itself, with the aim of destabilizing government (Ryan 2013: 168). This led the Saudis to engage all aspects of national security power—in this case, including "soft" counterterrorism.

Like counterradicalization programs in Western liberal democracies, the primary audience for Saudi prevention programs is "not extremists themselves, but the larger population that may sympathize with extremists and those who do not condemn the beliefs that lead to extremism" (Boucek 2008b: 8). A substantial portion of the program is directed at deradicalizing prisoners convicted of terrorist offences including a prison deradicalization program, run by a group of well-respected clerics, who visit the prisoners individually to engage militant jihadis in discussions about their beliefs. The state also supports prisoners believed to be in danger of recidivism after they have left prison by supporting their integration into broader society: it funds employment programs, engages their families in prisoner rehabilitation, and even in some cases offers support in arranging marriages (Boucek 2008b).

The program also focuses on broader prevention measures. It includes diversionary activities and education programs for young men considered at risk of radicalization. These include government-approved summer programs and after-school programs, for example, as well as curriculum-driven programs in schools to encourage reflection by students on the impact of terrorism on society. In general, these programs draw on a non-violent interpretation of Islam and the impact of violence on Saudi Arabian society (Boucek 2008b: 10). The Ministry of Culture and Information has initiated a series of projects to this end using television, newspapers, and other forms of mass media. The program includes speaking tours, classes, and lecture series by religious sources in schools and mosques, to speak about the dangers of extremism. A two-week national awareness campaign carried out in 2005, for example, was titled the "National Solidarity Campaign against Terrorism and Extremism," and was described as part of a "strategy to combat extremism" and to "educate Saudi citizens about the true values of the Islamic faith and the importance of tolerance and moderation" (Kingdom of Saudi Arabia 2005).

The Saudi program also focuses on online radicalization. The Saudi Sakinah (religious tranquility) campaign is funded by the Ministry of Islamic Affairs. Through it, Islamic scholars interact online with individuals looking for religious knowledge, with the aim of steering them away from extremist sources (al-Saud 2017). The campaign seeks to refute so-called deviant interpretations of Islam and rebut extremist arguments. Intriguingly, and again laying bare the link between the integrity of political community and counterradicalization, a former State Department adviser has pointed out that the Sakinah program's scholars argued strongly against the Arab Spring uprisings as un-Islamic.[21]

More recent legislative moves confirm the link between internal order and counterterrorism: a royal decree introduced in early 2014 criminalized "participation in hostilities outside the kingdom" and targeted Saudi citizens fighting in IS battlegrounds. The Law Concerning Offenses of Terrorism and its Financing took effect on February 1, 2014. It introduced a wide definition of terrorism, including "disturbing the public order of the state," "destabilizing the security of society, or the stability of the state," "endangering its national unity," "revoking the basic law of governance or any of its articles," or "harming the reputation of the state or its standing." It also defines terrorism as all atheist thought, or thought or speech that calls into question the "fundamentals of the Islamic religion on which this country is based." The law also introduces penalties for those who assist or support organizations who engage in such activities or demonstrate affiliation or sympathy with them (Al-Rasheed 2014; Iaccino 2014). These new legislative efforts do not focus on counterradicalization or prevention, but clearly frame the problem of terrorism in terms of thoughts as well as actions and also clearly in terms of state stability and the relationship between the state and religion.

Morocco was one of the first Muslim majority states to move on counterradicalization, but did not move on deradicalization until 2016. Despite a history of encouraging certain strains of Salafism because of their political quietude, the government moved to address the problem of extremism and changed its approach to Salafism completely following bombings in Casablanca in 2003 linked to AQ elements in the Maghreb. The policy involved antipoverty measures, as well as several religious bodies, including the Higher Council of Ulemas (council of theologians), imams, mosques, and the religious affairs body of the Moroccan Community Abroad in discussions about the relationship between Islam and Moroccan identity. In his speech announcing a new policy direction focusing on the institutionalization of religious affairs as a measure against extremism, King Muhammad VI declared the creation of regional chapters of the council of theologians "so that the clerics . . . provide assistance in strengthening the spiritual security of the nation by ensuring the preservation of its religious doctrine which is tolerant Sunni Islam," and "guard the faith . . . and the Moroccan identity against the fundamentalists and extremists" (Bouasria 2015: 40; Touahri 2008; Masbah 2018). In 2004, the government announced plans to oversee training for imams and the licensing of mosques as part of a modernization of the teaching of Islam. Several religious scholars have argued that this has involved prioritization and support in financial and publicity terms of Sufism over other forms of Islam. This is because unlike Salafism, Sufism offers no obvious contradiction between religion and pledging allegiance to the state whereas Salafism (broadly put) sees the modern state as a violation of Islam and demands the politicization of religion through applying Sharia (Islamic law) (see Hassan 2010).[22] These endeavors have seen over 1,000 imams sent into towns and villages, preaching moderate Islam and respect for the role of the king as the leader of Morocco's Muslims (see, for example, Dlugoleski 2010). This was extended to the training of imams. For example, a program introduced in 2009 aimed to train 45,000 imams in skills appropriate to modern Moroccan society (see El-Katiri 2013 generally).

In Algeria, the government has increasingly turned to state control of religion in order to neutralize the threat of AQ-linked Salafism. As one scholar of Islamist extremist movements in North Africa notes of the post-9/11 environment, "[w]hereas Algeria's major Islamist parties in the 1990s tended to embrace politics, participate in the system, and discuss the concept of democracy, the new anti-state Salafi actors do not believe in working within the political system" (Boubaker 2011: 58). Boubaker (2011: 69) noted increasing depoliticization and re-Islamization among Wahhabi Salafists, and the re-dynamism of jihadi Salafism, both drawing their increasing popularity among young people in particular from their links to a broader, globalized worldview of AQ: "The Algerian government is aware that [AQ-inspired-Whabbism] is a social force with enormous political potential, greater than the openly political parties Islam ever had.... [and] question[s] its national loyalty." As a result, the state has invested heavily in sponsoring and monitoring religion as a way of countering the influence of AQ-inspired ideas among its citizens—a type of counterradicalization given its post-9/11 context.

As elsewhere, much of this has seen the government focus on promoting Sufism as an alternative to Salafism more in keeping with Algeria's national identity and to increasing existing state control over Islamic practice (Ghanem 2018). For example, the Ministry of Religious Affairs has openly stated that Salafi ideology "doesn't take into consideration the particular nature of Algeria... [noting] We are doing a lot to encourage people to come back to our traditional Islam: a peaceful, tolerant and open-minded Islam" (Reuters 2009). To this end, the government has created a television and radio station to promote Sufism, in addition to regular appearances by Sufi sheikhs on other stations—all tightly controlled by the state. In 2004 the government passed legislation regulating mosques, including requiring Friday sermons to be state approved, and in 2006 it introduced legislation to "curb certain religious practices deemed subversive or out of line with mainstream Islam and the state's law," including the regulation of the sale of Korans (Fethi 2006). Over 1,000 Salafi titles were banned from the 2007 and 2008 book fairs (Boubaker 2011: 69), and the minister of religious affairs has vowed that any work "of a subversive nature, putting forward ideas which are incompatible with our principles and values," imported from abroad, will be checked and possibly banned if necessary (Fethi 2006, 2007).

In 2015, Algeria's Ministry of Religious Affairs began to publicly attempt to dismantle IS's ideology on twitter in an attempt to counteract online radicalization.

It also announced the creation of a new governmental body called the National Observatory of the Struggle against Religious Extremism comprised of officials from Algeria's Ministries of Culture, Communications, National Education, Higher Education, Vocational Training, Religious Affairs, the Interior, and security agencies, as well as members of the mass media (Counter Extremism Project 2018).

In Mauritania, an increase in aggression by Al-Qaeda in the Islamic Maghreb (AQIM) (Boukhars 2011) saw the government step up both its hard and soft counterterrorism measures and for the first time introduce counterradicalization programs. These included structural incentives aimed at deterring young AQIM combatants. The provision of jobs and financial support has reportedly been successful, and in 2010 the government initiated a series of "dialogue" meetings with alleged radical Islamist prisoners, during which government officials and imams attempted to convince Islamist prisoners that their interpretation of Islam was wrong. In addition, the government hired about 500 imams to preach "moderate" Islam in the country's mosques (Jourde 2011), the goal of which was to "rehabilitate violent extremists as well as to demobilize and de-radicalize potential recruits" (Boukhars 2011). The government has also considered introducing internet monitoring, ostensibly in an effort to combat Islamic extremism (Idoumou 2012).

Other policies that link state control of religion and state security to counterradicalization goals either overtly or by default exist across the Muslim world, from Ethiopia to Bahrain (see US Department of State 2017). Both Muslim minority and Muslim majority states, then, engage in policies designed to counter the threat of radicalization among their own citizens. Despite considerable differences in jurisdictions, contexts, and capacities, these share an underlying integrationist approach. In some cases, especially China and Russia, this integrationist focus targets territory that has been the subject of separatist movements and is contained within a broader emphasis on regime stability.

## Counterradicalization, discourse, and persuasion

Importantly, counterradicalization programs in both Muslim majority and Muslim minority states exhibit an important feature within the broader category of integration that marks them as additionally distinctive to traditional counterterrorism policies—they are overwhelmingly discursive. They employ language, narratives, ideas, and beliefs as policy practices. Intuitively, this is a response in kind to the fundamentally discursive strategies employed by global jihadis in the context of recruitment of homegrown extremists, as discussed in Chapter 1.

Responding to discursive strategies is, unsurprisingly, an inherently discursive exercise.

In some (usually Western) states, such as the UK, Canada, the Netherlands, and Sweden, the concept of discourse—of providing a "counternarrative" as a counterterrorism measure—is explicitly detailed in policy documents. The Canadian policy, for example, focuses on providing:

> positive alternative narratives that emphasize the open, diverse and inclusive nature of Canadian society and seek to foster a greater sense of Canadian identity and belonging for all. Programs would be aimed at raising the public's awareness of the threat and at empowering individuals and communities to develop and deliver messages and viewpoints that resonate more strongly than terrorist propaganda. (Government of Canada 2013: 16–17)

Similarly, the first iteration of the Danish counterradicalization program had as one of seven specific areas of intervention "dialogue and information," providing alternatives to "extremist propaganda which to a high degree originates from outside the Danish borders" with " 'factual information' " (Government of Denmark 2009: 12, 15, 11). In the United States, the DHS runs meetings and roundtables with members of Muslim communities that provide "safe spaces for exchange of information, learning and discussion" (Institute for Strategic Dialogue 2008: 16–18). In the UK, the "Prevent" policy identifies as a key goal challenging the "ideology behind violent extremism" and supporting "mainstream voices" (HM Government 2008b: 83).[23]

Many states also engage in online counterradicalization, highlighting the discursive nature of many policies, and they focus on the way in which discourses are consumed by individuals—in this case online. In Saudi Arabia, the Sakinah campaign funds religious scholars to engage in theological debate online, while in the United States, the Barack Obama administration instituted the Center for Strategic Counterterrorism Communications in 2010. Until replaced by the similarly focused Global Engagement Center in 2016, its task was "to devise effective ways to counter the terrorist narrative" including, for example, the production of Youtube videos making fun of AQ narratives and exposing flaws in their logic. It also included an expanded version of the Digital Outreach Team, which began in the later years of the George W. Bush administration. This team "actively and openly engage[d] in Arabic, Urdu, Punjabi, and Somali to counter terrorist propaganda and misinformation about the United States across a wide variety of interactive digital environments that had previously been ceded to extremists" (US Department of State 2010). In the UK, the Research Information and Communications Unit is almost entirely covert but is tasked with orienting domestic government communications on terrorism-related issues. The

Netherlands has also produced an online magazine, *Ahlan*, designed to counter the persuasive effects of online radicalization. The Danish National Action Plan on Preventing and Countering Extremism and Radicalisation (Government of Denmark 2016) introduced the concept of "digital voices of reason" and critical thinking skills into new initiatives on countering online propaganda.

In some cases, policies explicitly focus on individuals and their thoughts and feelings about the world. A key counterradicalization measure in the UK is Channel, a police program initiated in 2007 and designed to "support individuals at risk." The program takes referrals from community-based agencies—schools, health services, sporting clubs, and so on—of individuals suspected to be at risk of radicalization and provides a mechanism for ensuring that individuals are referred to and assessed by a multi-agency panel, and where necessary, provides an appropriate support package tailored to an individual's needs.[24] In Germany, the Federal Office for Migration and Refugees runs a "radicalization hotline" for anyone who has questions on the topic or is concerned about the radicalization of a relative or acquaintance. In addition, the hotline is in touch with various local counseling facilities and can provide relevant contacts and networks (BAMF 2013). The Danish and Norwegian programs also include preventive measures of this sort—where neighbors, families, and others can work with government agencies to address individuals and beliefs as a way to prevent terrorist acts occurring.[25] The Danish program, meanwhile, included in its first incarnation "individual preventive talks," targeting "young people who are in an early process of radicalisation or who are affiliated with radical or extreme groups" (Government of Denmark 2009: 12).

In some cases, usually in Western liberal states, policies explicitly focus on individuals as both recipients and *generators* of ideas and values via discourse. For example, Amsterdam's counterradicalization program emphasizes training in debating skills for youth at risk of radicalization, so that they may not only be educated against radicalization themselves but may combat Islamist propaganda on the internet, or act as community representatives (Netherlands Ministry of the Interior and Kingdom Relations 2007: 44, 46). Denmark's national security and intelligence service (PET) has funded an ongoing dialogue with a number of representatives from Muslim communities, aimed at strengthening the "disagreeing dialogue" by entering into dialogue with individuals who represent controversial views (Government of Denmark 2009: 17). The UK government funds a toolkit for schools that aims to equip young people with the "knowledge and skills to be able to challenge extremist narratives" and community programs that provide forums for debates on politics and theology (HM Government 2009a: 89, 90). The Norwegian program also proposes debate and dialogue as a counterradicalization measure—for example, by providing funding for "strengthening dialogue and greater involvement" (Norwegian Ministry of

Justice and the Police 2011: 5, 31), and Australia's counterradicalization policy also includes several measures aimed at training young Muslims in debate and presentation skills (Australian Attorney-General's Department 2012).

This emphasis on discursive methods can be framed more broadly as an emphasis on *persuasion* rather than the overt coercive and repressive techniques that mark traditional counterterrorism policies. By persuasion, I mean the idea that the process of countering radicalization relies on individuals changing their minds about the way the world works, especially the nature of political community, or by embedding associated values, ideas, and beliefs about the world in individuals as a bulwark against future radicalization. Even where activities are undertaken at the community level, it is the extent to which individuals can commit violence, and inspire others to commit violence, which is at the core of the threat the programs seek to counter.

Harking back to the discussion in the first section of this chapter, counterradicalization approaches across Muslim minority and majority states share an emphasis on the psychological drivers of radicalization, although often combined with an understanding of structural factors, such as unemployment and education. This emphasis on persuasion, and the discursive techniques accompanying it, distinguishes counterradicalization policies from traditional counterterrorism policies, which find their effectiveness in physical coercion.[26] Scholars of counterterrorism note the preponderance of exceptional counterterrorism measures in the post-9/11 environment, especially in liberal democratic states, which can be classed as coercive because they impinge upon the rights or normal practices of citizens or introduce new coercive practices into existing measures. Pre-trial detention, ethnic profiling measures, or even torture of aliens suspected of terrorist activities may be classed in this way, as may no-fly lists or counterterrorism financing measures (Herman 2011; Wilkinson 2006; Donohue 2008).

But why do counterradicalization policies emphasize persuasion? As discussed in Chapter 1, they are, of course, responding to a problem that is almost entirely discursive: the problem of radicalization and recruitment by global jihadi groups. But an additional approach, which accords the agency of policymakers more weight, may also lie across two bodies of literature: on the relationship between political legitimacy and the effectiveness of traditional, coercive counterterrorism; and on the relationship between political legitimacy and consent.

Debates about whether respect for human rights in the context of terrorism prevention reduces, or increases, the likelihood of a terrorist attack, have been a longstanding part of traditional terrorism studies. Although definitions of terrorism and regime type vary, and generalizations are difficult, a significant body of work suggests that repressive or coercive counterterrorism policies can increase the danger of terrorist attacks or the longevity of a terrorist group. Daxecker and Hess (2013), for example, find that where liberal democratic states engage in repressive policies, terrorist groups persist for longer and further attacks are more likely to take place. Some studies are explicitly focused on the relationship between counterterrorism and respect for particular types of human rights: Abrahms (2007) finds that states that enforce civil liberties are less likely to be targeted by acts of terrorism. Piazza and Walsh (2010) focus on a subset of rights they describe as physical integrity rights, meaning rights that offer freedom from physical coercion. They find that, independent of the strength of democratic institutions, respect for physical integrity rights is consistent with fewer terrorist attacks. This is because coercive responses undermine a government's legitimacy and can increase overall support for a terrorist group, the number of potential recruits, and the resources available to the group. These findings build on and draw from a significant body of work in counterinsurgency literature which finds that state legitimacy plays a role in the success of counterinsurgency campaigns (see Joes 2004 for a summary). Legitimacy in this context is built on respect for rule of law, restraint by military and law enforcement operations, and respectful treatment of local populations (see Hashim 2006).

This body of research is supported by work on the role of the rule of law in counterterrorist regimes which suggests that suppressive policies may subvert the legitimacy of counterterrorism efforts in the context of members of the ethnic and religious communities in which potential terrorists have their roots, diluting valuable community support in counterterrorism initiatives (Donohue 2008; Wilkinson 2006; Dragu and Polborn 2014). Research on the experiences of targeted minority groups in a counterterrorism context is also relevant here. Scholarly work on Arab American, British Muslim, and Australian Muslim experiences of racism in the post-9/11 environment support the concept that where individuals experience their identity in a political community primarily via counterterrorism policies, their feeling of inclusion and integration in that community decline, sometimes with effects on cooperation with national security goals (Wray-Lake, Syvertsen, and Flanagan 2008; Tyler, Schulhofer, and Huq 2010; Cherney and Murphy 2017; Huq, Tyler, and Schulhofer 2011).

Literature on traditional counterterrorism, then, suggests that government legitimacy in the eyes of terrorists, potential terrorists, and the community at large can play a strong role in ensuring the success of counterterrorist regimes and that legitimacy is related to the absence of coercion. But there are no explicit statements of counterradicalization policies learning from the impact of coercive, traditional counterterrorism in other states. And in most states where counterradicalization takes place, the policies are enacted in an environment where traditional forms of counterterrorism also exist, often with levels of coercion intensified in the post-9/11 environment. Some former policymakers suggest that decision-makers have learnt the lessons of past policy failure regarding undue or excessive coercion because of their impact on state legitimacy. This can be seen, for example, in British reluctance to act coercively in the context of counterradicalization given policymakers' cognizance of the failures of coercive measures in Northern Ireland, and the way they radicalized the Northern Irish population.[27] A significant body of work on the unintended consequences of coercive policies in Northern Ireland makes a similar point (see, for example, LaFree and Dugan 2009; Gill, Piazza, and Horgan 2016; Dixon 2009; Bigo and Guitett 2011).[28]

Similarly, public discourse in the United States repeatedly emphasizes the lessons of inherently coercive Japanese internment and McCarthy-era anticommunism in the context of homegrown extremism (Feinstein 2011). As one interviewee noted, "You [also] had the history with Hoover and the FBI [Federal Bureau of Investigation]—the stigma that attaches to monitoring ideology. If you look at the rhetoric around it, the FBI will never concede that what they are doing is monitoring ideology . . . The NYPD [New York Police Department] say precisely the same thing. There is a huge stigma attached to monitoring ideology in the US."[29] And in Indonesia, for example, authorities have been reluctant to introduce preemptive measures, including counterradicalization, because of fears of stigmatizing Islam and its practitioners, especially given the context of the Suharto years and political unrest (Sumpter 2017; IPAC 2014: 4).

The broader point may come from the inherent and intuitive relationship between political legitimacy and consent. This link is intimated by the research on legitimacy and the effectiveness of traditional coercive terrorism outlined in the preceding paragraphs. The underlying premise of this research is that coercion of individuals is unlikely to produce feelings of attachment in that individual to the state that engenders a coercive policy, meaning that individuals and potentially their community are less likely to cooperate with the overarching policy goal of security of the broader political community—the state—including by abstaining from violence and by assisting security forces.

In contrast, counterradicalization is concerned with persuasion, rather than coercion. With the broader goal of integration, counterradicalization policies seek to persuade individuals to think in a certain way about the world. Persuasion has a particular relationship with consent. If an individual is *persuaded* of something, they may be said to *consent* to it, even if only in the abstract. In the context of counterradicalization policy, if an individual is persuaded to think in a particular way about the world, then they may be said to consent to at least thinking about the world in that way. This is particularly important in the context of integration. If a policy aims to foster a feeling of inclusion in targeted individuals—to make them feel more "British" or "American" or "Indonesian" in an attempt to ward off or address radicalization—then persuading them to think in a certain way about the world means securing their implicit consent that the world *is* indeed that way. Individuals who *are* persuaded consent to the fact that they are, in fact, British or American, or Indonesian, contrary to other ways of viewing the world and their place in it. As the literature on traditional counterterrorism suggests, coercion does not breed consent.

In the context of counterradicalization and integration, it is also important to consider that consent is a vector for political legitimacy. Literature on the origins and maintenance of political power draws strongly on voluntarist traditions in Lockean[30] thought to show how political authority is secured and sustained by the function of legitimacy, which is in turn secured by the consent of those governed by it.[31] In his analysis of the role of legitimacy in sovereignty, Hurd (1999) highlights the role of internal ordering of the world by individuals in the function of state legitimacy. Drawing together the strands of intricate debates of political theory on this issue, he adopts a definition from Mark Suchman, an organizational sociologist, who describes legitimacy as "a generalised perception or assumption that the actions of an entity are desirable, proper or appropriate within some socially constructed system of norms, values, beliefs and definitions" (quoted in Hurd 1999: 387). The inclusion of perception in this definition highlights the role of an internal adjudication of the world, but places it within the context of socially constructed norms. Counterradicalization, then, seeks to secure the legitimacy of the political authority of the state by persuading individuals of their place within it as a way to secure implicit consent. Studies of traditional counterterrorism have shown that coercion is counterproductive in this sense, and counterradicalization's concern with persuasion in the context of integration speaks to a deeper concern with political legitimacy and with combatting alternative models of political community proffered by the similarly discursive models of global jihadi propaganda.

# 3
# For Queen and country
## Counterradicalization and political community in Britain

In his response to the July 7, 2005 (7/7) bombings of 2005, committed on British soil by British citizens, Prime Minister Tony Blair explicitly linked British identity and citizenship to counterterrorism: "people who want to be British citizens should share our values and our way of life" (Blair 2005). Counterradicalization policy measures in Britain routinely deal in the language of citizenship that Blair espoused. For example, the Islam and Citizenship Education (ICE) project, first piloted in 2008, aims to "demonstrate to young British Muslims that their faith is compatible with wider shared values, and that being a good Muslim is also compatible with being a good British citizen" (HM Government 2008c: 41). And the Luton Ambassadors for Islam project funded twenty-four young men during the period 2007–2008 to take part in classes taught by a "British-born Islamic scholar," with the aim of helping them to "assert their British identity" (HM Government 2008a: 20). Indeed, every policy since 2011 relies on a definition which frames extremism as "vocal or active opposition to fundamental British values" (HM Government 2011a: 107). But what *are* British values and what does it mean to be British in this context?

### Formal and informal political community in the UK

The boundaries of the formal political community of the UK are relatively recent, dating from Acts of Union between England and Wales in 1535 and 1542, Scotland in 1707, and Ireland in 1800, and the creation of Northern Ireland and the Irish Free State in 1922. While its official title is now the United Kingdom of Great Britain and Northern Ireland, Great Britain and Britain are often used as synonyms for this sovereign state, with "Britishness" a synonym for the values, beliefs, and identities that define it—the informal political community of "Great Britain." Because it conflates several smaller political communities, the UK does not possess the "historiography of a nation-state," meaning that there is not, and was not even at its very inception, an underlying and inevitable link between the values and identities of a cohesive *informal* political community and its formal structures: "Britain" is an "invented nation" (Scott 1990: 168; see also Pocock 1982). Formal citizenship beyond subjectship (of the monarch) was only introduced in 1981, with the British Nationality Act. And the absence of an official constitutional document[1] means the UK has "no constitutional statement or declaration enshrining our objectives as a country; no mission statement defining purpose; and no explicitly stated vision of our future" (Brown 2006; see also Rose 1977; Dyson 1988).

This relatively weak link between formal and informal political community has been further shaped in the modern era by Britain's experiences of empire. The expansion of the British empire to territories entirely foreign to the experiences of most of its inhabitants has helped to define a cohesive British identity against an inherent Other: "possession of such a vast and obviously alien empire encouraged the British to see themselves as a distinct, special, and-often-superior people . . . Whatever their own differences, Britons could feel united in dominion over, and in distinction from, the millions of colonial subjects beyond their own boundaries" (Colley 1992: 324, 2005).[2]

The effects of this core/periphery model of empire and British political community emerged clearly in the post–Second World War era. In the declining stages of the empire, membership as formal "subjects" was accessible to all, technically without regard to race or heritage. This facilitated the great post-war influxes of former colonial subjects, as the British Nationality Act of 1948 invested some eight million subjects of empire with the right of entry and settlement in the UK. In response to social unease at this process, the post-war period involved successive redefinitions of gradations of membership between alien, subject, citizen, and national (see Joppke 1999 for an overview). These redefinitions were increasingly restrictive—incrementally limiting the right of entry and access to the formal political community based on (effectively racial) heritage—over successive legislative efforts from 1948 onward: "preventing the outer reaches of empire from moving toward the centre" (Joppke 1999: 101). These new pieces of legislation were introduced usually without explicitly stating the restriction of post-colonial immigration as a policy goal, given the liberal underpinnings of the British polity (see Spencer 2002). From 1981 onward, however, and in the face of greater diversity of immigration and the politics of asylum, UK immigration policies have increasingly incorporated notions of heritage (*jus sanguinis*) and "British" values into processes for immigration and citizenship (Joppke 2010: 130–131; Everson 2003: 77; Goulbourne 1991). The 1981 British Nationality Act codified the idea of formal UK citizenship, and in doing so, based it on ideas of heritage in, and birth on, UK soil, rather than membership of empire.

Despite these attempts to limit access, the UK still affords a variety of social and political rights and benefits to those outside the inner circle of formal citizenship.

These rights and benefits correspond to the expansion of the post-war welfare state, the impact of EU expansion, and the demands of a transnational immigration market (see Soysal 1994; Hansen 1999: 427; Feldblum 1998; Sainsbury 2012: 47–48). As Everson (2003: 77–79) notes, historically, given the "emptiness" of British citizenship, the focus of the British conception of citizenship has not been contractualist. Instead of inherent and unassailable rights (and responsibilities), formal British citizenship is based on a gradation of privileges: from welfare, to residency and so on, which may also be extended to non-citizens.[3]

## Britishness, integration, and citizenship

Articulations of the relationship between informal and formal citizenship have been relatively recent in the UK given the narrow "subject" identity that dominated much of the formal aspects of citizenship until relatively recently. The issue became more prominent in the post-war years, as emerging race relation problems were linked with a post-colonial immigration influx of "formal co-nationals" without "substantive ties of belonging," the result of "political boundaries that had been too expansively and indistinctly drawn as the boundaries of empire" (Joppke 1999: 100; Freeman 1979: 309). Croft's (2012: 132–153) analysis of the evolution of post-war Britishness is relevant here. He writes of the importance of the post-war years in imbuing Britishness with a sense of social justice, as embodied by the Clement Attlee government's welfare reforms, and the "phlegmatic" yet moral stance that defined Britain's Second World War experiences. Croft argues that this commitment to social justice saw the emergence of an emphasis, in cultural products and official discourse from the late 1960s, on Britain's emerging nature as a kind of "post-class" meritocracy, capable of tolerance and inclusion. Croft links this to official attention at the time to tolerance and inclusion as being British undertakings.

Accordingly, integration policy in the UK has traditionally taken the form of attention to rights and group identities as a matter of social harmony. This has resulted in official national level soft multiculturalism in the form of anti-discrimination legislation. Here, attention to informal political community is conducted by proxy attention to race relations and associated concepts of tolerance and non-discrimination. Home Secretary Roy Jenkins famously expressed this strategy in 1966:

> Integration is perhaps rather a loose word. I do not regard it as meaning the loss, by immigrants, of their own national characteristics and culture. I do not think that we need in this country a "melting pot" which will turn everybody out in a common mold, as one of a series of carbon copies of someone's misplaced

vision of the stereotypical Englishman. I . . . define integration, therefore, not as a flattening process of assimilation but as equal opportunity, accompanied by cultural diversity, in an atmosphere of mutual tolerance. (Jenkins 1967: 267)

As part of this approach, attention to immigrant identities as an issue of social cohesion has continued in Britain into the third and fourth generations of postwar immigrants (Spencer 2011).[4] However, increases in migration diversity, increases in European migration, and challenges associated with the changing nature of international asylum movements, mean that in the years immediately prior to and following 9/11, the government's attitudes to integration shifted substantially in ways that are arguably important for counterradicalization policy. Historically, the "Right" in Britain had been more explicit in its argument for the necessity of an established informal political community in Britain, marked by active commitment to clearly defined national values, and associated with the formal aspects of political community such as citizenship and welfare rights (Kim 2011). New Labour had come to power in 1997 on a platform that emphasized both individual and collective community rather than state responsibility for delivering social outcomes, and which pointed to the role of shared values and experiences in facilitating such an appropriate collective community identity (see Giddens 1998; Advisory Group on Citizenship 1998). The party largely maintained a framework of multiculturalism, managed via race relations and anti-discrimination legislation.

However, concepts of collective community identity, individual responsibility, and "active citizenship," were conflated with race relations, integration, and migration in the government response to a wave of unrest that swept the north of England during the summer of 2001. This reframed the concept of tolerant multiculturalism to embrace a more specific conceptualization of the values and beliefs underpinning British political community as a response to problems of public order, especially those linked to migration.

In the summer of 2001, violence erupted in several Northern English towns with strikingly disparate racial communities. Involving pitched street battles between rival ethnic groups, the riots resulted in £27 million worth of damage and 282 arrests, the majority of which were described by police as "Asian males" (Travis 2002; McGhee 2005: 59). The riots predominantly involved groups of young white men and young men of Pakistani and Bangladeshi heritage, and built on a long history of racial unrest in economically deprived areas in the north (Denham 2001: 8).

The concept of social cohesion, community cohesion, and associated tropes of integration and strong, united communities had, of course, been present in Labour social policy for many years prior to 2001.[5] However, the use of the term "community cohesion" specifically in the context of public order and security, especially regarding ethnic communities, emerged only after the disturbances in the summer of 2001 (Worley 2005: 486), heralding a "new politics of community" (Robinson 2008: 15; see also Pilkington 2008).

In response to the riots, the government established a Ministerial Review Group on Community Cohesion and Public Order in July 2001 and a Community Cohesion Unit in the Home Office in August 2001. Two major, national-level reviews were commissioned. The report of the Ministerial Group on Public Order and Community Cohesion, known as the Denham Review, and the report of the Independent Community Cohesion Review Team, known as the Cantle Review, were both commissioned in August 2001 and released in December 2001. These reports focused strongly on the links between community cohesion and security outcomes, making several clear integrationist recommendations that would later resonate with counterradicalization policy. The reviews found that the two most important factors causing the riots were "the lack of a strong civic identity or shared social values to unite diverse communities" (Denham 2001: 11) and the effective segregation of culturally diverse communities, living "parallel lives" (Cantle 2001: 9).[6] The Denham Review in particular framed the response to the problem of a shared civic identity as an especially urgent task against the backdrop of the 2001 terrorist attacks in New York and Washington, DC, and linked the issue particularly to the immigration, asylum, and citizenship white paper due for publication in 2002. Explicitly placing the issue of citizenship and informal political community in the context of social cohesion, the review argued that "[c]itizenship means finding a common place for diverse cultures and beliefs, consistent with our core values" (Denham 2001: 20). The Cantle Review also emphasized the link between citizenship and social cohesion, arguing that: "the responsibilities of citizenship need to be more clearly established" in the context of an "honest and open national debate" (Cantle 2001: 20; for further discussion, see Robinson 2008; Husband and Alam 2011). In doing so, both reviews employed an influential application of values-based community cohesion as a bulwark against violence that was to find its echo in counterradicalization policies from 2005.

In February 2002, the home secretary introduced the 2002 white paper, *Secure Borders, Safe Havens: Integration and Identity in Modern Britain*,[7] which argued that the foremost challenge posed by migration was to "our national identity and citizenship" (Home Office 2002: 9). It directly referenced the 2001 riots as a problem of social cohesion caused by the lack of a shared sense of national identity. Linking social cohesion to the point of migration, the white paper recommended "light touch" citizenship education for all new migrants and a sharpening of naturalization requirements by means of a citizenship test. This found its expression in a citizenship test via the Nationality, Immigration and Asylum Act 2002, which was formalized in the "life in the UK" test, introduced in 2005 (see Van Oers 2016: 116–123 for a discussion of parliamentary debate on the act and the citizenship test). The 2005 version of the test focused largely on life in England and included questions on British history and society, its institutions, and political system. The test's introductory booklet included information on these topics but also on practical issues such as employment, healthcare, education, and using public services like libraries. It made a reference to British values but did not test applicants on them, noting simply that: "To be British mean[s] that we respect the laws, the parliamentary and democratic political structures, traditional values of mutual tolerance, respect for equal rights" (HM Government 2004b: 15). The test was revised slightly in 2007 and was at this point introduced into requirements for settlement as well as citizenship. In 2013, the test was revised substantially to focus on what the Home Office described as "values and principles at the heart of being British," encouraging "participation in British life" (BBC News 2013). This included questions on British history, culture, and sporting achievements (Express 2013). Rules for citizenship ceremonies and an English-language test for applications, for both naturalization and permanent residency, were also introduced at this time (Byrne 2017).

Debates in the past decade about the "politics of Britishness" (Mycock 2010: 339) have drawn on turn-of-the-century community cohesion initiatives outlined above and are set against wider debates about devolution, Europe, and asylum and immigration. They have laid bare the fact that British identity—the informal political community which binds the UK alongside its formal structures—is contested and opaque. As one key adviser to the Blair government on counterradicalization put it: "The UK has been struggling to articulate what these shared values are all about: post-second World War, post Blair Britain—it is difficult to articulate anything which isn't too wishy washy or morally relative."[8] Occasionally the nature of these values is outlined in more detail. In a significant speech in 2004, the then chancellor, Gordon Brown, outlined the role of British values in "just about every central question about our national future" and drew on a "golden thread which runs through British history of the individual standing firm for freedom and liberty against tyranny and the arbitrary use of power" to define core values, including the "passion for liberty anchored in a sense of duty and an intrinsic commitment to tolerance and fair play" (Brown 2004). These words echo scholarly references to British values as strongly informed by a (Protestant) moral code and democratic "procedural values" embodied in key national institutions—significantly the "cult of parliament" (Colley 2005: 54; see also Newman 1996; McGlynn, Mycock, and McAuley 2011).

The trajectory of citizenship education for UK citizens also offers some clues. First introduced in response to the violence of June–July 2001, citizenship education in England[9] was built on findings from the report of the Advisory Group on Citizenship (1998), also known as the Crick Report, named after the chair,

Professor Bernard Crick (see Starkey 2018 for an overview). The report saw its goal explicitly in the context of the thinness of British informal political community, arguing that:

> a main aim for the whole community should be to find or restore a sense of common citizenship, including a national identity that is secure enough to find a place for the plurality of nations, cultures, ethnic identities and religions long found in the United Kingdom. Citizenship education creates common ground between different ethnic and religious identities. (Advisory Group on Citizenship 1998: 17)

There were no references to the flag or the head of state in the Crick Report, but a clear reference to "values and dispositions." These were framed in essentially global terms, as "concern for the common good," for human rights, and for the environment; "commitment to equal opportunities and gender equality," active citizenship, and voluntary service; and "belief in human dignity and equality . . . respect for the rule of law, [and] determination to act justly" (Advisory Group on Citizenship 1998: 44). In 2007, in the context of the 2005 London bombings, the government ordered a review of citizenship education in England. The Ajegbo review recommended students be educated further on issues of identity and diversity (Ajegbo 2007: 97). Citizenship education was further reviewed in 2014, this time explicitly in the context of counterradicalization, as discussed in Chapter 8. At this point, schools were told to promote "fundamental British values." The phrase first appeared in the 2011 version of the UK's counterradicalization strategy in a definition of extremism: "Extremism is vocal or active opposition to fundamental British values, including democracy, the rule of law, individual liberty and mutual respect and tolerance of different faiths and beliefs" (HM Government 2011a: 107).

In 2014, the phrase and this associated definition of "fundamental British values" was adopted by the Department for Education, initially in a statement of teacher standards, and subsequently in advice and guidance on the standard for all schools to promote the spiritual, moral, social, and cultural (SMSC) development of pupils. According to the Education (Independent School Standards) Regulations 2014, the standard is met when a school "actively promotes the fundamental British values of democracy, the rule of law, individual liberty, and mutual respect and tolerance of those with different faiths and beliefs" (Part 2, Section 5(a)) and was expected to be delivered at a whole-of-school level, rather than simply as a standalone citizenship class. The 2014 guidance outlined SMSC as included in the school inspection regime as a priority area of concern. As discussed further in Chapter 8, the duty of schools to implement and teach these values went beyond citizenship education and even SMSC, as in 2015 it was embedded in a "Prevent Duty" for educational institutions in section 26 of the Counterterrorism and Security Act 2015. Under this legislation, educators were required to undertake training in the Prevent duty, to become aware of when it was appropriate to refer Prevent-related concerns about students or colleagues, to a "Prevent officer" in the institution, and to themselves exemplify these values in their educational practice.

The history of the political community of the UK is of an historically indeterminate conception of "Britishness" revived with some specificity in the context of violence, social order, and, more recently, counterterrorism. This occurs against a backdrop of a—historically speaking—relatively indeterminate formal political community, given the changing nature of citizenship in the context of the decline of empire. As the following chapters show, debates over the definition of this community—both formal and informal—underpin the discourse of counterradicalization policy.

## Citizen violence and the state in the UK

The relationship between the state and its citizens in the UK is marked by the absence of a constitutional document. Policymaking on the relationship between citizens and the state in the UK proceeds, then, not as a series of iterative events marked by decision-making against consideration of a constitutional document—as in the United States—but as a series of policy decisions informed by the successes and failures of previous policies.

Unsurprisingly, such policy decisions have been undertaken most prominently in times of war. Both the First and Second World Wars saw the UK inter its own citizens based on their political beliefs or associations, or their heritage (see Vorspan 2005; Bird 1986; Simpson 1992). Legislation such as the Defence of the Realm Act of 1914, and the Emergency Powers (Defence) Act of 1939, also saw formal rights of membership in the political community (such as access to a jury trial or free movement and expression) diluted considerably based on the informal aspects of political community—political beliefs and/or heritage—as the state came under threat. Measures included the criminalization of dissent and incitement to disaffection in both cases, used against not only enemy aliens but also to quell labor unrest and address pacifist sentiment (see Fox 2012; Simpson 1992). Such legislation also introduced barriers to entry and denaturalization provisions based on similar concepts. Overall, wartime measures expired or were withdrawn as hostilities ceased. Indeed, the National War Aims Committee 1917 (Millman 2000: 229–251; Monger 2012: 37–62), the Local and Regional Speakers Bureau, and the Ministry of Information/Home Intelligence Bureau in the Second World War (Fox 2012), are among the few non-legislative parallels to modern-day counterradicalization policy regarding the management of citizen political beliefs and opinions. Broadly speaking, they involved the creation of specific communication policies designed for local audiences often thought to be at risk of expressing violent dissent. Ultimately, however, these policies were concerned with maintaining a home front, rather than creating one, as counterradicalization policies arguably do.

Emergency powers legislation was a key feature of the government's legislative response to Irish nationalism and associated acts of terrorism, and indeed formed the basis of the Terrorism Act 2000 (discussed in detail in Chapter 7). This response was driven by successive re-enactments of legislation that were meant to be temporary. Most relevant were those introduced during the period of direct rule of Northern Ireland by the UK parliament in Westminster between 1972 and 1998.[10] Foremost among these was the Northern Ireland (Emergency Provisions) Act 1973, following the introduction of direct rule in 1971. This act built on measures introduced by the Northern Ireland government in the Civil Authorities (Special Powers) Act (Northern Ireland) 1922, which empowered the Parliament of Northern Ireland to impose curfews; proscribe organizations; censor printed, audio, and visual materials; ban meetings, processions, and gatherings; restrict the movement of individuals to within specified areas; and detain and intern suspects without bringing charges. The act also authorized extensive powers of entry, search, and seizure. The Northern Ireland (Emergency Provisions) Act 1973 retained the government's extensive powers of detention, proscription, entry, search, and seizure. In addition, the statute eliminated juries from the court system and established certain crimes as "scheduled" offenses, regardless of the perpetrator's motivation. The act was designed to be temporary. However, as Chapter 7 shows, it was extended without debate until the implementation of the Terrorism Act 2000.

Importantly, the UK government's response to violence in Northern Ireland, especially between 1972 and 1998, is regularly compared to current domestic counterterrorism measures. Indeed, a former senior security and intelligence coordinator in the early UK response to post-2001 homegrown extremism explicitly linked early policies to the lessons of community policing drawn from responses to terrorism in Northern Ireland.[11] However, despite important similarities in the coercive aspects of the policies (see Hickman et al. 2012; Heath-Kelly 2013; McGovern 2013), policy responses differ markedly. Unlike present-day counterradicalization policies, measures such as internment, restriction of movement, and preemptive detention aimed at curbing terrorism in Northern Ireland were almost wholly coercive and involved scant measures that could be described as either concerned with persuasive measures or as "integrationist." Certain early measures did draw on counterinsurgency measures and an understanding of "root causes" to try and address social causes of the unrest (Kennedy-Pipe and McInnes 1997: 14; Bennett 2010), but these were largely abandoned during direct rule. Similarly, media policy driven by the UK parliament focused on "persuasive" measures to address some problems of perception of the conflict by the people of Northern Ireland. However, these were not only limited after the introduction of direct rule in 1972 and in the years immediately prior, but were also arguably designed to influence perceptions of UK military intervention for military operational reasons rather than to function as a preemptive counterterrorism measure (see Miller 1993; Dixon 2009). During the period of direct rule—and indeed during the larger period of unrest associated with Irish nationalism—there was no attempt to integrate individuals into the broader informal British political community via the inculcation of values: the response was dominated by the use of force by traditional, formal arms of the state.

In the UK, then, as in most liberal democracies, the relationship between the formal and informal markers of political community are strained in times of war and in times of societal unrest considered dangerous by the state (Wilkinson 2011; Donohue 2008). This means that during those periods, citizens whose beliefs, heritage, or values are framed as dangerous are subject to having the formal aspects of their citizenship—which they might otherwise enjoy— challenged. But as Chapters 7 and 8 show, measures adopted in the post-2001 era differ substantially from those described here.

## 2001 and homegrown extremism in the UK

Unlike comparable experiences in the United States, post-2001 homegrown extremism in the UK was considered a threat from the earliest days following 9/11. This judgment drew on the country's large South Asian Muslim population, a history of transnational Islamic activism, terrorism taking place in or from the UK, and the clear involvement of significant mosques in London with transnational terrorist activity (Winnett et al. 2011).[12] Initially, however, as discussed further below, such a judgment was based on UK citizens being directed from abroad or fighting in foreign theaters.[13]

In the months and years following September 11, British Muslims were arrested in large numbers on terrorism-related charges, although few were actually charged. For example, 500 British Muslims were arrested between September 11, 2001, and December 2003. In one key raid, 150 police stormed the Finsbury Park mosque in North London in January 2003 (Muir 2003). However, in the early years following 9/11, British security services saw the threat of homegrown extremism as emanating from the activities of British citizens or residents directed by AQ-core: meaning the plots were generated outside Britain.

As former chief of the Metropolitan Police, Peter Clarke (2007: 20) put it: "The spectre of a home-grown terrorist threat was not yet with us." This explains, for example, the fact that radical preachers formerly housed at the Finsbury Park mosque were permitted to continue preaching despite concerns about their links to, and support for, AQ after police raids in 2003. These raids uncovered significant evidence of international links to terrorist activities, and both preachers' avowed support for AQ. Some commentators suggest that this apparent lack of concern resulted from norm competition in UK discourses. That is, increasingly prominent norms of securitization competed with long-held norms of the freedom of speech, respect for community identities, and respect for political asylum (Foley 2013: 54), meaning that the threat from homegrown extremism was not recognized and/or acted upon as it might have been otherwise.

However, statistics on the activities of the security services show that norms did not prohibit surveillance, and also suggest that between 2001 and early 2004, UK security services simply did not put much weight on the threat from homegrown extremism and were unwilling to act. For example, in 2001 there were 201 targets related to "Islamic radicalism" under surveillance by MI5, the UK's domestic counter-intelligence and security agency. In September 2005, this had increased only to "several hundred." In November 2006, after the 7/7 bombings, this had increased to 1,600, and by November 2007, to 2,000. By 2009–2010, there were 200 investigations underway (Foley 2013: 255). Given increases in counterterrorism funding in the years following 2001, and the introduction of increasingly repressive terrorist legislation even before 2001 (as discussed in Chapter 7), norm competition appears to be not the only or even the most prominent reason for an apparent lack of concern at this early stage. Instead, the threat appeared to be perceived as more likely to emerge outside the UK and to be linked to strong and already identified AQ networks, although with an acknowledgement of the increasing threat of UK citizens being involved in such plots. This explains the immediate focus on banning terrorist organizations and organizational funding and on border control in the early years following 2001. As Clarke (2007: 21) noted, "there was still no indication that there were plans for British citizens to mount attacks in the UK. By and large, in 2003 the UK was a net exporter of terrorism" (although see Intelligence and Security Committee 2006a: 25–26).

However, this judgment had changed by early 2004 when evidence and assessments began to suggest that the "home-grown element" would become more prominent. In 2006 the Parliamentary Intelligence and Security Committee judged that "over the next five years the UK would continue to face a threat from 'home-grown' as well as foreign terrorists" (Intelligence and Security Committee 2006b: 25). In March 2004, the largest counterterrorism operation mounted in the UK led to the arrest of eight UK-born citizens and one naturalized UK citizen in Operation Crevice, which uncovered a plot to blow up a nightclub, a shopping center, and the gas network, in concert with operatives in Canada. In August 2004, Operation Rhyme uncovered a plot by thirteen UK citizens to bomb installations in the United States and the UK. In both these cases, the plots were linked to core AQ operatives, indicating that the organization's methods had changed to increasingly involve the recruitment, training, and funding of terrorist operations on UK soil by UK citizens. In contrast, previous models saw plot preparation taking place wholly within AQ-core and outside the UK.

The events of July 2005 brought this new model into extreme relief. The London bombings of July 7 killed fifty-two people, and injured over 700. Conducted by a group of UK citizens, with assistance or oversight from AQ-core (Intelligence and Security Committee 2006b: 26; Hoffman 2009), the bombers were undetected prior to the explosions and the events changed the UK's response to homegrown extremism substantially. Three of the bombers were UK citizens of Pakistani descent, and one was a UK resident of Jamaican descent who had converted to Islam. The July 7 bombings were followed by a similar attempted bombing on July 21 in London by six UK citizens. This attempt failed and is largely considered a copycat attack. Unlike the 7/7 attackers, the July 21 bombers were not second-generation immigrants of largely South Asian descent, but were refugees who had come to the UK from East Africa—mainly Somalia and Eritrea—as children or young adults (Tumelty 2005).

Following 2005, the threat profile of homegrown extremism in the UK continued to diversify. Some plots continued to be driven by AQ-core, while others were wholly internally generated, and still others were a combination. For example, the three individuals convicted of the most serious charges in the 2006 US-UK plot to bomb transatlantic airliners (directed by core AQ operatives, as well as most of their co-conspirators) were British citizens of Pakistani descent, while a 2007 plot to kidnap and behead a UK soldier was conducted by UK citizens without AQ-core oversight—although at least one member of the plot had some links to AQ in Pakistan.

A striking development was the increase in threats by self-radicalized cells and individuals (Pantucci 2011). For example, in 2010 four citizens were arrested for planning attacks on the London stock exchange, inspired by AQ propagandist Anwar al-Awlaki's online sermons (Naik 2012). Studies suggested that the threat from self-radicalized "lone wolf" attacks increased over the period 2005–2010 (Pantucci 2011). For example, in February 2010 a "self-radicalized" individual who had worked for British Airways was jailed for thirty years after being found to have volunteered his services to Al-Qaeda in the Arabian Peninsula, while in 2013 the beheading of a UK soldier was committed by two UK citizens, apparently self-radicalized, at least one of whom had fought in Somalia with al-Shabaab.

The threat rating for terrorist activity in the UK decreased in July 2011 from severe (meaning an attack is highly likely) to substantial, and a House of Commons inquiry into the root causes of radicalization heard from experts in 2011 that the threat from radicalization was decreasing (House of Commons Home Affairs Committee 2012: 7). However, the 2012 annual report on the government's counterterrorism policy marked a "trend towards homegrown extremism," and the Deputy Assistant Commissioner of Police Stuart Osborne assessed the threat as similar to one 7/7 attack thwarted every year (HM Government 2013b: 10; Sky News 2013). In 2013, the Home Office warned that the ongoing conflict in Syria was a "game changer" for British homegrown extremism (Whitehead 2013). The terrorism threat rating changed back to severe in 2014, as the foreign fighter problem increased. By 2016, 800 UK-linked fighters were estimated to have travelled to Syria and Iraq since the conflicts began in those countries. Fifty percent of these foreign fighters were thought to have returned to the UK (House of Commons Home Affairs Committee 2016: 3). Researchers had also noted a surge in far-right terrorism and the re-emergence of some aspects of Northern Irish terrorism, although policy responses to these phenomena had not yet emerged by the end of 2016 (Hamilton 2016).

# 4
# Legislating against homegrown extremism in Britain

What does counterradicalization look like in the UK? One way of answering this question involves tracing its framing of the problem of homegrown extremism and its response in law. Building on Neal's (2012b) analysis of counterterrorism law in the UK, this approach notes that lawmaking is cumulative, even in the context of terrorism, where lawmaking is often viewed as an exceptional process. Rather than focusing on new laws as if they emerged anew in response to catastrophic events, this chapter takes the approach that "[l]awmaking is cumulative, with each law always in a relationship to others, adding to them, amending them, replacing them, or, in the case of security laws, often escalating their provisions beyond what was regarded as 'exceptional' the last time around" (Neal 2012a: 261). This is particularly true in the UK, where counterterrorism lawmaking takes place in an historical context of domestic terrorism. This approach also allows us to elucidate what lawmakers mean by homegrown extremism and their response to it in the absence of definitive research. It allows us to trace the historical antecedents of this approach.

The chapter traces the UK's legislative approach to the relationship between citizens and the state in the context of homegrown extremism,[1] showing that such legislation addresses the problem within a broader framework of political community. It examines three types of legislative measures: those which establish the framework through which the relationship between citizen and state is viewed in the context of post-9/11 counterterrorism; those which seek to prevent "citizen terrorism" directly; and those which respond to homegrown extremism via immigration and citizenship legislation. Doing so offers insights into the way that the problem and response are framed in the UK, showing that the concept of political community is key. In particular, it offers clues as to the nature of the inchoate British informal political community outlined in Chapter 3: the meaning of Britishness is clearly outlined in several pieces of legislation responding to homegrown extremism, showing the importance of the idea as a response to the problem.

## Establishing the citizen–state relationship post-9/11

### The Terrorism Act 2000

The Terrorism Act 2000 was intended to streamline cumbersome rolling emergency legislation—long a feature of the UK's response to violence in Northern Ireland—in order to address the expiration of enabling legislation, the passage of the Human Rights Act 1998, and important shifts in the Northern Ireland peace process (Walker 2000). Although it is removed from the problem of homegrown extremism I address in this chapter, the act is important for understanding of the relationship between the citizen, the state, and terrorism in the UK for four reasons. First, and most importantly, it introduced a broad definition of terrorism that decoupled the concept from Northern Irish terrorism for the first time in the UK. In doing so it defined terrorism on political, religious, and ideological grounds, substantially expanding the concept from definitions that had previously focused more on the material act of violence itself. It combined international and domestic terrorism into one definition in a way that highlighted the importance of the values, beliefs, and ideas motivating terrorist acts. This arguably provided the basis for later legislative and policy interventions that both criminalized and problematized the link between values, beliefs, and actions—emphasizing the role of informal political community in counterterrorism. Second, the act introduced the notion that terrorism was destructive of the system of British values, therein defining the informal political community associated with the jurisdiction through a counterterrorism lens. Third, the new legislation introduced the concept of incitement, further linking thoughts and values to acts of terrorism and emphasizing the power of certain ideas and beliefs in defining terrorism. Finally, it introduced many practical measures such as the removal of limits on intercepts and certain restrictions on warrants and stop and search powers that were designed to increase the preventative powers of police in the UK, although these measures had to some extent already been present in Northern Ireland in some form or other.[2]

The most important aspect of the Terrorism Act 2000 was the expansion of the definition of terrorism. The Northern Ireland (Emergency Provisions) Act 1996 (EPA) and the Prevention of Terrorism (Temporary Provisions) Act 1989 (PTA) had up until then been the source of the definition of terrorism for the UK and differed only slightly from the definition in the Prevention of Terrorism Act, which covered Northern Ireland. The definition in the EPA 1996 and the PTA 1989 drew on the original Northern Ireland (Emergency Provisions) Act 1973, and read:

(IV) 28(1) "terrorism" means the use of violence for political ends, and includes any use of violence for the purpose of putting the public or any section of the public in fear.

That definition was limited, in that the powers and offenses applied only to terrorism connected with Northern Ireland and to international terrorism. The definition introduced in Section 1 of the Terrorism Act 2000, is as follows:

(1) In this Act "terrorism" means the use or threat of action where—
   (a) the action falls within subsection (2),
   (b) the use or threat is designed to influence the government or to intimidate the public or a section of the public, and
   (c) the use or threat is made for the purpose of advancing a political, religious or ideological cause.

Section 1(c) of this definition introduces ideological and religious terrorism, moving the definition into the ideational realm. Part II of the act uses the definition as the basis for proscription of terrorist organizations.[3] The following paragraphs outline the basis for this considerable expansion.

Key to the expansion was Annex 1 of Lord Lloyd's 1996 review of terrorist legislation, which had been instituted by the Conservative John Major government (Lloyd 1996). Annex 1, written by academic and government adviser Professor Paul Wilkinson, dealt exclusively with the changing nature of the terrorist threat and was hugely influential in formulating both Lloyd's findings and new government policy on the matter (Brown 1996), particularly on the need to define terrorism more broadly given both the permanence of the proposed legislation, and the changing nature of the terrorist threat. As Walker (2000: 11) shows, prior to the Terrorism Act 2000, the definition had not only been restricted to Northern Ireland, it had been restricted by the express listing of particular offenses within that jurisdiction. The new definition was designed to counter as yet unknown threats: the emphasis was on countering the unknown and demonstrating how wildly terrorism could deviate from what the UK had already experienced.

The government drew on Wilkinson's work to argue that "the powers in the new legislation should be capable of being used in relation to any form of serious terrorist violence whether domestic, international or Irish" (HM Government 1998: para. 3.13), noting "the last few years has seen a marked increase in terrorism motivated by religious idealism . . . today over a third of the world's active international terrorist groups are predominantly motivated by religious fanaticism" (HM Government 1998: para. 2.4).

The government thus introduced definitions of terrorism based on actors' political and religious motivations, meaning the beliefs, values, and ideas that informed it, rather than the effect it had on sections of the public—"inspiring fear" in the original definition in the Terrorism Act 2000. To differentiate terrorism from the normal realms of political protest, then Minister of State at the Home Office Charles Clarke highlighted the importance of motivation—and indeed a particular type of motivation—in determining whether the threshold for action could be reached. He argued in Parliament that: "The test for terrorism is not 'any use of violence'. Acts that intimidate the public but for which no qualifying motivation can be demonstrated are no longer caught by the Bill." He noted that: "The fundamental thrust of what we should be trying to achieve is a definition of terrorism as an attempt to undermine democratic processes by the use of violence.... We chose the phrase 'advancing a political, religious or ideological cause' because it summed up what we were trying to achieve. It encompasses the use of violence in an attempt to undermine the democratic process better than any other description" (Clarke 2000). Then Home Secretary Jack Straw espoused a similar vein of thought when he noted in the same debate: "Although all crime to some degree plainly threatens the stability of the social and political order, terrorism differs from crime motivated solely by greed in that it is directed at undermining the foundations of government" (Straw 1999).

Both ministers thus emphasized that religious, political, and ideological motivations were important on the whole, because when defined as terrorism they amounted to an attempt to undermine certain democratic processes and preexisting foundations of government. In doing so, they emphasized that, for the first time, the definition of terrorism in UK legislation required consideration to be paid to the thoughts, beliefs, and values behind a terrorist act, rather than to the effects of the act itself. In addition, these thoughts, beliefs, and actions were linked by Clarke to the values that underpinned Britain's informal political community—emphasizing democratic and parliamentary processes. The act thus laid the basis for further considerations of such factors in designing counterradicalization programs and in other measures addressing the problem of "citizen terrorists."

## Incitement

The Terrorism Act 2000 also introduced the notion of incitement into counterterrorism legislation for the first time, in this case applied extraterritorially.[4] Incitement is important to our understanding of counterradicalization, and the problem of citizen terrorism more generally, because it involves the role of thoughts, values, and ideas of citizens, as precursors to terrorism and the symbolic power inherent in the narratives they construct. The Terrorism Act 2000 applied this specifically to terrorism, but specifies that the terrorist act should take place at least in part outside the United Kingdom. Section 59(1) (4) of the Act reads:

(1) A person commits an offence if—
   (a) he incites another person to commit an act of terrorism wholly or partly outside the United Kingdom...
(4) For the purposes of subsection (1) it is immaterial whether or not the person incited is in the United Kingdom at the time of the incitement.

As Walker (1992: 23–27) notes, the UK had long been struggling to manage the issue of dissidents or diasporas acting on UK soil in the name of foreign struggles.[5] In response to criticism that the act would target activists unnecessarily, it framed the issue in terms of the link between informal political community and terrorism, in ways that would later prove important for counterradicalization.[6] Clarke (2000) argued that:

> The distinguishing feature of a democracy as opposed to other forms of organisation of society is that we promote those causes within our democratic system, rather than having recourse to violence and other means. It is important to be clear as to whether there is any doubt—I do not believe that there is—that the Bill does not suggest that it is wrong for people to have causes or that to have causes adds up to behaving as a terrorist. On the contrary, the Government and all hon. Members strongly want to promote a society in which people have views and causes, campaign and take up issues, but do so inside the democratic tradition that we embody by virtue of our election rather than outside it in any direct way.

In debating the definitional and incitement provisions of the bill, the government made clear that certain sorts of values, beliefs, and ideas were targeted: those which sought to undermine the current system of government and democratic processes. These processes—the "cult of Parliament" (Colley 2005: 52)—underpin the values, beliefs, and ideas which define the UK's informal political community, and this is certainly the way legislators described them in the associated debate.[7] The Terrorism Act 2000, then, redefined the relationship between citizen beliefs, values, and the state in the context of terrorism. The following chapters show that this was fundamental to post-9/11 legislation outlined below.

## The Anti-Terrorism, Crime and Security Act 2001

Like legislation introduced around the world in response to the events of September 11, 2001, the Anti-Terrorism, Crime and Security Act 2001 was striking in the breadth of measures it introduced, the speed with which it was passed, and its severity—a leading UK constitutional scholar called it "the most draconian legislation Parliament has passed in peacetime in over a century" (Tomkins 2002: 205). Like similar US legislation, the act, introduced two months after September 11, focused on coercive measures such as the freezing of suspected terrorist assets, detention of non-British citizens for unspecified periods of time when they were suspected of terrorism, enhanced airport security control measures, and collection and retention of personal data. The 124-page act was passed in just over one month, with much of it never debated. Indeed, the House of Commons let the bill pass without proposing any amendments, although the House of Lords considered it in some detail—albeit quickly—with a record five defeats for the government in one session (see Gearty 2005 and Fenwick 2002 for a general discussion).

The most controversial of the new provisions was an innovation related entirely to the new terrorism environment, and one which recalls the link between terrorism and informal political community established in the Terrorism Act 2000. These provisions focused on detention and deportation and were especially controversial because they required the government to institute a derogation from the European Convention on Human Rights. The government did so under Article 15 of the convention, which authorizes such action where the executive judges this is "strictly required" on account of a "public emergency" "threatening the life of the nation."

Part IV of the Act included measures for the detention without trial of non-British citizens and those without legal right of abode suspected of international terrorism. Under Sections 21 and 22 of Part IV, the home secretary can issue a certificate of detention and deportation for such a person on the basis of (a) reasonable belief that their presence in the UK is a risk to national security[8] or (b) reasonable suspicion that he or she is a terrorist. Importantly, via Section 21(2), the definition of a terrorist draws on the broad definition introduced in Section 1 of the Terrorism Act 2000, including, as a result, action where the use or threat of action is "made for the purpose of advancing a political, religious or ideological cause," and including, under Section 59(1) incitement "to commit an act of terrorism ... outside the United Kingdom," where that person is inside or outside the UK. Section 23 of the Anti-Terrorism, Crime and Security Act 2001 effectively provided for detention of non-citizens indefinitely in circumstances where deportation was prevented either by some practical consideration or because to do so would subject individuals to a risk of torture.

Given non-refoulement requirements under the Human Rights Act, this meant that where individuals could not be deported, they were to be detained indefinitely, for ideas, values, and beliefs in effect framed in the earlier legislation as incommensurate with "British values."[9] In their derogation from the

European Convention on Human Rights, these measures withdrew the protection of due process previously offered to non-citizens. This meant that in practice the boundaries of formal political community were tightened immediately following 9/11, including according to newly ideational definitions of terrorism. The act redefined the *status* of residents who were previously the legal equivalent of citizens in terms of due process rights, theoretically based on issues of values, beliefs, and ideas—*identity*—as well as violent acts themselves.

## The Prevention of Terrorism Act 2005

The Prevention of Terrorism Act, passed in March 2005, was largely a response to a court case, *A (FC) v Secretary of State for the Home Department*, in which the House of Lords held that the indefinite detention of foreigners under Part IV of the Anti-Terrorism, Crime and Security Act 2001 was unlawful. The new act introduced a system of control orders,[10] whereby instead of locking up those suspected of preparing for terrorist acts as under the 2001 act, individuals could be subjected to control orders which allowed them to live in the community under significant restrictions, including curfews, restrictions on visitors and access to places of worship, and compulsory wearing of electronic tags. Importantly, under the new act, control orders could be applied to UK citizens, whereas indefinite detention under the 2001 act was restricted to non-citizens.[11]

Section 2(1)(a) allows that to impose a control order the secretary of state must only "have reasonable grounds for suspecting that the individual is or has been involved in terrorism-related activity," while Section 1(9) of the act specifies that involvement in terrorist activity may include:

(a) the commission, preparation or instigation of acts of terrorism;
(b) conduct which facilitates the commission, preparation or instigation of such acts, or which is intended to do so;
(c) conduct which gives encouragement to the commission, preparation or instigation of such acts, or which is intended to do so;
(d) conduct which gives support or assistance to individuals who are known or believed to be involved in terrorism-related activity.

Section 1(9) contains the seeds of the crime of encouragement introduced in the Terrorism Act 2006, marking the encouragement[12] of an act—the transmission of ideas and values—as dangerous in itself, separate from the act, emphasizing the role of symbolic power in the problem. In doing so, these elements focus on the concept of persuasion, and persuasiveness, as important facets in post-2001 terrorism.

## Preventing "citizen terrorism": The 2005 London bombings and beyond

The London bombings of July 7, 2005, (7/7) killed fifty-two people and injured over 700. Conducted by four British citizens, with some oversight from AQ-core, the bombers went undetected prior to the plot. The London bombings initiated extensive, integration-focused counterradicalization policies aimed at deterring citizens from engaging in terrorism against the state. The legislative response was rather more coercive, but engaged in the management of the informal political community—of British values, beliefs, and ideas—in ways similar to those of broader policy measures. These legislative efforts also frame the problem of terrorism itself in terms of symbolic violence and the problem of persuasion, setting the stage for persuasive rather than coercive measures.

### The Terrorism Act 2006

Drafted in October 2005 and passed in March 2006, the Terrorism Act 2006 slightly broadened the definition of terrorism contained in the 2000 act and created a new series of offenses, including the encouragement of terrorism, the dissemination of terrorist publications, preparation of terrorist acts, training for terrorism, making terrorist threats, making devices to be used for terrorist acts, and attendance at a place used for terrorist training.[13]

In introducing the bill, Home Secretary Clarke laid out the government's intent to link British values with counterradicalization. Beginning his second-reading speech by outlining the political values held dear by the political community that the bill aimed to protect, he argued:

> Of all the societies throughout the world, perhaps that of the United Kingdom is the society that laid the basis for the values that we here seek to defend: valuing and building free speech and freedom of expression, including a free media; believing in a society that respects all faiths, races and beliefs; believing in a society founded on the rule of law; wanting every citizen to have a democratic stake in our society; valuing the free economy, which has built prosperity, including high-quality public services on which we all depend; and valuing the fact that women can play a full role in our society. (Clarke 2005b)

Noting that "ideas drive those people forward," Clarke went on to argue that the ideas behind such AQ-inspired terrorism were marked by "nihilism" toward democratic values rather than any foreign policy considerations and stated that "our societies would cease to be a target only if we were to renounce all the values of freedom and liberty that we have fought to extend over so many years. Our only answer to this threat must be to contest and then to defeat it, and that is why we need this legislation" (Clarke 2005c).

With its new crimes of glorification and encouragement of terrorism and dissemination of publications, this legislation was introduced in a context which very clearly defined terrorism as antithetical to British values and established counterterrorism as concerned with managing the thoughts, values, and beliefs associated with terrorism, including those held by British citizens. These measures are ultimately concerned with counterradicalization because they approach the symbolic power inherent in narrative propagated by citizens and their capacity to radicalize others.[14] The new offenses are listed in Section 1 of the act as follows. Their novelty is such that it is worth quoting them in full:

Encouragement of terrorism

(1) This section applies to a statement that is likely to be understood by some or all of the members of the public to whom it is published as a direct or indirect encouragement or other inducement to them to the commission, preparation or instigation of acts of terrorism or Convention offences.

(2) A person commits an offence if—
   (a) he publishes a statement to which this section applies or causes another to publish such a statement; and
   (b) at the time he publishes it or causes it to be published, he—
      (i) intends members of the public to be directly or indirectly encouraged or otherwise induced by the statement to commit, prepare or instigate acts of terrorism or Convention offences; or
      (ii) is reckless as to whether members of the public will be directly or indirectly encouraged or otherwise induced by the statement to commit, prepare or instigate such acts or offences.

(3) For the purposes of this section, the statements that are likely to be understood by members of the public as indirectly encouraging the commission or preparation of acts of terrorism or Convention offences include every statement which—
   (a) glorifies the commission or preparation (whether in the past, in the future or generally) of such acts or offences; and
   (b) is a statement from which those members of the public could reasonably be expected to infer that what is being glorified is being glorified as conduct that should be emulated by them in existing circumstances.

(4) For the purposes of this section the questions how a statement is likely to be understood and what members of the public could

reasonably be expected to infer from it must be determined having regard both—
   (a) to the contents of the statement as a whole; and
   (b) to the circumstances and manner of its publication.
(5) It is irrelevant for the purposes of subsections (1) to (3)—
   (a) whether anything mentioned in those subsections relates to the commission, preparation or instigation of one or more particular acts of terrorism or Convention offences, of acts of terrorism or Convention offences of a particular description or of acts of terrorism or Convention offences generally; and,
   (b) whether any person is in fact encouraged or induced by the statement to commit, prepare or instigate any such act or offence.

These measures introduced offenses of indirect encouragement and glorification into UK legislation for the first time, and linked them directly to terrorism.[15] Indirect encouragement, unlike "incitement," decouples the link between thinking and talking about an act to others and the commission of the act: it highlights the importance of the ideas and values held by individuals themselves—specifically ideas antithetical to British values—and the symbolic power inherent in the ability to communicate those ideas and values to others. For example, Section 1(5)(b) makes it clear that there is no necessary link between the encouragement of terrorism and the actual commission of a terrorist act. Similarly, glorification is referred to as an example of encouragement and is defined as "any form of praise or celebration" of any act in the past, present, or future (Section 20(2)). Contrary to Clarke's originally stated plans, the final form of the act removes the requirement for intent, requiring only that the person act "recklessly." In this, the act maintained an "objective" test for recklessness which ran against then recent common law decisions, which had moved toward a "subjective" test (see *Regina v G*). Simply put, this meant that the wording of the act made an offense of a much broader range of activities, in the sense that a speaker's individual understanding or judgment of the effects of their words would not be taken into account, only those of a "reasonable person."

The government paid particular attention to the role of the publication of certain materials in giving oxygen to ideas that led to the radicalization of British citizens, arguing: "We should not ignore the contributory role that radical texts and extremist pamphlets have in radicalisation. They serve to propagate and reinforce the extremist and damaging philosophies which attempt to justify and explain the motivations of terrorists" (Scotland 2006). To combat this problem, Section 2 of the Terrorism Act 2006 introduced a new offense of the dissemination of terrorist publications. A publication is a "terrorist publication" if it is likely "to be understood . . . as a direct or indirect encouragement . . . of terrorism" (Section 2(3)(a)). Section 2(4) defines "matter that is likely to be understood . . . as indirectly encouraging" terrorism as any matter which (a) glorifies terrorist acts and which, under the circumstances, (b) "could reasonably be expected" to cause a person to believe that they should emulate the glorified acts of terrorism. Like the encouragement of terrorism offense, the dissemination offense does not require intent, and allows for a person to be charged if they are simply "reckless as to whether his conduct" encourages or assists in the commission of terrorism.[16]

Under Section 3, this offense included provisions for publications on the internet for the first time. Dissemination offenses include the act of making available information on bomb-making on a website. Relatedly, Sections 3 and 4 of the act establish an internet "Notice and Takedown" procedure under which as content providers, editors and hosts of websites can be required to remove or amend material considered to be unlawfully terrorism-related. As discussed further in Chapter 5, this provision has led to the deletion of thousands of websites.

## The Counter-Terrorism Act 2008

The Counter-Terrorism Act 2008 was unusual in the sense that it was passed without the sense of urgency of other post-9/11 acts and did not immediately follow a terrorist incident. There was instead a relatively leisurely seventeen months between introduction and assent of the act and a long consultation period. Its design also encompassed a 2007 review of counterterrorism legislation (the Carlisle Review) and the government's response. The government framed the act as a preparation for future, as yet unknown, risks. Many of the provisions can be categorized as moving the state's reach temporally backward and forward, attempting to manage as yet unknown risks in ways characteristic of the "preventive state" (Steiker 1998: 771). In this way the act is relevant to counterradicalization although it does not directly address it. The act included, for example, measures such as longer terrorism sentences, provisions for post-charge questioning, changes to the collection and use of evidence including intercept evidence, powers to seize terrorist assets, and provisions for judges to implement more severe sentences for offenses merely associated with terrorism, rather than being terrorist offenses themselves.

The most controversial measure was Part 2, Section 22 of the bill, which proposed the introduction of an extended period of pre-charge detention from twenty-eight to forty-two days, following on from the government's failed attempt to introduce a ninety-day pre-charge period in 2005. The measure was defeated in the House of Lords after a controversial and hotly debated passage through the House of Commons. As Walker (2011: 293) notes, these restrictions drew on similar individual-level monitoring restrictions found in the context of violent and sexual offenders in the Criminal Justice Act 2003 under certain provisions of the Criminal Justice and Immigration Act 2008 and other provisions used against football hooligans or drug traffickers. However, the particular restrictions proposed in the Counter-Terrorism Act 2008 are distinctive in that they seek to "monitor without the more positive social intervention aspects" of other, similar measures in other contexts (Walker 2011: 293). They are preventive but permanently so, without the promise of "rehabilitation"—they represent a permanent exclusion from the normal due process rights otherwise accorded British citizens, based on a broad definition of terrorism.

## Counter-Terrorism and Security Act 2015 (Prevent Duty)

The Counter-Terrorism and Security Act 2015 was developed in response to increasing concerns about foreign fighters, as well as existing concerns about processes of radicalization. In responding to these concerns, the act introduced a new duty directly relevant to counterradicalization and two new powers particularly designed to address the issue of foreign fighters. In Section 26(1), the act imposes a legal requirement on certain bodies (a range of public authorities including schools, universities, and hospitals) to demonstrate "due regard to the need to prevent people from being drawn into terrorism" (HM Government 2015a: 5) better known as the "Prevent Duty." The term "due regard" means workers in designated parts of the public sector are required to "demonstrate an awareness and understanding of the risk of radicalisation in the area, institution or body" (HM Government 2015a: 6). This includes identifying and reporting an individual's proclivity for extremist ideologies and reporting concerns. To demonstrate effective compliance with the duty, specified authorities must demonstrate evidence of productive cooperation, in particular with local Prevent coordinators, the police, and local authorities, and coordination through existing multi-agency forums, for example Community Safety Partnerships (HM Government 2015a: 7). In Section 36, the act also introduced, relatedly, provisions for local Prevent boards to assist with identifying and managing individuals who had been identified and in instituting reporting requirements for local authorities. Intriguingly, the act did not refer to "radicalization," preferring the phrase "drawn into terrorism" and using the definition of terrorism drawn from the Terrorism Act 2000. This effectively broadens the scope for monitoring and reporting activity and removes the need for specific signposts or markers of radicalization.

Updated guidance on the Prevent Duty specifically for universities was released in 2015, addressing the special duties attached to managing extremist speech in the higher education sector—given government concerns about radicalization via speaking tours to university Islamic groups. The guidance was informed by the newly formed Extremism Analysis Unit, housed in the Home Office. The unit found that in 2014, there were at least seventy events involving speakers known to have "promoted rhetoric that aimed to undermine core British values of democracy, the rule of law, individual liberty and mutual respect and tolerance of those with different faiths and beliefs" (HM Government 2015b). New powers introduced in the act also specifically addressed the problem of foreign fighters. They enabled the seizure and retention of the passport of a person suspected to be leaving the UK for the purpose of a terrorism activity outside the UK (Section 1, Schedule 1) and allowed for the temporary exclusion of other citizens on this basis (Sections 2–5, 9–10). The act also introduced new measures for TPIMs, allowing individuals to be relocated to different parts of the country to reduce their ability to radicalize others (see Fenwick 2016).

## Managing homegrown extremism via immigration and citizenship legislation

### The Nationality, Immigration and Asylum Act 2002

The Nationality, Immigration and Asylum Act 2002 was part of a broader Labour government response to citizenship issues, but transcended those original goals in the newly defined post-2001 security environment. As with other migration-focused acts discussed in this chapter, it is included here because government discourse linked it strongly to counterterrorism policy and to the problem of "citizen terrorists."

Riots in summer 2001 in cities in the north of England with large Muslim populations resulted in two inquiries into community cohesion that touched upon issues of immigration and integration. These inquiries built on concerns about active citizenship, which had been evident under Labour since 1998, but focused on them in the context of community cohesion and social order following the 2001 riots (Spencer 2007). As discussed in Chapter 3, the response to the violence of summer 2001 laid the conceptual and discursive groundwork for the association of community cohesion with immigration, integration, counterterrorism, the maintenance, delineation and promotion of certain national values, and a particular mode of citizenship.

Emerging links between originally relatively disparate agendas of social order, citizenship, immigration, integration, and counterterrorism were made clear in a key essay by Home Secretary David Blunkett in September 2002. Addressing the meaning of citizenship in the context of globalization, he linked defense of democracy, and counterterrorism, with community cohesion and citizenship. Following a description of AQ and the Taliban as perpetuating attacks on democracy, he argued: "It follows that the strongest defence of democracy resides in the engagement of every citizen with the community, from activity in the neighbourhood, through to participation in formal politics" (Blunkett 2002: 69). Here, the practice of citizenship is portrayed not only as a good in its own right, but as a legitimate and effective counterterrorism measure.

The Nationality, Immigration and Asylum Act 2002 was enacted in this environment. The act introduced substantial changes to the asylum regime, extending the power to detain asylum seekers. It also made substantial changes to the conceptualization of citizenship in UK immigration law. For example, Section 1 introduced requirements for "knowledge of life in the United Kingdom" and English-language proficiency as part of the naturalization process and introduced citizenship ceremonies in the UK for the first time. The Life in the United Kingdom test introduced for citizenship applicants included not only knowledge about the political system but also values,[17] drawing on a booklet "Life in the United Kingdom: A Journey to Citizenship" which included sections on "the rights and duties of a citizen," "human rights," and religion and tolerance (HM Government 2004a: 128, 132, 54).[18]

The act also introduced substantial changes to measures for the deprivation of citizenship, the first being a change to the required standard. The British Nationality Act 1981 had listed reasons for denaturalization and deprivation as: disloyalty, trading with the enemy, and criminality, and included the requirement that, overall, denaturalization be conducive to the public good. Section 4(2) of the 2002 act outlined a new standard such that that the only requirement was that the secretary of state had to be satisfied that the person "has done anything seriously prejudicial to the vital interests" of the UK. The second change was that the deprivation of citizenship process was for the first time to apply to all types of dual-national citizens: native born, registered, and naturalized—previously, native-born citizens had been excluded. In practice, the act was only applicable to dual-national native-born citizens, since it retained the requirement from the British Nationality Act 1981 that no-one be rendered stateless in its application.

The application to dual nationals was justified on national security grounds (see Gibney 2013). The Home Office minister argued in committee, for example, that the bill modernized the deprivation procedure "in terms of national security threats and non-state threats, such as those from organisations that are organised globally but are not states" (Eagle 2002). Here, under the rubric of national security we see the boundaries of formal political community—the status of citizenship—redefined by the boundaries of informal political community, in a striking way.

In fact, at least one scholar argues that the government intended these provisions to apply to all citizens and was limited only by European Convention on Human Rights provisions, which meant individuals could not be rendered stateless in response to a state's actions. For example, in response to accusations that the measures were discriminatory, the government argued that it would have preferred the provisions to apply to all citizens, not just dual nationals, but was unable to do so (Filkin 2002; see also Gibney 2013: 648–649). This suggests that although in practice the provisions introduced a gradation of citizenship where none had existed before—a boundary between non-dual national and dual nationals in favor of the former—in fact the ultimate goal was to link all citizenship to behavior in the context of certain values, subverting the status of citizenship and the rights associated with it to the identity associated with that citizenship: the "behavioural aspects of individuals acting and conceiving of themselves as members of a collectivity ... or the normative conceptions of such behaviour imputed by the state" (Joppke 2007: 38).

## The Immigration, Asylum and Nationality Act 2006

This act was introduced in 2006 to give effect to certain counterterrorism measures prefigured in Prime Minister Tony Blair's immediate response to the 7/7 bombings but not addressed in the Terrorism Act 2006. The amendments in question were foreshadowed by Home Secretary Clarke's introduction of a new list of "unacceptable behaviours" in late August 2005 that would form the basis for the exercise of the home secretary's powers to exclude and deport non-nationals.

The home secretary had always had these powers under the Immigration Act 1971 on the grounds that such individuals' presence in the UK was not conducive to the public good. The list of "unacceptable behaviours" was intended to give substance to what was meant by "conducive to the public good" in the context of the post-7/7 environment. These built on initial amendments to the migration regime introduced in the Nationality, Immigration and Asylum Act 2002, which introduced for the first time the possibility of the removal of British citizenship for activities associated with terrorism. The new amendments went further in linking exclusion, deportation, and removal of formal citizenship to the promulgation of certain ideas incompatible with British values by definition.

Home Secretary Clarke published the final list of unacceptable behaviors on August 23, 2005. The preceding three-week consultation period saw the government drop one of its more controversial definitions of unacceptable behaviors from the original list—a clause specifying views "which the government considers to be extreme and that conflict with the UK's culture of tolerance" (Tempest 2005). The final list gives the following as unacceptable behaviors:

> Writing, producing, publishing or distributing material
> Public speaking including preaching
> Running a website
> Using a position of responsibility such as teacher, community or youth leader to express views which:
> - Foment, justify or glorify terrorist violence in furtherance of particular beliefs;
> - Seek to provoke others to terrorist acts;
> - Foment other serious criminal activity or seek to provoke others to serious criminal acts; or
> - Foster hatred which might lead to inter-community violence in the UK.
> (Article 19 2005: Appendix)

This list thus expanded the basis on which the Home Secretary could potentially deny applicants entry (including asylum seekers) to the UK because of political views they had expressed and allowed for their deportation based on those same views. The list was retrospective, meaning it could be used as the basis for exclusion or deportation based on acts of encouragement or dissemination undertaken before the list's very existence. This provision also operated to remove those with previous leave to remain in the UK, including students and temporary entrants, those in the UK with infinite leave to remain or as students, workers, asylum seekers, and refugees. The secretary also announced that in conjunction with the introduction of the list of unacceptable behaviors, the Home Office, Foreign and Commonwealth Office, and intelligence agencies would be compiling a "database of individuals around the world who have demonstrated the relevant behaviours" (Clarke 2005d) which would then be made available to entry clearance and immigration officers.

Access to the UK itself was thus newly determined based on not only the holding but the communication of certain values encouraging, instigating, justifying, or glorifying terrorist violence—the definition of which had, in previous legislation, been expanded to include an almost limitless range of behaviors.[19] As in earlier legislation, the symbolic power of narratives communicated by individuals was newly legislated in the context of terrorism. Public discourse by key government officials had in turn, as described earlier, placed such behaviors in opposition to key British values. In the past, individuals had previously been denied entry to the UK on character grounds, but this was based on evidence of criminal behavior rather than the communication of ideas.[20]

However, not only did the amendments add this element to exclusion and deportation provisions, they also expanded the basis on which naturalized citizens could be stripped of their British citizenship to include the same practices. In doing so, they defined access to the ultimate marker of membership in a formal political community—citizenship—based on the expression of certain values: that is, on informal political community. In doing so, they sought to realign the boundaries of formal and informal citizenship as a counterterrorism measure. Importantly, the list included reference to "justifying" terrorist violence—a behavior not included in the list of behaviors defined as encouragement of terrorism in Section 1 of the Terrorism Act 2006, and perhaps linked more closely to practices of argument and debate than promotion of terrorism.

The ability to remove citizenship under the counterterrorism regime was not novel. Governments had previously held the ability to strip nationals of their British citizenship if they had committed an act "seriously prejudicial to the vital interests of the United Kingdom or a British overseas territory" under Section 4 of the Nationality, Immigration and Asylum Act 2002. In practice, this was only applied to dual nationals, as the operation of the clause could not legally render a person stateless. However, the 2006 amendments revised the Immigration and Nationality Act 1981 so that a dual national could be stripped of citizenship if the secretary of state deemed it "conducive to the public good" to deprive a person of his or her British nationality, informed by the list of unacceptable behaviors described above, a much weaker test (House of Lords House of Commons Joint Committee on Human Rights 2005). The use of these provisions has increased in recent years. Between 2010 and 2015, thirty-three people were stripped of their citizenship on terror grounds (Parsons 2016), with a peak of twenty in 2013, a fact largely attributed to the emergence of the "foreign fighter" problem (Ross and Galey 2013; see Anderson 2016 for an overview of the powers in practice).

The Immigration, Asylum and Nationality Act 2006 also extended the right to deprivation of citizenship to include removing the right of abode for Commonwealth citizens based on the same criteria. It also allowed that applicants who had not yet obtained British citizenship but were eligible to do so via registration—meaning minors, for example, who had been born in the UK—to be refused on the basis of these unacceptable behaviors in the course of proving to the secretary of state that they were of good character, a new requirement in itself. The option to exclude persons from citizenship based on good character had previously been applied to those seeking citizenship via naturalization, not registration. Here, as in the Nationality, Immigration and Asylum Act 2002, access to formal membership of the political community—citizenship status—was predicated on attachment to the ideas, beliefs, and values of the informal political community.

## The Immigration Act 2014

The Immigration Act 2014 inserted new provisions into the British Nationality Act 1981 concerning the deprivation of the citizenship of naturalized citizens. Section 66 allows the home secretary to deprive a naturalized person of their British citizenship on the grounds that this is "conducive to the public good because the person, while having that citizenship status, has conducted him or herself in a manner which is seriously prejudicial to the vital interests of the United Kingdom," even if this rendered them stateless and even if they had not committed an actual offense. This is possible as long as the home secretary has "reasonable grounds for believing that the person is able, under the law of a country or territory outside the United Kingdom, to become a national of such a country or territory" (Section 66(1)). Then Home Secretary Theresa May described the new test for deprivation as follows: "The amendment will allow the key consideration to be whether the person's actions are consistent with the values we all attach to British citizenship . . . this is encapsulated by the oath that naturalised citizens take when they attend their citizenship ceremonies" (May 2014). In doing so, she clearly linked the newly extensive powers with the nature of the informal political community in the UK.

Such a measure had previously been impossible given that inducing statelessness in a person who had previously held British citizenship would breach domestic and international law, specifically Section 40 of the British Nationality Act 1981 and Article 8 of the United Nations Convention on the Reduction of Statelessness 1961. The measure was largely enacted in response to the Supreme Court case of Hilal Al-Jedda and in light of the number of British foreign fighters who had joined the Syrian civil war. Al-Jedda, an Iraqi refugee who was granted British citizenship, was accused of being involved in terrorist activities in occupied Iraq. In October 2013, the Supreme Court struck down the order to deprive him of his citizenship. The home secretary repeatedly referred to the case in the House of Commons debate on the bill, making it clear that these new powers sought to counter homegrown terrorism by British citizens by linking the retention of citizenship to the practice of "British values." This concept is defined in the Immigration Act 2006, in the Nationality, Immigration and Asylum Act 2002 in the context of the "public good," and in the context of the ideational elements of the newly broadened definition of terrorism in the Terrorism Act 2000. In effect, this amounts to a long-term plan for the congruence of formal and informal political community, as a measure to counter the threat of homegrown extremism. The measures allow the government to exclude individuals who had participated in global jihadi conflicts—especially in Syria, an issue of increasing concern raised by the home secretary in debate on the bill.

# 5
# A suspect community
## Countering radicalization in Britain

How do policymakers approach the problem of countering radicalization when the underlying science is not conclusive? This chapter outlines relevant UK policy responses to the problem of radicalization. Together with Chapter 4, this analysis also creates a timeline of counterradicalization policy in the UK, allowing us to see the policies and the ideas they express as a continuum rather than a response to emergency events, and allowing us as a result to chart the ideas underpinning the various iterations of policy responding to the problem of homegrown extremism. This timeline shows that the policies have shifted and developed over time, in response to events. It also shows, in discussion, that certain themes persist throughout. For example, it shows that in the absence of underlying research the policies adopt "taken for granted understandings" (Schwartz-Shea 2015: 123) about radicalization and its solution. These understandings frame "British Muslims" as part of a larger transnational community of Muslims whose values, beliefs, and ideas are not necessarily congruent with the informal political community delineated by "British values." They drive policy responses that deal in the language and practices of British values, integration, and cohesions, which are themselves somewhat "taken for granted" in that they are opaque at best. Unlike the equivalent discussion of US policy initiatives (Chapter 8), the analysis of persistent themes in the UK context is embedded in the timeline itself. This is because the UK has many more relevant policy documents than the United States, with abundant detail.

## Early policy initiatives

Civil society groups, largely driven by Muslim communities, had been active in counterradicalization since the early days following 9/11. According to Oliver McTernan, head of a faith-based charity: "Prior to 7/7 [July 7, 2005] we gave a dossier to Downing Street which clearly said there was a real risk of 7/7 happening. That was clear from concerns within the communities."[1] The government responded relatively slowly. In November 2002, the newly appointed UK intelligence coordinator in the Cabinet Office, David Omand, started work on a coordinated, multi-agency counterterrorism policy program, which had emerged in the wake of September 2001. This policy was presented to cabinet in February 2003, but remained classified until it was updated and made public in 2006, following the 7/7 bombings.[2] The policy, known as Contest, was a slim document of no more than twenty pages. It established four pillars of the government's approach, which were to resonate with emerging counterradicalization and broader counterterrorism policy: (1) preventing terrorism by tackling the radicalization of individuals; (2) pursuing terrorists and those that sponsor them; (3) protecting the public, key national services, and UK interests overseas; and (4) preparing for the consequences.

This policy is not discussed in detail here as it is not possible to ascertain that this text was used in 2003, rather than in 2006. But in 2003 the Prevent pillar was the most underdeveloped of the four (HM Government 2009a: 82), whereas in 2006 this was not the case so it is unlikely the texts are exactly the same. And one analyst stated that in 2003 the policy was largely expressed in terms of community policing.[3] An initiative within Special Branch, the Muslim Contact Unit, would later be absorbed into Prevent but at its inception in 2002 it was primarily an intelligence collection mechanism and an avenue for community engagement, in classic community policing style—providing a channel for communication between communities and policing services about issues and individuals of concern.[4]

A former senior British official working on counterradicalization policy noted that outside developments in community policing in Northern Ireland, with some attention to the negative impact of coercive policies employed by British forces there, experiences in that conflict had very little to do with policy design.[5] Instead the policy drew on understandings of community cohesion established during the government's response to the riots of summer 2001, discussed in Chapter 3:

> There were a couple of initiatives which I think were critical. One was the riots in England in 2001. In response to them the Home Office set up a community cohesion unit. This was part of the same administrative division as the faith communities unit. They were both the brainchild of David Blunkett [Home Secretary at the time], who wanted an approach to communities based on active citizenship. His views were influenced by US thinkers like [Robert] Putnam who wrote about the importance of preserving and building social capital.
>
> Those sorts of ideas influenced the measures that substituted for a Prevent in the first couple of years of Contest, the UK's counterterrorism strategy. This is because after 9/11 the emphasis was much more about the Pursue part of the Contest. This was given the greatest priority. The Prevent side was really left to this community-based approach, without the security officials really taking that

much interest in it. For two years the part of the Home Office concerned with counterterrorism, had only one and a half policy officials working on Prevent. There were a larger number than in the communities divisions and they developed policies in lieu of a Prevent policy proper. This was unfamiliar ground for the officials in the counterterrorism field and so they seemed to think "we've got other things to do, let's leave it to them."[6]

Prevent 1, as it came to be known, marked the beginnings of government thinking regarding the role of British citizens in acts of terrorism against the British state. In February 2003 government thinking on homegrown extremism was developing, but was still focused on the threat emanating from outside the UK. Even at this early stage, however, it appears policymakers were linking counterradicalization to integrationist concerns, which came to characterize later versions of the policy. These concerns resonate with preexisting discourses around community cohesion, integration, and immigration described in Chapter 3.

A leaked document from May 2004 outlining a cabinet meeting on "Relations with the Muslim Community" indicated that the security services had identified a growing threat from disaffected members of the British Islamic community. It referred to a joint Home Office and Foreign Office paper on "Young Muslims and Extremism," which amounted to an audit of the British Muslim community. It aimed to identify the disaffection which was producing the threat and to identify a path of recruitment into terrorism (Winnett and Leppard 2004). In fact, the Home Office had begun collaborating with the Foreign and Commonwealth Office (FCO) in the period 2001–2005, establishing a pattern of characterizing British Muslims in this context as part of a larger, deterritorialized community defined by faith. In September 2004, the FCO established the Engaging with the Islamic World (EWIW) group, which undertook a range of activities in the UK and abroad, working closely with the Home Office and MI5 (Winnett and Leppard 2004). Its goals were listed as:

- countering the ideological, and theological underpinnings of the terrorist narrative, in order to prevent radicalisation, particularly among the young, in the UK and overseas;
- increasing the understanding of, and engagement with, Muslim countries and communities, and working with them to promote peaceful, political, economic and social reform. (FCO 2007)

The group's activities included "outreach work" explaining foreign policy to domestic audiences, including lending support to independent Muslim organizations that give voice to mainstream Muslim opinion. The Radical Middle

Way, one of EWIW's key projects, took internationally respected scholars on a series of roadshows around Britain to tackle the theological arguments and misinterpretations of Islam used by extremists. The leaked 2004 document, for example, lists activities undertaken by the FCO and Home Office within Britain, including: "Ministerial outreach, customised information resources for young Muslims, participation in campus debates" and "sponsorship of activities of Muslim student groups," as well as interfaith dialogue and engagement with Muslim communities on "faith issues in schools." Likely referring to the then just-formed EWIW program (discussed further later in this chapter), the document also notes that the British Council was working internationally to facilitate emerging British Muslim leaders to work with counterparts around the globe and support preparatory classes in Pakistan for imams due to take up posts in the UK (Winnett and Leppard 2004).

In May 2004 the government launched a consultation process on a new community cohesion strategy aimed at a "vision of a successful integrated society that recognises and celebrates the strength in its diversity," in the face of the challenges of the "impact of exclusion and racism, the rise in political and religious extremism and segregation that can divide our communities" (HM Government 2004c: 1). The strategy's discussion paper built on links between community cohesion, public order, and integration identified in the government's response to the riots of 2001. However, this document, and those that would follow in its wake, linked community cohesion more closely with immigration and national security than earlier discourses emanating from the summer of 2001, stating for example: "The rise in international terrorism, new patterns of migration and the effects of globalization, can all contribute to people's sense of insecurity and fear" in the context of "community cohesion" (HM Government 2004c: 10). In doing so, it conflated new arrivals and old immigrant minority communities in terms of integration and reduced community identities, including faith communities, to a static, monolithic taxonomy, a pattern that was to continue throughout government responses to the issue. As one former senior official noted, "[i]n the absence of direction from security officials about what Prevent should be or do it was left to the communities division to develop it. They, in turn, did not know much about security and counter terrorism so naturally their ideas about what was needed were based on ideas about communities and cohesion and multiculturalism."[7]

This suggests that the form of the policy was being driven, at least to some extent, by the politicization of Islam and migration in Britain more broadly, a process stemming back to the Salman Rushdie affair of the 1990s and present in government responses to the violence during the summer of 2001 (Kundnani 2009; Modood 2003). This argument underlies much of the existing literature on British counterradicalization policy in the critical terrorism studies literature

(Heath-Kelly 2012; Jackson 2009; McDonald 2009). For example, Croft (2012) links the emergence of such community cohesion policies with a "crisis of Britishness" driven by fears about migration and explicitly links the emergence of counterradicalization policies to these fears. He writes: "new Britishness" has developed in part because of the "new terrorism; the new British Self is being constructed against those who support home-grown terrorism, who are the Internal Other" (Croft 2012: 198).

At this point in time the government also had in place a Muslim Engagement Action Plan (MEAP) which served "as a sort of proxy" for Prevent. A former senior official noted of the period: "Between 2003 and 2005, although there wasn't a prevent policy there was a Muslim Engagement Action Plan . . . MEAP consisted of about fifty different measures—most were things which were already happening but which could be regarded as contributing to Muslim engagement." These measures spanned a huge range of program areas in a manner that was to characterize later versions of Prevent. "At one end, there was a proposal to increase the educational performance of Muslim children—school certificate performance levels—and at the other were hugely ambitious things like 'what can we do that will improve the situation in Israel and Palestine'. MEAP continued up until the 7/7 bombing. After that the emphasis changed to being more Prevent oriented, but not immediately."[8]

These links between immigration, global politics, community cohesion, and terrorism, were further established in a major speech by Home Secretary Blunkett in July 2004, in which he stated:

> Instability and insecurity are a feature of the modern world. People are moving across borders more than ever . . . Taken together with the rise in international terrorism and organised crime, neither of which respect national borders . . . there is a growing feeling that globalisation is more a threat than an opportunity. In many ways, local communities are a microcosm of this global phenomenon . . . People move in and out more frequently. In our inner cities especially, many of us don't know our neighbours as well as we might. Old networks based on a sense of place have given way to new and looser networks. (Blunkett 2004: 1)

The community cohesion strategy that was outlined in the 2004 discussion paper was released in January 2005 and laid out the government's plans clearly:[9]

> Our underlying vision is of a greater sense of inclusive British citizenship, supported by a society in which:
> i. young people from different communities grow up with a sense of common belonging;

ii. new immigrants rapidly integrate;
iii. people have opportunities to gain an understanding of the range of cultures that contribute to our strength as a country;
iv. people from all backgrounds participate in civic society;
v. racism is unacceptable; and
vi. extremists who promote hatred are marginalised. (HM Government 2005a: 21)

An inquiry that same year into links between terrorism and community cohesion saw the government clearly link emerging themes of integration, Muslim communities, and counterradicalization for the first time. The House of Commons Home Affairs Committee directly referenced the Cantle Report commissioned by the government in response to the riots of summer 2001 in its conclusions and recommendations:

> Questions of identity may be inextricably linked with the reasons which may lead a small number of well-educated and apparently integrated young British people to turn to terrorism. No one should be forced to choose between being British and being Muslim and we do not believe the two are in any way incompatible. The relationship between rights and responsibilities and opportunities in this country cannot be separated from the concept of Britishness. These issues were raised by the Cantle Report in 2001. They have not lost their relevance today, and we endorse the Cantle Report's conclusion that a wider debate, in which young people must play a leading role, about a modern British identity should be developed. (House of Commons Home Affairs Committee 2005: 52)

In the same report, the committee prefigured the government's intentions to review antiterrorist legislation and noted the need for "a coherent strategy, developed with the Muslim community for tackling extremism," which should "explicitly and specifically set out how British Muslim leaders will be supported in assisting British Muslims in resisting extremist views" (House of Commons Home Affairs Committee 2005: 65, 66).

## The 2005 London bombings: The policy response

In many ways the government response to 7/7 built on preexisting agendas of community cohesion and active citizenship outlined above, despite the fact that the threat was framed by policymakers and politicians alike as fundamentally novel (see Croft and Moore 2010 for a discussion of the various threat narratives in the British counterterrorism response). Indeed, in his immediate response to the bombings, Prime Minister Tony Blair made it clear that the problem was framed in terms of formal political community and migration, despite the fact that all but one of the 7/7 bombers were London-born:

> The rules of the game have changed. We welcome people here who are peaceful and law abiding. People who want to be British citizens should share our values and our way of life. But if you come to our country from abroad, don't meddle in extremism. If you meddle in it or engage in it, then you're going to go back out again.

He went on to announce a Commission on Integration and Cohesion, framing the problem as also one of informal political community, noting that the commission would "advise on how, consistent with people's complete freedom to worship in the way they want and to follow their own religion and culture, there is better integration of those parts of the community presently inadequately integrated" (Blair 2005).

Initially, the government response focused on dialogue with Muslim communities. In the days following the bombings, Prime Minister Blair and Home Secretary Charles Clarke convened a number of summits with Muslim leaders. By August, the Home Office had convened seven Preventing Extremism Together working groups with leading British Muslims and other members of government and civil society, leading to a controversial report released some two months later, which many participants rejected as unrepresentative of their views and failing to deal adequately with the impact of British foreign policy on radicalization (Preventing Extremism Together Working Groups 2005; Briggs, Fieschi, and Lownsbrough 2006).

A former senior official noted that the policy environment at the time favored the community cohesion agenda already in place, observing that: "When 7/7 came along, the security side of the Home Office didn't quite know what to do on the Prevent front. So they left it pretty much to the communities division to come up with whatever they could. That's when we had the Preventing Extremism Together initiative. This was an intensification of the same kind of approach to engagement that had been going on for the past couple of years but with a bit more focus."[10] This process suggests not only a lack of research and understanding of the problem, but a desire to respond using pre-established "taken for granted" frameworks of understanding (Schwartz-Shea 2015: 123).

From 7/7 onward, UK counterradicalization policy was expressed via a series of three revisions of the national counterterrorism policy known as Contest, in 2006, 2009, and 2011. Contest contained the stream of counterradicalization policy known as Prevent, and via guidance on the Prevent aspect of this policy issued by a variety of agencies, most notably the Department for Communities and Local Government (DCLG), which assumed responsibility for Prevent in 2006, released an action plan in 2007 and updated guidance for implementation in 2008 and 2009. The newly formed Office for Security and Counterterrorism released a short Strategy for Delivery outline for Prevent in May 2008 (HM Government 2008b). The new Conservative government released a stand-alone version of the policy after a period of review in 2011.

As already noted, the first publicly available version of UK counterradicalization policy, released in 2006, outlined four strands of counterterrorism policy: prevent, pursue, protect, and prepare. This version of Contest linked the processes of radicalization to globalization and the concept of transnational Muslim community grievances to the "spread of radical ideas," especially via the internet (HM Government 2006: 10). As solutions, it proposed three measures. The first, "tackling disadvantage and structural reforms," listed ways to address broader sociological root causes such as housing and employment and also formalized the link between community cohesion, integration, and counterradicalization, highlighting the recently formed Commission on Integration and Cohesion as a counterradicalization initiative. The second focused on deterring facilitation—including by addressing the spread of radical ideas on the internet and via legal measures to outlaw incitement to violence (outlined in Chapter 8)—while the third aimed at "challenging the ideological motivations that extremists believe justify the use of violence." In practice, this meant establishing a National Imams and Advisory Commission, convening regional forums for discussing extremism, and supporting engagement with communities via, for example, ministerial visits and the "roadshows" by scholars and community leaders mentioned earlier. Significantly, this measure also included international engagement, affirming the conceptualization of British Muslims as members of a larger transnational Muslim community by listing initiatives in foreign policy and aid in the Muslim world as counterradicalization initiatives in the domestic context (HM Government 2006: 11).

The conceptualization of British Muslims as members of a larger transnational faith community above and beyond their British identity was to prove an ongoing feature of Prevent. From 2007, the FCO increasingly took on duties within the UK itself, addressing Muslim communities there in an unprecedented manner (HM Government 2011a: 48). The FCO's EWIW program built on earlier FCO initiatives stemming from the late 1990s whereby senior embassy staff were encouraged to visit diaspora communities within the UK when "at home." As Frances Guy, the first head of the EWIW unit, stated: "It was a recognition, I think, of the changing nature of the United Kingdom, of the more multicultural aspect of the United Kingdom. The FCO should be representing all facets of the UK and so part of that is making sure that HOM [Head of Mission] principally, but also other members of the mission, understand that part of the UK now often has its own links to the country in which you are serving. So it was already a tendency building up, there was already some encouragement of that, before the group was established."[11]

However, the EWIW unit was itself an innovation in the sense that it saw the FCO engaging with British Muslims specifically, and the Islamic world in general, in targeted information-based initiatives.[12] Initially, the unit had been established not for counterextremism purposes, but in recognition of the increasing problems with the way UK foreign policy was perceived in the Muslim world after the invasion of Iraq in 2003,[13] although there was also some recognition of its role in domestic counterextremism:

> The genesis of it was explaining our foreign policy. The recognition was that this was an issue for the Muslim community and the underlying motivation was that that could become a problem. And that some extremist elements of the Muslim community could use that to their advantage. But I wouldn't say that that was the principal motivation at the beginning. We started in 2004. It was only after the bombings in London that we became much more intensely involved, especially in dealing with DCLG. We were already engaged in outreach with the British Muslim community, but that was very specifically about explaining British foreign policy. There was an underlying hint that that was a problem, but we weren't doing it as a motivation part of Prevent at the time—that came later.[14]

The unit expanded considerably in the period 2007–2010. It conducted roadshows within the UK and to thirteen other countries, including Saudi Arabia, Indonesia, and Pakistan, to explain UK policies and the role of Muslims in UK society (HM Government 2009a: 16). This involved speaking *to* British Muslims as well as *about* and *with* them, as isolated from the broader British community. Between March 2008 and August 2009, for example, FCO staff took part in forty-five events aimed at British Muslims, largely comprising debates and presentations about UK foreign policy. The foreign secretary, David Miliband, for example, held "question time" style events with audiences of up to one hundred young Muslims in four locations, and also addressed 2,500 worshippers at a mosque in Bradford—the first cabinet minister ever to address worshippers at a mosque (HM Government 2009a: 18). As the 2011 version of Contest stated clearly: "there is very often no clear distinction between international and what is sometimes called 'home grown' terrorism," and "the strategy must be implemented in conjunction with communities here and overseas, who are often better able than Government to disprove the claims made by terrorists and challenge their views" (HM Government 2011b: 17, 62).[15] In senior meetings with US officials, UK officials described the positive and negative impacts of "strong linkages between the British Muslim community and Pakistan." For example, officials emphasized that large numbers of British Muslims watched Pakistani television, so that news coverage of such initiatives in Pakistan ultimately reached domestic audiences. The officials emphasized that "taking advantage of this international-domestic connection" was essential for domestic counterradicalization policy effectiveness (US Department of State 2009). The policy was substantially redesigned following the election of David Cameron's government in 2010 and an associated review of British counterradicalization policy. This redesign accompanied a shift away from work on community cohesion, and toward a focus on "technical assistance," and explicit engagement with countries which had a strong diaspora presence in the UK. The Countering Terrorism and Radicalisation Programme was at this point devolved and responsibility accorded to local posts (Home Office 2011.

## A discrete domestic policy emerges

In October 2006 Ruth Kelly, then secretary of state for the newly formed Department for Communities and Local Government, prefigured a forthcoming action plan for counterradicalization as her department took control over implementation of the Prevent aspect of Contest. The secretary linked the program clearly to issues of informal political community, listing Britain's key values as respect for the law, freedom of speech, equality of opportunity, respect, and responsibility toward others, and arguing in the context of counterradicalization that: "Security responses alone will not be enough. There is a battle of ideas here—it is all about us reasserting shared values and winning hearts and minds... It is only by defending our values that we will prevent extremists radicalising future generations of terrorists" (Kelly 2006).

The first moves toward DCLG's action plan for counterradicalization came with the announcement of the "Preventing Violent Extremism (Prevent) Pathfinder Fund" in October 2006. This fund made available an initial £6 million for 2007–2008, via regional government offices, to seventy local authorities of communities whose populations included 5 percent or more Muslims. Its strategic objectives were to develop a community in which Muslims in the UK:

- identify themselves as a welcome part of a wider British society and are accepted as such by the wider community;
- reject violent extremist ideology and actively condemn violent extremism;
- isolate violent extremist activity, and support and co-operate with the police and security services; and,
- develop their own capacity to deal with problems where they arise and support diversionary activity for those at risk. (HM Government 2007b: 3)

Sir David Omand, author of initial versions of Prevent and the overall Contest strategy, saw the creation of a program to channel money toward work with Muslim communities through the DCLG, which was also concerned with local authorities, equality, and community cohesion as a way of avoiding the targeting of "British Muslims" per se, and instead as a way to "de-ethnicize the program" by linking it to local communities. He noted that it involved:

> looking at communities not in terms of ethnic origins but looking at communities as communities rather than where people had come from. In that way you would also minimize a right-wing backlash—"they only got a swimming pool because they throw bombs at the government" and so on. There was a bit of that in Northern Ireland as well, so there was a bit of learning from Northern Ireland that you have to be careful about how you balance this work across communities. We decided at that point that quite a lot of the Prevent work might be better off badged not as Prevent at all but should be badged under a title such as "strengthening communities," or "healthy communities" and should be given to people who had been working on these issues for years—reducing racial tension, improving community cohesion, youth work and all the rest of it. Anything they did that improved the situation would have a benefit for those of us working in counterterrorism, but the reason for doing that was because Britain wanted healthy communities, not first and foremost because those communities are terrorists. So that at this point the work bifurcated and the cabinet secretary, the social policy departments and the economic departments took that agenda about communities, leaving the counterterrorism community with the harder edged Prevent work.[16]

However, this funding model attracted a wide range of criticism as it conflated divisions within Muslim faith and practice into one, securitized identity (Kundnani 2009). It is important to note that despite this integrationist focus, research on the integration of British Muslims suggests that the story of alienation driven by religious identity is not entirely clear. Indeed, the 2007–2008 Home Office citizenship survey, conducted at the height of this integrationist move, suggested that practicing Muslims were less likely to feel a conflict between their religious and national identity than non-practicing Muslims (HM Government 2009b: 31), a position supported by the government's own research (Travis 2008). Similarly, although a report commissioned by the Preventing Extremism Unit in the DCLG highlighted research which found that while religion was a very important marker of identity for British Muslims, hybrid identities such as "British Muslim" were more popular than monolithic identities (Choudhry 2007: 7–8). This analysis complicates the picture in a manner not reflected by counterradicalization policies and associated measures.

In March 2007, various elements of the government's counterterrorism apparatus were consolidated in the new Office for Security and Counter-Terrorism (OSCT). Tasked with providing advice to ministers and developing policy and security measures to combat terrorism, this unit was placed under the control of the home secretary. It had six areas of oversight, the first of which was: "implementing strategies to stop people becoming terrorists or supporting violent extremism; and for the strategic communications to support this" (House of Commons Home Affairs Committee 2009: 6). The OSCT drove a restructuring and formalizing of Prevent over its next few iterations. To this end, the aims and logic of the initial approach for local funding via the DCLG were outlined publicly in the April 2007 publication "Preventing Violent Extremism: Winning Hearts and Minds," which marked the government's first post-7/7, detailed exposition of its counterradicalization program under its new implementation arrangements. The policy had previously been split between the Home Office and the DCLG, with the latter dealing with the "soft" aspects of the policy and the Home Office dealing with more traditional counterterrorism.[17]

The policy outlined the government's approach to combating radicalization via four goals: (1) promoting shared values; (2) supporting local solutions; (3) building civic capacity and leadership; and (4) promoting the role of faith institutions and leaders. The first of these directly linked counterradicalization to conceptions of citizenship, proposing broadening of the provision of citizenship education in supplementary schools and madrassahs, ensuring the most effective use of the education system in promoting faith understanding. It also sought to bring communities otherwise out of reach of government—such as women of Pakistani and Bangladeshi heritage—into employment (HM Government 2007a: 5). Indeed, the narrative of community cohesion continued to influence the policy: "The 2007 strategy was still using the same thinking and paradigm as MEAP and Preventing Extremism Together. Its basic premise was the promotion of community development within which Muslims were regarded as a distinct community."[18]

One of the key outcomes of this goal was the Islam and Citizenship Education project, funded by the DCLG and the Home Office in 2008, which developed material for schools. The project's goal was "[t]o demonstrate to young British Muslims that their faith is compatible with wider shared values and that being a good Muslim is also compatible with being a good British citizen" (HM Government 2008c: 41). By 2011, the program had expanded to 300 madrassahs and one hundred independent faith schools (HM Government 2011a: 69). The program involved approximately forty-four lessons at two different levels (ages 9–11 and 11–14), arranged around a definition of citizenship based on four key principles: belonging, interacting, rights, and responsibilities.

These principles are strongly integrationist. As the project's implementing agency put it, for example, belonging means "sharing our country's values in things like respect, tolerance and freedom"; interacting means "taking part in the life of our country"; rights means "your rights to live and worship and take part in democratic elections," "the rights of others to do the same," and "government rights over you, for example, in making sure you obey the law"; while responsibilities means "your responsibilities towards each other . . . not interfering with the rights of others, obeying the law and going to school" and include government responsibilities such as "protecting your rights as a citizen" (Islam and Citizenship Education 2010: 14). Lesson titles include "Being a British Muslim," "British or Muslim or British Muslim," "Good Muslim, Good Citizen," and "Understanding Democracy" (Coles 2010: 45). The program also includes a module on the "skills of citizenship and Islamic enquiry," focused on encouraging young Muslims to, for example, "ask those who know when you do not know" and showing that "the key to ignorance is to question" (Islam and Citizenship Education 2010: 17). This process arguably reinforces traditional sources of Islamic knowledge over increasingly disparate sources of Islamic authority in the Islamic world, which had been identified as a source of radicalization.

Similarly, the National Resource Centre for Supplementary Schools was launched in January 2007 to provide guidance to, and best practice in, registered supplementary schools, including those hosting the approximately 10,000 children who attended madrassahs. The centre has released good practice guidelines for the schools that explicitly highlight the need to promote shared British values of toleration and respect for diversity. Separate projects were funded under the Local Government Pathfinder fund announced in late 2006, which ran until 2010. For example, the Barnet region's Madrassah Citizenship Programme trained local youth workers to deliver a ten-week course to teenagers highlighting the links between Islamic sacred texts and good citizenship (HM Government 2008a: 41).

The second goal of the 2007 policy outline was to support local solutions as a counterradicalization measure. In pursuit of this, the policy increased Pathfinder funding and extended its reach to seventy local authorities, increasing the number of local forums on extremism and counterradicalization already funded (HM Government 2007a: 9). The 2007 strategy's third goal—building civic capacity and leadership—meant engaging with as wide a range of community partners in pursuit of the second goal as possible, including women and young people, and rebalancing engagement "towards those organisations that uphold shared values and reject and condemn violent extremism."[19] This goal also included an affirmation of the transnational nature of British Muslims, vowing to "[p]romote links between Muslim communities here and overseas to develop joint projects to support the promotion of shared values and to tackle violent extremism," building on existing roadshows by the FCO mentioned earlier (HM Government 2007a: 10).[20] The Radical Middle

Way roadshows were a key component of this activity, delivering over 170 events across the UK, attended by an excess of 75,000 people, between 2005 and 2012 (Radical Middle Way 2012).

The fourth goal, strengthening the role of faith institutions and leaders, included measures to regulate the immigration of foreign imams, improve mosque governance, and develop state approved and regulated training for mosque leaders, as well as "[s]upporting platforms for mainstream interpretations of the role of Islam in modern societies" including by continuing to support the FCO roadshows (HM Government 2007a: 8).[21] This emphasis on the need to integrate Islam in particular was also evident in a range of measures designed to contextualize "British Islam"—integrating not only its practitioners and leaders, but the faith itself. Projects funded under Pathfinder also focused on British Islam. For example, the Luton Ambassadors for Islam project funded twenty-four young men to take part in classes taught by a "British-born Islamic scholar," with the aim of their becoming "ambassadors for mainstream Islam" and helping them to "assert their British identity" (HM Government 2008a: 20). The Contextualising Islam in Britain project, meanwhile, funded academics to research the role of Islam in the UK and the dissemination of their discussions to a wider audience (Suleiman 2009). Similarly, the Forward Thinking charity, funded by the Home Office, ran a series of workshops across England with young Muslims on the role of Islam in a pluralistic society (HM Government 2006: 15). Measures to professionalize mosque leadership also emerged from these initial policy documents. A Continuous Professional Development program for faith leaders was introduced in September 2007 and has been funded by Prevent continuously since its introduction, delivered by the National Institute of Adult Continuing Education (HM Government 2010: 51). Croft's (2012) work on the securitization of Britishness is relevant here. He argues that the integrationist impulse of Prevent and associated security discourses reflect wider uncertainty about the meaning of "Britishness" present even before 2005. Building on work by Hansen (2006) and Connolly (1991) he shows that the securitization of British identity in this context creates a "radical other" and an "Orientalized other" which buttress a core notion of the British self.

## The policy adjusts

Prevent was adjusted and expanded in 2008, following further research that expanded understanding of the causes of radicalization. This research, commencing in mid-2007, was driven by the OSCT (House of Commons Home Affairs

Committee 2009: 201; US Department of State 2008) and led to the release of new policy guidance documents in mid-2008 (HM Government 2008). It was also reflected in the 2009 update of Contest, the government's overall counterterrorism strategy. Updated Prevent policy guidance released by the OSCT in 2009 (following on from previous updates in 2008) had five "key strands" in "support of the overall aim of stopping people becoming or supporting terrorists or violent extremists" (HM Government 2009c: 6):

- Challenging the violent extremist ideology and supporting mainstream voices
- Disrupting those who promote violent extremism and supporting the institutions where they are active
- Supporting individuals who are being targeted and recruited to the cause of violent extremism
- Increasing the resilience of communities to violent extremism
- Addressing the grievances that ideologues are exploiting.

The policy guidance included two new cross-cutting work streams: "Developing Understanding, Analysis and Information" and "Strategic Communications" (HM Government 2009c). These changes signaled a shift toward understanding radicalization as a phenomenon of individuals and ideology rather than simply a problem of integration. However, although "shared values" no longer featured as prominently in the goals of Prevent itself, the policy continued to emphasize "mainstream voices" and civic ideals as solutions to radicalization. Funding for community cohesion work delivered by local authorities and the DCLG was not removed, rather it was de-emphasized and centralized (see Heath-Kelly 2017: 297–298).[22] Indeed, a review of funding delivered through 2009–2010 and 2010–2011 revealed the primary role that integration measures played in counterradicalization policy: 40 percent of total Prevent funding delivered through local government during this period went to programs aimed at general cohesion and integration (HM Government 2011a: 29).

Integration of religion into state identities continued with official funding of the Mosque and Imams National Advisory Board (MINAB) in 2008, which continued to be funded throughout later versions of Prevent (HM Government 2011b: 83; Bunglawala 2009). MINAB was charged not only with the development of "leadership skills for imams and mosque officials" but also the "accreditation of imams, progress in the inclusion of young people and women, and supporting mosques to contribute to community cohesion and tackling extremism" (HM Government 2007a: 12). This theme was reflected in the establishment of the National Muslim Women's Advisory Group in January 2008 and the Young Muslim Advisory Group in late 2008. These groups were intended to facilitate engagement between the national government and Muslim communities, and also to act as role models. Importantly, MINAB in particular is charged with being a role model emphasizing "civic responsibility" and the promotion of demonstrably British values such as the participation of women. By virtue of its funding, these behaviors are linked to counterradicalization policy (MINAB 2020). To this end, MINAB outlines standards for mosques as:

1. Members apply principles of good corporate governance.
2. Members ensure that services are provided by suitably qualified and/or experienced personnel.
3. There are systems and processes in place to ensure that there are no impediments to the participation in the activities, including governance, for young people.
4. There are systems and processes in place to ensure that there are no impediments to the participation in the activities, including governance, for women.
5. Members ensure there are programmes that promote civic responsibility of Muslims in the wider society. (MINAB 2020)[23]

Projects reflecting the new understandings of radicalization included measures to address online radicalization for the first time as part of an increasing focus on combating ideology, which in turn saw a concern with persuasion and persuasive techniques emerge as a clear government priority. In mid-2007, the Home Office established a Research, Information and Communications Unit (RICU), designed to assist the government in understanding and countering the "communications challenge" across all communications media, including the internet.[24] The unit was staffed across three departments: the DCLG, the FCO, and the Home Office, emphasizing the transnational nature of the communications problem. Indeed, by 2009 a RICU official was spending extended periods of time in Pakistan, working closely with the FCO on the EWIW program and sharing strategic communications research with Pakistan's government in order to address the problem of radicalization on a transnational scale (US Department of State 2009).

RICU focused on government's understanding and communication with Muslim target audiences, analyzing extremist propaganda and dissemination, and providing advice on effective counter communications. As one former senior official noted, "at its inception it harked back to the research and information department in the FCO during the 50s and 60s and there were vague hopes that it might lead to a modern equivalent of the Congress of Cultural Freedom that was so successful in the Cold War."[25] Heavily classified, its early work included the design of key messages to be used in government communication including advice on specific language—for example, advice to avoid using the term "war on terror." It also trained local practitioners on communication skills and strategies, researched the effectiveness of various channels of communication, and provided advice on the best way to manage government responses to specific events such as the Dutch anti-Islam video (RICU 2007; Corera 2007; US Department of State 2007a, 2009). The unit delivered a weekly update for local Prevent delivery partners, providing facts on topical news stories and issues that resonated with target (Muslim) communities—seeking to manage those communities' interpretations of global events in a way conducive to counterradicalization goals. A former senior official noted, "RICU did some good things but there was enduring confusion about its role" which meant that at times "it was barely distinguishable from the Press Office."[26] RICU persisted through later versions of Prevent, shifting its focus on priorities, such as foreign fighters in the Syrian conflict, as they emerged, and has been regularly criticized for a lack of both transparency and effectiveness (Intelligence and Security Committee 2014: 78; House of Commons Home Affairs Committee 2016: 31).

Aside from RICU, the government also sponsored internet-based activities to target British Muslim communities and those overseas with the same policy initiative. For example, the (now inactive) website www.radicalmiddleway.co.uk was funded under Prevent to "promote debate within UK Muslim communities, using the internet to reach audiences in the UK and overseas" (HM Government 2009a: 95). This extended even to theological advice, as the FCO partnered with RICU to ensure that theological advice was available on the internet in a variety of languages (HM Government 2009a: 95).

The 2007 strategy increased attention on the role of individuals as generators and facilitators of terrorism. The Channel program is the most prominent example of this change in understanding and has emerged as one of the underpinnings of UK counterradicalization policy. First piloted in 2007 (HM Government 2009a: 15), it was designed to identify those at risk from violent extremism (primarily young people) and support them, mainly through community-based interventions. A former senior official noted bureaucratic contestation between the more traditional "case work" model that Channel invoked and an emphasis on community cohesion. These contestations were based not only on emerging understandings of the problem, but on contestation between ministers and departments. Contests for influence emerged, for example following the creation of the OSCT in 2007 and the move of what was then known as the Communities Division out of the Home Office to establish the Department of Communities and Local Government. The official noted in this context the importance of "big P" and "small p" politics, with the result that both strands of thinking were present in various policy iterations, observing: "The ideological framework was in the early stages, a community one, later it shifted to a more traditional casework approach which the police and security service felt more comfortable with."[27]

The 2009 version of Contest, in this vein, referred to the concept of "self-starting" radicalization for the first time, unlike the earlier version of Contest (HM Government 2009a: 44), and focused on the causes of radicalization as related to very personal, granular experiences. This was in contrast to the structural approach of previous strategies, which had focused on addressing inequality and racism as sources of grievance. For example, it noted that "radicalisation seems to be related directly to a feeling of not being accepted or not belonging" and "a lack of affinity with and disconnect from family, community and the state" (HM Government 2009a: 44). Support focused on individuals included such programs as the Mosaic Muslim Mentoring Scheme, introduced in late 2007, which recruited Muslim professionals to mentor disadvantaged young Muslims, aiming to "raise aspirations and reduce the sense of isolation experienced by young Muslims in marginalised communities, addressing one of the factors that can contribute to sympathy with violent extremist actions" (HM Government 2008a: 29). And despite the fact that a House of Commons inquiry into Prevent found that the Channel program was difficult to assess and a cause of resentment, the 2011 version of Prevent increased the focus on the policy (House of Commons Communities and Local Government Committee 2010: 11, 18; HM Government 2011a: 8, 55), referring to the concept of "unaffiliated" (lone) terrorists for the first time in official policy documents (HM Government 2011a: 14). By 2013, funding for the program had increased, even in an environment of extreme fiscal austerity: overall, 2,500 individuals had been referred between 2007 and 2012 (Travis 2013a). By 2015–2016, 3,994 people were referred annually (Halliday 2016).[28] Similarly, in concert with an increased focus on "strategic communications," and especially the internet, Prevent and associated legislative measures from 2008 onward increasingly came to focus on individuals as both generators of ideas and agents of terrorism. As the 2011 strategy put it, "the transmission of ideology for the purposes of radicalization also depends on people who both develop thinking about the case for terrorism and then set out to disseminate their views" (HM Government 2011a: 42). This built on thinking about incitement introduced in the Terrorism Act 2000.

## Domestic reactions

From the outset, Prevent attracted criticism from across the spectrum of British politics regarding—in effect—its framing of political community. The right, for example, saw it as a dubious use of taxpayers' money, with few measurable outputs and a corollary of engagement with organizations such as the Muslim Council of Britain whose activities and views many saw as inconsistent with mainstream values (TaxPayers' Alliance 2009; Maher and Frampton 2009). Criticism on the left largely echoed the criticism espoused more forcefully by Muslim communities. Many Muslim community groups shared and continue to share government concerns about extremist violence within their own communities. However, a poll conducted in 2007, for example, found that although 58 percent of British Muslims felt that Muslims should do more to prevent extremism, almost two-thirds felt the Muslim community did not bear any responsibility for the emergence of extremists willing to attack UK targets (Tran 2007).

A variety of Muslim groups benefitted financially from the large pools of funding available under Prevent, causing disunity and resentment within the community. As one commentator noted, the policies created such problems "by creating incentives for some Muslim voices to be funded as 'government approved' and as such privileged in national discourse" (Kundnani 2009). Often, these voices were seen as privileging one form of Islam over another, or one community group over another, depending on the government's preferred outcomes. McTernan noted that "[i]t just opened the door to opportunists. They spent millions on organizations that had no constituency, no influence in the community."[29] Indeed, the relationship between Muslim identity and funding opportunities also saw resentment building from other faith and community groups regarding the opportunism that the policies engendered. As Dr. Indarjit Singh of the Network of Sikh Organisations remarked, the policies had resulted in a "sort of favoured status as a result of radicalisation" (House of Commons Communities and Local Government Committee 2010: 18).

Many Muslim commentators also saw Prevent work as facilitating spying and intelligence gathering. McTernan, the head of Forward Thinking, disengaged his organization from previous work with Home Office visits to Muslim communities, because "they confused community cohesion and capacity building with intelligence gathering [and] we thought our own credibility was under threat. [Charles] Farr [the head of Prevent by this time] was playing around with... these visits and intelligence gathering."[30]

Such allegations stemmed not only from community engagement with security services themselves (Lambert and Spalek 2008), but also from a groundbreaking newspaper investigation in mid-2009, which alleged Prevent to be "the biggest spying programme in Britain in modern times," alleging that policymakers used community engagement programs to identify informants and gather primary intelligence (Dodd 2009). Despite the government's stringent assertions that the policies were not in fact used to gather intelligence, a House of Commons committee found that the effectiveness of Prevent was under threat because of widespread allegations of intelligence gathering and surveillance under the Prevent program (House of Commons Communities and Local Government Committee 2010: 3).

The bulk of community objections described were centered on the way that Muslim communities were framed in the policies as defined by a cohesive identity indicated primarily by religion, and addressed by government solely in a counterterrorism context. This construction of British Muslims as a "suspect community" (Pantazis and Pemberton 2009: 646) was driven by several factors and reflected a broader, preexisting construction of Islamic identity in Britain as separate from mainstream British identity (see Modood 2003). Most importantly, the construction emerged from the early policies' determination of funding to local government areas based on the number of Muslims living within each area. As outlined earlier, this directly equated the presence of Muslims in a community with the need for counterterrorism funding. Such an approach also failed to conceive of diversity within the Muslim community, in the process essentializing layers of identity involved in modern British citizenship. As discussed further later, the policy documents more generally supported this framing of "Muslim" as a cohesive identity linked by definition to the danger of radicalization, offering very little in the way of nuance in either the design or application of the policies.

In response to such misgivings, the House of Commons Select Committee for Communities and Local Government—the independent group of backbench Members of Parliament charged with scrutiny of the work of the DCLG—established an inquiry into Prevent, with a call for written evidence released during summer 2009 and hearings commencing in December 2009. The inquiry attracted over seventy responses from a range of Muslim community organizations and heard from over one hundred witnesses. The committee found that the reductionist identities employed by Prevent meant that "Muslim communities have felt unfairly targeted and branded as potential terrorists. The strategy has contributed to a sense of frustration and alienation amongst Muslims which may increase the risk of making some individuals more vulnerable to radicalisation" (House of Commons Communities and Local Government Committee 2010: 11). In fact, the committee found that Prevent's association with community cohesion work furthered this sense of alienation, questioning the "appropriateness of the Department of Communities and Local Government—a Government department which has responsibility for promoting cohesive communities—taking a leading role in counter-terrorism initiatives" and noting that "*Prevent* risks undermining positive cross-cultural work on cohesion and capacity building to combat exclusion and alienation in many communities" (House of Commons Communities and Local Government Committee 2010: 3).

This perception was reinforced by calls within the early policy documents outlined earlier for all Muslims to work together in combating radicalization.

This not only unnecessarily portrayed Muslims as "vulnerable" to radicalization (see Richards 2011) despite evidence to the contrary, but also placed a burden on non-radicalized Muslims that was not shared by non-Muslim communities. As one influential analyst of the policies noted, "the problem with attempting to mobilise all these Muslims against 'extremism' is that it, in effect, constructs Muslims into a 'suspect community,' in which the failure of Muslim individuals or organisations to comply with this mobilisation makes them suspect in the eyes of the counter-terrorist system" (Kundnani 2009: 15).

The bipartisan committee enquiry of 2009 made several strong recommendations that drew on the concerns presented by Muslim communities. These focused on the need to separate community cohesion and counterradicalization work, to change the funding model for local authorities, and to improve communication of Prevent's goals. These recommendations were largely taken up by the new government elected in 2010.

## A new government, a new policy of sorts

The newly elected Conservative/Liberal Democrat coalition government under Prime Minister Cameron decided to review Prevent in November 2010, under the independent oversight of Liberal Democrat peer Lord Carlile, although it decided explicitly not to examine the allegations of "spying." The review was eventually published in June 2011 and informed the revised Prevent strategy published in the same year. The revised strategy outlined the following three objectives:

- respond to the ideological challenge of terrorism and the threat we face from those who promote it;
- prevent people from being drawn into terrorism and ensure that they are given appropriate advice and support; and
- work with a wide range of sectors and institutions [including education, faith, health, and criminal justice] where there are risks of radicalisation which we need to address. (HM Government 2011a: 7)

These objectives were repeated in an updated Contest strategy published in July 2011 (HM Government 2011b). The new strategy did not stray far from previous iterations in terms of its goals, removing only an emphasis on increasing the resilience of communities and addressing grievances, and retaining an emphasis on individuals and ideology. It also removed the bulk of Prevent's work from the DCLG, shifting it to the Home Office, leaving the DCLG concerned specifically with cohesion and integration. The revised version also changed the rules for funding allocation away from the Muslim percentage calculation under earlier versions of Prevent. The policy was now to focus on work in twenty-five areas identified as "hotspots" of potential radicalization, with local coordinators to be funded directly by the Home Office in order for them to direct local Prevent-funded activity.

The new policy ostensibly shifted Prevent's focus away from obvious integration as a counterradicalization measure, noting that "apparently well-integrated people have committed terrorist attacks" (HM Government 2011a: 27). However, debates within the new coalition and within the Conservative Party itself—about assertion of British values as a response to counterradicalization— saw the policy still intertwined with integration concerns and the discussion of informal political community (Bagehot 2011). This debate revolved in part around actual beliefs about the role of integration in counterradicalization and in part around political concerns about engaging with "extremist" partners for the delivery of the program—one of the persistent critiques of Prevent from the right. This meant that beliefs, values, and ideas still played an important role. For example, in a major speech on radicalization and extremism immediately prior to the introduction of the new policy, Prime Minister Cameron referred to the need for a "muscular liberalism" when introducing it (Cameron 2011). The new document clearly linked the firming of informal political community to counterradicalization, stating: "Work to deal with radicalisation will depend on developing a sense of belonging to this country and support for our core values" (HM Government 2011a: 13).

Building on a similar theme, in making the case for its approach to dealing with organizations it defined as "extremist," the policy stated: "We are concerned that insufficient attention has been paid to whether these organisations comprehensively subscribe to what we would consider to be mainstream British values: democracy, rule of law, equality of opportunity, freedom of speech and the rights of all men and women to live free from persecution of any kind" (HM Government 2011a: 34). The new policy also instituted checks on proposed free schools and published new teachers' standards which stated that teachers' actions in the classroom must not undermine "fundamental British values" (Maylor 2014).

In doing so, it extended Prevent work to non-violent extremism as well as violent extremism (HM Government 2011a: 63), a direction which was met with much criticism. The policy defined extremism, in a departure from earlier definitions in policy documents, as "active opposition to fundamental British values, including democracy, the rule of law, individual liberty and the mutual respect and tolerance of different faiths and beliefs" (HM Government 2011a: 34). In outlining the nature of its first objective under the new policy, "challenging the ideology that supports terrorism and those who promote it," the government clearly linked these values to a collective—and thus integrated—identity bound by common values. It stated: "Challenging ideology is also about being confident in our own values—the values of democracy, rule of law, equality of opportunity, freedom of speech and the rights of all men and women to live free from persecution of any kind" (HM Government 2011a: 44). The new policy also increased funding and implementation of the Channel program (Travis 2013a) and introduced the concept of mental health services into the government's Prevent work, noting that "people with mental health issues or learning disabilities . . . may be more easily drawn into terrorism," following the sentencing in separate terrorism cases in 2008 of at least two people who could be described as mentally ill (HM Government 2011a: 69).

The 2011 version of Prevent was the most explicit yet in its focus on persuasion, listing its first of three goals as: "respond to the ideological challenge of terrorism" (HM Government 2011a: 7). It outlined the government's goal of engaging in a "clearer explanation" of its own arguments (HM Government 2011a: 50) and rebutting key AQ texts, "providing information about what those texts are" so that communities and theologians might explain why they are wrong (HM Government 2011a: 51). Similarly, the 2011 version of Contest highlighted the importance of AQ's ideology as extant outside of central AQ-core actors, suggesting that "the ideology which has come to be associated with Al-Qa'ida will be more resilient than Al Qa'ida itself" (HM Government 2011b: 41).

Indeed, a former senior official argued that aside from the strong influence of pre-2005 community cohesion initiatives, overall, Prevent drew far more strongly on the persuasive elements of counterinsurgency and Cold War information initiatives than traditional counterterrorism lessons from Northern Ireland, arguing:

> I don't think they [persuasive approaches] are a new thing. These kinds of approaches have been around forever. There have always been attempts to win people over through persuasion rather than coercion. Look at the book *Who Paid the Piper*, about the soft methods used by both sides during the Cold War. I won't say this was directly influential, but it was the kind of thing that people in senior positions were reading during the mid-2000s. And if you look at industrial policy and the British colonial wars in, say, in Malaya or India there were often attempts to work with the groups that were less radical than the real extremists, and that is similar to the sort of thing that was being done during this period.[31]

As the focus on persuasion and strategic communication increased, so did a focus on the role of communications technology. Early versions of the policy did not refer explicitly to the role of communications technology, although the

2006 iteration highlighted the internet as a factor facilitating the spread of extremist ideas (HM Government 2006: 10). Emerging research highlighted the increasing danger from internet radicalization, and policy focused on online measures among a larger focus on communicative techniques (see Stevens and Neumann 2009). For example, the 2009 version of Contest listed the internet as a problem for the very first time in a special section on the internet and Prevent (HM Government 2009a: 90, 43) and the 2011 policy also had its own section dealing with the internet (HM Government 2011a: 64). Concrete measures included the establishment of RICU in 2007 and the Counter-Terrorism Internet Referral Unit in 2010.

The new government also expanded its online activities. The updated policy pledged to increase the confidence of civil society activists to "challenge online extremist content effectively and to provide credible alternatives" (HM Government 2011a: 52), and to work with social media enterprises like Facebook in this endeavor. By 2012, fifteen civil society groups had been helped in this manner (HM Government 2013a: 22). Indeed, the 2011 version of the policy listed "The Internet" as a sector equivalent to education, faith, and health (HM Government 2011a: 77). It heralded the introduction of internet filtering of extremist material, stating "we want to ensure that users in schools, libraries, colleges and Immigration Removal Centres are unable to access unlawful material" (HM Government 2011a: 79). The policy pledged to further develop the Counter-Terrorism Internet Referral Unit, including terrorist video referral mechanisms, and to incorporate material on online extremism in outreach and awareness programs associated with Prevent (HM Government 2011a: 79). The unit, first piloted in 2010, was one of the first initiatives to focus exclusively on the internet as an agent of radicalization. It sought to remove extremist material from UK-hosted websites, recognizing its persuasive potential. The unit removed online content referred by the public, which it assessed against the Terrorism Act 2006. The unit works closely with international agencies, but has been hamstrung by the problem of international hosting, although from 2010 to 2013 over 5,000 websites had reportedly been taken down (see House of Commons Home Affairs Committee 2012: 24; HM Government 2009a: 94; Wintour and Jones 2013). Similarly, RICU's activities changed under the Cameron government in order to focus more on the online environment.

The next policy move to shape counterradicalization policy in the UK occurred in response to the murder of a British Army soldier, Fusilier Lee Rigby, in London in May 2013. Brigadier Rigby was murdered in broad daylight by two British-born citizens of Nigerian descent, both converts to Islam, in retribution for British military activities in Iraq and Afghanistan. The attackers were filmed in the immediate aftermath justifying their actions, and this footage was shown on British TV, generating significant controversy.

In response to the attacks, Prime Minister Cameron announced the creation of the Extremism Task Force, a cabinet-level body that brought the overall strategic design of counterradicalization directly under the prime minister. This continued moves to centralize counterextremism policy in government, which had been evident from the shift between the 2006 and 2011 versions of Prevent. The taskforce issued a report in December 2013 that offered responses to what it saw as four problem areas, most of which can be described as concerned with the role of persuasion in radicalization and counterradicalization. For example, the first priority area was designated "disrupting extremists"—the report announced measures to make it "harder for extremist preachers and groups to spread extremist views which can lead people into terrorism, while at the same time being careful not to contravene existing laws on incitement to violence or glorifying terrorism." This included consideration of proposals to investigate powers to "ban groups which seek to undermine democracy or use hate speech" (HM Government 2013c: 3). The second area of focus, "countering extremist narratives and ideology," also targeted persuasive measures. In particular it targeted the "poisonous messages of extremists" (HM Government 2013c: 3). The report announced measures including training community groups to counter extremist messages online, filtering online extremist content, working with internet companies to restrict access to terrorist material hosted outside the UK but which breached the UK's laws, and using existing legislation to exclude those outside the UK from entry if they posted extremist material online.

The report also emphasized the role of institutions in providing opportunities for extremists to "share their poisonous messages with others." To this end, it prefigured tougher inspection regimes for schools, for example, in an effort to "ensure that schools support fundamental British values" and improved oversight of religious supplementary schools. The report also announced new guidelines on counterextremism specifically tailored for universities, and new Prevent coordinators were deployed across the sector. It also introduced new measures for the prison system, including targeted faith-based initiatives for the most extreme prisoners, restrictions on the ability of extremist and terrorist prisoners to radicalize others by minimizing their contact with other prisoners, "tightening the rules on legal correspondence to minimize the chance of extremist material being smuggled into prison, and post-release programs for extremist prisoners" (HM Government 2013c: 6–7). Measures focused on institutions, including educational institutions, prefigured the imposition of Prevent Duty in the Counter-Terrorism and Security Act 2015.

Outside of this focus on persuasion, the report also emphasized integration, as previous versions of counterradicalization policy had done, although in a way which focused on the promotion—and thus the persuasive capacities—of successful integration rather more than measures to explicitly encourage integration, which marked earlier iterations of British counterextremism policy. It argued that "more resilient communities will be more resilient to the influence of extremists" (HM Government 2013c: 4). In support of integrationist measures, it proposed providing platforms for communities to demonstrate their success in integration and supporting projects which demonstrated the success of integration in other ways. The report also moved to further centralize Prevent within government. It explicitly stated that the taskforce would intervene if local governments were not "taking the problem seriously" (HM Government 2013c: 4) and raised the concept of a legal Prevent Duty and of the implementation of the Channel program as a legal requirement in England and Wales, again prefiguring measures introduced in the Counter-Terrorism and Security Act 2015.

In addition to the taskforce, the Intelligence and Security Committee of Parliament conducted an inquiry into Rigby's murder, which was published in November 2014. The issue examined possible intelligence failures in the lead-up to the attack, and found one significant factor—a conversation that had taken place between one of the attackers and an overseas extremist on Facebook, which had not reported the conversation at the time.[32] Noting that companies like Facebook did not regard themselves as under any obligation to ensure that threats emerging from exchanges on their platforms were identified or reported to the authorities, the report recommended several measures that went to the problem of persuasion. As well as recommending that more be done to deter individuals from accessing extremist material online, it addressed the problem that online conversations such as the key conversation in the Rigby matter could not be accessed by government agencies (Intelligence and Security Committee 2014: 168, 170). The committee recommended that communication service providers like Facebook should accept their responsibility to review known terrorist accounts and share relevant information with the appropriate authorities. The report also recommended that the prime minister and the National Security Council should prioritize the issue (Intelligence and Security Committee 2014: 171). Indeed, in September 2014, Prime Minister Cameron announced a special cabinet-level envoy on intelligence and law enforcement data sharing specifically to address this issue.[33]

# 6
# To form a more perfect union
## Political community in America

Omar Mateen, a twenty-nine year-old US citizen who in 2016 pledged allegiance to IS and killed forty-nine people at a nightclub in Orlando, Florida, and injured fifty-three others, had a childhood described in the media as "All American." He played baseball, worked in his family's small business, and trained to become a police officer (Sullivan and Wan 2016; Doornbos 2016). Newspaper reports describe Ryan Anderson, a US military member convicted of providing material support to AQ, as "unremarkable." They depict a college graduate from a family with a US flag displayed outside their house and a former member of "Junior Statesmen for America," a group for students interested in political issues (Tizon 2004). The first American suicide bomber in the Syrian conflict is also described in media reports as an "ordinary" American. He grew up in Florida and played basketball and video games. But in 2014 he recorded a video showing himself tearing at his US passport with his teeth and setting it on fire. The next day he drove a truck packed with explosives into a government outpost in Syria (Giglio 2014).

This narrative of an "ordinary American" committing violence against his fellow citizens goes directly to the problem that US counterradicalization policy tries to confront. The narrative is seductive because it is at odds with popular understandings of what it is to be American or indeed a citizen of any country: someone who does not commit this sort of violence against fellow citizens in the name of a foreign power. This study argues that the idea of being an "American" and holding "American values" underpins US counterradicalization policy. These ideas about what an American *is* and *should be* and what American political community *is* and *should be* are the "taken for granted" understandings about the world (Schwartz-Shea 2015: 123) that frame policy in the absence of conclusive research.

This chapter establishes the basis of these common–sense understandings in three ways. The first section briefly outlines what it means to be "American" by examining the ways those values have been enacted in citizenship and immigration law. As Smith (1997: 31) argues, these sorts of laws and policies designate the criteria for membership in a political community and the key prerogatives that constitute membership. He writes that they are "among the most fundamental of political creations . . . they proclaim the existence of a political 'people' and designate who those persons are as people." American identity, at least in these spheres, is dominated by constitutional patriotism, meaning an attachment to the values expressed in the constitution and civic engagement as a marker of identity, which precludes the "thick" approach to citizenship and immigration practices that mark other states such as Germany. However, US immigration practices have also been driven by ideas about race and values that privilege ideas of Anglo identity and of particular political attitudes. These suggest that the idea of American identity is more complicated and politically contingent than constitutional patriotism and civic engagement would suggest, although it remains surprisingly thin.

The second section looks at the ways federal policy has managed violence by citizens against the state prior to 9/11 and prior to the development of federal counterradicalization programs. It shows that such citizen violence has historically been associated with ideas and beliefs associated with existential threats to the state, which seek to overthrow the system of politics that defines the United States. These threats include political ideologies such as communism or anarchism, or enemy loyalties during wartime. Furthermore, although there are some antecedents to post-9/11 policies described in Chapters 7 and 8, there is no exact precedent. The chapter's third section is a brief overview of the emergence of the threat of homegrown extremism in the United States in the post-9/11 era, prior to the introduction of federal counterradicalization programs. Together, these three sections set the stage for a deeper analysis of US counterradicalization policies in Chapters 7 and 8. They outline the history of approaches that turn on similar issues and also the biases, framings, and understandings of political community which, I argue, underpin counterradicalization policies and their approach to the problem of homegrown extremism.

## "American values": Informal political community in the United States

### Constitutional patriotism

In the United States, the ideational and material elements of political community are combined in a particularly clear way because of the US model of political organization. The United States is based on a constitutional model of political community and offers its citizens codified rights. These reflect the founding values and beliefs that define American informal political community, at least in theory, giving it a particularly civic flavor, as the *informal* values and beliefs of that community are defined by the substance of the rights granted by the *formal*, legal, foundations of that community: the Constitution. As Schuck (2006: 7) describes it, in constitutional states the founding document is the result of violent disagreement and, at the end of the foundational struggles, "a constitution can often become the symbol, indeed the metonym or actual representation, of the rule of law and of the nation." Especially as a nation of immigrants, the US nation-state has a particular attachment to the values embodied in the constitution as the undergirding of a common identity: a "civic religion . . . binding together a nation of diverse peoples" (Schuck 2007: 50).

This approach, hinging as it does on the Constitution, amounts to what Smith (1997: 33) refers to as a *civic myth*, in that it "explains why persons form a people, who is eligible for membership, who is not, and why, and what the communities values and aims are." It can best be described as a type of constitutional patriotism.[1] This means that in theory, the beliefs and values which define American political community revolve around the protection and enforcement of constitutional rights for all citizens. The concept has particular resonance for immigrant communities and their incorporation into the US political community because these values and their protection apply regardless of heritage or ethnic identity. Section 1 of the Fourteenth Amendment of the Constitution makes this clear:

> All persons born or naturalized in the United States, and subject to the jurisdiction thereof, are citizens of the United States and of the state wherein they reside. No state shall make or enforce any law which shall abridge the privileges or immunities of citizens of the United States; nor shall any state deprive any person of life, liberty, or property, without due process of law; nor deny to any person within its jurisdiction the equal protection of the laws.

A key adviser to Tony Blair's government on counterradicalization, working on the issue in the United States, highlighted the role of such constitutional patriotism in discussions and policies concerning the prevention of terrorist violence by citizens, stating:

> Here, interestingly, this country is based and built on an ideology: you hear ordinary people talk about the free market, the rule of law, the constitution—it's there. People are ingrained in that patriotic mindset from school onwards. So your American Muslim here is as American and as patriotic as your evangelical white, Anglo-Saxon protestant Christian. They all sign up to something from a very young age and the country is built on those foundations.[2]

## Immigration and race

It is important to note that in practice, the application of constitutional rights within the American political community is less consistent than the values and beliefs outlined in the founding document might suggest. The practice of US constitutional values has always been distant from their letter, and struggles for recognition, and civil rights debates, show that protection of rights is not equal for all citizens, and significant race discrimination has existed since the polity's founding days (Lieven 2012; Smith 1993). Smith (1993) refers to this as the "multiple traditions" of American national identity—the idea that contradictory ideas of racism and gender exclusion can exist in policy at the same time as ideals of constitutional patriotism. As Karst (1989: 30–32) puts it, the American creed has self-contradictory elements. These are contradictory to a rhetoric of inclusive civic culture, not least because at least until the 1950s, they associated American identity with white, male, Protestant identity. But ideas about national identity are inherently normative—they do not necessarily, and in fact rarely, reflect the present. Joppke (2007: 38) notes this when describing the three aspects of citizenship as status, rights, and identity, with the latter reflecting "normative conceptions of individual behaviour imputed by the state" which are closely connected with the "semantics of nations and nationalism." Similarly, writing of the normative aspects of citizenship (distinguishing them from the positive), Schuck (1997: 1) argues that normative citizenship "serves as a proxy, or placeholder, for our deepest commitments to a common life."

Constitutional patriotism and associated civic engagement have played an important role in US citizenship and immigration policy, by ensuring it is focused on a thin rather than a thick identity—defined by rights rather than heritage. For example, as befits a "nation of immigrants," the US Constitution is free of markers of ethnic identity. And today, following a period of expansionism building on the Immigration and Nationality Act 1965 (also known as the Hart–Celler Act), US citizenship has low barriers to entry, largely requiring simply a period of residence and an oath of allegiance. A similar period of expansionism has extended the application of the rights of citizenship beyond formal citizenship. The period since 1985 has seen a trend in immigration law and policy toward the empowerment of non-formal members of the American political community, with due process rights and constitutional rights applied to permanent, temporary, and illegal immigrants, and to asylum-seekers (see Joppke 1999: 24–25; Schuck 1989: 39). As Heller (1997: 26–27) writes, in the United States citizenship as a legal category is "thin citizenship"—meaning it is easy to acquire if certain residence conditions are fulfilled and that, given the expansion of constitutional rights beyond citizens, it bestows few privileges beyond those already granted to legal permanent residents.

But this understanding of civic rights as the defining marks of American identity glosses overs significant racism in US immigration policy. Race-based immigration policies were a feature of US policy until 1965. The Naturalization Act 1790, for example, excluded African Americans, Asians, and native Americans from citizenship, limiting it to white immigrants of "good character"—a provision that remained in place until the Immigration and Nationality Act 1952. The Chinese Exclusion Act 1882 was the first law implemented to prevent all members of a specific ethnic or national group from migrating.[3]

The Immigration Act 1917, also known as the Asiatic Barred Zone Act, introduced literacy tests for all migrants, effectively barring some populations from entry. It also barred immigration from a zone extending from east of the Urals through China to Afghanistan and North and Southeast Asia, including India and much of Polynesia. The Asian Exclusion Act 1924, part of the Immigration Act 1924 (also known as the Johnson–Reed Act), prevented immigration from Asia completely, excluding Asians from a newly introduced national origins quota system, which also by definition restricted immigration from many non-Anglo countries, including much of Europe—for example, new restrictions were imposed on Irish and German immigration, reflecting anti-Catholic sentiment and post–First World War tensions (see King 2000: 204–215, 224–227 for a discussion of national origins quotas versus nationality quotas). This act clearly aimed at maintaining a mix of US racial components through selection of immigrants from countries whose racial origins, languages, traditions, and political systems were similar to white, Anglo, usually Protestant, America. The Immigration and Nationality Act 1952 (also known as the Walter–McCarran Act) retained the quota system for nationalities, but with new sensibilities that reflected its Cold War environment. It placed a limit on immigrants coming from the "Asia Pacific triangle" and colonial dependencies (see Daniels 1993). It also added to ideas about good moral character and eligibility for entry and naturalization that had existed since the 1917 act, adding affiliation with subversive organizations or advocacy of subversive doctrines (see Bennett 1966).

National origin quotas were removed in the Immigration and Nationality Act 1965, complementing other major democratic reforms of the period—the Civil Rights Act 1964 and the Voting Rights Act 1965. These were combined with policies expanding constitutional and civic rights to non-citizens (see Schuck 1997, 2007).[4] No racially based restrictions on immigration or citizenship have been introduced since the 1965 Act. There have been strong moves to limit the extension of rights to aliens and legal permanent residents in the aftermath of the 1995 Oklahoma bombings and September 11, 2001. And debates have emerged about denaturalization in the context of foreign fighters. But there have been no similar restrictions introduced on the *acquisition* of citizenship. Similarly, there have been surprisingly minimal changes made to naturalization policy. The main changes, most introduced immediately in the aftermath of 9/11[5] have been in entry and visa policy, and apply to non-citizens rather than citizens, although they have been applied to aliens or permanent residents previously enjoying those rights (Akram and Johnson 2001-2003).

## Becoming American: Naturalization and American identity

Naturalization procedures associated with the acquisition of citizenship have historically been limited in the United States compared to other countries. Just as access to citizenship requires relatively little of immigrants, the process itself requires relatively few pre or post hoc demonstration by immigrants of their "American" identity. Today, immigrants are required to do little more than recite an oath pledging their allegiance to the constitution and to demonstrate certain residency and criminal record requirements (Pickus 2014). But there have historically been more onerous legal aspects to naturalization: applicants have had to prove more fulsomely that they are of "good moral character," prove their attachment to the constitution, and demonstrate knowledge and understanding of the principles of the constitution. These obligations still exist in theory but are pursued with far less vigor in both legal and policy terms than previously. Analyzing the history of these requirements, however, outlines the shape of the informal aspects of the American political community with particular clarity. It shows what it has meant, historically, to be or to become an American. In doing so, it allows us to establish what is meant by the "American values" invoked by policymakers in the context of US counterradicalization policies, as discussed in Chapters 7 and 8.

The requirement that candidates for naturalization demonstrate "good moral character" was introduced in the US Naturalization Act 1795 when Congress first mandated these specific requirements for naturalization, having previously only required, in the Naturalization Act 1790, the demonstration of "good character." The newer requirements are still part of US citizenship and immigration law, and link entry to the formal US political community with particular types of moral attributes—that is, with entirely interior values and practices. The judgment is essentially a subjective one, and its practical impact has generally focused on behavior associated with sexual mores and, more recently, criminal behavior. The Immigration and Nationality Act 1952 provides the first list of actual behaviors that would demonstrate a lack of good moral character, including gambling, habitual drunkenness, and polygamy as well as criminal convictions for felonies. But in keeping with the expansive moral concerns of the McCarthy era, the act also included a catch-all phrase allowing that "[t]he fact that any person is not within any of the foregoing classes shall not preclude a finding that for other reasons such a person is or was not of good moral character." The Antiterrorism and Effective Death Penalty Act (AEDPA) 1996 substantially changed the list of crimes that were classed as felonies, expanding them to include what had previously been characterized as misdemeanors and thus substantially narrowing the application of the "good moral character" requirement.[6] Overall, these requirements link formal membership of the American political community—citizenship—to certain types of societal norms and associated interior values, and practices.

The requirement that individuals demonstrate attachment to the Constitution is similarly interior and has also proven relatively malleable. This requirement links American identity with particular types of political thought, again confounding the simple constitutional patriotism model somewhat by showing that certain interior beliefs and values are desirable, and that these can include beliefs and values that are inherently political. According to the Naturalization Act 1795, petitioners for naturalization must also demonstrate that they are "attached to the principles of the constitution of the United States, and well disposed to the good order and happiness of the same." Exclusions based on lack of attachment have historically been based on ideological convictions. For example, the Naturalization Act 1906 disqualified believers in anarchism or polygamy and advocates of political assassination. These grounds were expanded via the Nationality Act 1940 to include individuals who were affiliated with communist front organizations.[7] The Internal Security Act 1950 added the even more specific designation of support for the Communist Party and the "doctrines of world communism," and these provisions were included in the Immigration and Nationality Act 1952. We can see here that there is a strong precedent with associating American identity in its most formal iteration with certain political ideas—those which do not put the US mode of government at risk. As Chapters 7 and 8 show, counterradicalization policy in the United States (unconsciously) incorporates these ideas about interior political values and beliefs and outward attachment to the constitution as a mode of counterterrorism.

These ideological approaches were explicitly discarded in the latter part of the twentieth century. In 1977, Congress passed the "McGovern Amendment" requiring the attorney general to grant visas to people otherwise excludable under the Immigration and Nationality Act 1952 on the grounds of their affiliation with certain proscribed groups such as communists. In 1987, following attempts by President Ronald Reagan to circumvent the McGovern Amendment by allowing exclusion based on foreign policy interests, Congress passed the Moynihan-Frank Amendment, explicitly prohibiting the president from excluding foreigners based on their beliefs. The provision became permanent with the enactment of the Immigration Act 1990. It is significant to note that the Immigration and Nationality Act 1952, the primary governing act, does not itself eschew all forms of ideological discrimination. It still excludes from entry and naturalization communists, Nazis, and those who advocate the overthrow by force of the US government, the propriety of killing or unlawfully assaulting government officers, unlawful injury to property, or sabotage, and those who knowingly write or circulate publications advocating any of these ideas or who affiliate with an organization that does so. It defines "advocate" to include one who "'advises, recommends, furthers by overt act, and admits belief in' a doctrine" (Neuman 1994: 101). Here, within an overt national identity prioritizing attachment to constitutional values, the idea of "being American" or at least *becoming* American involves ideas about proper forms of government and the exclusion of threats to that form of government.

The final substantive requirement for US naturalization is demonstrating knowledge and understanding of the principles of the constitution. Policy approaches to this condition show the ways in which the state itself conceives of this aspect of American identity. The United States has had an English literacy test in some form as a component of access to citizenship since 1917, and a civics test was introduced in 1952. The test has historically focused on a range of knowledge about US geography, laws, and practices, and pass rates have always been high with the test not particularly onerous (see Orgad 2010). Following the events of 2001, conservative forces in government sought to make the test more meaningful in terms of appreciation of American civic values rather than the relatively unimportant trivia that had previously comprised the test. In doing so, it has shifted the focus of the test further toward a values-based orientation. It now focuses on individual rights, the rule of law, and divided powers, and includes questions about the contributions of various groups to American life. In doing so, the test does not seek to make the process more difficult, and in fact supporters sought to maintain previously high pass rates (Pickus 2014). As Joppke (2010: 124) notes, in the post-2001 climate, "such moderation is astonishing." That is, the policy approach to US civics education and testing is surprisingly thin, suggesting that in practice it is the most minimal version of attachment to the constitution that defines American identity.

It is important to note, however, that the period of "Americanization" associated with significant nativist movements in the early part of the twentieth century, saw the development of a more comprehensive approach to immigration and citizenship policy which clearly emphasized American identity in ways that are less apparent today but which persist in political discourse around immigration and, ultimately, counterradicalization. This nativist approach saw its bureaucratic apogee in the development of the Bureau of Naturalization in 1914, at a time when American anxiety about the First World War and the United States' place in the world was peaking (Smith 1997). The education programs that the bureau developed focused on helping immigrants assimilate as part of a broader program aimed at preparing them for citizenship and integration into American life. The programs designed by the bureau focused on the "moral character" of good US citizens in an effort to promote assimilation. Classes on aspects of American life as diverse as civics and hygiene were delivered by state departments of education, local school boards, and private corporations—the bureau ran largely on private funds (Schneider 2001: 61). The naturalization drive of this period was not successful in improving migrant take up of citizenship. Following the financial crises of the late 1920s and 1930s, the programs fell out of favor with the organizations that were delivering them, and the bureau was merged with the Bureau of Immigration in 1933. This process of decline continued as restrictions on immigration and access to citizenship were lifted. As Schneider (2001) notes, from the mid-1960s, the already declining roles played by the immigration service and other federal agencies in furthering US citizenship education diminished further, and today they play almost no role. This fact was recognized by the US Commission on Immigration Reform, which called for a "new Americanization" in an attempt at reclaiming the term from its racist undertones.

The concept of citizenship education and, implicitly, Americanization, was re-emphasized in the aftermath of 2001. In 2006, President George W. Bush inaugurated the Task Force on New Americans within the DHS, aimed at encouraging successful immigrant assimilation. The task force developed online information resources to help new arrivals to "fully embrace the common core of American civic culture" as well as directions to English-language classes. It also developed a civics toolkit for delivery to immigrant-serving organizations and online resources for incorporating civics education into English as a second language teaching. In 2008 it released a report titled "Building an Americanization Movement for the Twenty-First Century" (US Department of Homeland Security 2008). Although the report did not provide for federal funds, it encouraged volunteerism among US citizens and corporations, hoping to replicate earlier public/private partnerships on the issue.

The Barack Obama administration also tackled the issue of immigrant integration via the establishment of a White House Task Force on New Americans in 2014. Unlike the Bush-era approach, this task force was housed in the White House, not the DHS, effectively desecuritizing it, at least comparatively. In this case, the task force was framed as encouraging immigrants to take up citizenship as part of a broader effort at immigration reform rather than as a response to a security issue. It provided relatively small amounts of federal funding to encourage local immigrant integration efforts, including developing civics materials and resources for increasing access to "linguistic integration" (Task Force on New Americans 2015). Unlike the Bush-era Task Force, it purposefully avoided the terms "assimilation" and "Americanization." Neither of these initiatives substantially changed the process of naturalization, or devoted large amounts of federal funds to the issue. But they did show that better integration and citizenship practices have even in recent years been seen as desirable, including in a securitized context.

In general, however, and in keeping with its relatively laissez-faire approach to the acquisition of citizenship (Pickus 2014), the United States has not implemented strong post-naturalization integration policies, preferring to leave integration of new migrants, including new citizens, to the "self-regulatory forces" of the economy and society (Joppke 1999: 147). This lack of attention to integration and the maintenance of immigrant identity in the face of a monoethnic national identity is what is known as America's melting pot approach to integration and national identity (Bloemraad 2006): adherence to civic values, not ethnicity, is the most important marker of an expansive American identity. In practice, integration policies are often left to states, if they exist at all. Situating American identity in the context of counterradicalization then requires a difficult balance between a traditional melting pot approach and an approach to ethnic identities when one primary identity—American Muslim—is associated by policymakers with acts of violence. Overall, it also means that US policies focus on constitutional patriotism as a way to define American identity in this context, but with an historical undercurrent that problematizes its application, especially in wartime.

## Citizens, violence, and the state: A brief history

As well as informing immigration and citizenship policy, the constitution has directly informed the way the US federal government has responded to citizen violence against the state throughout US history, which sets the stage for how policymakers today frame homegrown extremism. Although it is generally targeted at fellow citizens or representatives of the state, as discussed in the Introduction to this book, homegrown extremism inspired by global jihadi terrorism clearly focuses on the state on a conceptual if not always a material level. Violence of this sort has historically been framed by lawmakers as seditious, clearly situating these behaviors as insurrection against the foundations of the state. Historically, lawmakers have responded to seditious acts, or times where the foundations of the state have been seen as under pressure, by limiting the rights of citizens to otherwise fundamental rights in these contexts. This means that historically, where the basis of US formal political community has been threatened, the constitutional rights associated with US informal political community have been diluted.

This approach has persisted from the days of the Alien and Sedition Acts 1798 through the Espionage Act 1917, the Sedition Act 1918 of the First World War, and the Alien Registration Act 1940, known as the Smith Act (Stone 2004). In practice, this has meant regulation of freedom of speech in the context of national security, contrary to the First Amendment. For example, the Sedition Act 1798—"perhaps the most grievous assault on free speech in the history of the United States" (Stone 2004: 19)—penalized "any false, scandalous and malicious" statements against the president, Congress, or the government made with intent to defame, to bring into disrepute, or to "excite against them the hatred of the good people of the United States." The Sedition Act 1918 prohibited language disloyal to the American form of government and the Constitution, or the use of language intended to promote the cause of the enemies of the United States. The Smith Act, meanwhile, made it an offence for anyone, including citizens, to "advocate, teach or advise" the "overthrow" of the United States (Section 2385), again contrary to the First Amendment. Legislation of this sort, which limits constitutional rights in the context of national security, has been introduced in times of both peace and war, although more generally the latter. In wartime, such legislation, like the Sedition Act 1918, has focused on enemies and dissenters. In peacetime, such legislation has been associated with the emerging threat of war, the management of industrial unrest (see, for example, the Smith Act 1940), or the management of a perceived ontological threat to the state (see the Communist Control Act 1954).[8]

Similar legislation also introduced barriers to entry, or even denaturalization provisions, based on political beliefs or practices of potential citizens in times where the state has been under threat. For example, as discussed, the Nationality Act 1940 collated a number of earlier laws, including those from the First World War, restricting admission on the basis of political beliefs as well as race. It also restricted the conditions for the acquisition of naturalized citizenship by resident aliens along similar lines and provided for the removal of such citizenship under certain circumstances. These restrictions built on similar provisions from the First World War to the effect that persons already in the United States who "oppose or assist organizations that oppose organized government or promote the overthrow of the U.S. government" were not eligible for citizenship (Section 305).

Non-legislative activity has also addressed the problem of citizen activity regarded as seditious. Anti-communist congressional committee hearings of both the Second World War and Cold War eras, for example, targeted citizens' political beliefs and behaviors. Internment of citizens of Austrian, German, and/or Italian descent in both world wars, and especially Japanese Americans in the Second World War, has also exemplified the diluting impact of wartime on constitutional rights, especially for citizens holding non-majority views or of certain minority ethnic heritages (see Preston 1994; Stone 2007).

However, the Supreme Court has historically acted as a check on such measures. Although largely upholding legislation enacted during wartime, important dissenting cases such as *Abrams, Schiedermann, Baumgartner*, and *Yates* have established a precedent for judicial intervention when such laws and practices responding to the problem or threat of citizen violence against the state have infringed upon constitutional rights. Some policymakers have, in turn, responded to the role played by the Supreme Court as a brake on policies designed to manage citizen violence against the state. For example, Vietnam-era policies designed to deal with significant domestic unrest took the form of increased surveillance of citizens rather than active legislative programs, arguably because of the precedent set by key Supreme Court decisions overturning legislation that restricted political expression and association during the Cold War (see, for example, Stone 2004, 2007; Goldstein 2001; Heale 1990; Goldsmith and Sunstein 2002; Cole 2003). And arguments and congressional debates outlined further in Chapter 8 suggest this history of judicial activism has played a role in the design and implementation of counterradicalization policy, with regular references to constitutional constraints.

Importantly, there have been no federal level, non-legislative, or non-coercive responses to citizen-generated violence in the past, other than standard wartime home-front propaganda campaigns—the current counterradicalization policy represents the first such attempt. US counterterrorism laws have historically focused on a criminal justice approach to the problem, rather than the persuasive, discursive approach that characterizes counterradicalization policy (Donohue 2008: 345–350; Wilkinson 2011).[9] The form of US government is also important in considering the potential for implementing counterradicalization policies at the federal level. Unlike the UK, which is a unitary state, as a republic, the United States does not have the authority to wield multi-agency programs at the national level in the same way as the UK, making federal policy generally more difficult to imagine and implement (see Donohue 2011).

During the period on which this book focuses, very little federal attention in any sense has focused on the ongoing problem of so-called sovereign citizen violence which has dogged the United States since its inception, although it has become increasingly prominent in the post–Cold War era (Bjelopera 2013). In fact, in 1999, the Federal Bureau of Investigation (FBI) reported that "[d]uring the past 30 years, the vast majority—but not all—of the deadly terrorist attacks occurring in the United States have been perpetrated by domestic extremists" and most of those by far-right extremists (FBI 2000: 16).[10]

Indeed, the deadliest attack perpetuated on US soil by a US citizen was committed by far-right extremist Timothy McVeigh. He bombed a federal building in Oklahoma City in 1995, killing 168 people and injuring over 600, in retaliation for FBI action against far-right groups, and in hopes of inspiring an uprising against the federal government (Michel and Herbeck 2001). The government's legislative response—the AEDPA 1996—was thin and was subjected to heated debate in Congress about the rights of citizens. It contained no new definition of terrorism, retaining the definition in the Foreign Intelligence Surveillance Act 1978, which referred only to "international terrorism." And McVeigh was charged not with terrorism but with murder and conspiracy. The AEDPA also failed to limit access to certain types of ammunition or sale of the fertilizers McVeigh had used to build his bomb. Instead, the AEDPA was almost entirely based on anti-terrorism legislation drawn up before the Oklahoma bombing, which focused on international terrorism in response to the 1993 World Trade Center bombing and increasing concerns about international terrorism on US soil (Whidden 2001). Indeed, the bulk of the AEDPA's provisions focused on measures to address international terrorism.

Perhaps somewhat counterintuitively, the USA PATRIOT (Uniting and Strengthening America by Providing Appropriate Tools Required to Intercept and Obstruct Terrorism) Act 2001, passed in the aftermath of 9/11, introduced a definition of domestic terrorism (Section 802) into federal law for the first time, despite the fact that the acts were committed by non-US citizens. In doing so it brought the post-2001 environment into contact with the sphere of politically motivated citizen activity against the state in a manner approaching, if not replicating, earlier sedition acts.

As discussed in detail in Chapter 7, Title VIII of the PATRIOT Act alters the definitions of terrorism and establishes or redefines rules with which to deal with it. It substantially increases the tools available to the state to investigate and prosecute international terrorism, including that committed by US citizens (see Sinnar 2019), which are discussed further in Chapters 7 and 8. But importantly, in the context of previous approaches to citizen violence, the act expanded the definition of terrorism to include "domestic terrorism." According to Section 2331(5) of Title 18, United States Code, domestic terrorism occurs primarily within US territorial jurisdiction, and involves:

(A) ... acts dangerous to human life that are a violation of the criminal laws of the United States or of any State;
(B) appear to be intended—
    (i) to intimidate or coerce a civilian population;
    (ii) to influence the policy of a government by intimidation or coercion; or
    (iii) to affect the conduct of a government by mass destruction, assassination, or kidnapping.

Interestingly, the PATRIOT Act introduced no federal charge of domestic terrorism, despite introducing a definition. Federal charges remain restricted to international terrorism. Nor did it introduce methods by which domestic terrorist organizations could be proscribed, as Congress did for international organizations in 1994. However, by including the definition in the act, it allowed expanded surveillance contained elsewhere in the legislation (Section 219) to be applied to acts meeting this definition.

The issue of domestic terrorism is contentious because it raises issues concerning the constitutional rights of US citizens, especially First Amendment rights concerning free speech, freedom of assembly, and freedom of political thought. In addition, and as discussed further in Chapter 7, scholars argue that counterterrorism laws and practices in the United States proactively target American Muslim citizens despite increasing acts of violence by US citizens associated with the far-right (see Sinnar 2019; Akbar 2013, 2015; Rascoff 2010). In 2010, for example, the DHS redacted a report which suggested that at that time far-right extremism perpetuated by citizens presented a greater threat than Islamic extremism (US Department of Homeland Security 2010). The author of this report said the redaction was "politics, pure and simple," arguing that the report's findings were unpalatable because they implicated "white, patriotic" US citizens.[11] Today, counterextremism policies do not target far-right terrorism in any cohesive manner.

A former State Department official framed the problem as one concerning the boundaries of informal political community: that is, of ideas about membership and American identity that go beyond formal citizenship status:

> Politically it is extremely difficult. Right-wing extremists and the more moderate right-wing in this country don't like their extremists being talked about under the rubric of terrorism because 1) that is something that is supposed to be for brown people, not us and 2) they don't like that it casts a pall on the entire movement, if we have people who are rational actors who are permitting violence in the name of our political causes that is more worrisome. They don't want to see it framed in that way.[12]

Noting that a report from the West Point Military Academy with similar findings received a similar reception, he went on to say, "[t]he reception of those reports shows that politically it is an extremely difficult thing to do for the Obama administration to launch a broader campaign against terrorist recruitment of all varieties."[13]

In the years following 2011, attacks associated with domestic terrorism—largely from the far right—began to increase, from five or less per year between 2007 and 2011 to fourteen per year between 2012 and 2016 (Jones 2018). In June

2014, the Department of Justice announced the re-establishment of its Domestic Terrorism Executive Committee, which had lain dormant for several years (NBC News 2014). Despite this increase, by the time of the 2016 presidential election, there were no comprehensive policies in place to specifically address the threat of far-right extremism.

Overall, existing and historical approaches to violence by citizens against the state suggest that violence against the state by citizens has historically—that is, prior to 9/11—been targeted by lawmakers largely in times of war, or other forms of perceived existential threat. This targeting has taken the form of specific legislative approaches, rather than federal policy measures. Responses have focused on diluting constitutional rights to freedom of association and speech as a way of diminishing the threat, but judicial activism has curtailed the government's freedom to act in many of these cases. Here, courts have acted to protect US citizens' constitutional rights of freedom of speech and association against charges of seditious activity, even in wartime, implicating the role of the Constitution in American values. As a result, in the context of counterradicalization policy, the varied history of policies to counter citizen violence leaves no easy or direct path available to policymakers, constitutional considerations are paramount, and there are few policy-driven rather than legislative approaches to provide any sort of template.

## Post-9/11 homegrown extremism: An emerging threat

September 11, 2001, was the largest terrorist attack ever on US soil and moved the country onto a war footing in a way that far-right extremism never had. This section outlines changes in the nature of the threat of homegrown AQ-inspired extremism during the post-9/11 years. It shows how policymakers came to conceive of homegrown extremism as an existential threat, framing their eventual policy responses, as discussed in Chapters 7 and 8.

Initially, US policymakers did not register the threat from homegrown extremism as a priority. US foreign fighters had been active in AQ battlegrounds before 2001: estimates suggest that between 1,000 and 2,000 American Muslims engaged in violent jihad during the 1990s in Afghanistan, Bosnia, and Chechnya (Wiktorowicz 2005: xv; Vidino 2012: 5). In the years following 2001, US policymakers and commentators saw the risk of such attacks in the United States as much lower than in Europe or the UK, and attributed this to the difference in integration, wealth, and education between Muslim minorities in the United States and in the UK and Europe (Vidino 2012). As a former head of UK counterterrorism stated, the United States saw its population—correctly, in the eyes of many commentators—as "more dispersed, more highly educated and more integrated," and saw this as an indicator of a lower level of threat. This meant that despite high-level meetings on the issue between the UK and the United States from the earliest days following 9/11, the "US persisted in approaching the issue in this context."[14]

Early plots uncovered in the United States largely concerned US citizens training to travel to Afghanistan or Pakistan to fight against US troops. The "Lackwanna six" plot of 2002, for example, involved six young Americans of Yemeni descent accused of training at an AQ camp in Afghanistan in the summer of 2001, while the "paintball network" uncovered in 2003 involved nine US citizen converts of mixed Middle Eastern heritage planning to travel to Pakistan for training. Similarly, one of the most prominent cases of homegrown extremism, Jose Padilla, first came to public attention in 2002 connected with training in an AQ camp in Afghanistan. A US-born convert, Padilla was accused of having been recruited by top AQ operatives to create and detonate a radioactive "dirty bomb."[15] The first prison-based terrorist cell was disrupted in 2005, and influenced the first legislative response to the issue in 2007 (Harman 2007b: 1).

Despite the London bombings of 2005, US officials and policymakers continued to see the threat as external to the United States, and the US experience as providing somewhat of a buffer. Plots uncovered in Toronto in 2006 shocked the US policymaking establishment and inspired the first congressional committee field trip on these issues (Harman 2007b: 2). However, even by 2007 there was no unified high-level agreement on the severity of the domestic threat: in a hearing by the Senate Committee on Homeland Security and Governmental Affairs in 2007, then secretary of the DHS, Michael Chertoff, stated that the United States had less of a problem with homegrown radicalization than the rest of the world, specifically Europe and the UK (Chertoff 2007: 1–2). During the same period, FBI Deputy Director John Pistole noted that although the threat from homegrown extremism was real and increasing, "[m]any, if not most, of those cases are dealing with material support for terrorism. These are not bomb-throwers; these are people out there raising money or recruiting" (*Washington Times* 2006), and the 2007 National Intelligence Estimate persisted in describing the threat from homegrown extremism as not "likely to be as severe as it is in Europe," and downplayed it in response to the threat from AQ-core (National Intelligence Council 2007: 7).

This assessment changed with an increase in homegrown extremism beginning with a spike in activity in 2009, when forty US citizens were charged with terrorist-related activity, compared to just five the year before (Bergen, Sherman, and Salyk-Virk 2019). Two successful attacks in the years between 2009 and 2011, when a total of 105 US citizens were charged, included a shooting by Army Major Nidal Hasan at Fort Hood and another shooting by convert Abdulhakim

Mujahid Muhammad at an army recruiting center in Little Rock, Arkansas.[16] Overall, there was little high-level preparation involved in these plots: those aiming at executing violence on US soil involved low-level preparation only, meaning that plots involved firearms or badly executed bombs. This "spike" in activity was dominated by lone actor terrorism rather than active recruitment and coordination by AQ-core (Bjelopera and Randol 2010: 34).[17] From 2012 onward, attacks were characterized by a shift to quicker planning, simple tactics, and softer targets, and the threat from IS-inspired extremism grew, compounded by increasing numbers of foreign fighters leaving the United States for IS battlefields. US officials have not released clear figures, but focused on between 250 and 300 recruits, with the flow of fighters beginning in 2011 and peaking in 2015.[18]

Attacks grew more successful, with four attacks and five fatalities in 2013, including the Boston bombings when two brothers killed three people and injured hundreds of others. Between 2014 and 2016, IS-linked plots dominated the homegrown violent jihadist landscape, accounting for fifty-seven of sixty-six total plots. Eighty Americans were charged in 2015, including Rizwan Farook and Tashfeen Malik, a married couple who killed fourteen people in San Bernadino, California, and fifty-three were charged in 2016 (Bergen, Sterman, and Salyk-Virk 2019).

By 2016, the Director of National Intelligence testified before Congress that US-based homegrown actors would "probably continue to pose the most significant Sunni terrorist threat to the U.S. homeland in 2016" (Clapper 2016), and the Director of the FBI testified that foreign fighters and homegrown extremists remained the "highest priority," marking a clear turning point in the government's recognition of the problem, which matched the development of new policy responses that are outlined in Chapter 8 (Comey 2016). Demographic analysis of jihadi terrorist-related arrests in the United States in the period from 2001 to 2016, suggest that approximately 8 percent of those were citizens or permanent residents, with approximately 30 percent converts with an average age of twenty-nine (Bergen, Sterman, and Salyk-Virk 2019). Other research shows that IS recruitment attracts different demographics than AQ recruitment. According to this research, US IS recruits were less likely to be Arab American and more likely to be African American, Caucasian, or Latino; they were also more likely to be converts (Vidino and Hughes 2015).

Overall, these more recent trends toward decentralized, autonomously radicalized homegrown extremists are consistent with a larger global trend. Federal US counterterrorism policy documents and new legislative initiatives following the increase in attacks from 2009 show US policy responses framing homegrown extremism as a high-level threat, consistent with the threat posed in the UK and elsewhere.

# 7
# Legislating against homegrown extremism in America

Counterradicalization in the United States is constitutionally complex because at its heart it is about regulating the behavior of US citizens, and federal lawmaking involving citizens requires delicate and highly controversial maneuverings around constitutional protections. But, precisely because of these sensitivities, laws that target homegrown extremism or the relationship between citizen and state in the context of counterterrorism treat citizenship in a notable manner. Such treatment engages "taken for granted" understandings of political community, which shape the way homegrown extremism and counterradicalization problems are addressed by lawmakers in the United States in the absence of definitive research or prior legislation that specifically addresses the issue.

This chapter presents a history of legislative attempts to address the issue of citizen terrorists in the United States, either directly or indirectly. It focuses on legislation that is either successful in the sense that it has become law or notable in the sense that it represents an authoritative attempt to create such law. Despite a plethora of congressional activities on homeland security, including multiple investigative hearings into counterradicalization in both houses of Congress, surprisingly few pieces of legislation have been enacted that approach the issue of citizen behavior in the context of homeland security. Unlike similar legislation in the UK, legislation in the United States on counterradicalization is confined to the post-9/11 period—the issue of US citizen terrorists was not addressed in legislative form prior to this time.[1] I begin with relevant provisions in the PATRIOT Act 2001, which establishes the framework through which the relationship between the citizen and the state is viewed in the context of post-9/11 counterterrorism. The chapter moves on to the failed Violent Radicalization and Homegrown Terrorism Prevention Act 2007 and tracks provisions dealing with citizen terrorists in the National Defense Authorization Acts (NDAAs) 2012–2016, and the Enemy Expatriation Act 2011. Each of these pieces of legislation have either become public law or represent a significant congressional attempt to enact legislation, with significant bipartisan and/or bicameral support.

Legislative attempts to deal explicitly with the problem of homegrown extremism clearly show the link between the concept of radicalization as a problem and the application of "national values" as its solution. In doing so, such legislation draws the boundaries of informal political community more clearly and more closely, especially in the context of constitutional patriotism and its place in the delineation of American national values. Post-9/11 legislation dealing with the problem of citizen terrorism problematizes the constitutional patriotism that defines US political community by diluting the equal application of rights and by framing the problem of radicalization as one of insufficient attachment by certain individuals to the US political community, often defining those individuals by their immigrant heritage. It reduces rights previously extended to lawfully resident non-citizens and significantly broadens the definition of terrorism. This legislation also broadens the ways in which terrorism is investigated to include a wide range of political activities, beliefs, and values and in doing so restricts the boundaries of informal political community by placing limits on freedoms that are otherwise constitutionally protected.

## The PATRIOT Act 2001

The PATRIOT Act 2001 was passed speedily through Congress and marks the immediate legislative response to the events of September 11, 2001. The post-9/11 environment was characterized by presidential and public discourse which emphasized the informal values of US political community as both under attack and as a bulwark against terrorism (see Croft 2006).

The PATRIOT Act does not focus on homegrown extremism; indeed, the threat from homegrown extremism was considered relatively limited at the time it was passed. However, the act contains several measures that re-map the boundaries of formal and informal political community: it reduces rights previously accorded to permanent residents, introduces a definition of domestic terrorism, and changes the way federal surveillance of citizens is regulated.

### Expanding the definition of terrorism

The most significant effect of the PATRIOT Act in the context of homegrown extremism and the problem of "citizen terrorists" was its expansion of the definition of terrorism. Section 802 of the act amends the criminal code to add a new definition of "domestic terrorism," the first time such a definition had been introduced into federal legislation. In doing so it reconfigures the relationship between citizens and the state: defining domestic terrorism as more likely to take place on US territory increases the likelihood it will involve US citizens.[2] The relevant section reads:

(5) the term "domestic terrorism" means activities that:
   (A) involve acts dangerous to human life that are a violation of the criminal laws of the United States or of any State;
   (B) appear to be intended:
      (i) to intimidate or coerce a civilian population;
      (ii) to influence the policy of a government by intimidation or coercion; or
      (iii) to affect the conduct of a government by mass destruction, assassination, or kidnapping; and
   (C) occur primarily within the territorial jurisdiction of the United States.

The definition is not linked to a new federal charge of domestic terrorism—as many analysts have pointed out, the introduction of such a charge would be highly controversial because it would clearly set limits on constitutionally protected rights (McCord and Blazakis 2019). But in Section 219, the definition allows for the use of the term in establishing FBI-led investigations of terrorist activity on US soil and is thus more likely to involve US citizens. Previously, such activity was protected by constitutional constraints (Aden and Whitehead 2001–2002). Importantly, the definition does not link domestic terrorism solely to an act of violence. Instead, the act must only be: "calculated to influence or affect the conduct of government by intimidation or coercion or to retaliate against government conduct" (Section 219). This definition requires insight into the mental state of the perpetrator, does not specifically identify the necessary element of violence, and reduces the purpose clause to achieving political goals. And acts must only "appear to be intended" to intimidate or coerce or influence policy, requiring only a loose link between intent and action (see Chesney 2005 for a discussion of the shift to preemption in US national security policy following the events of 9/11).

Constitutional lawyers at the time problematized the new definition by pointing out that it endangered constitutionally protected political activity linked to the thoughts, beliefs, and values of US citizens: the substance of American informal political community. For example, Nancy Chang, senior litigation attorney for the Center for Constitutional Rights, noted that the act's definition of terrorism was "couched in such vague and expansive terms, it runs the risk of being read by federal law enforcement agencies as licensing the investigation and surveillance of political activists and organizations based on their opposition to government policies. It also runs the risk of being read by prosecutors as licensing the criminalization of legitimate political dissent." She argued that vigorous protest activities, by their very nature, could be construed as acts that "appear to be intended . . . to influence the policy of a government by intimidation or coercion." Further, clashes between demonstrators and police officers and acts of civil disobedience—even those not resulting in injuries and entirely non-violent—could be construed as "dangerous to human life" and in "violation of the criminal laws." For example, the blocking of an intersection or delays caused to ambulances by protest crowds, whether intentional or not, could be construed in this way. As a result, "[e]nvironmental activists, anti-globalization activists, and anti-abortion activists who use direct action to further their political agendas are particularly vulnerable to prosecution as 'domestic terrorists'" (Chang 2001: 144). This definition redefined the relationship between citizens, the state, and political behavior, and in doing so touched on the nature of informal political community in the United States, defined by rights to freedom of association, speech, and protest. Until this point, such behavior by citizens had been governed either by criminal laws, as had been the tradition in US domestic antiterrorism, or by treason and sedition laws—some dating back to the late eighteenth century. Indeed, such laws featured in several early post-9/11 indictments (Yost 2001).

## Inscribing the boundaries of formal political community

Although the PATRIOT Act's expanded definition of terrorism reconfigures notions of informal political community, many of its most controversial features focus on redefining formal community—on the tightening of borders and the associated allocation of rights.

### Non-citizens

Title IV, Subtitle B, Section 411 of the PATRIOT Act substantially enhances the provisions through which non-citizens associated with acts of terrorism may be barred from entry. The section states that anyone who is a representative of:

(aa) a foreign terrorist organization, as designated by the Secretary of State under section 219 or

(bb) a political, social or other similar group whose public endorsement of acts of terrorist activity the Secretary of State has determined undermines United States efforts to reduce or eliminate terrorist activities;

    (ii) in subclause (V), by inserting "or" after "section 219,"; and

    (iii) by adding at the end the following new subclauses:

"(VI) has used the alien's position of prominence within any country to endorse or espouse terrorist activity, or to persuade others to support terrorist activity or a terrorist organization, in a way that the Secretary of State has determined undermines United States efforts to reduce or eliminate terrorist activities."

Here, the right to refuse entry—the boundary of the formal political community—is defined by advocacy as well as action and based on membership or advocacy connected to "political or social groups," not only terrorist groups.[3] As Cole and Dempsey (2006: 153, emphasis in original) note:

> Under the immigration law that existed before September 11 aliens were deportable for engaging in or supporting terrorist *activity*. The PATRIOT Act makes aliens deportable for wholly innocent associational activity with a "terrorist organization," irrespective of any nexus between the alien's associational conduct and any act of violence, much less terrorism.

### Resident non-citizens

Not only did the PATRIOT Act restrict the rights of entry of foreign nationals; it also restricted previously held rights of foreign nationals legally resident in the United States. Such distinctions between otherwise legal residents and citizens were a feature of the anticommunist and wartime eras (Stone 2004; Cole 2003: 368–369, 385). The PATRIOT Act further diluted the rights of legal non-citizen residents, drawing more firmly the boundaries of formal political community. This was in contrast to more expansive pre-9/11 policies, which—as discussed in Chapter 6—had extended some rights to non-citizens. For example, in the years prior to 9/11, and following the loosening of migration restrictions in the mid-1960s, the US Supreme Court had held that constitutional rights of due process and access to a jury trial in criminal matters apply to all lawfully resident persons and temporary aliens: "a lawful resident alien may not ... be deprived of his constitutional rights to due process" (see *Shaughnessy*). These protections have even been extended to those whose presence in the United States is unlawful, involuntary, or transitory (Aden and Whitehead 2001–2002: 1094). As Cole (2003) argues, extension of constitutional protection of non-citizens had been relatively uncontroversial for approximately the last century.

Certain provisions in the PATRIOT Act systematically dilute these rights. Section 411, for example, provides that the expulsion of legal aliens be undertaken for the same reasons as the inadmissibility of new entrants described above: including incitement or endorsement of terrorist acts or organizations and membership of problematic political or social groups rather than simply terrorist organizations, directly implicating First Amendment rights of freedom of speech and association previously available to such residents (see Aden and Whitehead 2001–2002; Cole 2003).[4] Due process rights, meanwhile, are almost entirely reduced for foreign nationals in the United States who are convicted of terrorism: the act condemns such individuals to a military tribunal rather than a civilian court hearing.

## Material support

Aside from its effect on the rights of non-citizens, the PATRIOT Act also dilutes the rights of citizens through new measures targeting material support. For example, Section 805 expands on controversial "material support" elements of mid-1990s counterterrorism,[5] expanding the meaning of material support to include "monetary instruments" and "expert advice or assistance" and in the process invoking First Amendment concerns regarding freedom of speech and association.

In practice this has expanded the meaning of support to a variety of ideational rather than traditionally material activities, including maintaining websites, providing training, translating documents, and providing advice on peaceful conflict resolution and human rights to a listed terrorist organization (Cole 2012; Abdo 2012; Murray 2012).[6] Interestingly, within this, there is a provision that distinguishes between domestic and foreign terrorist organizations, even though both concern citizens. To be convicted of material support for a domestic terrorist organization, for example, the individual concerned must know or intend that the support provided may be used in support of terrorism—that is, for acts of violence. In the case of international groups, individuals can be convicted of material support for simply "knowingly providing" support for terrorist *organizations*—that is, without knowing or intending that the support may be used for violence (see Sections 2339A, 2339B). Because the charge may also apply to conspiracy to support rather than actual support it may apply to scenarios in which, for example, individuals agreed with others to travel abroad to join a terrorist group but did not actually do so: attempt or conspiracy to provide material support are common charges in international terrorism cases (Sinnar 2019).

The new charges mean that members of diasporas are more likely to be convicted of support because their donations are more likely to flow to international organizations and the definition of material support is looser (Sinnar 2019).[7] Perhaps unsurprisingly, conviction rates for material support have been overwhelmingly weighted toward American Muslims and other diaspora members (see Aziz 2014). As Cole (2012: 148, 168) points out, in establishing such broad provisions for material support, the United States has reverted to outdated principles from the anticommunist era, which saw government diluting First Amendment principles on national security grounds. Current apparent dilution of such rights is compounded by the arguably unequal effect of the provisions on US citizens depending on their heritage.

## Surveillance

Section 218 of the PATRIOT Act changed the relationship between citizens and states in the context of surveillance, especially surveillance linked to international terrorism. It allows for surveillance of citizens by federal intelligence agencies without those agencies having to provide direct evidence of a citizen's links to a "foreign power,"[8] as had been the case in the past. Section 218 specifically altered the Foreign Intelligence Surveillance Act (FISA) 1978, which had in part been designed to respond to Richard Nixon–era executive branch abuse of the surveillance of citizens. Responding to these abuses, FISA was intended to serve as a wall between foreign and domestic intelligence gathering by creating a clear distinction between domestic criminal investigations and foreign intelligence investigations. In this way, FISA served to protect the Fourth Amendment rights of US citizens in criminal investigations, requiring probable cause before a search warrant could be issued and preserving freedom from unreasonable search and seizure. Under FISA, these Fourth Amendment protections did not apply in full force in foreign intelligence investigations, allowing law enforcement agencies to get court orders for wiretaps and searches with a much lower standard of proof than that required in a criminal investigation. In these cases, investigators did not need to demonstrate probable cause of criminal activity and could have a surveillance order issued by demonstrating that the purpose of the investigation was to gather foreign intelligence information (see Donohue 2006).[9]

Section 218 of the PATRIOT Act amended FISA to provide that "foreign intelligence information" need not be the only purpose of such a warrant, but merely a "significant purpose," allowing information to be collected, including on citizens, without that cause being established.[10] In addition, Section 203 introduces a definition of "foreign intelligence information" to include information, whether or not concerning a US citizen, with respect to a foreign power or foreign territory that relates to (among other activities): "sabotage or international terrorism by a foreign power or an agent of a foreign power."[11] This ensures that some types of activities—in this case "international terrorism"—are clearly defined as engendering foreign intelligence information. The PATRIOT Act does not define international terrorism, but in the context of changes to surveillance outlined above, in FISA it is defined as activities that either "occur totally outside the United States," or "transcend national boundaries in terms of the means by which they are accomplished, the persons they appear intended to coerce or intimidate, or the locale in which their perpetrators operate or seek asylum" (Section101(C)(3)). As Sinnar (2019) shows, this definition is expansive: legal interpretations by the US Department of Justice suggest that domestic activities conducted merely with the intent to influence a global audience would qualify, given that the audience or persons they appear "intended to coerce or intimidate" transcend national boundaries. In practice, this has meant, for example, that citizens merely planning to travel to IS battlefields have been surveilled under these provisions (Sinnar 2019: 1346). It also means that, in practice, internet communications or consumption of online material counts as "conduct which transcends international boundaries"—the definition is loosely applied. Sinnar (2019) argues that this means the activity is more likely to frame the activities of American Muslims as international terrorism, removing constitutional protections, than it is the activities of other US citizens. In doing so it prioritizes certain informal aspects of political community—ideas, values, and beliefs—over formal citizenship, in theory diluting the application of particular rights in situations where the beliefs of certain individuals, often American Muslims, are inappropriately held.

In fact, between the 109th and 113th Congresses (2009–2013), the House Homeland Security Committee held fourteen hearings dealing directly with homegrown extremism, while the Senate held eight, and the issue regularly arose in the course of other hearings. Two of the House hearings specifically on the issue were extensive, multi-day hearings resulting in the publication of reports totaling close to 1,000 pages. This "parade of hearings" arguably reflected the politicization of the issue as much as the issue itself,[12] and so for this reason the next section focuses on a particular set of hearings revolving around the only piece of post-2001 legislation dealing in homegrown extremism that has ever managed to pass one house of Congress.

## The Violent Radicalization and Homegrown Terrorism Prevention Act 2007

The Violent Radicalization and Homegrown Terrorism Prevention Act 2007 was the first legislation passed by Congress that addressed homegrown extremism in any substantial form. Responses to it in committee are useful evidence of broader policymaking thinking on these issues and of the discourse surrounding it more broadly, which revolves almost exclusively around conceptions of formal and informal political community. The congressional hearings also show that thinking on the main provisions of the eventual US policy to counter violent extremism, which emerged in 2010—online counterradicalization and dialogue based on civil rights—had emerged outside government as early as 2006.

The bill was introduced by Representative Jane Harman in April 2007.[13] But the committee had already held one hearing and one field trip on the issue of homegrown extremism, which likely informed the bill. This section analyses that first hearing, in 2006, to see the ways in which the issue was framed. It then examines the two hearings on the bill and the final version of the bill itself, including the congressional findings on the issue. It shows that the issue was discussed by committee members and witnesses as both lacking an appropriate research base and as inherently a problem of informal political community.

The initial hearing, titled The Homeland Security Implications of Radicalization, was held in September 2006[14] in Washington, following a

July 2006 field trip to Toronto, inspired by a plot uncovered in the summer of 2006: the so-called Toronto 18, Canadian citizens plotting attacks on political installations and public figures (Teotonio 2010). As the committee's chairman, Representative Robert Simmons, put it, the first hearing was designed to:

> become the beginning of a conversation—a conversation that we might initiate here in this subcommittee but that we can then extend out into our districts and into our states, to talk with our friends and neighbors in the Muslim community, to meet in their meeting places, to gather to exchange views, so that we can attempt to better understand what their issues might be and then attempt to better understand what the issues of other Muslims elsewhere in the world might be. (Simmons 2006: 2)

In his opening statement, Simmons established two things: first, that the issue of radicalization revolved around American Muslims, not all Americans. Second, that the issue was framed in terms of American Muslims having an active global rather than a national identity in this context—as representatives of Muslims globally rather than as US citizens. It was indelibly rendered an issue of integration and of multiple, informal political communities.

The issue of civil liberties and constitutional protection was raised early in the hearing by the chairman, who framed the issue in questions to senior US DHS, FBI, and National Counterterrorism Center staff:

> [W]e are concerned about freedom of speech, academic freedom, religious freedom. These are fundamental freedoms that those of us who have served in uniform felt we were fighting for and want to protect... Have either of your three agencies encountered legal difficulties in trying to examine more closely these nodes [of radicalization]? Have you been either restricted by the staff attorneys or been given advice and guidance? And how does that issue, the issue of individual liberties and freedom, interfere, let's say, as you try to address radicalization in these different nodes? (Simmons 2006: 22)[15]

The two collection agencies, the FBI and the DHS, answered: "The FBI is very aware of the rights of freedom of religion and also freedom of speech" (Van Duyn 2006: 22), and "we have the same concerns with the tension between civil liberties and the ability to further investigate potential activities that could cause harm in the US" (Ali 2006: 22–23).

Following its introduction on April 19, 2007, the bill was immediately referred to the Homeland Security Committee's subcommittee on Intelligence, Information Sharing and Terrorism Risk Assessment, and the House Judiciary committee (which reported it immediately and passed it unanimously).

From there, the bill underwent two hearings directly related to its provisions. Chairwoman Harman opened the first meeting by emphasizing that the committee did not want to focus on "people from any particular ethnic, political or religious group" (Harman 2007c: 1–2), doing little to ameliorate the obvious implication of featuring a series of representatives from American Muslim groups and none from any other ethnic, political, or religious group. In opening questioning of senior government witnesses regarding how best to combat radicalization, Representative Daniel Lungren (2007: 30) outlined the problem, explaining it in terms of informal political community:

> We are dealing here with a phenomenon of radicalization to the extent of attempting to destroy the very essence of society we live in. That is different than many of the white skinheads we had. Ku Klux Klan was a terrorist group but they thought they were promoting their crazy version of American ideals which was radicalization of a different type... Here we are dealing with a question of an etiologically based radicalization which goes beyond just committing crimes. It goes to committing crimes for the purpose of destroying the structures of our society. That is different in form and substance than what we have done before.

Later testimony linked this to American Muslim identity specifically. In particular, one of the most influential witnesses repeatedly linked the issue to problems of integration. The RAND Corporation's senior counterterrorism analyst, Brian Jenkins, appeared before the committee four times on this issue and in total has appeared before congressional committees on this issue over thirteen times since 2006. A former member of the Clinton administration's counterterrorism commission, and hired as RAND's first counterterrorism analyst in 1972, Jenkins is extremely influential in US counterterrorist policymaking circles (see Reid 1997; Reid and Chen 2007). Prior to his appearance before the committee, he had authored two reports on US homegrown terrorism, including one specifically on the role of the internet in radicalization and was introduced by Chairwoman Harman (2007c: 42) as a "close friend."

Jenkins (2007a: 42) described the problem as one of a "marginalized immigrant subculture," noting that "as a nation of immigrants, we don't demand cultural assimilation as a prerequisite to citizenship... These are inherent strengths we have as a nation of immigrants." Directly comparing the US and European experiences he noted:

> As a nation of immigrants we have been successful at integrating new arrivals without specific policies beyond guaranteeing equal opportunity and fairness so long as they obey our laws. This success makes one wary of government

programs aimed at specific ethnic or immigration groups. Faith alone should never be the basis for suspicion but religion should provide no shield for subversion.

Jenkins focused his recommendations on the need for a commission of investigation, especially given the absence of understanding about processes of radicalization. He linked such a commission to the race riots commissions of the late 1960s, the Kerner Commission and the Eisenhower Commission, cementing his framing of the problem as one of integration and political values—that is, of informal political community (Jenkins 2007a: 10). He was not alone. A senior FBI analyst for the Los Angeles region concurred when she outlined the definition of homegrown Islamic extremism used at the federal FBI level: "US persons who may appear to be assimilated, but reject the cultural values, beliefs, and environment of the United States. They identify themselves as Muslim on some level and on some level become radicalized in the United States" (Fedarcyk 2007: 15).

Not only the problem but also its solution was framed throughout the hearings as one of informal political community. The senior civil rights and civil liberties adviser for the DHS, David Gersten, agreed, and recommended specific programs aimed at encouraging formal integration into civic and political life:

> Specifically, we need community leaders to convince more of their young people to consider public service as a career. One of our priorities as a government has to be to get young people from American Arab and Muslim families to join government service... we need to challenge community leaders to extol the virtues of public service... we also need to challenge these communities to help us increase the integration and assimilation of new immigrants, particularly those from the Arab and Muslim worlds. (Gersten 2007: 52)

Notably, the committee focused on the problem of internet radicalization, with Harman and other senior committee members focusing on it in their introductory remarks and questioning in both hearings. And although several respondents noted the First Amendment problems of action to combat online radicalization (Lungren 2007: 55–56; Gersten 2007: 57), Jenkins referred to the US Information Agency of the Cold War era as an appropriate tool, focusing on counternarratives rather than censorship. He argued for a "single point" within the State Department linked closely to the intelligence agencies to produce counternarratives (Jenkins 2007a: 40), in a format that closely resembled the later Center for Strategic Counterterrorism Communications formalized in 2011, as described in Chapter 8. After the bill passed the House of Representatives, the committee held two more hearings in 2007–2008 on the internet as a source of radicalization, with no other hearings on the other "nodes" of radicalization discussed in the initial hearings on the bill, prisons and mosques.

## Civil society opposition

Civil society was active on the issue of homegrown extremism in terms of problematizing it as early as 2003, including activism by American Muslim civil society groups. Such groups were also present in the hearings. The Muslim Public Affairs Committee appeared twice before the committee and highlighted the concern felt by American Muslims on the issue of radicalization, as well as the problem of stigmatization of the community by lawmakers and the media. Traditional civil rights groups were also active on the issue but did not appear before the committee. Key civil liberties activist groups including the American Civil Liberties Union (ACLU), the Center for Constitutional Rights, and Human Rights Watch, took issue with the bill and continued to lobby on the issue of counterradicalization from a broader constitutional perspective. Drawing comparisons to the McCarthy era, the Alien and Sedition Acts, and Nixon-era abuses of government power, such opposition focused on the argument that by acting to change and/or stigmatize political and ideological beliefs, the act mitigated First Amendment rights, including rights to free speech online, tagging it a "thought crimes bill" (Giraldi 2007; Lithwick 2007; Center for Constitutional Rights 2007; ACLU 2007). These criticisms highlight the mismatch between formal and informal political community induced by legislation addressing the behavior of citizens in this context.

Criticism was such that the majority committee took the unusual step of issuing a fact sheet after the bill had passed the House of Representatives stating: "*This legislation in no way restricts thought or speech.* Both of these are legal activities that should be encouraged by all segments of our society and are welcomed in our system of open debate and dialogue. Radical thinking is not a crime and this legislation does not turn radical thinking into criminal behavior" (Committee on Homeland Security 2007: 1, emphasis in original). In an unusual show of bipartisanship, the bill was facilitated by the House Judiciary Committee and passed the House unanimously on October 16, 2007 (Harman 2007a). In passing the bill, the key congressional findings emphasized the nature of the threat as minimally understood and driven by persuasive techniques— that is, by symbolic rather than actual violence. They also framed the problem and its response in terms of civil liberties, and specifically referred to ethnic and religious identities (Section 899B):[16]

FINDINGS.
The Congress finds the following:

(1) The development and implementation of methods and processes that can be utilized to prevent violent radicalization, homegrown terrorism, and ideologically based violence in the United States is critical to combating domestic terrorism.
(2) The promotion of violent radicalization, homegrown terrorism, and ideologically based violence exists in the United States and poses a threat to homeland security.
(3) The Internet has aided in facilitating violent radicalization, ideologically based violence, and the homegrown terrorism process in the United States by providing access to broad and constant streams of terrorist-related propaganda to United States citizens.
(4) While the United States must continue its vigilant efforts to combat international terrorism, it must also strengthen efforts to combat the threat posed by homegrown terrorists based and operating within the United States.
(5) Understanding the motivational factors that lead to violent radicalization, homegrown terrorism, and ideologically based violence is a vital step toward eradicating these threats in the United States.
(6) The potential rise of self-radicalized, unaffiliated terrorists domestically cannot be easily prevented through traditional Federal intelligence or law enforcement efforts, and requires the incorporation of State and local solutions.
(7) Individuals prone to violent radicalization, homegrown terrorism, and ideologically based violence span all races, ethnicities, and religious beliefs, and individuals should not be targeted based solely on race, ethnicity, or religion.
(8) Any measure taken to prevent violent radicalization, homegrown terrorism, and ideologically based violence and homegrown terrorism in the United States should not violate the constitutional rights, civil rights and civil liberties of United States citizens and lawful permanent residents.
(9) Certain governments, including the United Kingdom, Canada, and Australia have significant experience with homegrown terrorism and the United States can benefit from lessons learned by those nations.

The bill also defined violent radicalization, homegrown terrorism, and ideologically motivated violence for the first time in US legislation (Section 899A):

For purposes of this subtitle:

(2) VIOLENT RADICALIZATION—The term "violent radicalization" means the process of adopting or promoting an extremist belief system for the purpose of facilitating ideologically based violence to advance political, religious, or social change.

(3) HOMEGROWN TERRORISM—The term "homegrown terrorism" means the use, planned use, or threatened use, of force or violence by a group or individual born, raised, or based and operating primarily within the United States or any possession of the United States to intimidate or coerce the United States government, the civilian population of the United States, or any segment thereof, in furtherance of political or social objectives.

(4) IDEOLOGICALLY BASED VIOLENCE—The term "ideologically based violence" means the use, planned use, or threatened use of force or violence by a group or individual to promote the group or individual's political, religious, or social beliefs.

This definition is slightly different to the definitions introduced in the initial bill. The main differences are the addition of "violent" to the term "violent radicalization,"[17] added on the advice of witnesses (Harman 2007a).

The bill also clearly laid out its impact on the substance of informal political community. (Section 899F) Protecting Civil Rights and Civil Liberties while Preventing Ideologically Based Violence and Homegrown Terrorism states (a) "the Department of Homeland Security's efforts to prevent ideologically based violence and homegrown terrorism as described herein shall not violate the constitutional rights, civil rights and civil liberties of United States citizens and lawful permanent residents." It also provided for a national center of excellence on combating homegrown extremism and a national commission on preventing homegrown extremism.[18]

The bill passed the House of Representatives under a suspension of rules used only for uncontroversial bills. It passed in a landslide 404 votes for and six votes against in a show of bipartisanship not seen since initial votes on the war in Iraq, with dissent split evenly between Republicans and Democrats. Indeed, hearings on the substance of the bill, the final mark-up sharing, and the introduction of the bill into the chamber were marked by comments on the bipartisan nature of the committee, which passed the bill from the subcommittee and the full committee unanimously (Harman 2007a). An identical bill was introduced into the Senate on the same day and was referred to the Homeland Security and Government Affairs Committee as Section 159, where it remains. Congresswoman Harman attributed this to "civil liberties concerns," writing of the bill's stagnation: "Sadly, a misguided view over privacy concerns by the civil liberties community blew up the bill when it hit the Senate. Today, we're left with fewer tools than we need to stop the next homegrown plot" (Harman 2013).

The congressional findings, the testimony, and the text of the legislation itself, show the conceptualization of homegrown extremism as a new type of threat requiring a new type of response. This threat was clearly identified in the hearings as a problem of informal political community—of integration and of ideas and values—exacerbated, or even driven, by problems associated with immigration, integration, and the internet. This is reflected in the new definitions that the bill would insert into the Homeland Security Act. As civil society responses show, these definitions raise issues of informal political community in distinctly US terms of constitutional rights. Potential solutions to the problem by lawmakers and committee participants were also framed in the context of informal political community: ideas about the communication of civic values as an avenue to greater integration and an antidote to extremism appear in influential expert witness testimony, despite general agreement on a lack of information about the causes of radicalization. These ideas also appear in further iterations of US counterradicalization policy.

## The National Defense Authorization Act for Fiscal Year 2012

The United States has passed a defense authorization bill every year for fifty years, and the bill is an important measure used to adjust military funding to deal with changing military circumstances. In 2011 a bipartisan provision inserted into the bill by the leaders of the Senate Armed Services Committee, Senators John McCain and Carl Levin, saw the management of citizen terrorists and homegrown extremism raised controversially in the context of the National Defense Authorization Act for Fiscal Year 2012 (NDAA 2012). Specifically, Section 1021, Subtitle D of the act, passed in December 2012, provides for the indefinite military detention of US citizens engaged in terrorist activity on US soil.[19] In doing so, the legislation imposed a conceptual disjunct between formal political community—citizenship—and informal political community by authorizing the detention of citizens on the basis of acts such as material support based on beliefs which might otherwise be protected by the Constitution. As the act's sponsor, Senator Lindsey Graham (2011a: S8088) noted in the furious debate in the Senate on the provisions, "the homeland is part of the battlefield." The relevant provision reads as follows:

Subtitle D (Section 1021)

(b) (1) A person who planned, authorized, committed, or aided the terrorist attacks that occurred on September 11, 2001, or harbored those responsible for those attacks.

(2) A person who was a part of or substantially supported al-Qaeda, the Taliban, or associated forces that are engaged in hostilities against the United States or its coalition partners, including any person who has committed a belligerent act or has directly supported such hostilities in aid of such enemy forces.

The bill was introduced in the context of increasing pressure on President Barack Obama to fulfil an election promise to close Guantanamo Bay and in the face of a vastly reduced Senate majority and a hostile House. However, Graham also specifically linked the detention provisions in the bill to homegrown extremism, stating that the issue involved: "what to do with an American citizen who is suspected of collaborating with al-Qaida or an affiliated group" (Graham 2011a: S8088), having noted previously in the debate that "they don't have a home country, they have a home idea" (Graham 2011c: S7667). Graham linked the act to earlier anti-sedition laws enacted during the Second World War and "efforts by German saboteurs," and stated clearly:

Since homegrown extremism is a growing threat . . . under the current law, if an American citizen becomes radical, went to Pakistan and trained with Al-Qaida or an affiliated group, flew back to Dulles Airport, got off the plane, got a rifle, went down to the Mall right behind us and started shooting people . . . under the law as it exists today that person could be held as an enemy combatant, that person could be interrogated by our military and intelligence community and we could hold them as long as necessary to find out what they know about any future attacks or any past attacks and we don't have to read them their Miranda rights [(Graham 2011b: S8088)

Both liberal and libertarian critics argued that Section 1021(b) of the bill effectively legalized the indefinite military detention of US citizens. Proponents argued the bill merely codified existing executive authority under the Authorization for Military Force which had come into existence on September 11, 2001, and which authorized the detention of US citizens and had been affirmed by a Supreme Court decision in *Hamdi*. The White House disagreed, arguing that such force did not need codification and that in fact, the bill would complicate intelligence matters. In fact, the president threatened to veto the act based on these provisions (White House 2011e: 1–2, 3).

The bill passed in a relatively bipartisan fashion through both the House and the Senate, although no hearings were held on the detention provisions. On its return to the Senate the bill engendered furious debate and attempts at amendment. One amendment (1107) to strike the detention provision from the bill failed,[20] while Senator Dianne Feinstein proposed an amendment (126) explicitly stating that the law did not apply to US citizens. She argued that without such a provision, "Congress is essentially authorizing the indefinite imprisonment of American citizens without charge or trial" (Feinstein 2011: S7962). She also incorporated a newspaper article by the National Executive Director of the Japanese American Citizens League directly comparing the provision to the detention of Japanese Americans during the Second World War (Feinstein 2011: S7963)—a comparison repeated by other senators. However, a compromise version of the amendment, which later passed, simply inserted wording specifying only that the act does not override "existing law or authorities" concerning US citizens or legal residents.[21] Substantial objections from civil rights organizations in this vein persisted throughout the passage of the bill. Human Rights Watch, for example, directly linked the bill with earlier anti-sedition legislation, noting: "The far-reaching detainee provisions would codify indefinite detention without trial into US law for the first time since the McCarthy era when Congress in 1950 overrode the veto of then-President Harry Truman and passed the Internal Security Act" (Human Rights Watch 2011).

On signing the act, President Obama delivered a relatively unusual presidential signing statement, usually used to aid in constitutional interpretation, which emphasized the administration's discomfort with the detention provisions,[22] stating: "My administration will not authorize the indefinite military detention without trial of American citizens. Indeed, I believe that doing so would break with our most important traditions and values as a Nation. My administration will interpret section 1021 in a manner that ensures that any detention it authorizes complies with the Constitution, the laws of war, and all other applicable law" (White House 2011f).

Amid ongoing debates within both sides of the political divide about the sections' legality, recent legal challenges have sought to highlight the law's alleged unconstitutionality. The most prominent of these (*Hedges*) was brought against President Obama and the defense secretary and directly challenged the application of Section 1021(b) to citizens. The case's initial success at a federal court hearing was subject to a successful appeal brought by the Obama administration, and in July 2013 the initial case was struck down and an application to have the case heard in the Supreme Court while under appeal failed (Greenwald 2012; Mariner 2011, 2012a; Savage 2013). The act has also been subject to substantial attempts to repeal the provisions by amendment, but none have been passed (Mariner 2012b).[23] Indeed, both the NDAA 2013 and the NDAA

2014 also contain subtitles addressing US detention policy, although neither addresses detention matters as comprehensively as did the NDAA 2012: the NDAA 2015 and the NDAA 2016 essentially maintain the status quo (Elsea and Garcia 2016).[24]

## The National Defense Authorization Act for Fiscal Year 2013

Aside from ensuring the continuation of the controversial detention measures of the NDAA 2012, the NDAA 2013 also contained measures that changed the State Department's ability to communicate with US citizens in the pursuit of foreign policy goals. This change was not only the result of essential bureaucratic reorganization to take account of changes to the communications environment wrought by the internet, but also because of the effect of older legislation on the government's ability to effect counterextremism measures (Thornberry 2012). In their focus on targeting citizens, these measures indicated the way that lawmakers conceptualized formal citizenship in the context of homegrown extremism—as overlaid with and foregrounding diaspora membership rather than formal US citizenship and associated political identities.

Section 208(B) of the NDAA 2013 amended the Smith-Mundt Act and the Foreign Relations Authorization Act 1987 to allow for materials produced by the State Department and the Broadcasting Board of Governors—one of the State Department's premier public diplomacy institutions—to be released within US borders and struck down a long-standing ban on the dissemination of such material in the United States.

The original Smith-Mundt Act 1948 had been passed in an environment of virulent anticommunism. At the time, members of Congress suspected that the State Department was a hotbed of leftist activism and so prohibited the department from disseminating inside the United States its information products designed for audiences abroad. US public diplomacy had undergone a reinvigoration in the years following September 11, 2001, and changes to Smith-Mundt can be directly related to these efforts. Under the George W. Bush administration, reform of public diplomacy had started early in 2001, and became an increasingly prominent aspect of the Bush administration's foreign policy efforts after the 2004 presidential elections. These efforts were inextricably linked to the global war on terror (Peterson 2002; Glassman 2010). For example, the first ever comprehensive national strategy for public diplomacy was released in 2007 and had three strategic objectives, with one focusing on the problem of extremism for the first time: "With our partners, we seek to isolate and marginalize violent extremists who threaten the freedom and peace sought by civilized people of every nation, culture, and faith" (US Department of State 2007b: 3).

In 2011, the US Advisory Commission on Public Diplomacy heard from senior State Department and counterterrorism policymakers that the Smith-Mundt Act presented a serious threat to strategic public diplomacy, specifically the ability to engage diaspora and expatriate audiences within the United States in a new media environment, noting that State Department media agencies were:

> currently prohibited by law from producing content for distribution inside the U.S. and will continue to comply with the law. However, anecdotal communication to closed foreign publics through expatriate communities within the U.S. or via diaspora communities in other nations seems to be an effective way to reach those closed communities, so legal paths to employ that strategy should be explored.
>
> Expat populations within the U.S. have access to foreign media content intended to influence them but access to the U.S. government perspective is limited. The resulting dissonance in what foreign audiences hear from the U.S. Government abroad and what they hear from relatives in the U.S. and media based in the U.S. creates unnecessary challenges. (United States Advisory Commission on Public Diplomacy 2011: 6)

Domestic diaspora communities played an important role in counterradicalization efforts, meaning the NDAA 2013 also played a role in facilitating domestic counterextremism. In fact, a former under-secretary for public diplomacy described this as the "main driver" of the legislative changes, noting that it "came out of the House Armed Services Committee interest in combating violent extremism. They were concerned that the US was becoming a source for bad guys and the US media is simply not doing its job on reporting what is going on abroad."[25] One of the bill's sponsors, representative Adam Smith, explained in a press release that: "Smith-Mundt restrictions are incredibly problematic when trying to combat the spread of violent extremist ideologies and extremist recruitment efforts . . . Smith-Mundt's restrictions on domestic distribution of material for foreign audiences through new technologies directly interferes with our efforts to get factual information out in a timely manner to counter the misinformation spread by violent extremists" (Smith 2013).

In response to concerns that the modernization could facilitate government propaganda targeted at the domestic population more broadly, he referred directly to a key cluster of AQ-inspired homegrown extremism in the Somali population in Minnesota, noting that,

> the bar on the US government doing domestic propaganda remains in place. What we amended was the ability of them, if asked, to provide that same content domestically. So one of the examples was that Voice of America had been

providing, in Somalia and in those areas, sort of a counter-radicalization method. And in Minnesota, where they have a substantial Somali population, they had asked, you know, well, can we have that information. Smith-Mundt barred them from providing it. So we amended it to say if somebody asks and if it's information that has already been created for an international audience, then yes, you can provide it. The government still cannot provide purely for domestic consumption any sort of information campaigns, so it was a very limited exception. (Smith 2013)

Notably, as discussed in Chapter 8, the government had already engaged in online counterextremism which by default—and to productive effect—could be consumed by US audiences. Prior to the NDAA 2013, such programming raised Smith-Mundt Act sensitivities. The Center for Strategic Counterterrorism Communications, for example, was established within the State Department in late 2010 and as one former senior government official noted, during his time (before the NDAA 2013), the Center was always "careful to broadcast in languages other than English" because of such sensitivities.[26] Here, then, we see the characterization of diaspora communities, including citizens, as part of a broader transnational community whose ideas, values, and beliefs are by definition separate to those of the United States.

## The Enemy Expatriation Act 2011

The US has a long history of linking access to formal political community—citizenship—with political beliefs and practices, often barring entry to those who have been convicted of certain crimes or who are not of a certain moral character, as outlined briefly in Chapter 4. The PATRIOT Act extended such exclusion provisions to include those activities associated with terrorism, broadly defined. These measures have extended to deportation of those who might otherwise be considered to have the formal legal protections of citizenship (Cole 2003). Denaturalization (the removal of citizenship from those who acquired it in adulthood) and denationalization (the removal of citizenship from those who acquired it at birth) have both featured in the legislative arsenal of governments in times of war extending back to the Civil War era and the Alien and Sedition Acts 1798 (Weil 2013; Aleinikoff 1985; Schuck 1989: 9). This section examines an ultimately unsuccessful piece of legislation that, however, is striking in its attempts to enforce denationalization in the context of homegrown extremism. Despite its failure, the associated debates help to delineate the context of current concerns about, and approaches to, citizen terrorists in the United States.

The Nationality Act 1940 expanded the automatic loss of citizenship to include denaturalization provisions for several categories of US-born citizens, for example those who had engaged in foreign military service or had been convicted of treason—material acts all. Such persons were considered to have voluntarily renounced their citizenship. Further denaturalization provisions were codified in the Immigration and Nationality Act 1952 (known as the McCarran-Walter Act) and under the Smith Act 1940. Here, immigrants had to prove a commitment to the Constitution and could not have been members of a subversive organization within five years of naturalization. Refusal to testify before a congressional committee became grounds for denaturalization, as did rebellion or insurrection, participation in a seditious conspiracy, or advocating the violent overthrow of government (Jones 1979: 132–134). Both acts came under judicial pressure from the late 1950s, as the Supreme Court began to raise the standard needed for denaturalization in particular, although decisions were by no means consistent. The most definitive case came with *Afroyim* in 1967, when the court held that the constitution grants Congress no express power to strip people of their citizenship, holding that "the Fourteenth Amendment was designed to, and does protect every citizen of this Nation against a congressional forcible destruction of his citizenship, whatever his creed color or race" (Black 1967: 267–268). Such provisions have rarely been used since then, and since 1990 the State Department has held that a US citizen does not intend to expatriate unless they *voluntarily* perform an expatriating act such as taking another citizenship or serving in a foreign army, with the intent of giving up their US citizenship.

Attempts to implement denaturalization measures are present in post-9/11 legislative discourse surrounding homegrown extremism, although such attempts are yet to come to fruition. For example, the Domestic Security Enhancement Act 2002 (known as PATRIOT 2) was leaked before its introduction to Congress (Lewis and Mayle 2003). The substance of the bill was hugely controversial for several reasons, including provisions concerning citizenship. If passed, it would have allowed the presumptive stripping of citizenship from anyone who supported even the lawful activities of an organization deemed terrorist by the executive branch (Section 402). This would have substantially redefined the boundaries of formal political community—citizenship—according to essentially informal, values-based definitions of terrorism, given the broadening of behaviors targeted in the context of already broad definitions in the PATRIOT Act. Importantly, Section 402 broadened the crime of providing material support to terrorism to include any material support in the name of supporting terrorist activities, even if support were either not intended for or not given to any organization listed as a terrorist organization by the government (Mariner 2004).[27]

PATRIOT 2 was withdrawn in the face of public outcry and was never introduced to Congress. However, the Terrorist Expatriation Act 2010 was introduced in both houses and with bipartisan support just days after US citizen Faisal Shazad was arrested for an attempt to bomb New York's Times Square in May 2010. Reintroduced in 2011 as the Enemy Expatriation Act, the bill seeks to amend the Nationality Act such that citizenship can be revoked from all citizens who provide support to terrorist groups like AQ or who attack the United States or its allies. Section 2(8) expands the meaning of "voluntary" expatriation to mean: "providing material support or resources to a foreign terrorist organization," which in turn means:

(B) engaging in, or purposefully and materially supporting, hostilities against the United States; or
(C) engaging in, or purposefully and materially supporting, hostilities against any country or armed force that is—
   (i) directly engaged along with the United States in hostilities engaged in by the United States; or
   (ii) providing direct operational support to the United States in hostilities engaged in by the United States.

The bill thus provides that a US citizen would lose their citizenship for "providing material support or resources to a Foreign Terrorist organization," or by actively engaging in hostilities against the United States or its allies, relying in the process upon broad definitions of material support in the PATRIOT Act as described earlier, and clearly drawing on the material of PATRIOT 2. Importantly, the bill does not require a conviction for providing material support, simply an administrative finding based on the secretary of state's listing of organizations.

In introducing the bill into the Senate, its principal sponsor, Senator Joseph Lieberman, clarified its links to homegrown extremism in the context of the Nationality Act 1940, which stripped the citizenship of those who joined the German or Japanese military during the Second World War, stating in a summary of the bill: "US nationals who join al-Qaeda and other FTOs [foreign terrorist organizations], declare America to be enemy soil, and take up arms with the goal of killing Americans should forfeit their rights to American citizenship or other nationality status, just as they would if they had joined the armed forces of any nation with whom the United States was at war" (Lieberman 2010; Fox News 2010). Critics including civil society representatives and senior Republicans argued that the bill was unconstitutional. Christopher Anders, ACLU senior legislative counsel argued: "This is an extreme bill that would give government bureaucrats the O.K. to strip Americans of their citizenship, based on nothing more than suspicion. American citizenship is too precious to be left to the whims of government bureaucrats" (quoted in Karaman 2011; Savage and Hulse 2010).

The bill was introduced with sponsors from both sides of politics and referred to committees in both the House of Representatives and the Senate with bipartisan support.[28] However, the bill died in committee and has not received any hearings since the first version was introduced in 2010. Lieberman has since retired, and the bill faces opposition from both the left and the conservative right. In general, the legislative measures leading up to and including the Enemy Expatriation Act 2011 show that the cause of homegrown extremism is neither understood nor settled. Instead, these pieces of legislation show the issue to be understood and discussed instinctively as one of political community, and especially as a problem of informal political community. Responses to the problem draw on these concepts in ways that reflect wartime measures discussed in Chapter 6—the Alien and Sedition Acts, for example. But these more recent approaches dilute the bond between formal and informal citizenship in the complex home "front" of homegrown extremism, driven by "taken for granted" assumptions about the nature of citizenship, American identity, and the problem of homegrown extremism itself.

# 8
# Civics, rights, and wrongs
## Countering radicalization in America

US policymakers refer to countering violent extremism (CVE) rather than counterradicalization. As prefigured in the introduction to this book, in effect both these terms refer to policies meant to stop individuals progressing along a path of radicalization leading to violent acts of terrorism and so are used interchangeably here. DHS, the lead agency on the US CVE taskforce during the period covered by this book, defines CVE as "proactive actions to counter efforts by extremists to recruit, radicalize, and mobilize followers to violence." It notes, "[f]undamentally, CVE actions intend to address the conditions and reduce the factors that most likely contribute to recruitment and radicalization by violent extremists" (US Department of Homeland Security 2016b). US CVE policy at the federal level has emerged slowly, and by 2016 it was still only relatively limited despite the threat being acknowledged as pressing. The emergence of CVE policy has been dominated by bureaucratic confusion and underfunding driven by interagency competition. This is not new. As Crenshaw (2001) has shown, the politics of counterterrorism in the United States have historically led to confusion and ineffectiveness. However, CVE policymaking is hindered additionally by the controversial and constitutionally delicate nature of CVE in the United States. Understanding the emergence of this policy, and the concepts deployed in policy documents, helps us to understand how the US bureaucracy—largely the executive branch—frames the threat and its solution, especially given the absence of scientific consensus on what causes radicalization (indeed what it *is*) and how to solve it.

In this chapter I offer a brief history of US CVE and identify the persistence of ideas about informal political community therein. These ideas, about what an American political community *is* and *should be*, form "taken for granted" understandings about the world (Schwartz-Shea 2015: 123) that appear in policy in the absence of conclusive research. This chapter shows that ideas about a strong informal political community as a valid response to the problem of homegrown extremism appear in much of the thinking behind counterradicalization measures in the United States. These measures consistently frame tightening the

*Hold Your Friends Close.* Sarah Logan, Oxford University Press. © Oxford University Press 2023.
DOI: 10.1093/oso/9780190920326.003.0009

borders of informal political community as a response to the problem of radicalization, via an emphasis on community engagement with the agencies of government and on community cohesion against agents of radicalization.

## Initial policy responses

Policy interventions specifically aimed at targeting US citizens in the context of homegrown extremism did not begin in the United States[1] until 2006, and ideas about informal political community did not inform policy directives at the federal level until 2010.[2] The George W. Bush administration had been engaging in work to counter the narratives of AQ recruiters in a minor way since 2005, focusing exclusively on international terrorists rather than domestic extremists. The Barack Obama administration aimed to build on this and add a new dimension to the broader counterterrorism effort both internationally and domestically. As one former senior State Department counterterrorism official noted:

> The Obama administration came in with the belief that the Bush administration had been incredibly good at what Dan Benjamin, the incoming coordinator for counterterrorism called "practical counterterrorism" i.e. kinetics, military operations and law enforcement. The Obama administration also felt that the Bush administration had not done enough to address what John Brennan had called the "upstream factors." That was the initial framework—it was about "upstream." The belief was that you had to have a more holistic approach to counterterrorism and a lot of the people formulating this found not a shift in policy but an expansion of policy, because the Bush administration had been thinking in similar terms—it was just that the Obama administration wanted to do more of it.[3]

The first congressional hearing on the issue was in 2006 (Harman 2007b), and in 2006–2007 the DHS was beginning its engagement with Muslim communities, focusing on regular meetings with leaders and the establishment of "incident response teams," which brought together federal agencies and community leaders in the aftermath of relevant incidents such as the Fort Hood shootings, for example.[4] Late 2006 saw the formation of a branch within the DHS Office of Intelligence and Analysis that focused exclusively on radicalization and extremism in the homeland (Chertoff 2007).

The FBI had begun establishing community outreach programs as early as 2006 (Fedarcyk 2007) in an effort to build relationships with local Muslim groups,[5] building on early approaches to the problem as one similar to community policing initiatives, and in November 2008 the Department of Justice (DoJ) established a specialized community outreach team staffed by special agents and other staff members with cultural and language skills (Bjelopera 2013). The unit was designed to assist field offices in establishing contacts with important but "hard to reach" communities such as the Somali American communities of Denver, Columbus, Minneapolis, and Seattle. A 2009 Building Communities of Trust (BCOT) pilot, led by the DoJ, sought to "improve information sharing and collaboration in order to protect our local communities," knowing that "[t]he knowledge about communities that comes from trust-based relationships among such partners is critical because it allows law enforcement officers and analysts to distinguish between innocent cultural behavior and that indicative of criminal activity" (Wasserman 2010: 7).

By 2010, analysts were increasingly wary of the threat of homegrown extremism (Blair 2010: 11). In early 2010 the secretary of the DHS, Janet Napolitano, created a Countering Violent Extremism Working Group within the Homeland Security Advisory Council.[6] At the same time, thirty-two US attorneys' offices began a pilot program introducing CVE into some existing conversations with communities around federal protection of civil rights and liberties. A National Task Force on Community Engagement was established in November 2010 to coordinate community engagement activities, including on CVE. Activities included roundtables conducted by the DHS Office for Civil Rights and Civil Liberties, State Department discussions on foreign policy with domestic communities, the production of brochures by DoJ on civil rights protections, and expansion of the BCOT initiative to focus on reporting suspicious activity and the protection of civil rights and liberties.

The Obama administration's first national security statement, delivered in May 2010, addressed the issue for the first time and showed that the threat had increased to the point where a federal-level response was necessary.[7] The statement outlined the US response to "new challenges," which included "combating violent extremism" as well as "stopping the spread of nuclear weapons and securing nuclear materials" and "forging cooperative solutions to the threat of climate change," ranking the threat by implication as not only novel but extremely serious. In addition, it cited "empowering communities to counter radicalization" as one of five key goals to "strengthen security and resilience at home" (White House 2010: 19).

Following the announcement of the national security strategy, the administration established an accelerated process, led by National Security Council staff, to develop a coherent approach to CVE. An interagency policy committee was established, including high-level representatives from the departments of State, Treasury, Defense, Justice, Commerce, Labor, Health and Human Services, Education, Veterans' Affairs, Homeland Security, the FBI, and the National Counterterrorism Center (NCTC)—a coordinating analytical body established after 9/11 (White House 2011c). The NCTC assumed a lead role in the committee, coordinating interdepartmental cooperation and information exchange on the issue. The policy response as a whole was driven by the National Security Council, in the executive branch. US intelligence and policy leaders also undertook intensive research on counterradicalization programs already underway elsewhere in the world, largely in Europe.

The administration particularly sought to learn from the UK's experience, given its innovative and whole-of-government response to a serious threat of homegrown extremism in the form of the Prevent policy and to avoid repeating its mistakes.[8] By late 2009, the UK policy was increasingly under fire for being not only expensive but also so ill-conceived as to act as a radicalizing agent by securitizing and alienating state relationships with Muslim communities (House of Commons Home Affairs Committee 2012).[9] Key to development of the US policy in this regard was US academic Quintan Wiktorowicz, based in London at the US embassy until early 2009.[10] Wiktorowicz joined the National Security Council in January 2009 as its first adviser on counterradicalization and remained skeptical about some aspects of UK policy, including the arguable securitization of community services.[11]

The Obama administration's first National Strategy for Counterterrorism was released in June 2011 and highlighted the threat from homegrown extremism, stating: "We are working to . . . build resilience within our communities here at home against al-Qa'ida inspired radicalization, recruitment, and mobilization to violence." The strategy highlighted "Information and Ideas: Al-Qa'ida Ideology, Messaging, and Resonance" as one of its ten key areas of focus, the others being geographical (White House 2011a: 11, 17). At this point, there was little consensus on the causes of radicalization: "contestation around causes [was] still ongoing. The DHS and NCTC will agree . . . that this religious conveyor belt theory is just bunk . . . and within the FBI now there is a tussle . . . If you talk to FBI agents on the ground they will tell you. FBI agents don't necessarily believe those theories."[12]

## A concrete policy emerges

The first part of the White House strategy on CVE, developed by the interagency policy committee, was released in August 2011. Empowering Local Partners to Prevent Violent Extremism in the United States outlined three key goals and areas of priority action: (1) Enhancing Federal Engagement with and Support to Local Communities that may be Targeted by Violent Extremists; (2) Building Government and Law Enforcement Expertise for Preventing Violent Extremism; and (3) Countering Violent Extremist Propaganda While Promoting Our Ideals.

The document did not detail plans for implementing the programs, but emphasized a "community based approach," stating: "The best defenses against violent extremist ideologies are well-informed and equipped families, local communities, and local institutions" (White House 2011b: 6, 2).

In pursuit of this approach, the document outlined the government's intention to leverage CVE programs off existing community-based measures, local partnerships, and community-oriented policing as part of a "broader mandate of community safety," stating that "[r]ather than creating a new architecture of institutions and funding, we are utilizing successful models, increasing their scope and scale where appropriate" (White House 2011b: 3). This focus on extension of existing institutions was in stark contrast to UK policy, which instituted extensive new funding streams and new architectures of policy development. In the US strategy, community policing initiatives were to be modeled on anti-gang initiatives developed in the 1990s and programs intended to prevent school shootings.

The second part of the White House strategy was released in December 2011. A longer document than its predecessor, the "Strategic Implementation Plan for Empowering Local Partners to Prevent Violent Extremism in the United States" outlined how the government was implementing the national strategy delivered in the earlier document. Three priorities were emphasized: "(1) enhancing engagement with and support to local communities that may be targeted by violent extremists; (2) building government and law enforcement expertise for preventing violent extremism; and (3) countering violent extremist propaganda whilst promoting [US] ideals" (White House 2011c: 2). Four fundamental activities were essential to the strategy's success: "(1) whole-of-government coordination; (2) leveraging existing public safety . . . (3) coordination of domestic and international CVE efforts . . . and (4) addressing technology and virtual space" (White House 2011c: 4). The Strategic Implementation Plan (SIP) designated the ninety-four US Attorney General's Offices throughout the country as the federal leads in the field for CVE-related community engagement and placed responsibility for implementation of the plan as a whole on four agencies: the DHS, the NCTC, the FBI, and the DoJ.

The policy did not provide guidance on federal-level oversight or offer significant new funding streams, so there was no lead agency on CVE, while including in its avowed "whole-of-government approach" agencies as diverse as Health and Education (McCants and Watts 2012). The DHS had at this point congressional authority to be the lead department to counter ideologically driven violence and handled the bulk of tasks associated with CVE but was required to share tasking with the DoJ. Both ran a taskforce with the NCTC, which was announced in 2011 and informed CVE policy, but each agency had—and continues to have—their own internal policy guidelines. The bulk of activities at this early stage were funded by preexisting funding streams or practices rearranged to incorporate new priorities (Aziz 2014; United States Government Accountability Office 2012: 61). Many of the practices to be continued or expanded included those begun in pilot community engagement practices by the DoJ and the DHS in 2010, as outlined earlier.

New initiatives included the establishment of a CVE Coordination Office in the FBI, the development of an online portal by the DHS to disseminate information, allocating funding for research, standardizing law enforcement training materials and expanding the quantity of training, providing grants to community groups to counter violent extremist narratives, brokering connections between private sector actors, and promoting international exchange programs to build expertise for countering extremist narratives.

The April 2013 Boston marathon bombing and later the rise of IS triggered a renewed focus on CVE. In 2014, then Attorney General Eric Holder announced a federal revamp of CVE efforts with a three-city pilot of different approaches to counterradicalization: societal approaches in Minneapolis-St Paul, community engagement in Los Angeles, and targeted interventions in Boston.

The review was followed by a White House summit on CVE in early 2015, which focused on discussion of best practice and was used to receive feedback on the three city pilots. A review of federal policy in 2015 saw representatives from eleven government departments identify four priorities to further progress the counterradicalization agenda. These were: (1) "infrastructure to coordinate and prioritize CVE activities" across the Federal Government and with stakeholders; (2) "clear responsibility, accountability, and communication" internally and with the public; (3) broad "participation of relevant departments and agencies outside of national security" issues; and (4) "a process to assess, prioritize and allocate resources to maximize impact" (US Department of Justice 2016). In September 2015, the DHS created the Office of Community Partnerships to manage CVE within the department.[13] The new office was funded by Congress for US$3.1 million and primarily brought together staff working on CVE in different areas of the department rather than hiring new staff. Similarly, it did not replace the Office for Civil Rights and Civil Liberties (OCRCL), which had previously managed community relations in this context—the office committed to using the OCRCL to drive community engagement as it had done previously. In response to the review, an interagency CVE taskforce was established in January 2016, with experts from the DHS, the DoJ, the FBI, the NCTC, and six other nontraditional security agencies. The taskforce was to be led on rotation—initially by the DHS, then by the NCTC for two years, and so on. And in July 2016, the DHS announced US$10 million in grants for CVE projects, to be managed by the Office of Community Partnerships (Biery 2016; Homeland Security Advisory Council 2016). The grant funding, and funding for the office itself, represented the first targeted package directed specifically at CVE and managed by a new, dedicated body. The grants were to be allocated based on five priorities: developing resilience, training and engaging with community members, managing intervention activities, challenging the narrative, and building capacity of community-level, nonprofit organizations active in CVE.

In October 2016, the White House released an updated SIP (White House 2016a). It outlined four "lines of effort" for work under the 2011 National Strategy for Counterterrorism's areas of priority action: research and analysis, community engagement and technical assistance, interventions, and communications and digital strategy. The first two lines of work were extensions of existing work in the 2011 SIP. The 2016 document introduced the concept of interventions—crystallizing US policy reactions to targeted, multiagency interventions of individuals identified as on the path to radicalization. The controversial concept mirrors to some extent the Channel initiative in the UK and was criticized in the United States specifically because of its implications for constitutionally protected rights (see for example Brennan Center for Justice 2016; ACLU v 2016). The idea found its initial expression in the US in a controversial 2015 FBI program for "shared responsibility committees" whereby community multiagency groups made up of community members would identity individuals at risk of radicalization and decide on appropriate treatment measures (Brennan Center for Justice 2016).

The fourth line of work also presented a shift in focus. Like the 2011 SIP, it emphasized communications and digital strategy—"countering violent extremist propaganda whilst promoting [US] ideals" (White House 2011c: 2). But the 2016 SIP introduced a new focus on collaboration with the private sector—for example, by convening forums with both government and private sector participation to discuss the potential of emerging technologies for radicalization and to identify technology solutions.

Overall, US CVE policy has remained underfunded, disjointed, and lacking in leadership. About half of the forty-four tasks identified in the 2011 SIP had been completed by 2016. A Homeland Security Advisory Council review in 2016 recommended significantly increasing funding, noting:

> Despite increased public and policy focus on CVE, federal funding has not matched the scope of this very real and present challenge. The initial national CVE strategy released in 2011, "Empowering Local Partners to Prevent Violent Extremism in the United States" provided unfunded or under-funded roles and responsibilities for federal, state, local, and community partners on prevention. For five years, the Department has been placed in the untenable position of implementing a national strategy with no new funding. (Homeland Security Advisory Council 2016: 8–9)

The review also recommended developing an as yet non-existent national architecture across all fifty states and establishing and funding the Office of Community Partnerships to lead DHS CVE efforts, including establishing regional offices around the country to facilitate DHS/Office of Community Partnerships collaboration across state and local jurisdictions (Homeland Security Advisory Council 2016: 6, 9).

This suggests that the form that counterradicalization takes in the United States is shaped in important ways by the fact that it targets citizens by definition, so policies are inevitably, and inherently, framed by considerations of the constitutional rights accorded to US citizens. Congressional hearings and discussions, the role of the OCRCL in delivering the policy in the United States, and responses by civil society show that the policy is shaped in important ways by constitutional constraints in ways that other counterterrorist measures are not. This arguably underlies the failure of two specifically targeted pieces of legislation and the relative paucity of policy responses, despite the fact that the threat was listed alongside nuclear weapons and climate change in the 2010 national security strategy. US counterradicalization policy is very thin: it is largely rhetorical and, unlike the UK approach, does not involve the allocation of large amounts of new funding or the design of new systems of delivery. As one analyst noted, "I wouldn't even call it a policy at all."[14] Another observed: "I think the whole thing was a rhetorical step. I think it is extraordinarily dangerous. The only thing that keeps me quiet is that I don't think they are going to do anything. They can't give direct money. They can't say 'we are going to fund this.'"[15]

These same two analysts largely attributed this thinness to constitutional constraints on policymaking to do with political and religious thought.[16] One suggested that this thinness was due to strong constitutional constraints, which meant that despite "an aspiration to be holistic in a very robust British way that never panned out . . . it was more a shout-out to that."[17] Indeed, for example, as discussed in Chapter 7, the Fourteenth Amendment conceptually limits extensive post-facto attention to immigrant integration. Demonstrating government attentiveness to protecting the civil rights of migrant communities (via OCRCL outreach, for example) is, then, arguably the only way the government can address integration concerns. This outreach, discussed later, largely comprises roadshows by the OCRCL to discuss the ways in which migrants' constitutional rights are protected by the government and to educate migrant communities on those rights. It reinforces *already existing* membership of the formal political community rather than enforcing integration more literally in a CVE context as is the case in the UK. One analyst also suggested that the thinness of the policy was a result of interagency battles about the worthiness of CVE itself. This position is supported to some extent by government studies of differences between

DHS and DoJ approaches to funding CVE-related training, which suggests that the FBI, for example, preferred not to engage in new program design or funding delegation for CVE training, opting simply to continue existing community engagement activities and acknowledging their relevance for CVE, whereas the DHS was far more active in designing new programs and reallocating funding (United States Government Accountability Office 2012: 58, 61). The analyst, a former employee of the OCRCL within the DHS, argued that "Those people [who support 'soft' counterterrorism] may have won the battle of ideas in the rhetorical sense, but they may not have won the budgetary one. They may have gotten what they wanted rhetorically in terms of acknowledging CVE but if there is no money then it shows they haven't made much headway against traditional counterterrorism. The money is still with traditional counterterrorism."[18]

## Common themes in US CVE policy

### More research is needed

Despite making clear policy prescriptions, all three federal policy documents (White House 2011b, 2011c, 2016a) emphasize the need for further research. This suggests that the overarching policy directions in US CVE are not informed by rigorous understandings of the problem or its solution. The 2011 policy document has as its second priority Building Government and Law Enforcement Expertise for Preventing Violent Extremism, necessitating "ongoing research and analysis" (White House 2011b: 6), as well as further training for law enforcement and information exchange with stakeholders and international partners. The 2011 SIP outlines existing research, largely housed in government, and expands on this by outlining the importance of "increased research, analysis, and partnerships with foreign governments, academia, and nongovernmental organizations" (White House 2011c: 12). The 2016 SIP brings "research analysis" to the forefront, with research and analysis the first line of effort. This foregrounding and the additional detail included in it suggests that the need for research has become more acute, not less, as programming has developed. The document recommends mapping and cataloguing all existing federally funded CVE research and increasing stakeholder access to that research. It also focuses on efforts to "increase the applicability of CVE research and analysis" to "ensure research and analysis can be used to inform program development," including "create[ing] a scientific basis for CVE programs" and ensuring that research and analysis informs CVE training (White House 2016a: 6). It also urges that evaluation methods for all federal CVE programs be implemented.

## A cohesive civic community is a valid counterradicalization measure

All three federal policy documents and a range of activities by federal agencies project the concept of a cohesive political community, bound by shared values and institutions, as a bulwark against radicalization. This consistency is striking in that it exists despite the similarly prominent shared theme drawing attention to the need for more research. The importance of political community was prefigured in Obama's 2011 State of the Union speech, which addressed extremism in this format for the first time. He framed the problem explicitly as one of political community: "And as extremists try to inspire acts of violence within our borders, we are responding with the strength of our communities, with respect for the rule of law, and with the conviction that American Muslims are a part of our American family" (Obama 2011).

As this speech suggested, rhetoric concerning constitutional rights and protections play an important role in US federal CVE policy. All three federal policy documents emphasize the protection of constitutional rights as fundamental to CVE practices. Policy documents consistently portray respect for constitutional values as a driver of stronger political communities, encouraging integration of diverse political identities into a common whole by providing a shared identity and an outlet for grievances managed in accordance with nonviolent, law-abiding US practices. Protection of constitutional rights is of course, fundamental to any US policy endeavor. But in the case of CVE, policy attention to the protection of constitutional rights, especially of migrant and minority communities, is a policy measure in itself, with a desired outcome of increased national unity and a shared sense of constitutional patriotism. As the DHS argues: "Protecting civil rights and civil liberties is paramount in itself and helps to counter violent extremism by safeguarding equal and fair treatment, ensuring nonviolent means to address grievances, and making it more difficult for violent extremists to divide communities" (US Department of Homeland Security 2016b). Vidino and Hughes (2015: 4) describe US CVE policy as shaped by "a national culture, reinforced by core constitutional values protecting freedom of conscience, that does not believe law enforcement should grapple with ideological and even indirectly religiously-related issues."

These sentiments are evident throughout the strategy documents, placed as overarching statements framing and introducing policy measures. In his introduction to the 2011 overarching strategy document, President Obama noted that the strategy "reaffirms the fundamental American principles that guide our efforts . . . We will defeat Al-Qa'ida and its affiliates. We will uphold the civil rights and civil liberties of every American. And we will go forward together, as Americans, knowing that our rich diversity of backgrounds and faiths makes us stronger and is key to our national security" (White House 2011b). Half of the eight guiding principles of the original strategy focus on the role of constitutionally protected rights as a CVE measure and/or as a framing device for CVE policy (White House 2011b: 7–8). The 2011 SIP reaffirms this approach. In the section titled Compliance with the Rule of Law, it states that "the Federal Government's actions must be consistent with the Constitution and in compliance with US laws and regulations ... Compliance with the rule of law, particularly ensuring protection of First Amendment rights, is central to our National Strategy for Empowering Local Partners and the execution of the SIP" (White House 2011c: 4). It also notes that the process of developing the first SIP was framed by constitutional ideals: "Given the complexities of addressing this threat and the uniqueness of the operating environment in the United States, the Administration recognizes the potential to do more harm than good if our Nation's approach and actions are not dutifully considered and deliberated. Throughout this process, careful consideration was given to the rule of law and constitutional principles, particularly those that address civil rights and civil liberties" (White House 2011c: 3).

The 2016 SIP, meanwhile, also highlights the role of constitutional values in framing CVE policy. In a section titled "Promoting American Ideals," it notes that "protecting civil rights and civil liberties is paramount in itself and helps to counter violent extremism by safeguarding equal and fair treatment ... Protection of individual privacy and freedom of expression is essential to this work and will be woven into all efforts." The strategy notes that when developing programs, federal departments and agencies will "analyze potential privacy, civil rights, and civil liberties considerations with their legal counsel ... as appropriate," and that state and local authorities may request the DoJ provide guidance on similar issues for local level programming (White House 2016a: 3).

Importantly, the primary DHS body engaged in CVE policy delivery has historically been the OCRCL. The office was established by the Homeland Security Civil Rights and Civil Liberties Protection Act 2004 (subtitle C). A key statutory amendment implemented by that act ensured that "the civil rights and civil liberties of persons are not diminished by efforts, activities, and programs aimed at securing the homeland," and established the OCRCL as a point for complaints and policy design relevant to these issues. Until 2008, the OCRCL was relatively inconsequential in CVE terms, but since the introduction of the Obama administration's CVE policies, the office has served as the hub for DHS activity on CVE and in effect assumed one of the most visible soft CVE roles in the federal government. This is particularly relevant given the lead role that the DHS seems to have assumed in the early years of CVE policy in the US. Bjelopera (2014: 20) notes that: "It appears that DHS is cited as a lead agency in 43 of the 62 future activities and efforts discussed in the SIP. Because it is a key player and decision maker in more than two-thirds of the SIP's impending plans, it seems that DHS may be the de facto lead agency in charge of U.S. CVE activity in the near future." Indeed, as outlined earlier, the DHS was at the time of writing the lead agency on the interagency CVE taskforce (though this was to be a rotating position shared with the DoJ), and although the Office for Community Partnerships had been funded to house CVE measures across the agency, the OCRCL remained in charge of delivering community engagement programs.

The emphasis on constitutional rights may also to some extent be a rhetorical device aimed at dampening and responding to criticism of CVE in the United States as discriminating against American Muslims. Significant criticism of the policy has emerged from constitutional perspectives. A February 2016 Freedom of Information Act lawsuit launched against federal CVE initiatives by the American Civil Liberties Union was driven by the serious risks CVE programs pose to US citizens' constitutional rights and the government's failure to release information about the programs. The lawsuit focuses particularly on the constitutional issues raised by CVE programs that seek to monitor speech or make it politically sensitive, especially in the case of American Muslims: "By framing First Amendment-protected activities as potential indicators or predictors of violence, Defendants' CVE initiatives encourage law enforcement and other government agencies to target individuals based on such activities or use them as a basis for other action" (ACLU 2016: 8-9).

## Community engagement can lead to a more cohesive political community

The concept that a cohesive political community is a strong response to, and protection from, radicalization, is also evident in the second group of policy measures (aside from research) common to all federal policies: community engagement. Engagement in this setting means using the arms of government— federal, state, and local—to engage with (usually Muslim) American communities and to engender stronger communities, with an underlying integrationist impulse. For example, after introducing community engagement measures as the second block of activity supported by this overarching policy, the 2016 SIP offers this guidance: "Federal outreach and engagement activities should aim to decrease exclusion and isolation, avoid stigmatization, encourage civic engagement, and empower potential partners to demonstrate how a thriving, inclusive community is the strongest front against violent extremism" (White House 2016a: 7). The policy supports measures "enhancing federal engagement with and support to local communities that maybe targeted by violent extremists" and aims to "improve the depth, breadth and frequency of Federal

Government engagement with and among communities on the wide range of issues they care about, including concerns about civil rights, counterterrorism security measures, international events, and foreign policy issues." The contribution of this sort of engagement is made clearer: "violent extremist narratives espouse a rigid division between 'us' and 'them' that argues for exclusion from the broader society and a hostile relationship with government and other communities. Activities that reinforce our shared sense of belonging and productive interactions between government and the people undercut this narrative and emphasize through our actions that we are all part of the social fabric of America" (White House 2011c: 8).

The 2011 strategy document and the 2016 SIP share this emphasis.

The 2011 strategy document emphasizes community engagement as an essential feature of good governance and highlights as a guiding principle that "we must use a wide range of good governance programs—including those that promote immigrant integration and civic engagement, protect civil rights, and provide social services—that may help prevent radicalization that leads to violence" (White House 2011b: 8). The 2016 document argues similarly that: "Violent extremist narratives espouse a rigid division of 'us' and 'them' that often promote an individual's exclusion and isolation from his or her community and broader society and encourage a hostile relationship with government and other defined groups" (White House 2016a: 7). Both the 2011 strategy document and the 2016 SIP note the importance of community engagement and emphasize the importance of integrating communities targeted for CVE practices into broader community engagement practices so that they do not feel marginalized (White House 2016a: 7).

The practical measures implemented by agencies delivering on the CVE priorities outlined above support the concept of community engagement as aimed at the development of a stronger informal political community as a bulwark against counterradicalization. The DHS's primary approach to CVE has been community engagement. For example, in congressional testimony the agency has consistently highlighted that the bulk of its CVE activities are facilitation of regular roundtables for community and government leaders—usually over one hundred events including roundtables and panels, which it sees as supporting CVE goals.[19] In 2010 the agency also initiated a series of annual "roundtables on liberty and security" for 150 young leaders, held in Washington, DC. The DHS officer in charge noted they were designed to "welcome young people in American Arab, Muslim, Sikh and south Asian communities to join our nation's collective security efforts: we must empower them to be connected rather than alienated" (Schlanger 2010: 12). The DHS strategy on CVE, delivered in October 2016, made this clear. Its third goal (of four) was to support community-based efforts to counter violent extremism by promoting (as its first objective) a "national message of inclusion, respect, and non-discrimination" (US Department of Homeland Security 2016a: 10).

One of the early US CVE–oriented community engagement initiatives was run jointly by the DHS and the DoJ and drew directly on the first goal of the SIP, "enhancing engagement." The Building Communities of Trust initiative was highlighted in the 2011 SIP as an appropriate program on which CVE initiatives could draw. As mentioned earlier, BCOT focuses on "developing relationships of trust between law enforcement, fusion centers, and the communities they serve, particularly immigrant and minority communities, so that the challenges of crime control and prevention of terrorism can be addressed" (Wasserman 2010: 3) and has been implemented in fifteen locations. It is undertaken specifically under the auspices of the Nationwide Suspicious Activity Reporting Initiative, created on the recommendation of the National Commission on Terrorist Attacks Upon the United States, also known as the 9/11 Commission—that is, despite the reference to crime, it focuses almost entirely on terrorism. BCOT is, arguably, primarily aimed at gathering intelligence from a community policing perspective but has controversially been framed as part of the CVE response (Hovington 2010; Schlanger 2010; Aziz 2014) and in the 2011 SIP as an inclusive measure generating increased bonds of political community.[20]

The DHS also runs three initiatives that explicitly target terrorist incidents and their potential to radicalize communities further and engender fear and sees these as community engagement exercises, even though they are more explicitly focused on situational response. In 2010 and 2011, it developed two initiatives with the NCTC. The Community Awareness Briefing (CAB) is designed to share unclassified information on the threat of radicalization with local communities who may be at risk—this can include, for example, information about recruiting strategies, particular individuals involved, narratives in play, and so on. The Community Resilience Exercise (CREX) is designed to simulate a response to an attack by a radicalized individual within a community. It engages local emergency and community services and civic leaders to role play a response. Other engagement initiatives have focused on the development of an "incident community coordination team" to disseminate information to affected communities in times of crisis that strain their relations with the federal government. Such communities are those (Muslim) where such incidents—for example Koran burnings by US troops in Afghanistan in 2012—can cause disquiet and unrest.

Other agencies also participate in community engagement activities as part of CVE programming. By 2016, thirty-eight FBI field offices had established community engagement councils/multicultural advisory councils in order to consult with local leaders and run town hall–style meetings concerning issues of Muslim-focused law enforcement. The FBI has also counted its "citizen academies"—where members of the public undertake a short course in

FBI activities—as a CVE/BCOT initiative and builds on existing youth outreach programs (Hovington 2010: 14). Overall, federal attorneys have become key points of interaction on DoJ initiatives, including BCOT (McCants and Watts 2012). The initiatives have included integrationist activities. For example, in 2011 the District of Minnesota established the Young Somali-American Advisory Council, in response to al-Shabaab's recruitment of young men within the greater Minneapolis-St. Paul Somali community. Among the outreach activities tied to the council, the US Attorney's Office instructed community members on civics and constitutional values (Jones 2012).

The most visible extra funding for CVE saw the DHS award US$10 million for CVE grants to community groups, in a highly unusual move for federal grantmaking practices, which usually avoids directly funding sub-state bodies. In January 2017, the DHS released the list of thirty-one CVE grant recipients. Approximately US$2 million was allocated for "developing resilience." Similar amounts were awarded for training and engagement activities and on intervention programs, while approximately US$2.7 million was allocated to challenging the narrative. A final fund of just over US$1 million was awarded for "building the capacity" of community-level nonprofit organizations active in CVE.[21] Across the list of twenty-six grant recipients, seventeen referred to "civic engagement" as a method employed to counter violent extremism. A project run by the Arlington Police Department, for example, pledged to foster "civic pride and increase civic participation amongst attendees," who were judged to be at risk of radicalization. Another, led by the Nebraska Emergency Management Agency, proposed that "high civic engagement leads to ownership of solutions and strategies for improving life for community members, which enhances community resilience in a sustainable manner." Another successful application, from the sheriff's office in Minnesota, outlined its CVE measures as "presenting our American model of self-government and the rule of law, [as] an alternative to the radical message and ideology, a model of freedom and opportunity, education, dignity and hope." Another, from Houston's Office of Public Safety and Homeland Security, proposed running leadership and civic engagement courses for youths from communities vulnerable to radicalization. These courses included information about "government, the political process and service" and included a line item for printing resources about constitutional rights (for details of these grants, see US Department of Homeland Security 2017a).

## American Muslims as a transnational political community

The bulk of US CVE policy has its basis in engagement with and focus on American-Muslim communities. The overly securitized nature of this engagement is furiously contested by many Muslim community members and by civil rights activists. Community members and civil liberties and human rights organizations argue that this engagement frames American Muslims as separated from the rest of the American community by virtue of their religion, despite formal citizenship (see Aziz 2011-2012, 2014; Markon 2011a; Brennan Center for Justice 2016; Lieberman 2011–2012 for an overview of tensions). This speaks to the framing of American Muslims as something "other" than Americans, who must be integrated into the American system of values to inoculate them against radicalization, or to respond to latent dangers of radicalization.[22] This aspect of CVE is part of the domestic politicization of the issue of Islam and Islamic minority communities (see, for example, Kundnani 2009; Patel 2011; Aziz 2014).[23] The politicization of the issue is certainly evident in much of the US congressional discourse, which regularly frames Islam and Muslim as distinct identities hostile to the United States. Similarly, the "parade of hearings" on radicalization has been directly linked to domestic political incentives.[24] It is important to note in this context that despite the problematization of American Muslim integration in counterradicalization discourse, American Muslims are historically far better integrated than equivalent communities in Europe. Indeed, a senior UK intelligence official noted that for a long time this led to US government officials' convictions that the United States did not and would not suffer from the same problems of radicalization as much of Europe.[25]

Perhaps the most striking part of CVE programming concerning American Muslims is the link between domestic and international community outreach efforts which frame American Muslims—and Muslims in other Muslim minority states—as comprising a transnational community by virtue of faith, rather than, or as well as, a political community defined by formal citizenship. Coordination of Domestic and International Efforts is one of the four key cross-cutting supportive activities outlined in the 2011 SIP (White House 2011b). While at pains to note the importance of relevant laws and regulations separating the two spheres, the SIP notes that "the delineation between domestic and international is becoming increasingly less rigid. Violent extremists operating abroad have direct access to Americans via the Internet, and overseas events have fueled violent extremist radicalization and recruitment in the United States. The converse is also true: events occurring in the United States have empowered the propaganda of violent extremists operating overseas" (White House 2011c: 5).

In practice, this means that the DHS and the State Department work together on this issue in relatively innovative cross-border ways. In doing so they frame the "Muslim" community globally as a key transnational actor separate from, but linked to, a smaller "American" identity. In fact, this sort of engagement between the State Department and American Muslims was in place prior to the introduction of a domestic CVE strategy as part of programs delivered by the State Department's counterterrorism unit and Bureau of International Information Programs to "support projects to counter violent extremist ideology" (Burns 2007; Glassman 2010). These projects focused on international counterextremism rather than domestic counterextremism, and so focused largely on Muslim majority countries. However, they also targeted diaspora communities, including those in the UK. For example, the State Department funded travel by American Muslims to London to showcase the message of American Muslims "proud to be both American and Muslim," as a "powerful message" that would "open British Muslim eyes to American cultural and religious diversity as well as encourage reflection on the part of the British Muslim community in a positive, self-defining direction" (US Department of State 2008: para. 5).

These efforts are largely a development in traditional public diplomacy initiatives through a counterterrorism lens and are important because they target Muslims as a transnational community rather than communities defined by states, the usual targets of public diplomacy initiatives. A further innovation in this sense is the emerging practice of briefings by State Department officials to diaspora communities within the United States, an innovation there as it is in the UK.[26] For example, the State Department has worked with DHS and FBI outreach teams to deliver relevant briefings on foreign policy matters of concern during broader community outreach initiatives. The Bureau of Near Eastern Affairs conducted eighty such briefings with Somalian, Arab, Egyptian, and Afghan community organizations within the United States during Fiscal Year 2010–2011. In addition, through its Foreign Service Institute, but working closely with the NCTC and the DHS, the State Department piloted specialized CVE training for US government officials working on CVE in the United States and abroad. The State Department also sponsored a speaker series and exchanges between international CVE practitioners and US communities targeted by violent extremist recruiters to better understand effective models for countering violent extremism (White House 2011c: 19).

Similarly, the Transatlantic Initiative with US-UK Pakistani communities, run by the DHS in concert with UK counterparts, is a useful example. The initiative aimed to build a long-term network of Pakistani Americans and Pakistani Britons and to foster integration and civic engagement (US Department of Homeland Security 2013). From 2011, the OCRCL collaborated with the State Department and international partners to coordinate CVE activities of a similarly transnational character in the City Pair Program. In this program, the OCRCL coordinated and cohosted a two-part CVE community engagement exchange program that involved a US delegation comprised of Muslim community and civic leaders, law enforcement, and government officials from US cities. The group traveled to cities with CVE-style programming and issues with radicalization in Brussels, Sweden, and Germany. Leaders, law enforcement officials, and community members likewise traveled to cities in the United States. The program aimed to "address community engagement best practices that support CVE and also promote immigrant integration, youth empowerment, resolution of grievances, and protection of rights and liberties" (US Department of Homeland Security 2016c: 18). The DHS also regularly conducted its CAB and CREX activities with overseas communities. In reporting, it combined statistics for these programs into one measure, further encouraging the conceptualization of Muslims as a transnational community defined by faith rather than citizenship. In 2016, for example, the DHS delivered CAB sessions in twelve US cities and four foreign cities, engaging "1,000 community members." It delivered four CREX briefings in the same year, two domestic and two internationally (US Department of Homeland Security 2017b: 16).

## Online CVE: Countering violent extremist propaganda while promoting our ideals

All three US CVE documents highlight the role of the internet in disseminating problematic narratives, especially regarding the third key goal of the 2011 policy document: "countering violent extremist propaganda whilst promoting our ideals." The document states: "We will work to empower families and communities to counter online violent extremist propaganda, which is increasingly in English and targeted at American audiences" (White House 2011b: 6). Foreshadowing the development of a specific online CVE policy, the 2011 SIP outlines "addressing technology and virtual space" as one of four "crosscutting and supportive activities," noting:

> The Internet has facilitated violent extremist recruitment and radicalization and, in some instances, attack planning, requiring that we consider programs and initiatives that are mindful of the online nature of the threat. At the same time, the Federal Government can leverage and support the use of new technologies to engage communities, build and mobilize networks against violent extremism, and undercut terrorist narratives. (White House 2011c: 5)

The 2016 SIP contained a section titled "communications and digital strategy," which focused on strengthening the online dissemination of CVE materials and engaging with the private sector to counteract messaging.

However, there are few if any government-funded programs targeted directly (at least overtly) at the domestic sphere. Pursuing these goals has taken several different forms. In 2013, the White House announced the creation of a new Interagency Working Group to Counter Online Radicalization to Violence. It was chaired by National Security Council staff at the White House and involved specialists in countering violent extremism, internet safety experts, and civil liberties and privacy practitioners from across the United States government. The working group was responsible for developing plans to implement an internet safety approach to address online violent extremism, coordinating the federal government's activities and assessing its progress against these plans, and identifying additional activities to pursue for countering online radicalization to violence (Wiktorowicz 2013). By 2016, the working group had largely been superseded by other interagency efforts focusing specifically on IS or other terrorist groups (OSCE 2020), and it does not appear in reporting to Congress. Additionally, attention to online radicalization has been a feature of several coercive counterradicalization measures. For example, several material support of terrorism charges have been brought successfully for online activity focused on ideas and beliefs, such as Facebook "likes," online translation, and consumption of YouTube videos (*Mehanna*; FBI 2012; Murray 2012). Commentators suggest the relative paucity of federally funded domestic online CVE programs is largely due to constitutional concerns about freedom of religion and expression (Helmus, York, and Chalk 2013: 5, 8–10).

Comparatively free of such constraints, the State Department has been relatively active on this issue, as discussed in Chapter 7, and with some impact on domestic audiences. The Obama administration established the Center for Strategic Counterterrorism Communications in May 2011.[27] Executive Order 13584 of September 2011 increased the prominence of the center's work and established a separate budget, set initially at US$6.2 million for 2012 (US Department of State 2011). The center initially consisted of a team of about thirty analysts working in a variety of languages to counter extremist propaganda on internet forums and chat rooms, and the executive order stated that this goal would increase so that the center should "coordinate, orient, and inform Government-wide public communications activities directed at audiences abroad and targeted against violent extremists and terrorist organizations, especially al-Qa'ida and its affiliates and adherents, with the goal of using communication tools to reduce radicalization by terrorists and extremist violence and terrorism that threaten the interests and national security of the United States" (White House 2011d). These measures directly echo the Bourdieusian symbolic violence employed by jihadi strategists, as described earlier in this book:

(i) monitoring and evaluating narratives (overarching communication themes that reflect a community's identity, experiences, aspirations, and concerns) and events abroad that are relevant to the development of a

U.S. strategic counterterrorism narrative designed to counter violent extremism and terrorism that threaten the interests and national security of the United States;
(ii) developing and promulgating for use throughout the executive branch the U.S. strategic counterterrorism narratives and public communications strategies to counter the messaging of violent extremists and terrorist organizations, especially al-Qa'ida and its affiliates and adherents;
(iii) identifying current and emerging trends in extremist communications and communications by al-Qa'ida and its affiliates and adherents in order to coordinate and provide thematic guidance to U.S. Government communicators on how best to proactively promote the U.S. strategic counterterrorism narrative and policies and to respond to and rebut extremist messaging and narratives when communicating to audiences outside the United States, as informed by a wide variety of Government and non-government sources, including nongovernmental organizations, academic sources, and finished intelligence created by the intelligence community (White House 2011d).

Importantly, the center's guidelines neither prohibit nor explicitly state that its activities might controversially target domestic counterradicalization; as discussed in Chapter 7, associated legislative innovations theoretically removed barriers to the targeting and consumption of such material by US citizens on US territory. Similarly suggesting at least some domestic component, the initial Fiscal Year 2012 budget request for the center notes its cooperation with the DoJ and the DHS, the two key domestic CVE agencies (US Department of State 2011: 57).[28] Reporting to the Undersecretary for Public Affairs, the center conducted a number of activities, including coordination of interagency counternarrative efforts and the production of offline and online countermessaging material. In the online space, the center engaged in a number of covert and overt activities. Its digital outreach team focused exclusively on online counternarratives actively "trolling" jihadi social media accounts and running counternarrative campaigns, often badged as US government accounts. From 2012 to 2015, for example, it performed over 50,000 online "engagements" in four languages: Arabic, Urdu, Somali, and English (Cottee 2015).

The center struggled to combat the volume of jihadi social media content and was belittled for failing to make measurable headway against the narrative threat. Senior staff, meanwhile, argued that it was under-resourced (Fernandez 2012) and that government was "probably not the best platform to try to communicate with the set of actors who are probably vulnerable to this kind of propaganda and this type of recruiting" (Rasmussen 2015), acknowledging it was limited by constitutional restrictions, the inability to acquire and access necessary analytic data at speed, and the need to communicate authentically with an audience outside—and often hostile to—government.

In March 2016, Executive Order 13721 renamed the center the Global Engagement Center (GEC) and allocated and increased dedicated funding to it through legislation for the first time (the previous center had not received such funding; see Weed 2017). Still housed within the State Department, and still working with interagency deployees, it focused on engaging private sector partners and also broadened its remit beyond "Al Qaeda and its adherents" to include Islamic State of Iraq and the Levant and other organizations, recruitment and radicalization, with an explicit focus on CVE, including within the United States. Like the executive order of 2011, the 2016 order charged the GEC with combating symbolic violence employed by jihadi strategists, this time directly targeting recruitment strategies. Among other responsibilities, the GEC was tasked with:

> consulting and engaging, in coordination with agencies and the Countering Violent Extremism Task Force, as appropriate, with a range of communications related actors and entities, within the United States and abroad, including governments, private sector and civil society entities, in order to contribute to U.S. Government efforts to counter the communications-related radicalization to violence and recruitment activities of international terrorist organizations and other violent extremists abroad, while also building the capacity of partners to create resonant positive alternative narratives and to diminish the influence of such international terrorist organizations and other violent extremists abroad. (White House 2016b: 1-2)

The establishment of the GEC also saw the State Department take up partnerships with private sector actors (see Isacson 2018 for an overview of tech platforms and their role in CVE). Although information on the relationship between the US government and corporate actors in such partnerships is scarce, efforts by technology companies on the issue with a key public-interest CVE outcome has included work by Jigsaw (a Google subsidiary) and Microsoft. This has included the development of tools such as the Redirect Method, which uses Google advertising technology to direct those who view extremist material toward alternative narratives, including material produced by the US government, and the development of hashtag databases which facilitate the removal of extremist content. A range of US-based technology platforms established the Global Internet Forum to Counter Terrorism in 2017.[29]

# Conclusion

In 2008, the UK government funded a program called "British Muslim or Wot?" Among other things, the money was used to run summer workshops which "created a space for Muslim boys and young men to build a new narrative about being young, British and Muslim." They also "looked at the difference between religion and culture . . . separating culture and religion helped people think how they could be Muslim and British" (Crook 2008). An example from the United States tells a similar story. In 2012, the Barack Obama administration funded a range of community CVE pilot projects. These included resourcing Heartland Democracy, an organization in Minneapolis, home to a large Somali-American community that had been the site of recruitment by the Islamic State of Iraq and Syria (Xaykaothao 2016). Heartland Democracy received money for humanities-based education, civic engagement, and identity development, as well as providing a safe, confidential space for complex dialogue around politics, history, race, religion, and culture. In its grant application, Heartland Democracy argued that the success of the program would be measured by increased voting, greater participation in community politics, and "increased education and quality of life" (Heartland Democracy 2016: 12).

At the same time, both the UK and the United States were investing in traditional, explicitly coercive counterterrorism policies. Among other provisions, the UK Counterterrorism Act 2008, for example, allows for post-charge questioning of terrorist suspects and extended sentences for offenders convicted of offences with a "terrorist connection." It enables the police to request monitoring information from convicted terrorists and to prevent them from foreign travel. The US 2012 budget provided US$14.1 million extra funds for the Transport Safety Authority's Secure Flight Program, which checks a passenger's data against the FBI Terrorist Screening Center database, which integrates all available information on known or suspected terrorists into a central, federal repository. Access to it by the Transport Safety Authority facilitates the removal of terrorist suspects from flights.

Counterradicalization programs like "British Muslim or Wot?" and those run by Heartland Democracy are unusual and novel in both the US and the UK. But, as Chapter 2 showed, counterradicalization programs also exist in many other states across the world, from Indonesia to the Netherlands to Saudi Arabia. Globally, counterradicalization policies converge in two important ways. First, they are integrationist: despite targeting individuals who are already formal members of a political community defined by a nation-state—citizens or residents—these policies are concerned with drawing their target audiences deeper into this community by focusing on inculcating the ideas and values that define it. The programs are defined by questions about citizenship, belonging, and the nature of formal and informal political community. This explains the emphasis on civic education, on discussions about identity, and on programs designed to foster integration and inclusion. As Chapter 3 indicated, these programs respond to the symbolic violence of jihadi narratives that seek to pry apart the boundaries of formal and informal political community by fostering homegrown extremism as a strategic move. Counterradicalization programs seek to realign those boundaries.

Second, aside from sharing a focus on integration, counterradicalization policies are concerned with *persuasion* rather than explicitly with coercion, clearly delineating them from what might be termed more "traditional" counterterrorism policies. The policies change individuals' minds, persuading rather than forcing them to undertake certain activities. As Chapter 2 showed, this quality persists across Muslim minority and Muslim majority, liberal and less liberal states. This suggests that dealing preemptively with members of a political community in the context of homegrown extremism seems to invoke similar constraints across different types of political systems. In liberal states, these constraints mean that governments are precluded from acting coercively and preemptively, especially regarding the way their citizens think about the world. Some analysts in liberal Muslim minority states generally refuse to even entertain the thought that governments might act coercively in response to their citizens' thoughts, ideas, and beliefs,[1] and one former senior UK government official referred to the government's desire to avoid repeating the mistakes of "radicalizing a generation" via coercive policies in Northern Ireland.[2] But at least one analyst noted that even in comparatively illiberal states such as Indonesia and Saudi Arabia, governments had to consider the political effects of acting coercively on citizens regarding these issues.[3] This suggests that the choice to act persuasively rather than coercively is not just the result of liberal paradoxes in the sense that liberal states cannot easily act coercively and preemptively against their own citizens (Joppke 2010: 142–145). Although requiring future research, in the case of counterradicalization, it is also because the threat involves citizens whose thoughts, beliefs, and opinions about the world potentially pose the very threat to the state these policies seek to counter. In this context, coercive measures can act as radicalizing agents by obviously excluding certain citizens from the protections of membership in their political community that they might otherwise reasonably expect—the right to, or expectation of, free expression, equal treatment, or freedom of religion, for example.

This reluctance to employ coercion may also be the result of past experiences, at least in liberal states, perhaps suggesting a desire to avoid repeating repressive policies of the past. Literature on judicial activism in the "war on terror" suggests that courts in the post-9/11 era are more activist in protecting citizens' rights and limiting executive excesses in liberal states than they have been in previous eras of national security emergencies (Ip 2011; Bonner 2007; Dyzenhaus 2008). This certainly appears to be the case in the United States (see Cole 2007–2008: 47–48). Policy discourse repeatedly emphasizes the role that citizens' constitutional rights play in policy design even though, as scholars have repeatedly demonstrated, such respect has in the past meant little (Stone 2004). Similarly, judicial activism in the UK—on control orders, for example—indicates that in the post-9/11 era, UK courts have been more activist than previously on such issues involving citizens (Kavanagh 2009; Ip 2013; Davis 2010). However, despite some surprising resistance on behalf of a UK judiciary usually acquiescent in the context of emergency powers in wartime, most scholars agree that the situation is both too complex and too limited to draw any conclusions in this regard (see Ewing and Tham 2008; De Londras and Davis 2010; Davis 2010). The fact that indefinite detention of citizens has been legislated in the United States and that control orders and other measures to deprive citizens of their status have been successfully implemented in the UK, suggests that the influence of such learning from the past is at best limited in the face of executive power. Chapter 3 shows that similar policies exist in decidedly illiberal states, suggesting that the fact of counterradicalization itself is unlikely to be the result of concerns about citizen rights, although in the United States and the UK its *form* is certainly subject to such concerns. Further research would benefit from focusing on Muslim majority states, as compared to Muslim minority states, and across Sunni and Shia populations.

Within this broad convergence on the form of counterradicalization, there exist important divergences. This book has demonstrated these divergences through its primary empirical focus on counterradicalization in the United States and the UK. Perhaps paradoxically, the primary differences between the policies draw on differences in the nature of the political community in which they are implemented and which they seek to protect. There are obviously important and fundamental structural differences between the formal aspects of the US and UK political communities, which inform some of the differences between their counterradicalization policies. The difference between a unitary state and a federal system, for example, influences important differences in the capacity of each government to implement policy at all levels of government.

But differences between UK and US counterradicalization policies go beyond those dictated by formal structures of governance. Instead, they deal in the language of citizenship and of the interplay between formal and informal political community. In doing so they draw on long-held understandings, norms, and practices of citizenship and political community, which differ between nation-states because they draw on different histories and experiences. These different histories and experiences produce different norms and values around political community, and in the absence of conclusive research on the causes of, or responses to, counterradicalization, they form the "taken for granted" (Schwartz-Shea 2015: 123) understandings that inform counterradicalization. This explains, for example, the role that the US Constitution plays in shaping US counterradicalization policies. The constitution and federal/state relations obviously restrict the actions that government can take in many ways by limiting the reach of federal government into state practices and also into the lives of individuals. Nonetheless, at the same time, the constitution shapes many of the actions that the federal government *does* take, by providing a demonstration of the values that signify informal political community in the United States.

In the UK, these "taken for granted" understandings inform the variety and comparative incoherence of British values at play in counterradicalization policies. Without a constitutional document, and with a contested recent history of British identity, the informal political community that UK counterradicalization policies prioritize as an integrative measure is less clearly defined than in the United States. But without constitutional constraints and in a unitary system, counterradicalization policies can attempt to reach further into the thoughts, values, and beliefs that British individuals hold about the world, their state, and their place in it.

Both case studies examined policies and legislation that focus on migration and integration as part of their approach to countering radicalization— sometimes directly and sometimes more indirectly. In both cases, I argue, these approaches mirror larger historical narratives and experiences about inclusion and exclusion in their respective political communities. Differences in the reach and intensity of their respective policies draw on these varied experiences and the values associated with them—from a "melting pot" approach to immigration and integration in the United States to a history of post-empire multiculturalism in the UK. These findings confirm my core assertion: that ideas and values inform counterradicalization policy in important ways. This contributes to a growing constructivist literature on counterterrorism that asserts the role of ideational as well as material factors in counterterrorist responses and seeks to identify these factors and their influence. The literature also emphasizes the growing role that domestic counterterrorism plays in terrorism studies: in an age of homegrown extremism, the study of post-9/11 terrorism and counterterrorism can no longer be limited to the international domain.

The lessons for policymakers are uncertain. It is extremely difficult to judge the effectiveness or failure of certain policies that seek to prevent rather than induce certain activities. Indeed, one of the great challenges of counterradicalization is justifying funding by virtue of its effects: it is almost impossible to measure a negative effect, and effective program evaluations are rare. Indeed, the United States only devoted significant resources to producing its first fully evaluated program in late 2015. And despite considerable angst around the topic of proof and value for money, UK policies have yet to be subject to broad efficiency tests. In both cases, the "taken for granted" understanding of political community, which informs the values that frame counterradicalization, has driven some of their strongest criticisms. This criticism is especially strong when the effect is the securitization of target communities such as British and American Muslims (see Heath-Kelly 2013; Aziz 2011–2012). Some have argued that these policies actually *increase* the prospect of radicalization, expanding a sense of alienation from the political community into which they seek to draw target communities and individuals precisely by implying that those communities are outside the norms and values that define that political community and exist as a coherent bloc. Interrogating the exclusionary and arguably radicalizing influences of assumptions driving some counterradicalization policies can help mitigate these effects and drive more rigorous, evidence-based approaches.

## Shifts in policy

Despite underlying consistencies in approach, there have also been important shifts in US and UK policies showing that they are adapting to changes in the nature of the material threat they face, although within the parameters of certain already foregrounded ideas, beliefs, and values. In the UK, counterradicalization policymaking has become increasingly centralized, assuming cabinet-level prominence and minimizing the previously significant role of the then Department for Communities and Local Government. In effect, this has meant that policy has become less focused on the practical aspects of integration and less associated with integrationist impulses in UK social policy, which in some cases predate the 9/11 era. Instead, later incarnations of the policy make clear the "muscular liberalism" (Cameron 2011) at which the integrationist measures inherent in current incarnations of the policy aim. In effect, this has meant less prominence for funding to build links between security services and local Muslim communities more broadly and the end of broad-based allocation of funding by head of Muslim population as was the case in early versions of Prevent. Instead, the most recent iteration of the policy and associated legislation from 2015 allocates funding via a calculation of risk based on a number of demographic factors. It also allocates a Prevent Duty to schools, universities, and prisons associated with the promotion of "British values," and in so doing, elevates the role of the Channel program, which diverts individuals identified as at risk of radicalization. Adapting these central institutions of the state to the service of counterradicalization is arguably an integrationist move in itself in the UK, drawing individuals perceived at risk further under the umbrella of responsibility of central rather than local government institutions.

This move toward targeted interventions has also occurred in the United States, although shifts in US policy are harder to judge given its comparatively minimal approach. But at least one Minneapolis-based program funded in the 2012 CVE grants round uses an interventionist model to funnel individuals at risk into a range of community programs designed to integrate them further into their community and address their concerns by, for example, providing help in finding employment, addressing mental health issues, and so on. This and other CVE programs funded by these grants have been subject to a legal challenge by the ACLU as contravening rights to freedom of speech and association—a case still underway at the time of writing.

A further shift in both the United States and the UK is an increasing concern with the persuasive influence of online speech and associated material. Policy moves in both have shown an increasing focus on the online sphere, including the funding of new government measures to manage responses to online messaging and new partnerships with tech. Both have also attempted to institute the removal of citizenship in the context of returning foreign fighters. This book ends at a point in time when the Syrian conflict and IS territorial success in the region were emerging as a hub for foreign fighters, and in response both the United States and the UK attempted to institute measures to withdraw citizenship rights from their own citizens associated with fighting in those conflicts. Unsurprisingly, given constitutional constraints, these have been rather more successfully implemented in the UK than in the United States.

Finally, at the time of writing, both the United States and the UK are dealing with an increase in far-right homegrown extremism. This issue poses arguably even more issues of conceptual clarity regarding citizenship and political community than the issue of homegrown Islamist extremism as it removes the conceptual levers of migration and integration and embeds the issue more fully into the practice of domestic politics. Unsurprisingly, definitional difficulties abound, especially in the United States. Both the United States and the UK have seen increases in attacks and levels of threat assessment, and the issue is increasingly prominent in the EU, especially in the Nordic states and Germany (Koehler 2019; Jones 2018). In the UK, funds have been devoted to counterradicalization measures associated with the far-right. But as indicated in Chapter 8, addressing domestic extremism in the United States is often fraught, and none of the funds allocated in the first round of domestic CVE grants addressed the issue of far-right terrorism.

## Constructivist counterterrorism and beyond

A number of implications emerge from the empirical work conducted in this study. Further research on Muslim majority states, including across Shia and Sunni states, in illiberal states, and across different Muslim minority states, will test my central assertions concerning the impact of norms and values on counterextremism policy and the symbolic violence perpetuated by post-9/11 jihadi narratives. As mentioned earlier, these assertions contribute to an emerging body of work on constructivist counterterrorism studies. In contrast to traditional studies of counterterrorism, and following Katzenstein (1996, 2002), Leheny (2002), Omelicheva (2007), and others, I argue that domestic ideas and values about politics influence counterradicalization policy. This does not occur in isolation from the nature of the threat itself, but certainly informs the policies' formats and explains important differences between US and UK responses to the issue.

But the book's findings also speak to debates in two other literatures: citizenship studies and work on transnationalism in International Relations. The link between these two literatures and my contribution to constructivist counterterrorism studies lies in the role that ideas about political community play in counterradicalization. In the next section I briefly outline the relevant debates and show, hopefully, how this empirical material resonates elsewhere.

## Citizenship studies

Citizenship is the primary indicator of membership in a modern political community defined by the nation-state. In analyzing these ideas and values, I have adopted many of the tenets of citizenship studies, especially Joppke's (2010) elucidation of citizenship as comprising three aspects: status, rights, and identity. Some scholars argue that the rights-status-identity compact is becoming more expansive. Access to "citizen-style" rights for migrant workers in some countries is a useful example here, as is the "denationalized" identity associated with EU citizenship (Joppke 2009; Soysal 1994). However, this liberalization does not apply in the context of counterradicalization. In this, it accords with other work showing that the boundaries of formal citizenship have narrowed and firmed in the post-9/11 era in an atmosphere of increased turmoil concerning security and immigration, especially in Western liberal states in the context of Muslim immigration, integration, and terrorism (Sackmann, Peters, and Faist 2003; Kofman 2005; Cole 2003).[4] Such work instead points to the *re*valuation of formal citizenship as the distinction between aliens and citizens having been reasserted in the post-9/11 environment. Scholars see this process as having begun in Western liberal states in an environment of changed and intensified migratory flows prior to 9/11 and intensified by responses to it (Kofman 2005). Such changes are evident in the post-9/11 measures examined here, including, for example, measures to expel and exclude non-citizens based on certain behaviors and evidence of beliefs, values, and ideas, and measures to withdraw rights previously accorded to non-citizens on similar levels to citizens. Such a redefinition of access to status and rights has inevitably been driven in the context of counterradicalization by the beliefs, ideas, and values that define informal political community (Brubaker 1992) and thus of the *identity* aspect of citizenship in Joppke's formulation. Triadafilopoulos (2011) sees this process of the assertion of "Dutch," "British," or "German" values, in states that are in essence committed to universalist liberal values, as the practice of a type of "Schmittian liberalism" redolent of states under threat—real or perceived—in times of changed (and linked) immigration and security environments. Counterradicalization and associated measures that address "citizen terrorists" certainly support the findings of such scholarship. Here, the *identity* aspect of citizenship and political community is contracting rather than liberalizing, as we see access to membership of the informal political community of the nation-state being contested, for example, in the case of the "suspect communities" of British Muslims and American Muslims. This aspect, I argue, can be read as informing a commensurate narrowing of the *status* and *rights* of formal citizenship in this context.

The bulk of scholarship on this issue in citizenship studies concerns the point at which non-citizens may access the *status* of citizen and associated *rights*. I suggest that the reassertion of national *identity* and associated narrowing of *rights* and even *status* occurs even once the *status* of citizen is unassailable. That is, a "narrowing" process goes beyond the point of entry and is no longer necessarily exclusive to recent immigrants, but rather applies equally to longstanding citizens: the policies do not distinguish but rather conflate. As a result, my work builds on the comparatively more limited body of scholarship that examines varieties of citizenship within national borders (Bloemraad, Korteweg, and Yurdakul 2008: 154). This is because domestic counterradicalization is concerned entirely with the activities, beliefs, and ideas of citizens, often of second and third generations. At least in the United States and the UK, counterradicalization policies and associated legislation aimed at "citizen terrorists" not only implicitly reinvigorates the distinction between aliens and citizens but also creates a layer of informal political community—of adherence to national *identity*—over the formal *status* of citizenship, with inherent effects on the *rights* of those citizens who are thus excluded from the informal, if not the formal, political community. For example, in the United States, the NDAA 2012 effectively removes due process rights from citizen "terrorists" in the broadest sense of the word, on US soil. Critics also charge that CVE policies in the United States targeting religious identities in the context of counterradicalization dilute rights of freedom of association, religion, and speech. In the UK, as judicial challenges in the European Court of Human Rights show, coercive measures such as control orders and Terrorism Prevention and Investigation Measures substantially dilute rights to freedom of movement and association afforded to certain citizens in the context of counterterrorism and counterradicalization. Legislative measures designed to prohibit incitement to, and glorification of, terrorism by citizens, similarly arguably restrict previously available rights to free expression. Given the broadened definition of terrorism, such measures are theoretically based on the expression of values, beliefs, and ideas as well as, or instead of, violent acts. This is very clearly the case for glorification and at least theoretically so for incitement. In addition, civil society discourse charges that the creation of "suspect communities," in the rhetoric, implementation, and design of counterradicalization policies, in turn creates a class of citizens more subject to state targeting and interference than others, based on their—actual, potential, or imagined—beliefs, values, and ideas.

Counterradicalization and associated legislation associated with the problem of "citizen terrorists" also facilitates the removal of citizenship *status* based (theoretically at least) on terrorist beliefs, values, and ideas. Gibney (2013) shows that in the UK, such legislation draws on similar practices from earlier wartime periods. Announcements by government officials suggest that the procedures for denationalization may be loosened even further in the future (Travis 2013b). In the United States, such legislation has so far failed, but the prominence of the debate, and the fact that the relevant legislation was introduced and referred to committee bicamerally, suggests that the treatment of the issue holds weight in understanding responses to the problem of citizen terrorists in the post-9/11 era.

Scholars who argue that citizenship is liberalizing also argue that even the Schmittian liberalism arguably evident in liberal states' attempts to manage Muslim integration is inevitably universalizing rather than particular, because it relies on the application of inherently universalist liberal values such as tolerance and free speech (Joppke 2010: 138). In contrast, I argue that that the national identities—the informal political community—promulgated by counterradicalization measures in liberal states rather at least aim at particularism: the integrationist impulses of the policies revolve around "American values" and "British values" very clearly defined in particularist rather than universalizing terms. Because these policies attempt to persuade individuals about the desirability of certain thoughts, beliefs, and ideas, they are inherently illiberal and particularizing in that they are interested in "policing individuals inner dispositions" (Joppke 2010: 140–141). That is, counterradicalization policies target individuals' beliefs, values, and ideas, and in doing so, go beyond the

Rawlsian neutrality of the liberal state and "transgress the thin line that separates the regulation of behaviour from the control of beliefs" (Joppke 2010: 141) This is particularly striking in the UK, which links state control of religion, British values, and citizenship, including by the provision of citizenship education in Islamic schools, and the introduction of the Prevent duty across a range of state institutions. In its legislative attention to incitement and glorification, the UK has also outlawed the expression of certain beliefs about the world as incitement and glorification of terrorism, while the United States has criminalized the expression of largely ideational support for groups defined as terrorist. The role of counternarratives as counterradicalization policy in both cases—about foreign policy and about national values, for example—also suggests attempts to change individuals' beliefs rather than simply their behaviors.

Although not my primary purpose, the empirical material and analysis in this study contribute to debates about the liberalization of citizenship, ultimately falling on the side of the debate arguing that citizenship is, at least in this instance, being reproduced in nationally distinct ways in a manner that reaffirms the prominence of "normative citizenship identities" (Joppke 2010: 30) as a "mechanism of social closure" (Brubaker 1992: 31) equivalent to "nation membership" (Brubaker 1990: 381). This observation is largely within the exception of "Muslim integration in liberal states" which Joppke (2010) and others identify. However, Chapter 3 demonstrates that these policies also occur in Muslim majority states and illiberal states. That is, the policies are not only concerned with immigration and integration, they are also concerned with a material threat that does not—in countries like Saudi Arabia or Indonesia—emerge from a community that can be framed as "immigrant."

As a result, the tightening of citizenship outlined above is not restricted to liberal states facing certain pressures but is instead a response to a threat faced by many types of states. As Chapter 3 demonstrates, these processes are shared by a variety of states: liberal, illiberal, Muslim majority, and Muslim minority. The brief survey in Chapter 3 suggests they respond in a similar manner to a transnational ideational threat driven by engines of globalization, although without denying that domestic politics and other pressures play a role in the format of that response. Here, further research should also directly compare counterradicalization policies in Muslim majority and Muslim minority states and the extent to which counterradicalization policies interact with ideas of citizenship outside liberal states. Much citizenship scholarship is parochial in its attention to Western Europe and liberal states, and counterradicalization offers a useful opportunity to extend such scholarship by examining a citizenship-focused variable external to the state (the threat of homegrown extremism) common to liberal, illiberal, Western, and non-Western states.

## Transnational communities

Again, although not my primary purpose, this study contributes to an emerging body of work on transnational communities in International Relations. Most prominently in the two case studies, it shows states framing the problem and response as one of transnational diasporic and/or religious identities. The target audience for counterradicalization policies is identified as (American or British) Muslims, framing such "Muslims" as members of a larger transnational community not congruent with the state and, especially in the UK, making few practical distinctions between citizens and non-citizens. This approach is fostered in both cases by the novel involvement of the State Department and the Foreign and Commonwealth Office in domestic counterextremism. In the United States, it is also evident in changes to the Smith-Mundt Act in the NDAA 2013, which effectively dilute territorial boundaries between American Muslims and the broader Muslim community in the context of certain aspects of counterradicalization policy.

In this context, one can see the impact of non-diasporic transnational communities on international politics. Chapter 2 argues that counterradicalization has emerged as a response to the perceived impact of the efforts of AQ-inspired homegrown extremism. This self-described transnational, deterritorialized community deals explicitly in the language of informal political community—the ideas, values, and beliefs that bind people together—and directly contrasts these with traditional modes of political community. As Mendelsohn (2009b: 666) argues, one of jihadism's most distinctive features is its take on sovereignty: "jihadis reject the anchoring of political life in a secular institution such as the state, or the division of the global terrain into independent separate states bounded by rules and norms that are set through practice or man-made (rather than divine) decisions" (see also Mendelsohn 2005). Chapter 2 argues that AQ-inspired homegrown extremism is thus arguably a "post diasporic" and increasingly aspirational transnational informal political community. It is arguably a transnational reformulating of "identities-border-order" beyond a simple configuration of migrant/non-migrant (Vertovec 2007), which simultaneously draws on ideas *about* migration. On the impact of such communities, Castles (2002) has argued that new forms of identity and belonging under increased conditions of globalization induce debates about the significance of transnational communities as new modes of belonging and the nature of nation-state citizenship. Analyzing the responses of powerful Western states like the United States and the UK, the book suggests such transnational communities undermine "modes of controlling difference, premised on territoriality" and "present a powerful challenge to traditional ideas of nation-state belonging" (Castles 2002: 1157). Further research on this topic in the context of terrorism should address more clearly the question of whether jihadi-inspired, homegrown extremism does constitute an informal political community beyond the observations gathered here and the shape and nature of that political community through the variations of intra-jihadi politics: of the doctrinal differences between AQ and IS discussed in Chapter 2, for example, and of the effect—if any—of the AQ "franchise model" on this political community (Mendelsohn 2015).

Much research remains to be done on counterradicalization policy outside the two case studies selected here. Most importantly, such research should extend beyond liberal, Western states. As counterradicalization evolves in response to the changing dynamics of homegrown extremism—for example, as non-immigrant communities emerge as the vectors of far-right extremism in the United States and the UK—the topic offers rich terrain for studying the dynamics of citizenship and the relationship between counterterrorism and this particular set of ideas, values, and beliefs. Perhaps more importantly, interrogation of the assumptions behind existing policies and their relationship to unspoken ideas of national identity, national values, and beliefs about citizenship, can help to mitigate some of the damage unspoken exclusionary practices may inflict on counterradicalization efforts. As further research emerges on the most effective responses to the problem, "commonsense" and yet in some ways unhelpful assumptions driving some policies may yet be left by the wayside of more empirically informed, rigorous approaches.

# Appendix

## Legislation Cited

### United States

Uniting and Strengthening America by Providing Appropriate Tools Required to Intercept and Obstruct Terrorism (USA PATRIOT ACT) Act of 2001, Pub. L. No. 107-56, 115 Stat. 272 (2001).
Violent Radicalization and Homegrown Terrorism Prevention Act of 2007, H.R 1955, 110th Congress (2007–2008).
National Defense Authorization Act for Fiscal Year 2012, Pub. L. No. 112-81 (2011).
National Defense Authorization Act Fiscal Year 2013, Pub. L. No. 112-239 (2013).
Enemy Expatriation Act 2011, HR 3166, 112th Congress (2011–2012).

### United Kingdom

Terrorism Act 2000, c. 11. https://www.legislation.gov.uk/ukpga/2000/11/contents/enacted.
Anti-terrorism, Crime and Security Act 2001, c. 24. https://www.legislation.gov.uk/ukpga/2001/24/contents/enacted.
Nationality, Immigration and Asylum Act 2002, c. 41. https://www.legislation.gov.uk/ukpga/2002/41/contents.
Prevention of Terrorism Act 2005, c. 2. https://www.legislation.gov.uk/ukpga/2005/2/enacted.
Terrorism Act 2006, c. 11. https://www.legislation.gov.uk/ukpga/2006/11/contents.
Immigration and Nationality Act 2006, c. 13. https://www.legislation.gov.uk/ukpga/2006/13/contents.
Counterterrorism Act 2008, c. 28. https://www.legislation.gov.uk/ukpga/2008/28/contents.

## Cases Cited

### United States

Abrams v. United States, 250 U.S. 616 (1919).
Schneiderman v. United States, 320 U.S. 118 (1943).
Baumgartner v. United States, 322 U.S. 665 (1944).

Shaughnessy v. Mezi, 345 U.S. 206 (1953).
Yates v. United States, 354 U.S. 298 (1957).
Afroyim v. Rusk, 387 U.S. 253 (1967).
Hamdi v. Rumsfeld, 542 U.S. 507 (2004).
Hedges et al. v. Obama, No. 12-3176 (2d Cir. 2013).
United States v. Mehanna, No. 12-1461 (1st Cir. 2013).

## United Kingdom

Secretary of State for the Home Department v. Rehman House of Lords (2001) UKHL, 47. https://publications.parliament.uk/pa/ld200102/ldjudgmt/jd011011/rehman-1.htm

Regina v. G and another, House of Lords (2003) UKHL, 50. https://publications.parliament.uk/pa/ld200203/ldjudgmt/jd031016/g-1.htm

A (FC) and others (FC) (Appellants) v. Secretary of State for the Home Department (Responent) (2004) UKHL, 56. https://publications.parliament.uk/pa/ld200405/ldjudgmt/jd041216/a&oth-1.htm

# Notes

## Introduction

1. Contested definitions of terrorism means that cooperation on terrorism has long been fraught. See Romaniuk (2010) for an overview, and Mendelsohn (2009a) for a discussion of multilateralism in the post-9/11 environment.
2. The distinction between formal and informal political community explains the reason this book uses the terms "United States" or "United Kingdom" when referring to a formal, legal political community and uses the terms "America" or "Britain" when it is the informal political community under discussion, as in the book's title.
3. Phillips (2011: 19) distinguishes these as the authoritative and coercive forms of power wielded by political communities. See Mitzen (2006) on ontological security and statehood and Wight (2015) specifically on the link between terrorism, violence, and modern statehood.
4. This book's use of the term "global jihadi community" draws primarily on Hegghammer's (2006: 12–15) description of a "global jihadist movement" as a third type of militant Islamism appearing in the mid-1990s. He describes it as a "heterogeneous movement" consisting of actors with "partially diverging political and strategic priorities." He writes that they are "bound together by little more than an extreme anti-Americanism and a willingness to carry out mass-casualty attacks on Western targets." Work on transnational Islamist communities is also relevant to understanding the nature of the political community offered by global jihadism, as discussed further in Chapter 1. See Adamson (2005a); Mandaville (2001); Roy (2006). In this book, I take the broadest possible interpretation of *ummah* taking it to mean the "world community of Muslims" (Mandaville 2001: 2), noting the term's flexibility and adaptability as a referent for different forms of Islamic political community, as discussed, for example, in Mandaville (2001: 51–82).
5. See Bevir (1999: 13, 2003: 211) for a discussion of "common sense" understandings in the context of an interpretivist approach.
6. Crenshaw's (2001) work is linked to a broader body of work on the fundamental problems facing counterterrorism policymakers in liberal democracies, given their need to balance the rights of citizens with the security interests of the state. See also Wilkinson (2011); Donohue (2008).
7. This builds on works on terrorism as symbolic communication such as Schmid and de Graaf (1982); Crelinsten (1987), although unlike that body of work this study focuses on state responses rather than terrorist acts themselves.
8. Although see Kundnani (2014) and Lindekilde (2012) for work on the US and Danish policies respectively.

9. In this way, the book focuses on the *subjects of terrorist acts* as the basis for definition rather than, for example, their political, ideological, or religious aims. See Vasilenko (2004: 54). It does not engage, then, in debates about the definition of terrorism itself.
10. Intriguingly, counterradicalization policy documents in some states suggest that concerns about radicalization and far-right extremism in the wake of the 2012 Utoya massacre in Norway, stem from a similar emphasis on the role of networks of violence external to the state—that is, global networks of far-right extremists (Goodwin 2013; see also Berntzen and Sandberg 2014). The UK and other states are also increasingly turning their attention to the problem of far-right domestic terrorism, but global jihadist-inspired domestic extremism continues to consume the bulk of policy attention.
11. There is a conceptual link between counterradicalization policy and "hearts and minds" approaches to counterinsurgency dating from the postcolonial era, and this comparison has been applied explicitly to the problem of homegrown extremism (Kilcullen 2007). Ultimately, however, counterinsurgency campaigns differ from counterradicalization in three ways. First, counterinsurgency campaigns using "hearts and minds" techniques have historically been directed at state-building, largely in a postcolonial sense. In Malaysia, for example, the famed British "hearts and minds" campaign of the Malayan emergency was directed initially at drawing populations into secure camps, thus diffusing the threat of Maoist recruitment. As the campaign progressed, it included programs prescient of today's counterradicalization programs such as civic programs and interventions in schools for the sake of controlling recruitment, and extensive information campaigns about the dangers of recruitment by Maoists (Stubbs 1989). Similar projects in Kenya sought to quell the Mau Mau rebellion between 1952 and 1960 (Elkins 2005). Second, colonial counterinsurgency projects were aimed at preparing the target community for independence, not "educating" a particular population in particular national values as a measure against violence (Stubbs 1989). The two approaches differ in the temporal location of the identity they are trying to teach. Counterradicalization measures look backward, or at least not explicitly forward. The concept of "Britishness" espoused in UK counterradicalization policy documents discussed in Chapters 3, 4, and 5, for example, is a preexisting identity which the policies seek to protect, not a concept being developed in concert with a state identity, as the "Kenyan" or "Malaysian" identity is in counterinsurgency thinking. Third, the most important difference between "hearts and minds" processes and counterradicalization is that the former is inextricably linked to heavy-handed postcolonial violence. Unlike counterradicalization, it is explicitly coercive, not couched in the language of persuasion.
12. The concept of extremism is of course not confined to this timeframe, and neither is the concept of Islamic homegrown extremism. Chapter 2 outlines the heritage of these concepts prior to 9/11.
13. Similar research has found this also exists to a certain extent among Western Muslims who strongly denounce violence (Change Institute 2009). See Mandaville (2001) for research on such grievances globally.

14. In its attention to preemption and the management of associated risk, counterradicalization is indicative of a broader shift to a preventive logic in political practice, which Beck (1992) characterizes as "the risk society."
15. Importantly, in many Western democracies, governments are forbidden from acting coercively because the individuals concerned have yet to commit a crime. Legislative and judicial protection of individual rights forbids states from acting coercively in a preemptive manner. See Ashworth, Zedner, and Tomlin (2013) for a further discussion of this issue.
16. The first UN working group on counterradicalization defines it in appropriately broad terms: "counterradicalization refers to policies and programmes aimed at addressing some of the conditions that may propel some individuals down the path of terrorism. It is used broadly to refer to a package of social, political, legal, educational and economic programmes specifically designed to deter disaffected (and possibly already radicalized) individuals from crossing the line and becoming terrorists" (CTITF 2008: 5).
17. The failure of most counterradicalization policies to address grievances about foreign policy as a cause of radicalization is an arguably useful example of the problem of research on this highly political issue. For example, a leaked UK cabinet document shows that MI5 saw foreign policy grievance as a significant cause of radicalization (Travis 2008). In their work on radicalization in the Netherlands, Slootman and Tille (2006) find that the socioeconomic argument for radicalization is partly correct—that factors of employment and education do have an influence. They also found that socio-political factors play a role and that international political events such as military activity in Afghanistan or Iraq play a key radicalizing role and contribute to a feeling of injustice in the domestic context. Work by Demant et al. (2008) also suggests that there are some sociological factors, like exclusion from employment, but that foreign policy events also play a role, and research in Spain produced a similar finding (Alonso 2010: 215). These findings are supported by a study conducted by the Change Institute in 2008. It found that foreign policy grievances emphasized by AQ narratives were widely shared among European Muslims in general (Change Institute 2009: 54). It is also supported by extensive interview work with British Muslims by Briggs, Fieschi, and Lownsbrough (2006), which found that British foreign policy was one of the most significant sources of anger within Muslim communities in the UK. This finding is supported by work conducted by the Preventing Extremism Together Working Groups, founded by the UK government immediately after the 2005 attacks (Home Office 2006: 3). In addition, leaked British intelligence assessments link the Iraq war to the increased level of terrorist threat in the context of the 2005 attacks (Intelligence and Security Committee 2006b: 23).
18. Importantly for the concerns of this book, such "common sense" understandings often associate the problem with immigrant populations, especially in the West. By definition, homegrown extremism engages citizens and, in the West at least, a significant proportion of perpetrators are citizens of immigrant heritage, although often second and third-generation immigrants disengaged from traditional diasporic sources of authority (see Sageman 2008a: 71–88). Immigrant or diaspora status and

attendant problems with integration are often invoked as a cause of radicalization although, as the empirical case studies show, the picture is more complicated than such attributions attest (Sageman 2008a: 67; Pisoiu 2013; Mullins 2012; Humphrey 2013; Zimmerman and Rosenau 2009).

19. Although the period following these elections has seen several changes to counterradicalization policy in each jurisdiction, these two elections predated a period of substantial and potentially structural political turmoil in each jurisdiction that would arguably shift a study of counterradicalization policy in these periods into a study of change or resilience under pressure rather than an interpretivist study of the policies themselves. In the UK, this focused on its place in the European Union following the 2016 referendum on membership, which was part of the Conservative Party's 2015 election platform. In the US, the period following the 2016 elections has, at the time of writing, seen a period of substantial and unusual policy and administrative uncertainty under the Donald J. Trump administration. I argue that the period following each of these elections is a "dilemma" of governance that can induce change in the worldviews of policymakers and polity members, constituting a meaningful break with previous policymaking environments and practices (see Bevir 1999: 221–222).

20. This approach also allows the study to analyze variation and change over time (Caramani 2010: 40), noting the different tempo of policy introduction and development in the United States and the UK. The emphasis on convergence at the global level also allows us to in some ways account for the impact of globalization, which would muddy a study that assumed isolated and independent state units in a "shrinking world" (Caramani 2010: 42). See also Van Kersbergen (2010) for a discussion of the importance of understanding the sources of political phenomena, including social power, in comparative case studies and the utility of most similar studies for doing so.

21. In the UK, this legislation begins with the significant expansion of the definition of terrorism contained in the Terrorism Act 2000. In the US this emerged from the significant redefinition of terrorism contained in the USA PATRIOT (Uniting and Strengthening America by Providing Appropriate Tools Required to Intercept and Obstruct Terrorism) Act 2001. The US Anti-Terrorism and Effective Death Penalty Act 1996 created a federal crime of terrorism and relevant congressional debates referred to domestic terrorism by default. However, the resulting legislation did not distinguish between international and domestic terrorism and focused almost entirely on the former. In the US case study, the analysis includes an examination of two ultimately unsuccessful pieces of legislation, the Violent Radicalization and Homegrown Terrorism Prevention Act 2007 and the Terrorist Expatriation Act 2011. Many other legislative proposals dealing with homegrown extremism also failed during these years. These two pieces of legislation are included because they represent some form of bipartisan consensus and therefore indicate some form of "collective activity" relevant to this study's narrativist and interpretivist concerns. The former was introduced bicamerally, investigated in committee in an atmosphere of bipartisan support, and passed the House of Representatives with substantial bipartisan support. The latter

was introduced with sponsors from both sides of politics and referred to committees in both the House of Representatives and the Senate with bipartisan support.

# Chapter 1

1. See Guiraudon (2013) and Adler-Nissen (2013) on Bourdieu in International Relations, citizenship, and sovereignty.
2. For example, see Polletta and Jasper (2001); Samuel (2013); and Husu (2013) on Bourdieu, collective identity, social movements, and symbolic power.
3. A narrative is "a coherent system of interrelated and sequentially organized stories that share a common rhetorical desire to resolve a conflict by establishing audience expectations according to the known trajectories of its literary and rhetorical form" (Halverson, Goodall, and Corman 2011: 14).
4. This perspective has driven a great deal of online counternarrative work in counterextremism policy, as discussed in the empirical chapters of this book. See, for example, Braddock and Horgan (2016); Parker and Davis (2017); Archetti (2013).
5. See Mendelsohn (2005: 54) on the challenge religious terrorism offers to international society, as per the English School. He notes, for example, that religion itself offers a competing logic to the state system. For a discussion of master narratives in Islamic texts, and their relationship to transhistorical approaches to political authority, see, for example, Halverson, Goodall, and Corman's (2011: 43–45, 50–56) analysis of the narrative of the pharaoh and *Jahilliyah*.
6. See, for example, Ayman al-Zawahiri, quoted in Musallam (2005: 167): "Sayyid Qutb's call for loyalty to God's oneness and to acknowledge God's authority and sovereignty was the spark that ignited the Islamic revolution against the enemies of Islam at home and abroad. The bloody chapters of this revolution continue to unfold day after day."
7. See Mendelsohn 2012 for a discussion of the role of different approaches to religion and statehood in political Islam.
8. See Hoffman (2004) and Schmid (2014) for overviews of the broader, more concrete political projects within this broader narrative. The global "anti-systemic" narrative identified in this section is not new and is not exclusive to global jihadism. Scholars identify similar aspects in, for example, late nineteenth century anarchist movements, and to some extent Marxist terrorist groups of the 1970s and 1980s (Sageman 2008a: 33–35; Neumann 2009: 21). It is also important to note that the globalized, transnational Islamic community that such narratives reference is neither novel nor stable, nor is it the only nor even the primary form of transnational Islamic community or identity available to Muslims today. Muslim transnationalism itself is not new (Piscatori 1986; Roy 2006; Melucci, 1989). Mandaville (2011: 8) argues that Muslim transnationalism can take many forms, of which this "anti-systemic" activism is only a minor part. An unsophisticated debate about the "global ummah" versus the state is fundamental to the narratives described in the text, then, but should be noted in the

context of other transnational Muslim identities, which are not necessarily a rejection of the nation-state but rather an alternative to them that exists simultaneously.

9. See Mendelsohn (2005: 53–57) on ways in which AQ's attack on sovereignty and the international system go beyond the relationship between sovereignty and religion framed by other religious terrorist groups, which may reinforce sovereignty of a particular sort.

10. In many ways the anti-systemic narrative propagated by global jihadism reflects, engages with, and sustains broader political narratives initiated in the West in the years immediately following 9/11 that frame the US-led "war on terror" as a "battle of ideas" and a "battle for hearts and minds." Like the AQ-inspired narrative, the alternative narrative emphasizes supra-state values and divides the world into binary, oppositional transnational identities based not only on hard military alliances but shared values and worldviews. The 2002 US National Security Strategy outlined the "war of ideas" as a key weapon in the war on terror (National Security Council 2002: 6), while the 2006 strategy noted: "Our strategy also recognizes that the War on Terror is a different kind of war. From the beginning, it has been both a battle of arms and a battle of ideas. Not only do we fight our terrorist enemies on the battlefield, we promote freedom and human dignity as alternatives to the terrorists' perverse vision of oppression and totalitarian rule" (National Security Council 2006: 1). Such sentiments have been echoed by US representatives and allies and have framed significant aspects of international politics in the period since 9/11. Sageman (2008a: 153–156) notes that the two narratives—AQ-inspired narratives of a global ummah, and the alternative narrative of a "war on terror" driven by values of "freedom and human dignity"—can reinforce each other.

11. Mendelsohn's analysis builds on work which analyzes the role of religion in International Relations, including Philpott (2002) and Fox (2001), and on work which specifically focuses on the challenge posed by religion to world order—see Tibi (2007).

12. Adamson (2005b: 548) notes, "[s]uch a framework provides a possibility for beginning to map out the types of systemic-level political opportunity structures that individual agents draw upon in their attempts to promote normative change in world politics." Adamson focuses particularly on the concept of "discursive opportunity structures," and on ideologies as "overarching structures of meaning that are drawn upon by entrepreneurs in their attempts to affect normative change in world politics."

13. See Jackson and Loidolt (2013) for a useful discussion, including the problems of relying on texts for interpretation of strategic thinking.

14. See Hellmich (2005, 2008); Wiktorowicz (2006); Hegghammer (2006, 2013) for overviews of the history of militant Islamist thought in this context. This section draws strongly on Ryan (2013) as a source for translations of original texts.

15. See Zimmerman (2004), for example, for a discussion of references to Qutb's writings on sovereignty in al-Zawahiri's work. The official version, drafted in 2001 and published in 2009, rails against the moral values of the United States and highlights the "battle of ideas" between the West and Islam. The text outlines the need to inspire a global ummah to unite and act against the United States.

16. See Hegghammer (2006); Lia (2009); Brachman and McCants (2006) for a discussion of this text, the author, and his influence.
17. See Perliger (2012: 509) on the symbolic power of "exceptional events" in the sense of surprise attacks.
18. See Awan (2010:10) for a discussion of debates in the jihadi community about the validity of online activity and the increasing prominence of "virtual jihad."
19. In May 2008, al-Awlaki delivered another sermon, framing the then current Mohammed cartoons controversy as part of a war against Islam and calling on all Muslims to retaliate. At the time that it came to the attention of US authorities in 2008, the lecture received approximately 48,300 visitors per month from the United States alone, on only one site on which it was hosted. It was cited in a 2009 assessment by the US Department of Homeland Security's (DHS's) Extremism and Radicalization Branch, which warned that "English language transcripts and recordings that are circulating on the Internet and in hard copy of . . . *Constants on the path of Jihad* command U.S. Muslims to conduct violent attacks in the Homeland and against U.S. targets abroad . . . The sermon also attempts to inoculate readers against popular counter-violence messages" (quoted in Meleagrou-Hitchens 2011: 56). According to Howard Clark, a former senior intelligence analyst who was monitoring al-Awlaki's blog (established in 2008) for the DHS Office of Intelligence and Analysis, the majority of visitors to the site came from the UK and United States (Meleagrou-Hitchens 2011: 70).
20. Some analysts argue that the utility of *Inspire* as a radicalizing tool has been overstated by Western media attention, arguing that AQ has long produced English-language material, as have other jihadi and Salafist preachers and organizations (Brachman and Levine 2011; Watts 2012). This observation feeds into broader debates about the actual effect of online radicalization, as discussed further in the following sections. See Stenersen (2008, 2013) and Bartlett, King, and Birdwell (2010). Regardless, these English-language efforts, and the nature of the text, show a deliberate attempt by AQ-core and sympathizers/affiliates to engender homegrown extremist attacks, particularly in the West, whether they are actually effective or not.
21. *Dabiq* arguably reflected doctrinal differences between AQ and IS, with less emphasis on instructions to homegrown extremists and more on justification for the group's actions and intra-sectarian debate than direct exhortation and instruction. See Mahood and Rane (2017).
22. The Syrian war has also presented a paradigm shift. Indeed, in this "most socially mediated civil conflict in history" (Lynch, Freelon, and Aday 2014), IS media is notable for the sheer volume of its products facilitated by new technology: one researcher judges an average of three videos and more than fifteen photographic reports circulated per day (Winter 2015: 12). See Kohlmann and Alkhouri (2014); Farwell (2014) for further discussion.
23. Scholars working in the sociology of media have integrated Bourdieu's concepts of field, habitus, capital, and symbolic power into the study of media effects, including in the context of online cultures. See Couldry (2003); Benson (1999); Lindell (2017).

24. Sageman (2008a: 134–139) situates homegrown extremism within three waves of terrorists inspired by global jihad. He sees the first of these waves as Arabs fighting against the Soviets in Afghanistan in the 1980s and the second as Middle Eastern expatriates, often educated in the West, who travelled to AQ training camps in Afghanistan in the 1990s. He argues that the third wave is dominated by "homegrown" terrorists. This group has no physical sanctuary, is driven by a post-Iraq narrative of global Islam under threat, and is endogenous to host countries, often in the West, but driven by attachment to an identity which is defined by anti-Western values and politics. This study approaches Sageman's third category of homegrown extremism as a spectrum of post-9/11 terrorist activity involving homegrown extremists rather than a simple cohort.
25. See Sageman (2008b); Hoffman (2008) for a useful discussion of the complexities of including the 2005 7/7 bombings in an AQ "command and control" model.
26. The concept of lone-actor terrorism is not new. Indeed, the term was coined by members of the far right in the United States, and incidents of lone-wolf terrorism span the full range of inspiration—from nationalism to religious and political terrorism (Bjelopera 2013). Some studies suggest that the number of lone-actor attacks is increasing globally, and suggest new, global networks of inspiration (Pantucci 2011a; Goodwin, Ramalingam, and Briggs 2012). Other, more recent studies, suggest the typology is limited in its utility. See Schuurman et al. (2019) for a discussion of the issue.
27. See Hoffman (1998: 42) for a discussion of the analytic importance of separating out "terrorists" and "lunatic assassins." This book treats them as analytically similar in the post-9/11 environment given their treatment in policymaking circles as part of a continuum of terrorist activity.
28. See Mendelsohn (2011) for an explanation of this "franchise" phenomenon with reference to AQAP and Al-Qaeda in the Islamic Maghreb (AQIM).
29. See Bures (2018); Hegghammer (2013); Zelin (2013) on the important role of foreign fighters in the Syrian conflict, which erupted in 2012, and on the role of such foreign fighters in fostering homegrown extremism.

# Chapter 2

1. In 2006 the US State Department began including in its annual country reports on terrorism a section on incidents of homegrown extremism and measures adopted by states that it regarded as countering extremism.
2. Telephone interview with Associate Professor Peter Romaniuk, Senior Non-Resident Fellow, Center on Global Counterterrorism Cooperation, New York, September 25, 2013.
3. Note that even in this context, however, differences between states were important. A senior UN official outlined the process by which the United States forced the UK to propose resolution 1624 under Chapter VI of the UN Charter rather than Chapter

VII, given that Chapter VI deals with pacific resolution of disputes rather than military responses, noting: "The US was one of the states that said: 'If you are going to compel us to deal with this, we are going to have a problem with the first amendment. If you make it Chapter VII then we are not going to approve it. We want to make it Chapter VI so that states can take the right measures—they can be individualized. It is different from 1373 which had to be Chapter VII.' So the US was one of the states, I don't recall if France was another, but the rest of them had no problem with it. That [the unanimous vote] kind of made up for the lack of Chapter VII—it was too complicated to force states to take measures to stop incitement to terrorism that could run against some of the guarantees of free speech that they had." Interview with Dr Howard Stoffer, Director, United Nations Counterterrorism Committee Executive Directorate, New York, December 18, 2011.
4. See also Karlsson (2012). He argues that security communities such as the EU and NATO played a key role in determining the design of "hard" counterterrorism institutions among member states, particularly in the context of facilitating a certain threat perception. See also Lehrke and Schomaker (2014) on counterterrorism policy diffusion among EU states.
5. Telephone interview with Professor Rik Coolsaet, Member, European Network of Experts on Radicalisation, July 9, 2013; see also Meyer (2009).
6. Interview with Ms Marie-Ange Balbinot, Head of Sector, Fight against Terrorism, Home Affairs, EU Commission, Brussels, March 15, 2013.
7. Interview with Coolsaet; see also Capoccia (2010); Hellmuth (2015).
8. Interview with Associate Professor Peter Romaniuk, Senior Non-Resident Fellow, Center on Global Counterterrorism Cooperation, New York, January 5, 2011.
9. Interview with Mr Richard Barrett, Coordinator United Nations Al-Qaeda Taliban Monitoring Team, United Nations, New York, December 20, 2011.
10. Some initiatives countering far-right extremism and terrorism do exist, especially in northern Europe and Scandinavia. But as discussed in the Introduction to this book, the study outlined here focuses on policies that seek to counter global jihadi violence.
11. Some counterradicalization activities are explicitly directed at new arrivals. For example, the 2011 iteration of the "Prevent" policy in the UK funded internet controls on radical material accessed at immigration detention centers (HM Government 2011a: 75).
12. In January 2015, two gunmen killed twenty-two people and injured eleven others in the offices of the satirical magazine *Charlie Hebdo*. The assailants identified themselves as belonging to AQ's branch in Yemen.
13. In Muslim minority countries, such policy measures do not generally account for varying degrees of faith, the cultural rather than religious aspects of faith practice, ethnic divisions within Islam, or the difference between practice and heritage. This approach to Muslim identity essentializes Islamic identity in a manner which Roy (2006: 115) argues is typical of Western political communities. Such a process also ignores the essential diversity of the Muslim faith. It prioritizes a faith identity over an ethnic identity and simplifies complex divisions and allegiances within Islam.

14. It is particularly intriguing because it shows a non-liberal Muslim minority state engaging in ostensibly liberal practices of discourse and engagement on this issue. The Singaporean program could provide a regional model given its apparent success. Interview with Ms Sidney Jones, Senior Adviser, Asia Program, Human Rights Watch, Canberra, September 22, 2013.
15. This program operates in concert with a much more developed deradicalization program.
16. By using a national identity like "British" as a modifier of "Muslim," the impression is given that "British" and "Muslim," or "European" and "Muslim," are two separate identities. A Muslim, therefore, is not British or European, German or American by implication without this modifier attached.
17. Interview with Mr Mike Smith, Executive Director, United Nations Counterterrorism Committee Executive Directorate, New York, December 28, 2011.
18. An important difference between the two types of states is the extent to which they engage in post–prison release deradicalization programs. Indonesia, for example, has long engaged in ad hoc post–prison release deradicalization programs, as have Saudi Arabia and Yemen, whereas such programs are extremely rare in the West, although prison-based deradicalization is commonplace. An examination of this difference is beyond the scope of this book but is likely the result of considerations driven by the move toward a "preventive state" in Western liberal systems in a new crime prevention environment framed by risk (Zedner 2007; Ashworth and Zedner 2012). Here, aside from changed assumptions of risk, preemptive measures also keep citizens from the legal process that would otherwise accord them due process rights and thus, in liberal states, preclude states from acting on such risks. Such rights would prohibit intensive state control upon release from prison, for example. States such as Saudi Arabia and Indonesia have no such rights automatically accorded to their citizens. It should be noted, however, that strong opposition exists in Indonesia, for example, toward the type of individualized preemptive programs found in some Western countries, such as Channel in the UK. These programs are seen to unfairly stigmatize Islam. See Sumpter (2017: 125).
19. Interview with Jones.
20. Interview with Romaniuk, 2013.
21. Telephone interview with Professor Will McCants, former Senior Advisor for Countering Extremism, State Department 2009–2011, and Director, US Relations with the Islamic World, Brookings Institute, September 23, 2013.
22. For example, the government launched a series of lectures and seminars in order to familiarize Moroccans with the principles of Sufism and the philosophy behind its practices. See Muedini (2012).
23. The distinction between such practices can be usefully thought of in terms of a Foucauldian distinction between productive and deductive power (Dean 1999: 11). Productive power acts upon the subject's "desires, aspirations, interests and beliefs" and are a product of governmentality. They exist in contrast to the Foucauldian understanding of sovereign power as "deductive." Sovereign power removes things—like physical freedom, wealth, or property—from the subject. Such power, and the

practices associated with it, can usefully be associated with traditional counterterrorism powers and are closer to "rule" than governance.
24. The number of Channel referrals annually has increased from five in 2006/2007 to 7,631 in 2015/2016 (Association of Chief Police Officers 2014; Home Office 2017).
25. Policy updates, as in Denmark, for example, explicitly refer to families worried about individuals about to leave for IS battlefields—this is less a discursive measure than an alerting mechanism as a precursor to physical coercive measures taken by the state in response—for example, the removal of passports (Government of Denmark 2016).
26. It is important to note, however, that a concern with the persuasive powers of discourse can be coercive in effect. For example, many states seek to act on incitement to terrorism, banning or criminalizing certain types of discourse as a way to limit the spread of values, beliefs, and ideas. Here, discourse itself is seen as dangerous. The UK, France, and Norway have introduced legislation that criminalizes incitement to terrorism without the need for actual acts of terrorism to have taken place or to have been intended to take place. China introduced a similar element to the definition of extremism in its Counter-Terrorism Law 2016. These are in effect coercive acts in that they limit speech, although they are inherently concerned with persuasion. It is also important to note that discourses in themselves can have coercive, material effects. Research from scholars working in critical terrorism studies, for example, shows that counterradicalization discourse in the UK frames British Muslims as a "suspect community," which highlights the coercive effect of discourses, especially state-sponsored discourses, on individuals and communities (Breen-Smyth 2014; Heath-Kelly 2013).
27. Telephone interview with Professor Sir David Omand, Former Security and Intelligence Coordinator, Cabinet Office, 2002–2005, and Permanent Secretary, Home Office, 1997–2002, October 2, 2013. See also Donohue (2008); LaFree and Dugan (2009).
28. Donohue (2008: 130), for example, quotes from a newspaper editorial of the period: "[In] conditions of free political debate in the absence of an overwhelming public conviction concerning the objectives of policy, recourse to unaccustomed powers of coercion such as the suspension of normal rights and safeguards may confuse and embitter opinion in a way that actually works to the advantage of those against whom the special measures are directed."
29. Interview with Ms Faiza Patel, Co-Director, Law and National Security Program, Brennan Center for Justice, New York, November 30, 2011.
30. Note that legitimacy depends on consent, even in authoritarian states. As Boucek (2008b: 3–4) notes, for example, the government of Saudi Arabia views the struggle against violent extremism as part of a war of ideas "centered upon issues of legitimacy, authority, and what is permitted in Islam," and their counterradicalization policies draw on long traditions of state co-option of various groups to maintain legitimacy. See Gerschewski (2013) on the importance of legitimacy in the survival of repressive and authoritarian regimes, especially Saudi Arabia.
31. The literature on legitimacy and political authority is large, and it is beyond the scope of this book to analyze its many debates. For useful overviews, see Flathman (1993); Beetham (1991).

## Chapter 3

1. Counterterrorism—and therefore counterradicalization—is a reserved matter and the responsibility of the UK government. However, many of the sectors in which UK counterradicalization policy is most active, such as education, have been devolved to the governments of Wales, Scotland, and Northern Ireland.
2. See Newman (1996: 124–125) for a critique of Colley's work, particularly regarding the primacy of Protestantism, Otherness, and war-making. Croft (2012) also focuses on the role of war-making in British identity, but emphasizes instead the impact of anti-German feeling in the development of narratives of Britishness in the twentieth century.
3. These have been arguably intensified by Britain's integration into Europe. See Pocock (1992); Vertovec (2007). Croft (2012: 162–177) argues for a "crisis of Britishness" engendered by post-war change and highlights a challenge between a "temporal self looking back" and an "explicit political project" aiming at the "rebirth of Britishness" exemplified by the Blair government's approach.
4. The impact of the Salman Rushdie affair of the late 1980s—in terms of the politicization of British Muslims, and the creation of a synergy between that politicized identity, public order, and British values—should not be underestimated. It is beyond the scope of this chapter to investigate this issue more fully, but it is important to note the impact it had on the conceptualization in the broader British political discourse of an inherent tension between "Muslim" and "British" values. This impact persisted into the Blair years. See Modood (1990, 2003).
5. The government had engaged on the issue of race relations and multiculturalism early in its tenure. See, for example, the Parekh (2000) report, resulting from its initial sponsorship of an investigation into "multiethnic" Britain.
6. Other factors such as unemployment and the influence of far-right activists were also noted as important by both.
7. Links between formal citizenship and counterterrorism policies are discussed further in Chapter 7.
8. Interview with Mr Ed Husain, founder, Quilliam Foundation, Senior Fellow for Middle Eastern Policy, Council on Foreign Relations, Senior Adviser, Tony Blair Faith Foundation, New York, December 20, 2011.
9. There was no nation-wide curriculum at this point, as each constituent nation in the UK has its own education system.
10. The Good Friday Agreement of 1998 formally ended direct rule, although the Northern Ireland parliament was suspended (and direct rule re-imposed) five times between 1998 and 2007 under the terms of that agreement.
11. Telephone interview with Professor Sir David Omand, Former Security and Intelligence Coordinator, Cabinet Office, 2002–2005, and Permanent Secretary, Home Office, 1997–2002, October 2, 2013.
12. See Modood (2003) on transnational Muslim identities in Britain and the Rushdie affair and the history of transnational Islamic activism in the UK. Foley (2013: 54)

links long-held tradition of political asylum in the UK to the emergence of homegrown Islamic extremism post-9/11.
13. See Croft and Moore (2010) for the various "threat" narratives conceived of by British policymakers in the post-9/11 environment: from a centralized AQ-core to a disparate network and from homegrown extremism to a novel threat fostered by globalization.

# Chapter 4

1. In the UK even more so than the United States, this process entails tracking the "normalization" of otherwise exceptional legislation (Neal 2012a) in the sense that UK terrorism legislation has avoided the use of sunset clauses, whereas in the United States almost all major pieces of terrorist legislation have sunset clauses.
2. The Terrorism Act 2000 was introduced in recognition of the declining threat from Northern Irish terrorism. The then Conservative government instituted a review of terrorist legislation—the Lloyd (1996) review—in an attempt to normalize the legislative response to the problem, recognizing that rolling emergency legislation could no longer be justified. The Belfast Agreement 1998 reinforced this judgment. In the event, the act consolidated and superseded what had until then been two pieces of emergency legislation reviewed annually: the Prevention of Terrorism (Temporary Provisions) Act 1989 (PTA) and the Northern Ireland (Emergency Provisions) Act 1996 (EPA) In addition, the Human Rights Act had been assented to in 1998 and was due to come into force in 2000, necessitating a re-design of certain aspects of earlier legislation.
3. Section 3 states:
    (5) For the purposes of subsection (4) an organisation is concerned in terrorism if it—
    (a) commits or participates in acts of terrorism,
    (b) prepares for terrorism,
    (c) promotes or encourages terrorism, or
    (d) is otherwise concerned in terrorism.
4. Note that Section 3 of Part II allows "promotes or encourages" terrorism to be used as the basis for proscription. This definition appears broader than the definition of incitement. However, although not unproblematic, it draws on earlier wording in UK terrorist legislation—specifically the PTA and EPA, where the proscription applied only to Northern Irish terrorism. The Terrorism ACT 2000 extended the proscription power to domestic and international terrorism as well as Irish terrorism. See Intelligence and Security Committee (2006b).
5. Middle Eastern and Indian terrorism had historically been particularly problematic in the UK, with assassinations, bomb plots, and planning taking place in London from the early 1980s. Pressure had been building to mount a defense since the early

1980s, and in the late 1990s the UK government was under increasing pressure from its allies to act on the issue. See Walker 1992: (23–27). For example, in 1996, as the Lloyd review was being published, the UK government was under pressure from Saudi Arabia to act against Mohammed Al-Masarai, a dissident in exile in London. The Saudis threatened to cancel lucrative defense contracts unless the UK government complied with their demands.

6. The concept of incitement had not previously been linked directly to terrorism. In Northern Ireland, the Incitement to Religious Hatred Act (Northern Ireland) 1970 and the Public Order Act 1970 managed incitement as a public order issue and did not link it directly to terrorism, although that was certainly the underlying concern. Incitement had previously been managed in the context of public order under the Public Order Act 1986 and the Crime and Disorder Act 1998, although the issue of incitement to racial hatred had first been introduced in the Race Relations Act 1965. None of these pieces of legislation specifically linked incitement and terrorism, although in their focus on public order they arguably preview the government's later description of the motivations of terrorism as aimed at destroying the "foundations of government" (Straw 1999). As Malik (2009: 103–104) points out, incitement and public order regulations largely took the place of outdated sedition and blasphemy laws; and the issue was linked largely to public order in the UK.

7. See also Section 58 of the act, which made it an offense to collect or possess "information of a kind likely to be useful to a person committing or preparing an act of terrorism." This provision, for example, was later used against UK citizen Bilal Zaheer Ahmed for—among other offenses—possessing a copy of AQ's *Inspire* magazine (Davies 2011).

8. The concept of national security has been held in subsequent judgments to include the security of the UK's allies, potentially redefining traditions of political asylum. Delivering his judgment in *Rehman* one month after September 11, Lord Slynn emphasized that national security had been redefined by drivers of globalization, referring to the speed of communications and travel, and suggested that not only did national security include the security of the UK's allies but that there need not be any "direct or immediate" threat posed. In doing so, the influential judgment framed the threat of terrorism in terms of preemptive risk and in terms of the redefinition of the "national" under conditions of globalization (Slynn 2001: para. 16).

9. The Law Lords ruled against the detention provisions in *A v. Secretary of State for the Home Department*, a case brought by nine suspected terrorists detained under the Anti-Terrorism, Crime and Security Act 2001. As discussed later, the measure was effectively abolished the following March when it was up for review. Its powers were replaced with "control orders," brought in by the Prevention of Terrorism Act 2005, and later the Terrorism Acts 2008, 2011.

10. The act created two kinds of control orders: non-derogating and derogating. The distinction was created so that during a public emergency the government could derogate from Article 5 of the European Convention on Human Rights and restrict individuals to house arrest. Authors such as Zedner (2007: 184) note that the very concept of a derogating order under conditions of public emergency means that the

state of emergency is predicated on a "peculiarly individuated basis," making the claim of a "walking one-man emergency."

11. Control orders involve an extraordinary level of restriction and surveillance such that they have been described by a key UK legal scholar as "internment by another name" (Bonner 2007: 22). They were modified somewhat in the face of public disquiet and successful legal challenges by a series of legislative initiatives under David Cameron's government in 2012. The Terrorism Prevention and Investigation Measures (TPIMs) Act 2011 abolished control orders and replaced them with an ostensibly less onerous regime of TPIMs. However, although TPIMs significantly reduce some of the most onerous requirements of control orders, they do not fundamentally alter their underlying assumptions: that individuals are powerful generators of terrorist acts and that their communication of certain ideas, beliefs, and values is a key component of that power. In 2012 the government published in draft form the Enhanced Terrorism Prevention and Investigation Measures Bill 2011. At the time of writing it had not yet passed, but will allow additional restrictive measures which bring TPIMs far closer to control orders to be imposed on suspects for ninety days should exceptional circumstances arise. Although it is important to note the evolution of the TPIMs regime, it is important mainly to show, as in Neal (2012a, 2012b), that exceptional measures can be normalized over time, and become entrenched, even as they are modulated slightly.

12. Because control orders are non-criminal preventative executive tools, rather than criminal offenses, there was no legislative requirement to detail the meaning of "encouragement."

13. Highly controversial measures to increase pre-charge detention to twenty-eight days introduced in the Terrorism Act 2006 are not discussed in detail here because they do not substantially address the problem of counterradicalization. Instead, they sit further along the temporal spectrum at the point where an individual may have already committed an act relevant to the legislation's concerns. In effect, however, they diminish the formal rights of citizens in the name of the redefinition of terrorism outlined in the Terrorism Act 2000.

14. On July 15, 2005, Clarke wrote to key opposition politicians to ask their opinions on a legislative proposal to combat glorification of terrorism, making it clear that the proposals were already in progress before the July 7 bombings (Clarke 2005a). Indeed, proposals against glorification had been part of the Labour Party's 2005 election manifesto (Blair and Spearing 2005: 53) and a response to ongoing inflammatory commentary about foreign policy, including terrorist attacks, by prominent Muslim clerics in the UK. Clarke's letter noted that this would bring UK legislation into accordance with the Council of Europe Convention on the Prevention of Terrorism, which requires parties to have an extant offense of public provocation to commit a terrorist offence. Article 5 of the convention defines "public provocation" as "making a message available to the public with the intent to incite the commission of a terrorist offense . . . whether or not directly advocating terrorist offences." The UK legislation in effect goes much further because it introduces the concept of recklessness and thus dilutes the requirement of intent. Similarly, the drafters of the

Council of Europe Convention intended that even indirect incitement must still present a credible danger that an offense might be committed. As discussed later, the UK legislation does not require any actual danger that an act may occur. Similarly, UNSC Resolution 1624 of September 2005, sponsored by the UK, which deals with incitement to terrorism, merely repudiates the glorification of terrorism (see Saul 2005: 869–870).

15. Public, inflammatory statements on terrorist events had been a feature of UK discourse by controversial imams before 7/7 (O'Neill and McGrory 2006: 95–96). Section 21 of the Terrorism Act 2006 also introduces these offenses as the basis for proscription of organizations.

16. Like the encouragement offense, the dissemination offense considers whether the publication glorifies specific act(s)—as opposed to general act(s)—of terrorism to be irrelevant, as well as whether any person was actually encouraged by the publication to commit acts of terrorism. However, unlike the encouragement offense, the act creates a defense to the offense of dissemination of terrorist publication so that those who transmit material that does not reflect their views should not be charged, presumably to allow for satire and public debate.

17. The test and the accompanying booklets were revised in 2007 and 2013. Changes between the 2004 and 2007 editions were relatively minor. However, the 2013 revisions are explicitly linked to informal political community. The immigration minister argued that changes were necessary because the old version tested people's knowledge of "how to claim benefits" whereas the new test would "encourage participation in British life," including tests on history not previously included, more questions on sport, and a new section titled "unique" and focusing on such esoteric topics as the British sense of humor. The immigration minister argued that the "new book rightly focuses on values and principles at the heart of being British ... We have stripped out mundane information about water meters, how to find train timetables, and using the internet." Questions about public transport, credit cards, and job interviews were removed from the new publication, and applicants were to be tested on British history, which had not previously been the case (BBC News 2013).

18. See Etzioni (2007) for a discussion of the emergence of such tests in Western liberal democracies more generally.

19. See Anderson (2016: 8) for a discussion of the deprivation of citizenship based on notions of the public good and Fripp, Moffat, and Wilford (2014: 307, 403) for a discussion of exclusion and citizenship deprivation on the basis of unacceptable behavior in particular. Fripp, Moffat, and Wilford (2014: 403) note that information about the exercise of the "unacceptable behaviors" power is limited.

20. The Borders, Citizenship and Migration Act 2009 introduced a complementary provision of "probationary citizenship" where citizenship for long-term residents was based on demonstration of active citizenship commensurate with core British values. See Zedner (2010); UK Border Agency (2008: 29).

## Chapter 5

1. Interview with Mr Oliver McTernan, Founder and Co-Director, Forward Thinking, London, April 9, 2012.
2. Telephone interview with Professor Sir David Omand, former Security and Intelligence Coordinator, Cabinet Office, 2002–2005, and Permanent Secretary, Home Office, 1997–2002, October 2, 2013.
3. Ibid.
4. https://publications.parliament.uk/pa/cm200304/cmselect/cmhaff/886/886we02.htm https://publications.parliament.uk/pa/cm200405/cmselect/cmhaff/165ii/165we02.htm; Innes (2006).
5. Ibid.
6. Email interview with a former senior UK government official, October 15, 2013.
7. Ibid.
8. Ibid.
9. An asylum and integration strategy released in 2005 also drew on the same consultation paper and community cohesion strategy (HM Government 2005b). Note also that 2005 was an election year in which the Labour government faced increased right-wing voting patterns across Europe and extreme pressure domestically. See Whitely (2005).
10. Email interview with a former senior UK government official.
11. Telephone interview with Ms Frances Guy, former head, EWIW unit, FCO, 2004–2006, November 16, 2013.
12. Ibid.
13. Two individuals noted the importance of the high percentage of Muslims in then Foreign Secretary Jack Straw's (2001–2006) constituency of Blackburn, suggesting this meant he was attuned to the concerns of British Muslims. Telephone interview with Guy; Email interview with a former senior UK government official.
14. Telephone interview with Guy.
15. Although the 2011 review of Prevent sought to reduce FCO funding on what it perceived as supporting wider cohesion goals such as English-language training for imams, or empowerment of Muslim women, the strategy highlighted the need to engage more significantly with communities with a strong diaspora presence in the UK, as "in these countries, work to address radicalisation can have a significant domestic UK impact" (HM Government 2011a: 37).
16. Telephone interview with Omand. A 2008 review of Pathfinder activities showed that two-thirds of the funded projects "promoted shared values," with the most common projects being debates and discussion forums, although the scope of activities funded ranged from leadership training for mosque governance bodies, to plays about radicalization, to sporting contests (HM Government 2008d: 1–10, 42).
17. Email interview with a former senior UK government official.
18. Ibid.
19. Note this was a response to emerging criticism of the government's engagement with groups perceived as too radical, such as the Muslim Council of Britain.

20. The Radical Middle Way has delivered programs and events in Pakistan, Sudan, Indonesia, Mali, and Morocco as well as in the UK. The FCO's EWIW program had expanded by this time to include, for example, such programs as "Projecting British Islam"—a program of "media intensive" visits by British Muslims to Muslim majority countries, to counter misperceptions about Islam in Britain that were being exploited by extremists. Participants were encouraged to liaise with the DCLG on Prevent work when they returned (Howells 2007).
21. The Charities Act 2006 removed exemption from registration for certain places of worship, including mosques, and the 2007 Prevent policy funded a Faith and Social Cohesion Unit within the Charity Commission to encourage faith communities—especially mosques—to register, a process which would "ensure best practice, provide advice, guidance and training on issues such as governance, finance and the role of mosques as community centres" (HM Government 2007a: 11). This unit was discontinued in 2010.
22. For example, Home Secretary May emphasized that two elements of the Prevent strategy were "promoting unified, British values and building 'resilience in the community'" (US Department of State 2008).
23. New monitoring and reporting requirements for local government, "National Indicator 35," were designed in 2008 by the Home Office and linked local government performance indicators to counterradicalization goals from April 2009, measured by: "Understanding of, and engagement with, Muslim communities; Knowledge and understanding of the drivers and causes of violent extremism and the Prevent objectives; Development of a risk-based preventing violent extremism action plan, in support of delivery of the Prevent objectives; Effective oversight, delivery and evaluation of projects and actions" (HM Government 2008d: 10). See Thomas (2012: 86–87) on the controversy this caused, with some local government areas with large Muslim populations refusing to adopt this indicator.
24. These messages indicated the policies' continuing underlying focus on integration. For example, key message 1.3 stated: "We are determined that the terrorist threat will not undermine our commitment to a diverse and open society built on democracy and shared values" (RICU 2007: 3).
25. Email interview with a former senior UK government official.
26. Ibid. RICU's activities were streamlined under the Cameron government to focus more on online communications. This counternarrative approach was increasingly complemented by measures to take down offensive terrorist or radicalizing material under the Counterterrorism Internet Referral Unit, which emerged in the 2011 version of Prevent.
27. Email interview with a former senior UK government official.
28. Of these, 1,319 reports came from the education sector, linked to the Prevent duty imposed in 2015 by the Counter-Terrorism and Security Act (Prevent Duty) 2015 (HM Government 2017).
29. Interview with McTernan.
30. Ibid.
31. Email interview with a former senior UK government official.

32. The report found that the intelligence agencies had not paid sufficient attention to one of the attackers after he had returned from abroad, having joined a terrorist organization overseas. The committee noted this was a particular problem in light of increasing issues concerning returned foreign fighters (Intelligence and Security Committee 2014: 166–168) The committee also urged the government to do more to make domestic counterradicalization more effective as a matter of urgency, arguing that the Rigby attack showed that those programs were not working (Intelligence and Security Committee 2014: 2).
33. This appointment and the associated observations of the parliamentary committee were made in the context of ongoing discussions in government concerning the retention of British citizens' data including a controversial Draft Communications Data Bill (the so-called Snoopers Charter) first raised in 2012 (see Travis 2012; Wintour 2015) and the Data Retention and Investigatory Powers Act 2014, which was introduced in July 2014. These pieces of legislation were explicitly concerned with retention of data for the purposes of preventing and investigating terrorism as well as other forms of serious crime. The envoy appointed by Cameron was Sir Nigel Sheinwald, a former ambassador to the United States. Sheinwald has been part of significant shifts in the post-2015 environment regarding new models for information sharing between US-based internet companies and non-US security services (see Daskal 2018).

# Chapter 6

1. In addition to these models of what it means to be American in the context of a political community are a multitude of features identified by scholars analyzing US society more broadly. These features are social rather than political, but add nuance to arguments about constitutional patriotism and associated civic values. In his seminal survey work, sociologist Seymour Martin Lipset (1996: 19) found American values to be defined as "liberty, egalitarianism, populism, and laissez-faire," with egalitarianism functioning as an outpost of individualism. Lipset (1996: 9) found these to be markers of American exceptionalism, marking it as "the most anti-statist, legalistic and rights-oriented nation." More recent work has focused on shifts in American values following significant social change in the latter part of the twentieth century. In his work on the rise and fall of Anglo-American power in the US, Kaufmann (2004: 199), for example, highlights the ongoing role of individualism in American identity, but as part of a broader argument about the impact of modernism on American national identity. He describes an attachment to novelty and change, arguing that a "forward looking" aspect is fundamental to modern-day America. Recent work has shown that religious affiliation is still extremely important in American life, even though attendance at formal religious institutions has fallen in recent years (see Zuckert 2016).
2. Interview with Mr Ed Husain, Founder, Quilliam Foundation, and Senior Fellow for Middle Eastern Policy, Council on Foreign Relations, New York, December 20, 2011.

3. It built on the Page Act 1875, which banned Chinese women from migrating to the United States and introduced a ten-year moratorium on all Chinese labor immigration.
4. See Joppke (2010: 124) for a discussion of the surprisingly laissez-faire approach by US authorities on citizenship acquisition post-9/11.
5. See Whidden (2001) on the impact of earlier counterterrorism legislation (specifically the Antiterrorism and Effective Death Penalty Act (AEDPA) 1996) on rights for immigrants of Arab heritage.
6. The AEDPA also introduced substantial habeus corpus reform and, with the Illegal Immigration Reform and Immigrant Responsibility Act 1996, facilitated deportation proceedings for legal permanent residents in ways that significantly increased the value of US citizenship by comparison (Schuck 1997). The AEDPA was introduced in the context of the 1995 Oklahoma bombing and as such should be an indicator of immigration being linked with domestic terror concerns, in ways similar to post-2001 measures designed to combat homegrown extremism. But instead it focuses almost exclusively on international terrorism. Scholars see both of these acts as twin pieces of legislation driven by election-year politics rather than substantial event related policy reform (Schuck 1997; Whidden 2001).
7. See the discussion of *Schneiderman* in Fontana (2002) regarding debates around behavioral versus moral attachment to the constitution in the context of political values and beliefs. The case, from 1943, concerns an individual applying for citizenship who was a member of the Workers (Communist) Party of America but stated that he supported the constitution. He successfully won an appeal against the revocation of his citizenship by authorities during the Second World War by showing that he had "behavioral" if not "moral" attachment to the constitution, and that the constitution only required the former. Fontana (2002) argues for the relevance of this case in the context of the post-9/11 environment.
8. See Stone (2004) and Heale (1990) for further discussion of different state approaches to the management of citizen beliefs and behavior. Stone (2004) in particular shows that some acts were simply rhetorical exercises, while others had substantial effects on citizens' lives.
9. Citizen or industry-generated drives targeting dissenters with violence or propaganda were not unknown, however, and were on some occasions discreetly encouraged by government officials. See, for example, Murphy (1979: 94–95) on such measures early in the First World War.
10. Noting that environmental, civil-rights based, and animal liberation terrorism also occur to a significant (although lesser) degree (Bjelopera 2013).
11. Interview with Mr Daryl Johnson, former Senior Domestic Terrorism Analyst at the US Department of Homeland Security, Office of Intelligence and Analysis, Rockville, Maryland, March 27, 2013.
12. Telephone interview with Professor Will McCants, former Senior Advisor for Countering Extremism, State Department 2009–2011, and Director, US Relations with the Islamic World, Brookings Institute, September 23, 2013.
13. Ibid.

14. Telephone interview with Professor Sir David Omand, former Security and Intelligence Coordinator, Cabinet Office, 2002–2005, and Permanent Secretary, Home Office, 1997–2002, October 2, 2013.
15. As discussed further in Chapter 7, the case was groundbreaking in that the Bush administration asserted its right in his case to detain US citizens captured on US soil as "enemy combatants." See Cole and Dempsey (2006).
16. Note that calculating the number of attacks/plots is notoriously difficult because of the need to rely on often emotive press reporting, and because of controversies surrounding issues of entrapment (Patel 2011: 5–7), sealed indictments, and differences in state and federal terrorism and criminal statutes. Therefore, some sources report larger numbers of plots than those reported here (King 2011: 4; Nelson and Bodurian 2010).
17. Note this trend is not specific to AQ-inspired violence but reflects a trend toward lone terrorism across the spectrum.
18. Most of the American jihadist recruits mentioned by authorities have not been publicly identified, suggesting on-going investigations, sealed indictments, and some uncertainty (Meleagrou-Hitchens, Hughes, and Clifford 2018).

# Chapter 7

1. Although as Chapter 6 shows, the behavior of citizens was certainly addressed prior to 2001—for example in the Sedition Act 1918 and, regarding membership of political organizations, in the Smith Act 1940. But the idea of terrorists in particular was not addressed until after 2001, notably not even in the AEDPA 1996, passed in response to the 2005 Oklahoma City bombing perpetrated by a US citizen.
2. Some measures that would have affected citizens were quashed by Congress. For example, the proposal to introduce a national identity card would have acted as a preemptive information collecting tool, but was shot down in Congress. The Terrorism Information and Protection System, which proposed the creation of a "volunteer spy corps," was also rejected. Similarly, the Defense Advanced Research Projects Agency Total Information Awareness program—essentially aimed at gathering online data, including transactions and communications, and potentially including those of citizens—had its funding revoked by Congress after a public outcry. See Jonietz (2003); Whitaker (2006: 156–158).
3. The AEDPA had introduced the concept of a list of foreign terrorist organizations determined by the Secretary of State but without reference to "a political, social or other similar group." It also introduced the concept of material support to terrorism, but again in a more limited fashion—limited to, for example, direct and intentional financial contributions.
4. Significant deportations under these provisions took place in the months following 9/11. See Chesney (2005: 32).

5. See Chesney (2005) for a discussion of the development of the material support provisions in the AEDPA 1996.
6. This has even extended to the "liking" of certain Facebook groups related to terrorist activities being classed as material support (Murray 2012).
7. Note that these provisions (for foreign terrorism) were amended in the Intelligence Reform and Terrorism Prevention Act 2004, ostensibly to narrow the definition. However, as Abrams (2005: 32–35) points out, these provisions were unclear and may in fact broaden the definition by, for example, implying that persons receiving training may be providing personnel and that providing any service—such as cleaning, for example—may be included as material support.
8. "A foreign power includes 'a group engaged in international terrorism or activities in preparation therefor [sic]'. . . . a group need not be formally designated as a terrorist organization to qualify as a foreign power, and can include as few as two people engaged in international terrorism" (Sinnar 2019: 1344).
9. The PATRIOT Act was reauthorized according to its sunset provisions in 2005, making many of its expiring provisions permanent, except for the FISA provisions, which have been reauthorized at every opportunity since 2001, most recently in 2017.
10. These amendments were intended to facilitate information sharing between the FBI and the CIA (Central Intelligence Agency), in an attempt to avoid mistakes in information sharing that had been made previously, especially in the lead-up to September 11. See Piette and Radack (2006) for an overview.
11. Changes to FBI guidelines in 2002 further loosened provisions on surveillance of citizens, including at religious gatherings (Ashcroft 2002).
12. Interview with Dr. William McCants, former Senior Advisor for Countering Extremism, State Department 2009–2011 and Director, US Relations with the Islamic World, Brookings Institute, Washington, DC, September 23, 2013. The hearings were headed by Representative Peter King as chair of the House Homeland Security Committee, and were arguably were part of a larger campaign to put pressure on the Barack Obama Administration during the run up to the 2012 elections, given long-standing right-wing apprehension regarding the relationship between the president and Islam. Interview with Ms Faiza Patel, Co-Director, Law and National Security program, Brennan Center for Justice, New York, November 30, 2011; interview with Mr Ed Husain, Founder, Quilliam Foundation, and Senior Fellow for Middle Eastern Policy, Council on Foreign Relations, New York, December 20, 2011.
13. The bill also incorporated ideas included in Ranking Member David Reichert's bill H.R. 1695, The Preventing Radicalism by Exploring and Vetting its Emergence as a National Threat (PREVENT) Act, 26/3 2007, which failed to pass the House.
14. The Senate Committee on Homeland Security and Governmental Affairs held a series of hearings on Violent Islamic Extremism between September 2006 and February 2011, broadly related to the ideas expressed in this bill. However, these are not examined here because they are not attached to a piece of legislation that successfully passed one of the houses of Congress.

NOTES 225

15. In fact, the RAND Corporation's senior counterterrorism expert, Brian Jenkins, recommended in later testimony the inclusion of a constitutional lawyer on any commission on radicalization (Jenkins 2007b).
16. Note that congressional findings play a key and arguably increasing role in Supreme Court adjudications, and have the effect of a statement of fact (Frickey 1995–1996). Federal courts have also long held that Congress's findings of empirical fact are entitled to judicial deference (Borgmann 2009: 6).
17. According to the recording of the act's mark-up session, this change in definition was introduced in response to witnesses Jenkins, Frank Ciluffo, and Javed Ali, who had been questioned extensively by members on their thoughts on appropriate language (Harman 2007a). The later bill also saw definitive extension of the definition in clause (3) from the draft, to include persons "based and operating primarily within the United States" rather than simply "the civilian population" as the initial act listed it, presumably to extend the bill to lawful permanent residents, as in the congressional findings (see original bill H1955) introduced April 17, 2007.
18. Following Jenkins' (2007b) suggestion, this commission included a constitutional lawyer. The initial bill included provision for a federal grant system (for states) to prevent ideologically based violence and homegrown terrorism in "at-risk populations, as defined by the secretary" (Section 899C). Such funds could be used for such purposes as developing best practices, assisting with "educational outreach social services and integration into society," and "promoting civic engagement and community outreach programs." This section was struck out in the final version, on the advice of witnesses, and replaced by a commission of inquiry in recognition of the need to better understand the threat and the mechanisms of radicalization (Harman 2007a).
19. See Chesney (2005: 44, note 230) for a discussion of the emergence of debates around military detention of civilian terrorists in the wake of 9/11.
20. Note there was considerable opposition to the detention provisions, not only because of the civil rights issue, but because of objections by senior security and intelligence personnel that the presumption of military detention could cause serious problems with detainee and intelligence management which would otherwise be managed by the domestic services.
21. This amendment was explicitly removed in the NDAA 2013 (Gerstein 2012).
22. Although signing statements have become increasingly common since the Ronald Reagan administration and had featured heavily in the George W. Bush administration (Savage 2013; White House 2011f).
23. Only one, the Due Process and Military Detention Amendments Act 2012, has received a hearing by the Senate judiciary committee. This act repeals its application to citizens—reinstating the boundaries of formal citizenship while retaining application to non-citizens.
24. Debate on later NDAAs (2014–2016) focuses on the transfer of Guantanamo detainees, including US citizens—a narrower focus than that of the NDAA 2012, although the 2012 provisions have not been repealed.

25. Telephone interview with Mr Matt Armstrong, Governor, Broadcasting Board of Governors, and former Executive Director, United States Advisory Commission on Public Diplomacy (2011), October 24, 2013.
26. Interview with a former senior US government official, Washington, DC, June 20, 2013. Additionally, see LeBaron (2012) on the Center's founding.
27. The act also presaged the first congressional response to lone actors in Section 101, subtitle A, which redefined FISA powers for lone actors "to expand the definition of international terrorism" to include all persons engaged in international terrorism regardless of affiliation with a terrorist group, a measure later included in the Intelligence Reform and Terrorism Prevention Act 2004.
28. Such support did not necessarily fall along Republican/Democrat lines. Secretary of State Hillary Clinton noted that the State Department already had such power and was willing to examine the bill's provision, stating: "United States citizenship is a privilege . . . it is not a right," and Speaker Nancy Pelosi said she supported the "spirit" of the measure whereas the Republican leader of the House expressed doubts (both quoted in Savage and Hulse 2010).

# Chapter 8

1. Targeting of Muslim citizens outside the context of homegrown extremism began almost immediately following the 9/11 attacks. Responses in the immediate post-9/11 era targeted foreigners, citizens, and permanent residents of Muslim faith. Under the USA PATRIOT Act, for example, several thousand Arab and Muslim foreign nationals, including permanent residents, were detained within the United States in the initial period following 9/11, with many deported without due process rights (Cole 2003). In addition, seventy men of Middle Eastern descent, all but one of whom were Muslim and a quarter of whom were citizens, were detained between 2001 and 2005 under material witness laws, without due process rights (Human Rights Watch and American Civil Liberties Union 2005: 1–2).
2. Civil society arguably began actively engaging in counter-extremism discourse before the federal government. In 2007, the Chicago Council on Global Affairs formed a Task Force on Muslim American Civil and Political Engagement, funded and led by several prominent American Muslims. It released a paper on the integration of American Muslims, paying attention to the security ramifications of such integration (Kathwari, Martin, and Whitney 2007). The US Muslim Engagement Project, initiated in 2008, was similarly staffed by several prominent American Muslims, among others. It focused on Muslim engagement globally rather than simply on American Muslims, and many of its recommendations appear in later US domestic and international CVE policy (US Muslim Engagement Project 2008).
3. Interview with Dr. William McCants, former Senior Advisor for Countering Extremism, State Department, 2009–2011, and Director, US Relations with the Islamic World, Brookings Institute, Washington, DC, September 23, 2013. Note some

state agencies had paid attention to the problem—if not solutions—prior to this. For example, the New York Police Department had been (sometimes controversially) engaging in international consultation and training on the issue since 2003. See Rascoff (2012).
4. As mentioned in Chapter 1, Nidal Hasan, a US Army major, fatally shot thirteen people and injured more than thirty others in November 2014. Hasan had been in contact with AQ propagandist Anwar Al-Awlaki.
5. See Aziz (2014) for an outline of the role of these outreach measures as intelligence collection activities.
6. The Homeland Security Advisory Council provides advice and recommendations to the secretary on matters related to homeland security and comprises leaders from state and local government, first responder communities, the private sector, and academia. This 2010 process included a roundtable with Napolitano and twenty key Muslim Arab, South Asian, and Sikh leaders to discuss counterradicalization efforts (US Department of Homeland Security 2010).
7. By 2010, senior security officials were reporting an increase in threat levels. For example, the Director of the National Counterterrorism Center noted in congressional testimony that "the spike in homegrown violent extremist activity during the past year is indicative of a common cause that rallies independent extremists to want to attack the homeland. Key to this trend has been the development of a U.S.-specific narrative that motivates individuals to violence. This narrative—a blend of al-Qaeda inspiration, perceived victimization and glorification of past plotting—has become increasingly accessible through the Internet, and English-language Web sites are tailored to address the unique concerns of U.S.-based extremists" (Leiter 2010: 3). The Director of the FBI described the threat as evolving in complexity and intensity, noting: "Beyond the sheer number of disruptions and arrests that have come to light, homegrown extremists are increasingly more savvy, harder to detect and able to connect with other extremists overseas" (Mueller 2010: 4).
8. Interview with Ms Faiza Patel, Co-Director, Law and National Security program, Brennan Center for Justice, New York, November 30, 2011; Interview with McCants.
9. Existing differences between the two nations were evident in US attempts to counter homegrown extremism in the UK as part of its foreign policy (AFP 2011; Ross and Swinford 2011; Kennedy 2011).
10. Interview with Patel; Interview with McCants.
11. Although he reportedly remained supportive of more controversial measures such as engagement with non-violent extremists. Interview with McCants.
12. Interview with Patel.
13. The Countering Violent Extremism Act 2015 (HR 2899) was concerned with restructuring the bureaucracy of CVE, centralizing it within the DHS, and funding that new office for US$40 million. The bill failed to reach the Senate and was opposed largely on the basis of fiscal responsibility. Civil society opposition also focused on the ineffectiveness of CVE programs and their stigmatization and unnecessary surveillance of Muslim communities, and a failure to focus on far-right terrorism (Brennan Center for Justice 2015).

14. Interview with McCants.
15. Interview with Patel.
16. Ibid.; Interview with McCants.
17. Interview with McCants.
18. Telephone interview with Associate Professor Shahar Aziz, former Senior Policy Advisor for the Office for Civil Rights and Civil Liberties, Department of Homeland Security 2008–2009, November 5, 2013.
19. It is important to note that some of these events are not part of CVE efforts, although the DHS does not distinguish between them in official documents.
20. Community engagement initiatives have adapted to the changing nature of the threat from homegrown extremism over time. For example, DHS Community Awareness Briefings began in 2010. They were developed in conjunction with the NCTC and were designed to inform communities about specific threats from radicalization in their community (Brennan Center for Justice 2016). In 2014, these were redesigned to refocus on recruitment by IS. A Community Resilience Exercise was also designed by the NCTC and the DHS in 2014 to focus on recruitment by IS, involving community members—overwhelmingly those of Muslim heritage—in an exercise to understand various points of intersection by community and law enforcement members with the IS recruitment process.
21. Following the election of Donald J. Trump, five groups awarded funds stated that they would decline the funding in light of the Trump administration's apparent antipathy to Muslims and the program's overly broad focus on Islam (only one grant was awarded to a group working on far-right extremism).
22. In a 2014 letter to then Assistant to the President for Homeland Security and Deputy National Security Adviser, twenty-seven organizations, including Amnesty International USA and the Council on American-Islamic Relations, expressed concern about the targeting of Muslim communities under the auspices of CVE. These organizations argued that CVE may lead to the surveillance and monitoring of Muslim communities (ACLU et al. 2014). In 2015, a coalition of forty-eight organizations, led by the Brennan Center for Justice, also expressed their concern about community stigmatization and civil rights violations regarding the potential establishment of new CVE bureaucracy to the leadership of the House Committee on Homeland Security (Brennan Center for Justice 2015).
23. Telephone interview with Aziz.
24. Interview with McCants.
25. Telephone interview with Professor Sir David Omand, former Security and Intelligence Coordinator, Cabinet Office, 2002–2005, and Permanent Secretary, Home Office, 1997–2002, October 2, 2013.
26. Telephone interview with Ms Frances Guy, former head, Foreign and Commonwealth Office Engaging with the Islamic World Unit, 2004–2006, November 16, 2013.
27. This center was preceded by the Global Strategic Engagement Center (GSEC), founded in 2008 and also housed in the State Department's Public Affairs Section. The GSEC focused on terrorism, but not explicitly radicalization, and exclusively targeted foreign audiences outside the United States, working with the Department of

NOTES 229

Defense. The GSEC was preceded by the Counterterrorism Communication Center, which had been established in 2007 and was housed in the State Department's Bureau of International Information Programs, also established to work with the Department of Defense, and on operations outside the United States. See Weed (2017); LeBaron (2012) for useful overviews.
28. Interview with McCants.
29. See Helmus and Klein (2018) for a discussion of methods employed by a number of corporate actors following a Google-led summit on violent online extremism held in Dublin in 2011.

# Conclusion

1. Interview with Dr. William McCants, former Senior Advisor for Countering Extremism, State Department, 2009–2011, and Director, US Relations with the Islamic World, Brookings Institute, Washington, DC, September 23, 2013; Telephone interview with Professor Sir David Omand, former Security and Intelligence Coordinator, Cabinet Office, 2002–2005, and Permanent Secretary, Home Office, 1997–2002, October 2, 2013; Telephone interview with Mr George Selim, Senior Policy Adviser, Office of Civil Rights and Civil Liberties, US Department of Homeland Security, November 22, 2011; Email interview with a former senior British government official, October 15, 2013.
2. Telephone interview with Omand.
3. Interview with Ms Sidney Jones, Senior Adviser, Asia Program, International Crisis Group, Canberra, September 22, 2013.
4. Scholars who otherwise see the further liberalization of citizenship as an inevitable process into the future have highlighted the case of Muslims in Europe as important exceptions to their arguments (Joppke 2010).

# References

Abdo, Alex. 2012. "Rhetorical Support Is Not 'Material Support.'" American Civil Liberties Union, December 26. https://www.aclu.org/blog/free-speech/rhetorical-support-not-material-support.
Abrahms, Max. 2007. "Why Democracies Make Superior Counterterrorists." *Security Studies* 16, no. 2: 223–253.
Abrahms, Max. 2008. "What Terrorists Really Want: Terrorist Motives and Counterterrorism Strategy." *International Security* 32, no. 4: 78–105.
Abrams, Norman. 2005. "The Material Support Terrorism Offenses: Perspectives Derived from the (Early) Model Penal Code." *Journal of National Security Law & Policy* 1, no. 1: 5–36.
ACLU (American Civil Liberties Union). 2007. "ACLU Statement on the Violent Radicalization and Homegrown Terrorism Prevention Act of 2007." November 28. https://www.aclu.org/news/aclu-statement-violent-radicalization-and-homegrown-terrorism-prevention-act-2007.
ACLU (American Civil Liberties Union) et al. 2014. "Coalition Letter to Obama Administration on Countering Violent Extremism (CVE) Program." December 18. https://www.aclu.org/other/coalition-letter-obama-administration-countering-violent-extremism-cve-program?redirect=coalition-letter-obama-administration-countering-violent-extremism-cve-program.
ACLU (American Civil Liberties Union). 2016. "ACLU V. DHS—Complaint." February 10. https://www.aclu.org/legal-document/aclu-v-dhs-complaint.
Adamson, Fiona B. 2005a. "Globalisation, Transnational Political Mobilisation, and Networks of Violence." *Cambridge Review of International Affairs* 18, no. 1: 31–49.
Adamson, Fiona B. 2005b. "Global Liberalism versus Political Islam: Competing Ideological Frameworks in International Politics." *International Studies Review* 7, no. 4: 547–569.
Adamson, Fiona B. 2011. "Engaging or Contesting the Liberal State? 'Muslim' as a Politicised Identity Category in Europe." *Journal of Ethnic and Migration Studies* 37, no. 6: 899–915.
Adamson, Fiona B., Triadafilos Triadafilopoulos, and Aristide R. Zolberg. 2011. "The Limits of the Liberal State: Migration, Identity and Belonging in Europe." *Journal of Ethnic and Migration Studies* 37, no. 6: 843–859.
Aden, Steven H., and John W. Whitehead. 2001–2002. "Forfeiting 'Enduring Freedom' for 'Homeland Security': A Constitutional Analysis of the USA Patriot Act and the Justice Department's Anti-Terrorism Initiatives." *American University Law Review* 51, no. 6: 1081–1133.
Adler, Emanuel, Michael Barnett, and Steve Smith. 1998. *Security Communities*. Cambridge: Cambridge University Press.
Adler-Nissen, Rebecca, ed. 2013. *Bourdieu in International Relations: Rethinking Key Concepts in IR*. Abingdon: Routledge.

Advisory Group on Citizenship. 1998. "Education for Citizenship and the Teaching of Democracy in Schools: Final Report of the Advisory Group on Citizenship." London: Qualifications and Curriculum Authority on behalf of the Citizenship Advisory Group, September 22.

AFP (Agence France Presse). 2011. "US Feared London Mosque Was Extremist 'Haven': Wikileaks." April 26.

Ajegbo, Keith. 2007. *Diversity & Citizenship: Curriculum Review.* Nottingham: Department for Education and Skills.

Akbar, Amna. 2013. "Policing 'Radicalization.'" *UC Irvine Law Review* 3, no. 4: 809–883.

Akbar, Amna. 2015. "National Security's Broken Windows." *UCLA Law Review* 62, no. 4: 834–907.

Akram, Susan M., and Kevin R. Johnson. 2001–2003. "Race, Civil Rights, and Immigration Law after September 11, 2001: The Targeting of Arabs and Muslims." *New York University Annual Survey of American Law* 58, no. 3: 295–355.

Al-Barghouti, Tamim. 2008. *The Umma and the Dawla: The Nation State and the Arab Middle East.* London: Pluto Press.

Aleinikoff, T. Alexander. 1985. "Theories of Loss of Citizenship." *Michigan Law Review* 84, no. 7: 1471–1503.

Ali, Javed. 2006. "Testimony." Hearing before the Subcommittee on Intelligence, Information Sharing, and Terrorism Risk Assessment of the US House of Representatives Committee on Homeland Security: The Homeland Security Implications of Radicalization, September 20. https://fas.org/irp/congress/2006_hr/radical.pdf.

Almond, Gabriel A. 1956. "Comparative Political Systems." *Journal of Politics* 18, no. 3: 391–409.

Alonso, Rogelio. 2010. "Radicalisation and Recruitment among Jihadist Terrorists in Spain: Main Patterns and Subsequent Counter-Terrorist Measures." In *Understanding Violent Radicalisation: Terrorists and Jihadist Movements in Europe*, edited by Magnus Ranstorp, 207–230. Abingdon: Routledge.

Al-Rasheed, Madawi. 2014. "Saudi Arabia's Anti-Terror Law Not Enough." *Al-Monitor*, February 4. https://www.al-monitor.com/pulse/originals/2014/02/saudi-anti-terror-law.html.

Al-Saud, Abdullah bin Khaled. 2017. "The Tranquillity Campaign: A Beacon of Light in the Dark World Wide Web." *Perspectives on Terrorism* 11, no. 2: 58–64.

Al-Zawahiri, Ayman. 2005. "Zawahiri's Letter to Zarqawi." Combating Terrorism Center at West Point. https://ctc.usma.edu/harmony-program/zawahiris-letter-to-zarqawi-original-language-2/.

Anderson, Benedict. 1991. *Imagined Communities: Reflections on the Origin and Spread of Nationalism.* London: Verso Books.

Anderson, David. 2016. "Citizenship Removal Resulting in Statelessness: First Report of the Independent Reviewer on the Operation of the Power to Remove Citizenship Obtained by Naturalisation from Persons Who Have No Other Citizenship." Independent Reviewer of Terrorism Legislation, April. https://assets.publishing.service.gov.uk/government/uploads/system/uploads/attachment_data/file/518390/David_Anderson_QC_-_CITIZENSHIP_REMOVAL__print_.pdf.

AntaraNews. 2012. "Aceh Sets up Counter Terrorism Unit." August 8. https://en.antaranews.com/news/83837/aceh-sets-up-counter-terrorism-unit.

AQAP (Al-Qaeda in the Arabian Peninsula). 2011. "New Terrorists as Inspiration for Al-Qaeda Followers in the West." *Inspire*. http://www.memri.org/report/en/print4927.htm. Accessed 01/01/2013.

Archetti, Cristina. 2013. *Understanding Terrorism in the Age of Global Media: A Communication Approach*. Basingstoke: Palgrave Macmillan.

Article 19. 2005. "Home List of Unacceptable Behaviours: Freedom of Expression the Scapegoat of Political Expediency." London: Article 19, October.

Ashcroft, John. 2002. "Remarks of Attorney General John Ashcroft." May 30. https://www.fas.org/irp/news/2002/05/ag053002.html.

Ashworth, Andrew, and Lucia Zedner. 2012. "Prevention and Criminalization: Justifications and Limits." *New Criminal Law Review: An International and Interdisciplinary Journal* 15, no. 4: 542–571.

Ashworth, Andrew, Lucia Zedner, and Patrick Tomlin, eds. 2013. *Prevention and the Limits of the Criminal Law*. Oxford: Oxford University Press.

Association of Chief Police Officers. 2014. "Freedom of Information Request Reference Number: 000117/13." January 24. https://www.npcc.police.uk/documents/FoI%20publication/Disclosure%20Logs/Uniformed%20Operations%20FOI/2013/117%2013%20ACPO%20Response%20-%20Channel%20Project%20Referrals.pdf.

Asthana, Anushka, and Sam Levin. 2017. "UK Urges Tech Giants to Do More to Prevent Spread of Extremism." *The Guardian*, July 31.

Australian Attorney-General's Department. 2012. "Countering Violent Extremism." Canberra: Government Printing Office.

Australian Department of the Prime Minister and Cabinet. 2010. "Counter-Terrorism White Paper: Securing Australia; Protecting Our Community 2010." Canberra: Department of the Prime Minister and Cabinet.

Awan, Akil N. 2010. "The Virtual Jihad: An Increasingly Legitimate Form of Warfare." *CTC Sentinel* 3, no. 5: 10–13.

Aziz, Sahar F. 2011–2012. "Caught in a Preventive Dragnet: Selective Counterterrorism in a Post 9/11 America." *Gonzaga Law Review* 47, no. 2: 429–492.

Aziz, Sahar F. 2014. "Policing Terrorists in the Community." *Harvard National Security Journal* 5, no. 1: 147–224.

Baele, Stephanie, Gregorio Bettiza, Katharine A. Boyd, and Travis G. Coan. 2021. "ISIS's Clash of Civilizations: Constructing the 'West' in Terrorist Propaganda." *Studies in Conflict & Terrorism*, 44, no. 11: 887–919.

Baele, Stephanie, Katharine A. Boyd, and Travis G. Coan, eds. 2019. *ISIS Propaganda: A Full-Spectrum Extremist Message*. Oxford: Oxford University Press.

Bagehot, Walter. 2011. "A Coalition Disagreement over Engaging with Extremists." *The Economist*, March 3.

BAMF (Federal Office for Migration and Refugee). 2013. "The Federal Office and Its Tasks: Centre of Excellence for Asylum, Migration and Integration." Nürnberg: BAMF.

Baran, Zeyno. 2005. "Fighting the War of Ideas." *Foreign Affairs* 84, no. 6: 68–78.

Barkindo, Atta, and Shane Bryans. 2016. "De-Radicalising Prisoners in Nigeria: Developing a Basic Prison Based De-Radicalisation Programme." *Journal for Deradicalization* 7, Summer: 1–25.

Barnett, Michael N. 1995. "Sovereignty, Nationalism, and Regional Order in the Arab States System." *International Organization* 49, no. 3: 479–510.

Barrett, Richard. 2017. "Beyond the Caliphate: Foreign Fighters and the Threat of Returnees." New York: The Soufan Center.

Barry, Brian. 2002. *Culture and Equality: An Egalitarian Critique of Multiculturalism*. Boston, MA: Harvard University Press.
Bartlett, Jamie, Michael King, and Jonathan Birdwell. 2010. *The Edge of Violence*. London: Demos.
BBC News. 2013. "UK Citizenship Test 'to Cover Britain's Greats.'" January 28. https://www.bbc.com/news/uk-21221773.
Beck, Ulrich. 1992. *Risk Society: Towards a New Modernity*. London: Sage.
Beetham, David. 1991. "Max Weber and the Legitimacy of the Modern State." *Analyse & Kritik* 13, no. 1: 34–45.
Benhabib, Seyla. 2004. *The Rights of Others: Aliens, Residents and Citizens*. Cambridge: Cambridge University Press.
Bennett, Huw. 2010. "From Direct Rule to Motorman: Adjusting British Military Strategy for Northern Ireland in 1972." *Studies in Conflict & Terrorism* 33, no. 6: 511–532.
Bennett, Marion T. 1966. "The Immigration and Nationality (McCarran-Walter) Act of 1952, as Amended to 1965." *Annals of the American Academy of Political and Social Science* 367: 127–136.
Benson, Rodney. 1999. "Field Theory in Comparative Context: A New Paradigm for Media Studies." *Theory and Society* 28, no. 3: 463–498.
Bergen, Peter, David Sterman, and Melissa Salyk-Virk. 2019. "Terrorism in America 18 Years after 9/11." Washington, DC: New America Foundation, September 16.
Berntzen, Lars Erik, and Sveinung Sandberg. 2014. "The Collective Nature of Lone Wolf Terrorism: Anders Behring Breivik and the Anti-Islamic Social Movement." *Terrorism and Political Violence* 26, no. 5: 759–799.
Bevir, Mark. 1999. *The Logic of the History of Ideas*. Cambridge: Cambridge University Press.
Bevir, Mark. 2003. "A Decentered Theory of Governance." In *Governance as Social and Political Communication*, edited by Henrik Bang, 200–212. Manchester: Manchester University Press.
Bevir, Mark, and R. A. W. Rhodes. 2010. *The State as Cultural Practice*. Oxford: Oxford University Press.
Biery, Mary. 2016. "DHS Offers $10 Million Counterterrorism Grant." *Washington Examiner*, July 6.
Bigo, Didier, and Emmanuel-Pierre Guitett. 2011. "Northern Ireland as Metaphor: Exception, Suspicion and Radicalization in the 'War on Terror.'" *Security Dialogue* 42, no. 6: 483–498.
Bird, J. C. 1986. *Control of Enemy Alien Civilians in Great Britain, 1914–1918*. New York: Garland Publishing.
Bjelopera, Jerome P. 2013. "American Jihadist Terrorism: Combating a Complex Threat." CRS Report for Congress R41416. Washington, DC: Congressional Research Service.
Bjelopera, Jerome P. 2014. "Countering Violent Extremism in the United States." CRS Report for Congress R42553. Washington, DC: Congressional Research Service.
Bjelopera, Jerome P., and Mark Randol. 2010. "American Jihadist Terrorism: Combating a Complex Threat." Updated. CRS Report for Congress R41416. Washington, DC: Congressional Research Service.
Black, Justice Hugo. 1967. Majority Opinion, *Afroyim*, 387 US (Supreme Court of the United States of America).
Blair, Dennis C. 2010. "Annual Threat Assessment of the US Intelligence Community for the Senate Select Committee on Intelligence: Statement for the Record." February

2. https://www.dni.gov/files/documents/Newsroom/Testimonies/20100202_testimony.pdf.

Blair, Tony. 2005. "PM's Press Conference—5 August 2005." http://webarchive.nationalarchives.gov.uk/20040105034004/number10.gov.uk/page8041.

Blair, Tony, and Nigel Spearing. 2005. *Britain Forward Not Back. The Labour Party Manifesto 2005*. Annotated by Nigel Spearing, MP for Newnham South. London: Labour Party.

Bloemraad, Irene. 2006. *Becoming a Citizen: Incorporating Immigrants and Refugees in the United States and Canada*. Los Angeles: University of California Press.

Bloemraad, Irene, Anna Korteweg, and Gökçe Yurdakul. 2008. "Citizenship and Immigration: Multiculturalism, Assimilation, and Challenges to the Nation-State." *Annual Review of Sociology* 34, no. 1: 153–179.

Blunkett, David. 2002. "Integration with Diversity: Globalisation and the Renewal of Democracy and Civil Society." In *Reclaiming Britishness: Living Together after 11 September and the Rise of the Right*, edited by Phoebe Griffith and Mark Leonard, 65–77. London: Foreign Policy Centre.

Blunkett, David. 2004. "New Challenges for Race Equality and Community Cohesion in the 21st Century." Speech to the Institute of Public Policy Research, London, July 7.

Bodine-Baron, Elizabeth, Todd C. Helmus, Madeline Magnuson, and Zev Winkelman. 2016. "Examining ISIS Support and Opposition Networks on Twitter." Santa Monica, CA: RAND Corporation.

Bonner, David. 2007. *Executive Measures, Terrorism, and National Security: Have the Rules of the Game Changed?* Aldershot: Ashgate.

Booth, Ken. 2004. "Beyond Critical Security Studies." In *Critical Security Studies and World Politics*, edited by Ken Booth, 259–278. Boulder, CO: Lynne Rienner.

Borgmann, Caitlin E. 2009. "Rethinking Judicial Deference to Legislative Fact-Finding." *Indiana Law Journal* 84, no. 1: 1–56.

Bouasria, Abedlilah. 2015. *Sufism and Politics in Morocco: Activism and Dissent*. Abingdon: Routledge.

Boubaker, Amel. 2011. "Al-Qaeda in the Ismalic Maghreb and Algerian Salafi Networks." In *Interregional Challenges of Islamic Extremist Movements in North Africa*, edited by Muna Abdalla, 57–75. Pretoria: Institute for Security Studies.

Boucek, Christopher. 2008a. "Counter-Terrorism from Within: Assessing Saudi Arabia's Religious Rehabilitation and Disengagement Programme." *RUSI Journal* 153, no. 6: 60–65.

Boucek, Christopher. 2008b. "Saudi Arabia's 'Soft' Counterterrorism Strategy: Prevention, Rehabilitation, and Aftercare." Washington, DC: Carnegie Endowment for International Peace, September.

Boukhars, Anouar. 2011. "Mauritania Confronts Structural Problems as It Steps Up Counterterrorism Efforts." *Terrorism Monitor* 9, no. 31. August 4. https://jamestown.org/program/mauritania-confronts-structural-problems-as-it-steps-up-counterterrorism-efforts/

Bourdieu, Pierre. 1989. "Social Space and Symbolic Power." *Sociological Theory* 7, no. 1: 14–25.

Bourdieu, Pierre. 1991. *Language and Symbolic Power*. Cambridge, MA: Harvard University Press.

Bourdieu, Pierre. 1998. *Practical Reason*. Stanford, CA: Stanford University Press.

Bourdieu, Pierre. 2002. "Some Questions for the True Masters of the World." *Berkeley Journal of Sociology* 46: 170–176.

Brachman, Jarret M., and Alix N. Levine. 2011. "You Too Can Be Awlaki!" *Fletcher Forum of World Affairs* 35, no. 1: 25–46.

Brachman, Jarret M., and William F. McCants. 2006. "Stealing Al Qaeda's Playbook." *Studies in Conflict & Terrorism* 29, no. 4: 309–321.

Braddock, Kurt, and John Horgan. 2016. "Towards a Guide for Constructing and Disseminating Counternarratives to Reduce Support for Terrorism." *Studies in Conflict & Terrorism* 39, no. 5: 381–404.

Bravo, Fernando. 2010. "Islam in Spain." *Euro-Islam*, March 8. http://www.euro-islam.info/2010/03/08/islam-in-spain/.

Breen-Smyth, Marie. 2014. "Theorising the 'Suspect Community': Counterterrorism, Security Practices and the Public Imagination." *Critical Studies on Terrorism* 7, no. 2: 223–240.

Brennan Center for Justice. 2015. "Citing Civil Liberties Concerns, 48 Groups Oppose Countering Violent Extremism Act." New York: Brennan Center for Justice, July 14.

Brennan Center for Justice. 2016. "White House Introduces 2016 CVE Plan." New York: Brennan Center for Justice, October 19.

Briggs, Rachel, Catherine Fieschi, and Hannah Lownsbrough. 2006. *Bringing It Home: Community-Based Approaches to Counter-Terrorism*. London: Demos.

Brighton, Shane. 2007. "British Muslims, Multiculturalism and UK Foreign Policy: 'Integration' and 'Cohesion' In and Beyond the State." *International Affairs* 83, no. 1: 1–17.

Brown, Colin. 1996. "Ministers Said to Be Soft on Terrorism." *The Independent*, November 2.

Brown, Gordon. 2004. "Gordon Brown's Speech (Part 1)." *The Guardian*, July 8.

Brown, Gordon. 2006. "The Future of Britishness." Speech to the Fabian New Year Conference Who Do We Want To Be? The Future of Britishness. Imperial College, London, January 14.

Brubaker, Rogers. 1992. *Citizenship and Nationhood in France and Germany*. Cambridge, MA: Harvard University Press.

Brubaker, William Rogers. 1990. "Immigration, Citizenship, and the Nation-State in France and Germany: A Comparative Historical Analysis." *International Sociology* 5, no. 4: 379–407.

Bunglawala, Inayat. 2009. "Minab: Community Initiative, or Quango?" *The Guardian*, May 15.

Bures, Oldrich. 2018. "EU's Response to Foreign Fighters: New Threat, Old Challenges?" *Terrorism and Political Violence*, January 8: 1–18. https://doi.org/10.1080/09546 553.2017.1404456.

Burns, Quiana. 2007. "More Home-Grown Terror Attacks to Come?" ABC News, May 10. https://abcnews.go.com/Politics/story?id=3162824&page=1.

Byrne, Bridget. 2017. "Testing Times: The Place of the Citizenship Test in the UK Immigration Regime and New Citizens' Responses to It." *Sociology* 51, no. 2: 323–338.

Cameron, David. 2011. "PM's Speech at Munich Security Conference." February 5. https://www.gov.uk/government/speeches/pms-speech-at-munich-security-conference.

Camilleri, Raphaelle. 2012. "Impact of Counter-Terrorism on Communities: France Background Report." London: Institute for Strategic Dialogue. https://counterextrem

ism.org/resources/details/id/206/impact-of-counter-terrorism-on-communities-france-background-report.
Cantle, Ted. 2001. "Community Cohesion in Britain: A Report of the Independent Review Team." London: Home Office.
Capoccia, Giovanni. 2010. "Germany's Response to 9/11: The Importance of Checks and Balances." In *The Consequences of Counterterrorism*, edited by Martha Crenshaw, 285–334. New York: Russell Sage Foundation.
Caramani, Daniele. 2010. "Of Differences and Similarities: Is the Explanation of Variation a Limitation to (or of) Comparative Analysis?" *European Political Science* 9, no. 1: 34–48.
Carter, Joseph A., Shiraz Maher, and Peter R. Neumann. 2014. "#Greenbirds: Measuring Importance and Influence in Syrian Foreign Fighter Networks." London: International Centre for the Study of Radicalisation and Political Violence, King's College London.
Castles, Stephen. 2002. "Migration and Community Formation under Conditions of Globalization." *International Migration Review* 36, no. 4: 1143–1168.
Center for Constitutional Rights. 2007. "Factsheet: The Violent Radicalization and Homegrown Terrorism Prevention Act of 2007." November 19. https://ccrjustice.org/node/2502.
Chalk, Peter, and William Rosenau. 2004. *Confronting "the Enemy Within": Security Intelligence, the Police, and Counterterrorism in Four Democracies*. Santa Monica, CA: RAND Corporation.
Chang, Nancy. 2001. "The USA Patriot Act: What's So Patriotic about Trampling on the Bill of Rights?" *Guild Practitioner* 58, no. 3: 142–158.
Change Institute. 2009. "Security and Counter-Terrorism: Studies on Violent Radicalisation." London: Change Institute.
Cherney, Adrian, and Kristina Murphy. 2017. "Police and Community Cooperation in Counterterrorism: Evidence and Insights from Australia." *Studies in Conflict & Terrorism* 40, no. 12: 1023–1037.
Chertoff, Michael. 2007. "Written Testimony." Hearing before the US Senate Committee on Homeland Security and Governmental Affairs on Radicalization: The Threat from Islamic Radicalism to the Homeland. March 14. https://www.hsgac.senate.gov/imo/media/doc/031407Chertoff.pdf.
Chesney, Robert M. 2005. "The Sleeper Scenario: Terrorism-Support Laws and the Demands of Prevention." *Harvard Journal on Legislation* 42, no. 1: 1–89.
Choudhry, Tufyal. 2007. "The Role of Muslim Identity Politics in Radicalisation (A Study in Progress)." London: Department for Communities and Local Government.
Chrisafis, Angelique. 2015. "Copenhagen Shooting Suspect Omar El-Hussein—A Past Full of Contradictions." *The Guardian*, February 16.
Ciovacco, Carl J. 2009. "The Contours of Al Qaeda's Media Strategy." *Studies in Conflict & Terrorism* 32, no. 10: 853–875.
Clapper, James R. 2016. "Statement for the Record: Worldwide Threat Assessment of the US Intelligence Community." Office for the Director of National Intelligence. February 25. https://www.dni.gov/files/documents/Newsroom/Testimonies/HPSCI_Unclassified_2016_ATA_SFR-25Feb16.pdf.
Clarke, Charles. 2000. House of Commons Standing Committee Debates, Terrorism Bill. January 18. https://publications.parliament.uk/pa/cm199900/cmstand/d/st000118/am/00118s05.htm.

Clarke, Charles. 2005a. "Letter from the Home Secretary to Rt Hon David Davis MP and Mark Oaten MP." House of Commons Select Committee on Home Affairs, Annex A: Written Evidence 2005–2006. July 15. http://www.publications.parliament.uk/pa/cm200506/cmselect/cmhaff/462/462we03.htm.

Clarke, Charles. 2005b. House of Commons Debates. Column 323, October 26. https://publications.parliament.uk/pa/cm200506/cmhansrd/vo051026/debtext/51026-08.htm#51026-08_spmin0.

Clarke, Charles. 2005c. House of Commons Debates. Column 326, October 26. https://publications.parliament.uk/pa/cm200506/cmhansrd/vo051026/debtext/51026-09.htm#51026-09_spnew8.

Clarke, Charles. 2005d. House of Commons Debates. Column 1256, July 20. https://publications.parliament.uk/pa/cm200506/cmhansrd/vo050720/debtext/50720-04.htm#50720-04_spmin0.

Clarke, Michael. 2018. *Terrorism and Counter-Terrorism in China: Domestic and Foreign Policy Dimensions.* Oxford: Oxford University Press.

Clarke, Peter. 2007. "Learning from Experience: Counter-Terrorism in the UK since 9/11: The Inaugural Colin Cramphorn Memorial Lecture." London: Policy Exchange.

Council of the European Union. 2007. "Revised Media Communication Strategy: European Union Strategy for Combating Radicalisation and Recruitment through Effective Communication of EU Values and Policies." 5469/3/07, March 28.

Committee on Homeland Security. 2007. "Fact Sheet Prepared by the Majority Staff: Understanding H.R. 1955: The Violent Radicalization and Homegrown Terrorism Prevention Act of 2007." December. https://www.hsdl.org/?view&did=481975.

Cole, David. 2003. *Enemy Aliens: Double Standards and Constitutional Freedoms in the War on Terrorism.* New York: New Press.

Cole, David. 2007–2008. "Rights over Borders: Transnational Constitutionalism and Guantanamo Bay." *Cato Supreme Court Review* 2007–2008: 47–61.

Cole, David. 2012. "The First Amendment's Borders: The Place of *Holder v. Humanitarian Law Project* in First Amendment Doctrine." *Harvard Law & Policy Review* 6, no. 1: 147–177.

Cole, David, and James X. Dempsey. 2006. *Terrorism and the Constitution: Sacrificing Civil Liberties in the Name of National Security.* 3rd edn. London: New Press.

Coles, Maurice Irfan. 2010. "When Hope and History Rhyme." Discussion Paper. The ICE Project. http://www.theiceproject.com/uploaded/files/Conceptual%20overview%20-%20When%20Hope%20and%20History%20Rhyme.pdf.

Colley, Linda. 1992. "Britishness and Otherness: An Argument." *Journal of British Studies* 31, no. 4: 309–329.

Colley, Linda. 2005. *Britons: Forging the Nation, 1707–1837.* 2nd edn. New Haven, CT: Yale University Press

Comey, James B. 2016. "Statement." Hearing before the US Senate Committee on Homeland Security and Governmental Affairs: Fifteen Years After 9/11: Threats to the Homeland. September 27. https://www.fbi.gov/news/testimony/fifteen-years-after-911-threats-to-the-homeland.

Commission of the European Communities. 2005. "Communication from the Commission to the European Parliament and the Council Concerning Terrorist Recruitment: Addressing the Factors Contributing to Violent Radicalisation Commission of the European Communities." COM(2005) 313 final, September

21. https://eur-lex.europa.eu/legal-content/EN/TXT/HTML/?uri=LEGISSUM:l14501&from=NL.

Connolly, William E. 1991. *Identity/Difference: Democratic Negotiations of Political Paradox*. Ithaca, NY: Cornell University Press.

Conway, Maura. 2017. "Determining the Role of the Internet in Violent Extremism and Terrorism: Six Suggestions for Progressing Research." *Studies in Conflict & Terrorism* 40, no. 1: 77–98.

Coolsaet, Rik. 2010. "EU Counterterrorism Strategy: Value Added or Chimera?" *International Affairs* 86, no. 4: 857–873.

Corera, Gordon. 2007. "Don't Look Now, Britain's Real Spooks Are Right Behind You." *Sunday Times*, December 2.

Cottee, Simon. 2015. "Why It's So Hard to Stop ISIS Propaganda." *The Atlantic*, March 2.

Couch, Cullen. 2010. "Q&A with Daniel Sutherland '85, National Counterterrorism Center." *UVA Lawyer*, University of Virginia Law School. http://www.law.virginia.edu/html/alumni/uvalawyer/spr10/counterterror.htm.

Couldry, Nick. 2003. "Media, Symbolic Power and the Limits of Bourdieu's Field Theory." Media@LSE Working Paper 2. London: Department of Media and Communications, London School of Economics and Political Science.

Counter Extremism Project. 2018. "Algeria: Extremism & Counter-Extremism." https://www.counterextremism.com/countries/algeria.

Cragin, R. Kim. 2014. "Resisting Violent Extremism: A Conceptual Model for Non-Radicalization." *Terrorism and Political Violence* 26, no. 2: 1–17.

Crelinsten, Ronald D. 1987. "Terrorism as Political Communication: The Relationship Between the Controller and the Controlled." In *Contemporary Research on Terrorism*, edited by Paul Wilkinson and Alasdair M. Stewart, 3–23. Aberdeen: University of Aberdeen Press.

Crenshaw, Martha. 1981. "The Causes of Terrorism." *Comparative Politics* 13, no. 4: 379–399.

Crenshaw, Martha. 2001. "Counterterrorism Policy and the Political Process." *Studies in Conflict & Terrorism* 24, no. 5: 329–337.

Crenshaw, Martha. 2011. *Explaining Terrorism: Causes, Processes, and Consequences*. Abingdon: Routledge.

Croft, Stuart. 2006. *Culture, Crisis and America's War on Terror*. Cambridge: Cambridge University Press.

Croft, Stuart. 2012. *Securitizing Islam: Identity and the Search for Security*. Cambridge: Cambridge University Press.

Croft, Stuart, and Cerwyn Moore. 2010. "The Evolution of Threat Narratives in the Age of Terror: Understanding Terrorist Threats in Britain." *International Affairs* 86, no. 4: 821–835.

Crone, Manni. 2016. "Radicalization Revisited: Violence, Politics and the Skills of the Body." *International Affairs* 92, no. 3: 587–604.

Crone, Manni, and Martin Harrow. 2011. "Homegrown Terrorism in the West." *Terrorism and Political Violence* 23, no. 4: 521–536.

Crook, Jennifer. 2008. "Why Words Matter in Council's Fight against Terrorism." *The Guardian*, October 14.

Cruickshank, Paul, and Mohannad Hage Ali. 2006. "Abu Musab Al Suri: Architect of the New Al Qaeda." *Studies in Conflict & Terrorism* 30, no. 1: 1–14.

CTITF (Counter-Terrorism Implementation Task Force). 2008. "First Report of the Working Group on Radicalisation and Extremism That Lead to Terrorism." New York: United Nations.

Dalgaard-Nielsen, Anja. 2010. "Violent Radicalization in Europe: What We Know and What We Do Not Know." *Studies in Conflict & Terrorism* 33, no. 9: 797–814.

Daniels, Roger. 1993. "United States Policy towards Asian Immigrants: Contemporary Developments in Historical Perspective." *International Journal* 48, no. 2: 310–334.

Daskal, Jennifer. 2018. "Microsoft Ireland, the CLOUD Act, and International Lawmaking 2.0." *Stanford Law Review Online* 71: 9–16.

Davies, Caroline. 2011. "Radical Muslim Jailed for Calling for Jihad against MPs." *The Guardian*, July 30.

Davies, Lynn. 2018. "Review of Educational Initiatives in Counter-Extremism Internationally: What Works?" Report 5. Gothenburg: Segerstedt Institute, University of Gothenburg.

Davis, Fergal. 2010. "The Human Rights Act and Juridification: Saving Democracy from Law." *Politics* 30, no. 2: 91–97.

Dawson, Lorne L. 2018. "The Demise of the Islamic State and the Fate of Its Western Foreign Fighters: Six Things to Consider." ICCT Policy Brief. The Hague: International Centre for Counter-Terrorism, June.

Daxecker, Ursula E., and Michael L. Hess. 2013. "Repression Hurts: Coercive Government Responses and the Demise of Terrorist Campaigns." *British Journal of Political Science* 43, no. 3: 559–577.

De Graaf, Beatrice, and Bob De Graaff. 2010. "Bringing Politics Back In: The Introduction of the 'Performative Power' of Counterterrorism." *Critical Studies on Terrorism* 3, no. 2: 261–275.

De Londras, Fiona, and Fergal F. Davis. 2010. "Controlling the Executive in Times of Terrorism: Competing Perspectives on Effective Oversight Mechanisms." *Oxford Journal of Legal Studies* 30, no. 1: 19–47.

Dean, Mitchell. 1999. *Governmentality: Power and Rule in Modern Society*. London: Sage.

Dearden, Lizzie. 2017. "Manchester Attacker 'Made Bomb in Four Days.'" *The Independent*, June 3.

Della Porta, Donatella, and Gary Lafree. 2012. "Guest Editorial: Processes of Radicalization and De-Radicalization." *International Journal of Conflict and Violence* 6, no. 1: 4–10.

Demant, Froukje, Marieke Slootman, Frank Buijs, and Jean Tillie. 2008. "Decline and Disengagement." Amsterdam: Institute for Migration and Ethnic Studies.

Denham, John. 2001. "Building Cohesive Communities: A Report of the Ministerial Group on Public Order and Community Cohesion." London: Home Office.

Deutsch Islam Konferenz. 2013. "What Has Been Happening in the German Islam Conference since 2006?" http://www.wir-sind-bund.de/SharedDocs/Anlagen/DIK/EN/Downloads/Plenum/social-polarisation.html;jsessionid=163E88C720CEA2E4E854832D8E9FECB4.1_cid294?nn=3842444.

Dicey, Albert Venn. 1962. *Introduction to the Study of the Law of the Constitution*. 10th edn. London: Macmillan.

Dixon, Paul. 2009. "'Hearts and Minds'? British Counter-Insurgency Strategy in Northern Ireland." *Journal of Strategic Studies* 32, no. 3: 445–474.

Dlugoleski, Deirdre. 2010. "Religious Instruction for Counter-Terrorism: Morocco's Moderate Imams." *Yale Globalist*, December 19. http://tyglobalist.org/onlinecontent/blogs/religious-instruction-for-counter-terrorism-moroccos-moderate-imams/.

Dodd, Vikram. 2009. "Government Anti-Terrorism Strategy 'Spies' on Innocent." *The Guardian*, October 16.

Donohue, Laura K. 2006. "Anglo-American Privacy and Surveillance." *Journal of Criminal Law and Criminology* 96, no. 3: 1059–1208.

Donohue, Laura K. 2008. *The Cost of Counterterrorism: Power, Politics, and Liberty*. Cambridge: Cambridge University Press.

Donohue, Laura K. 2011. "The Limits of National Security." *American Criminal Law Review* 48, no. 4: 1573–1756.

Doornbos, Caitlin. 2016. "Transcripts of 911 Calls Reveal Pulse Shooter's Terrorist Motives." *Orlando Sentinel*, September 22. https://www.orlandosentinel.com/news/pulse-orlando-nightclub-shooting/os-911-calls-released-orlando-shooting-20170922-story.html.

Doyon, Jérôme. 2019. "'Counter-Extremism' in Xinjiang: Understanding China's Community-Focused Counter-Terrorism Tactics." *War on the Rocks*, January 14.

Dragu, Tiberiu, and Mattias Polborn. 2014. "The Rule of Law in the Fight against Terrorism." *American Journal of Political Science* 58, no. 2: 511–525.

DutchNews.Nl. 2014. "Dutch Somali Woman Faces Deportation to US over Terrorist Funding." July 24.

Dyson, Kenneth H. F. 1980. *The State Tradition in Western Europe: A Study of an Idea and Institution*. Oxford: Martin Robertson.

Dyzenhaus, David. 2008. "Introduction: Legality in a Time of Emergency." *Windsor Review of Legal and Social Issues* 24: 1–4.

Eagle, Angela. 2002. House of Commons Committee. Column 56, April 30. https://publications.parliament.uk/pa/cm200102/cmstand/e/st020430/pm/20430s15.htm

Edwards, Charlie, and Luke Gribbon. 2013. "Pathways to Violent Extremism in the Digital Era." *RUSI Journal* 158, no. 5: 40–47.

El-Katiri, Mohammed. 2013. "The Institutionalisation of Religious Affairs: Religious Reform in Morocco." *Journal of North African Studies* 18, no. 1: 53–69.

Elkins, Caroline. 2005. *Imperial Reckoning: The Untold Story of Britain's Gulag in Kenya*. New York: Henry Holt and Company.

Elsea, Jennifer K., and Michael John Garcia. 2016. "Wartime Detention Provisions in Recent Defense Authorization Legislation." CRS Report for Congress R42143. Washington, DC: Congressional Research Service, March 14.

Erviani, N. K. 2013. "Bali Residents Told to Remain Vigilant on Terrorism." *Jakarta Post*, June 6.

Etzioni, Amitai. 2007. "Citizenship Tests: A Comparative, Communitarian Perspective." *Political Quarterly* 78, no. 3: 353–363.

Everson, Michelle. 2003. "'Subjects,' or 'Citizens of Erewhon'? Law and Non-Law in the Development of a 'British Citizenship.'" *Citizenship Studies* 7, no. 1: 57–83.

Ewing, K. D., and Joo-Cheong Tham. 2008. "The Continuing Futility of the Human Rights Act." *Public Law* Winter: 668–693.

Express. 2013. "Handbook Explains How to Be British." January 28. https://www.express.co.uk/news/uk/373827/Handbook-explains-how-to-be-British.

Farr, Charles. 2014. "Evidence to the House of Commons Select Committee on Home Affairs, Enquiry into Counterterrorism. Question 187." Norwich: Stationery Office.

Farrell, Theo. 2002. "Constructivist Security Studies: Portrait of a Research Program." *International Studies Review* 4, no. 1: 49–72.

Farwell, James P. 2014. "The Media Strategy of ISIS." *Survival* 56, no. 6: 49–55.

FBI (Federal Bureau of Investigation). 2000. "Terrorism in the United States 1999: 30 Years of Terrorism; a Special Retrospective Edition." Washington, DC: Federal Bureau of Investigation.

FBI (Federal Bureau of Investigation). 2012. "Four Men Charged for Conspiracy to Provide Material Support to Terrorism." Press Release, Los Angeles Division, November 19. https://www.fbi.gov/losangeles/press-releases/2012/four-men-charged-for-conspiracy-to-provide-material-support-to-terrorism.

FCO (Foreign and Commonwealth Office). 2007. "Engaging with the Islamic World Programme." December. https://webarchive.nationalarchives.gov.uk/20080207191151/http://www.fco.gov.uk/servlet/Front/Print?pagename=OpenMarket/Xcelerate/ShowPage&c=Page&cid=1070989564809&print=true.

Fearon, James, and Alexander Wendt. 2002. "Rationalism v Constructivism: A Skeptical View." In *Handbook of International Relations*, edited by Walter Carlsnaes, Thomas Risse, and Beth A. Simmons, 52–72. London: Sage.

Fedarcyk, Janice. 2007. "Testimony." Hearing before the Subcommittee on Intelligence, Information Sharing, and Terrorism Risk Assessment of the US House of Representatives Committee on Homeland Security: Radicalization, Information Sharing and Community Outreach: Protecting the Homeland from Homegrown Terror. April 5.

Federal Office for the Protection of the Constitution. 2007. "Integration as a Means to Prevent Extremism and Terrorism: Typology of Islamist Radicalisation and Recruitment." Cologne: Federal Office for the Protection of the Constitution.

Feinstein, Dianne. 2011. *Congressional Record*. Senate. Vol. 157, No. 181, November 29. https://www.congress.gov/112/crec/2011/11/29/CREC-2011-11-29.pdf.

Feldblum, Miriam. 1998. "Reconfiguring Citizenship in Western Europe." In *Challenge to the Nation-State: Immigration in Western Europe and the United States*, edited by Christian Joppke, 231–270. Oxford: Oxford University Press.

Fenwick, Helen. 2002. "The Anti-Terrorism, Crime and Security Act 2001: A Proportionate Response to 11 September?" *Modern Law Review* 65, no. 5: 724–762.

Fenwick, Helen. 2016. "Responding to the ISIS Threat: Extending Coercive Non-Trial-Based Measures in the Counter-Terrorism and Security Act 2015." *International Review of Law, Computers & Technology* 30, no. 3: 174–190.

Fernandez, Alberto. 2012. "Testimony." Hearing before the Subcommittee on Terrorism, Nonproliferation, and Trade of the US Congress House Committee on Foreign Affairs: The State Department's Center for Strategic Counterterrorism Communications: Mission, Operations, and Impact, August 2.

Fethi, Nazim. 2006. "Algerian Government Curbs Extreme Religious Practices." *Magharebia*, December 22.

Fethi, Nazim. 2007. "Algerian Imams to Be Kept Out of Politics." *Magharebia*, March 15.

Filkin, Lord Geoffrey. 2002. House of Lords Debates. Column 282 183, October 9. https://api.parliament.uk/historic-hansard/lords/2002/oct/09/nationality-immigration-and-asylum-bill

Finn, John E. 2010. "Counterterrorism Regimes and the Rule of Law: The Effects of Emergency Legislation on Separation of Powers, Civil Liberties and Other Fundamental Constitutional Norms." In *The Consequences of Counterterrorism*, edited by Martha Crenshaw, 33–94. New York: Russell Sage Foundation.

Flathman, Richard E. 1993. "Legitimacy." In *A Companion to Contemporary Political Philosophy*, edited by Robert Goodin and Philip Pettit, 527–533. Oxford: Blackwell.

Foley, Frank. 2009. "Reforming Counterterrorism: Institutions and Organizational Routines in Britain and France." *Security Studies* 18, no. 3: 435–478.

Foley, Frank. 2013. *Countering Terrorism in Britain and France: Institutions, Norms, and the Shadow of the Past*. New York: Cambridge University Press.

Folk, William Anders. 2011. "Testimony." Hearing before the US House of Representatives Committee on Homeland Security: Al-Shabaab: Recruitment and Radicalization within the Muslim American Community and the Threat to the Homeland. July 27.

Fontana, David. 2002. "A Case for the Twenty-First Century Constitutional Canon: Schneiderman v. United States." *Connecticut Law Review* 35, no. 1: 35–90.

Fox, Jo. 2012. "Careless Talk: Tensions within British Domestic Propaganda during the Second World War." *Journal of British Studies* 51, no. 4: 936–966.

Fox, Jonathan. 2001. "Religion as an Overlooked Element of International Relations." *International Studies Review* 3, no. 3: 53–73.

Fox News. 2010. "Lieberman Aims Legislation at Terrorists." May 6.

Freeman, Gary P. 1979. *Immigrant Labor and Racial Conflict in Industrial Societies: The French and British Experience, 1945–1975*. Princeton, NJ: Princeton University Press.

Frickey, Philip P. 1995–1996. "The Fool on the Hill: Congressional Findings, Constitutional Adjudication, and *United States v. Lopez*." *Case Western Reserve Law Review* 46, no. 3: 695–730.

Fripp, Eric, Rowena Moffat, and Ellis Wilford, eds. 2014. *The Law and Practice of Expulsion and Exclusion from the United Kingdom: Deportation, Removal, Exclusion and Deprivation of Citizenship*. London: Bloomsbury Publishing.

Gearty, Conor. 2005. "11 September 2001, Counter-Terrorism, and the Human Rights Act." *Journal of Law and Society* 32, no. 1: 18–33.

Geddes, Marc. 2019. "The Explanatory Potential of 'Dilemmas': Bridging Practices and Power to Understand Political Change in Interpretive Political Science." *Political Studies Review* 17, no. 3: 239–254.

General Intelligence and Security Service of the Netherlands. 2010. "Resilience and Resistance: Current Trends and Developments in Salafism in the Netherlands." The Hague: General Intelligence and Security Service. https://www.yumpu.com/en/document/read/13852290/resilience-and-resistance-aivd.

Genkin, Michael, and Alexander Gutfraind. 2011. "How Do Terrorist Cells Self-Assemble: Insights from an Agent-Based Model of Radicalization." SSRN Scholarly Paper. Rochester, NY: Social Science Research Network.

Gerschewski, Johannes. 2013. "The Three Pillars of Stability: Legitimation, Repression, and Co-Optation in Autocratic Regimes." *Democratization* 20, no. 1: 13–38.

Gerstein, Josh. 2012. "Conference Committee Drops Ban on Indefinite Detention of Americans." *POLITICO*, December 18. https://www.politico.com/blogs/under-the-radar/2012/12/conference-committee-drops-ban-on-indefinite-detention-152352.html.

Gersten, David. 2007. "Testimony." Hearing before the Subcommittee on Intelligence, Information Sharing, and Terrorism Risk Assessment of the US House of

Representatives Committee on Homeland Security: Radicalization, Information Sharing and Community Outreach: Protecting the Homeland from Homegrown Terror. April 5.

Ghanem, Dalia. 2018. "State-Owned Islam in Algeria Faces Stiff Competition." Carnegie Middle East Center, March 13. https://carnegie-mec.org/2018/03/13/state-owned-islam-in-algeria-faces-stiff-competition-pub-75770.

Gibney, Matthew J. 2013. "'A Very Transcendental Power': Denaturalisation and the Liberalisation of Citizenship in the United Kingdom." *Political Studies* 61, no. 3: 637–655.

Giddens, Anthony. 1998. *The Third Way: The Renewal of Social Democracy*. Cambridge: Polity Press.

Giglio, Mike. 2014. "One Man's Journey to Become the First American Suicide Bomber in Syria." *BuzzFeed News*, August 6. https://www.buzzfeednews.com/article/mikegiglio/one-mans-journey-to-become-the-first-american-suicide-bomber.

Gill, Paul, James A. Piazza, and John Horgan. 2016. "Counterterrorism Killings and Provisional IRA Bombings, 1970–1998." *Terrorism and Political Violence* 28, no. 3: 473–496.

Giraldi, Philip. 2007. "The Violent Radicalization and Homegrown Terrorism Prevention Act." *HuffPost*, November 26. https://www.huffpost.com/entry/the-violent-radicalizatio_b_74091.

Glassman, James K. 2010. "How to Win the War of Ideas." *Foreign Policy*, March 10. https://foreignpolicy.com/2010/03/10/how-to-win-the-war-of-ideas/.

Government of Canada. 2004. "Securing an Open Society: Canada's National Security Policy." Ottawa, Ontario: Privy Council Office. http://publications.gc.ca/site/eng/9.686980/publication.html.

Government of Canada. 2013. "Building Resilience against Terrorism: Canada's Counter-Terrorism Strategy." Ottawa, Ontario: Government of Canada. https://www.publicsafety.gc.ca/cnt/rsrcs/pblctns/rslnc-gnst-trrrsm/index-en.aspx.

Government of Denmark. 2009. "A Common and Safe Future: An Action Plan to Prevent Extremist Views and Radicalisation among Young People." Albertslund: Government of Denmark, January. https://strongcitiesnetwork.org/en/wp-content/uploads/sites/5/2017/02/A-common-and-safe-future-Danish-Action-Plan-to-prevent-extremism.pdf.

Government of Denmark. 2016. "Preventing and Countering Extremism and Radicalisation: National Action Plan." http://uim.dk/publikationer/preventing-and-countering-extremism-and-radicalisation.

Goldirova, Renata. 2007. "Brussels Questions EU Capitals Over Approach to Islam." *euobserver*, July 6. https://euobserver.com/justice/24436.

Goldsmith, Jack, and Cass R. Sunstein. 2002. "Military Tribunals and Legal Culture: What a Difference Sixty Years Makes." *Constitutional Commentary* 19, no. 1: 261–289.

Goldstein, Robert Justin. 2001. *Political Repression in Modern America from 1870 to 1976*. Chicago: University of Illinois Press.

Goodwin, Matthew. 2013. "The Roots of Extremism: The English Defence League and the Counter-Jihad Challenge." London: Royal Institute of International Affairs.

Goodwin, Matthew J., Vidhya Ramalingam, and Rachel Briggs. 2012. "The New Radical Right: Violent and Non-Violent Movements in Europe." London: Institute for Strategic Defence.

REFERENCES 245

Goulbourne, Harry. 1991. *Ethnicity and Nationalism in Post-Imperial Britain*. Cambridge: Cambridge University Press.
Graham, Lindsey. 2011a. *Congressional Record*. Senate. Vol. 157, No. 183, December 1. https://www.congress.gov/112/crec/2011/12/01/CREC-2011-12-01.pdf.
Graham, Lindsey. 2011b. *Congressional Record*. Senate. Vol. 157, Part 13, December 1. https://www.govinfo.gov/content/pkg/CRECB-2011-pt13/html/CRECB-2011-pt13-Pg18591.htm.
Graham, Lindsey. 2011c. *Congressional Record*. Senate. Vol. 157, No. 176, November 17. https://www.congress.gov/112/crec/2011/11/17/CREC-2011-11-17.pdf.
Greenwald, Glenn. 2012. "Federal Court Enjoins NDAA." *Salon*, May 17. https://www.salon.com/2012/05/16/federal_court_enjoins_ndaa/.
Guiraudon, Virginie. 2013. "Citizenship." In *Bourdieu in International Relations: Rethinking Key Concepts in IR*, edited by Rebecca Adler-Nissen, 207–220. Abingdon: Routledge.
Gunning, Jeroen. 2007. "A Case for Critical Terrorism Studies?" *Government and Opposition* 42, no. 3: 363–393.
Gunning, Jeroen. 2009. "Social Movement Theory and the Study of Terrorism." In *Critical Terrorism Studies: A New Research Agenda*, edited by Richard Jackson, Marie Breen Smyth, and Jeroen Gunning, 170–191. Abingdon: Routledge.
Gunning, Jeroen, and Richard Jackson. 2011. "What's So 'Religious' about 'Religious Terrorism'?" *Critical Studies on Terrorism* 4, no. 3: 369–388.
Gutkowski, Stacey. 2011. "Secularism and the Politics of Risk: Britain's Prevent Agenda, 2005–2009." *International Relations* 25, no. 3: 346–362.
Haddad, Margot. 2015. "France Government Fighting Online War against Jihadist Youth Recruiting." *CNN*, February 23. https://www.cnn.com/2015/02/23/europe/france-anti-jihadist-campaign/index.html.
Halliday, Josh. 2016. "Almost 4,000 People Were Referred to UK Deradicalisation Scheme Last Year." *The Guardian*, May 21.
Halverson, Jeffry R., H. L. Goodall Jr., and Steven R. Corman. 2011. *Master Narratives of Islamist Extremism*. New York: Palgrave Macmillan.
Hamdan, Ali Nehme. 2016. "Breaker of Barriers? Notes on the Geopolitics of the Islamic State in Iraq and Sham." *Geopolitics* 21, no. 3: 605–627.
Hamilton, Fiona. 2016. "Surge in Far-Right Extremism as Spotlight Fell on Jihadist Threat." *The Times*, November 24.
Hansen, Lene. 2006. *Security as Practice: Discourse Analysis and the Bosnian War*. Abingdon: Routledge.
Hansen, Randall. 1999. "Migration, Citizenship and Race in Europe: Between Incorporation and Exclusion." *European Journal of Political Research* 35, no. 4: 415–444.
Harman, Jane. 2007a. "Markup Session for H.R. 1955, the Homegrown Terrorism Prevention Act of 2007." Video recording. US House of Representatives Committee on Homeland Security Subcommittee on Intelligence Information Sharing and Terrorism Risk Assessment.
Harman, Jane. 2007b. "Opening Statement." Hearing before the Subcommittee on Intelligence, Information Sharing, and Terrorism Risk Assessment of the US House of Representatives Committee on Homeland Security: Radicalization, Information Sharing and Community Outreach: Protecting the Homeland from Homegrown Terror. April 5.
Harman, Jane. 2007c. "Testimony." Hearing before the Subcommittee on Intelligence Information Sharing and Terrorism Risk Assessment of the House of Representatives

Committee on Homeland Security: Radicalization, Information Sharing and Community Outreach: Protecting the Homeland from Homegrown Terror. June 14.

Harman, Jane. 2013. "The Other War on Terror." *Foreign Policy*, May 24. https://foreignpolicy.com/2013/05/24/the-other-war-on-terror/.

Harris-Hogan, Shandon. 2013. "Anatomy of a Terrorist Cell: A Study of the Network Uncovered in Sydney in 2005." *Behavioral Sciences of Terrorism and Political Aggression* 5, no. 2: 137–154.

Hashim, Ahmed S. 2006. *Insurgency and Counter-Insurgency in Iraq*. Ithaca, NY: Cornell University Press.

Hassan, A. 2010. "Morocco Fights Islamist Extremism with Sufism." *Al-Arabiya News*, September 26. http://www.alarabiya.net/articles/2010/09/26/120366.html.

Heale, M. J. 1990. *American Anti-Communism: Combating the Enemy Within, 1830–1970*. Baltimore, MD: Johns Hopkins University Press.

Heartland Democracy. 2016. "Strengthening Community Resilience in the Heartland: Collaboration, Education and Empowerment to Prevent Violent Extremism." Application for Funding, Department of Homeland Security Countering Violent Extremism Grants. Submitted September 6. Application No. EMW-2016-CA-APP-00401.

Heath, Anthony F., Stephen D. Fisher, David Sanders, and Maria Sobolewska. 2011. "Ethnic Heterogeneity in the Social Bases of Voting at the 2010 British General Election." *Journal of Elections, Public Opinion & Parties* 21, no. 2: 255–277.

Heath-Kelly, Charlotte. 2012. "Reinventing Prevention or Exposing the Gap? False Positives in UK Terrorism Governance and the Quest for Pre-Emption." *Critical Studies on Terrorism* 5, no. 1: 69–87.

Heath-Kelly, Charlotte. 2013. "Counter-Terrorism and the Counterfactual: Producing the 'Radicalisation' Discourse and the UK PREVENT Strategy." *British Journal of Politics and International Relations* 15, no. 3: 394–415.

Heath-Kelly, Charlotte. 2017. "The Geography of Pre-Criminal Space: Epidemiological Imaginations of Radicalisation Risk in the UK Prevent Strategy, 2007–2017." *Critical Studies on Terrorism* 10, no. 2: 297–319.

Hegemann, Hendrik. 2011. "Governing the Fight against Terrorism: Comprehensive Counterterrorism Cooperation and the Contested Agency of International Organizations." Hamburg: Institute for Peace Research and Security Policy at the University of Hamburg.

Hegghammer, Thomas. 2006. "Global Jihadism after the Iraq War." *Middle East Journal* 60, no. 1: 11–32.

Hegghammer, Thomas. 2013. "Should I Stay or Should I Go? Explaining Variation in Western Jihadists' Choice between Domestic and Foreign Fighting." *American Political Science Review* 107, no. 1: 1–15.

Heller, Thomas. 1997. "Modernity, Membership, and Multiculturalism." *Stanford Humanities Review* 5, no. 2: 2–69.

Hellmich, Christina. 2005. "Al-Qaeda—Terrorists, Hypocrites, Fundamentalists? The View From Within." *Third World Quarterly* 26, no. 1: 39–54.

Hellmich, Christina. 2008. "Creating the Ideology of Al Qaeda: From Hypocrites to Salafi-Jihadists." *Studies in Conflict & Terrorism* 31, no. 2: 111–124.

Hellmuth, Dorle. 2015. "Countering Jihadi Terrorists and Radicals the French Way." *Studies in Conflict & Terrorism* 38, no. 12: 979–997.

Helmus, Todd C., and Kurt Klein. 2018. "Assessing Outcomes of Online Campaigns Countering Violent Extremism: A Case Study of the Redirect Method." Santa Monica, CA: RAND Corporation.

Helmus, Todd C., Erin York, and Peter Chalk. 2013. *Promoting Online Voices for Countering Violent Extremism*. Santa Monica, CA: RAND Corporation.

Heng, Yee-Kuang, and Kenneth McDonagh. 2011. "After the 'War on Terror': Regulatory States, Risk Bureaucracies and the Risk-Based Governance of Terror." *International Relations* 25, no. 3: 313–329.

Herman, Susan N. 2011. *Taking Liberties: The War on Terror and the Erosion of American Democracy*. Oxford: Oxford University Press.

Hickman, Mary J., Lyn Thomas, Henri C. Nickels, and Sara Silvestri. 2012. "Social Cohesion and the Notion of 'Suspect Communities': A Study of the Experiences and Impacts of Being 'Suspect' for Irish Communities and Muslim Communities in Britain." *Critical Studies on Terrorism* 5, no. 1: 89–106.

HM Government. 1998. "Legislation against Terrorism: A Consultation Paper." Cm 4178. London: Stationery Office.

HM Government. 2003. "Memorandum Submitted by the Home Office." https://publications.parliament.uk/pa/cm200304/cmselect/cmhaff/886/886we02.htm.

HM Government. 2004a. *Life in the United Kingdom: A Journey to Citizenship*. 2nd edn. London: Stationery Office.

HM Government. 2004b. "Life in the United Kingdom: A Journey to Citizenship." Norwich: Home Office.

HM Government. 2004c. "Strength in Diversity: Towards a Community Cohesion and Race Equality Strategy." London: Home Office.

HM Government. 2004d. "Memorandum Submitted by Association of Chief Police officers. https://publications.parliament.uk/pa/cm200405/cmselect/cmhaff/165ii/165we02.htm.

HM Government. 2005a. "Improving Opportunity, Strengthening Society: The Government's Strategy to Increase Race Equality and Community Cohesion." Norwich: Home Office.

HM Government. 2005b. "Integration Matters: A National Strategy for Refugee Integration." Norwich: Home Office.

HM Government. 2006. "Countering International Terrorism—The UK's Strategy." London: Home Office.

HM Government. 2007a. "Preventing Extremism: Winning Hearts and Minds." London: Department for Communities and Local Government.

HM Government. 2007b. "Preventing Violent Extremism Pathfinder Fund: Guidance Notes." London: Department for Communities and Local Government.

HM Government. 2008a. "The Prevent Strategy: A Guide for Local Partners in England." London: Department for Communities and Local Government.

HM Government. 2008b. "Preventing Violent Extremism: A Strategy for Delivery." Office for Security and Counter-Terrorism. Norwich: Stationery Office.

HM Government. 2008c. "Preventing Violent Extremism: Next Steps for Communities". London: Department for Communities and Local Government.

HM Government. 2008d. "Preventing Violent Extremism Pathfinder Fund: Mapping of Project Activities 2007/2008." London: Department for Communities and Local Government.

HM Government. 2009a. "Pursue Prevent Protect Prepare: The United Kingdom's Strategy for Countering International Terrorism." Norwich: Stationery Office.

HM Government. 2009b. "2007–8 Citizenship Survey: Identity and Values Topic Report." London: Department for Communities and Local Government.

HM Government. 2009c. "Delivering the Prevent Strategy: An Updated Guide for Local Partners." London: Home Office.

HM Government. 2010. "The Training and Development of Muslim Faith Leaders." London: Department for Communities and Local Government.

HM Government. 2011a. "*Prevent* Strategy." CM8092. Norwich: Stationery Office. https://assets.publishing.service.gov.uk/government/uploads/system/uploads/attachment_data/file/97976/prevent-strategy-review.pdf.

HM Government. 2011b. "CONTEST: The United Kingdom's Strategy for Countering Terrorism." Norwich: Stationery Office.

HM Government. 2013a. "CONTEST: The United Kingdom's Strategy for Countering International Terrorism." Norwich: Stationery Office.

HM Government. 2013b. "CONTEST Annual Report 2012." Norwich: Home Office.

HM Government. 2013c. "Tackling Extremism in the UK: Report from the Prime Minister's Task Force on Tackling Radicalisation and Extremism." London: Cabinet Office. https://www.gov.uk/government/publications/tackling-extremism-in-the-uk-report-by-the-extremism-taskforce.

HM Government. 2015a. "Prevent Duty Guidance: For England and Wales." https://www.rbkc.gov.uk/pdf/Prevent_Duty_Guidance_England_Wales.pdf.

HM Government. 2015b. "PM's Extremism Taskforce: Tackling Extremism in Universities and Colleges Top of the Agenda." Press Release, September 17. https://www.gov.uk/government/news/pms-extremism-taskforce-tackling-extremism-in-universities-and-colleges-top-of-the-agenda.

HM Government. 2017. "Individuals Referred to and Supported through the *Prevent* Programme, April 2015 to March 2016." Statistical Bulletin 23/17. London: Home Office.

Hoffman, Bruce. 1995. "'Holy Terror': The Implications of Terrorism Motivated by a Religious Imperative." *Studies in Conflict & Terrorism* 18, no. 4: 271–284.

Hoffman, Bruce. 1998. *Inside Terrorism*. New York: Columbia University Press.

Hoffman, Bruce. 2004. "The Changing Face of Al Qaeda and the Global War on Terrorism." *Studies in Conflict & Terrorism* 27, no. 6: 549–560.

Hoffman, Bruce. 2008. "The Myth of Grass-Roots Terrorism: Why Osama Bin Laden Still Matters." *Foreign Affairs* 87, no. 3: 133–138.

Hoffman, Bruce. 2009. "Radicalization and Subversion: Al Qaeda and the 7 July 2005 Bombings and the 2006 Airline Bombing Plot." *Studies in Conflict & Terrorism* 32, no. 12: 1100–1116.

Home Office. 2002. *Secure Borders, Safe Haven: Integration with Diversity in Modern Britain*. CM5387. Norwich: Stationery Office.

Home Office. 2006. "Countering International Terrorism: The United Kingdom's Strategy." CM6888. Policy Paper. London: HM Government, July.

Home Office. 2011. "Prevent Strategy." Cm.8092. Policy Paper, London. HM Government, June.

Home Office. 2017. "Individuals Referred to and Supported through the Prevent Programme, April 2015 to March 2016." Statistical Bulletin 23/17. London: Home Office.

House of Commons Communities and Local Government Committee. 2010. "Preventing Violent Extremism: Sixth Report of Session 2009-10." HC 65. London: Stationery Office.

House of Commons Home Affairs Committee. 2005. "Terrorism and Community Relations: Sixth Report of Session 2004–05: Volume I." HC 165-1. London: Stationery Office.

House of Commons Home Affairs Committee. 2009. "Project CONTEST: The Government's Counter-Terrorism Strategy: Ninth Report of Session 2008–09." HC 212. London: Stationery Office.

House of Commons Home Affairs Committee. 2012. "Roots of Violent Radicalisation: Nineteenth Report of Session 2010–12: Volume I." HC 1446. London: Stationery Office.

House of Commons Home Affairs Committee. 2016. "Radicalisation: The Counter-Narrative and Identifying the Tipping Point: Eighth Report of Session 2016–17." HC 135. London: Stationery Office.

House of Lords House of Commons Joint Committee on Human Rights. 2005 "Counter-Terrorism Policy and Human Rights: Terrorism Bill and Related Matters: Third Report of Session 2005–06." HL Paper 75-1, HC 561-1. London: Stationery Office.

Hovington, Brett. 2010. "Testimony." Hearing before the Subcommittee on Intelligence, Information Sharing and Terrorism Risk Assessment of the US House of Representatives Committee on Homeland Security: Working with Communities to Disrupt Terror Plots. March 17.

Howells, Kim. 2007. House of Commons Debates. Column 831W, December 13. https://publications.parliament.uk/pa/cm200708/cmhansrd/cm071213/text/71213w0017.htm#0712147002028.

Homeland Security Advisory Council. 2016. "Countering Violent Extremism (CVE) Subcommittee: Interim Report and Recommendations." Washington, DC: US Department of Homeland Security, June.

Human Rights Watch. 2011. "US: Refusal to Veto Detainee Bill A Historic Tragedy for Rights." December 14. https://www.hrw.org/news/2011/12/14/us-refusal-veto-detainee-bill-historic-tragedy-rights.

Human Rights Watch. 2014. "France: Counterterrorism Bill Threatens Rights." October 9. https://www.hrw.org/news/2014/10/09/france-counterterrorism-bill-threatens-rights.

Human Rights Watch and American Civil Liberties Union. 2005. "Witness to Abuse: Human Rights Abuses under the Martial Witness Law since September 11." New York: Human Rights Watch and American Civil Liberties Union.

Humphrey, Michael. 2013. "Migration, Security and Insecurity." *Journal of Intercultural Studies* 34, no. 2: 178–195.

Huq, Aziz Z., Tom R. Tyler, and Stephen J. Schulhofer. 2011. "Mechanisms for Eliciting Cooperation in Counterterrorism Policing: Evidence from the United Kingdom." *Journal of Empirical Legal Studies* 8, no. 4: 728–761.

Hurd, Elizabeth Shakman. 2009. *The Politics of Secularism in International Relations*. Princeton, NJ: Princeton University Press.

Hurd, Ian. 1999. "Legitimacy and Authority in International Politics." *International Organization* 53, no. 2: 379–408.

Husband, Charles, and Yunis Alam. 2011. *Social Cohesion and Counter-Terrorism: A Policy Contradiction?* Bristol: Policy Press.

Husu, Hanna-Mari. 2013. "Bourdieu and Social Movements: Considering Identity Movements in Terms of Field, Capital and Habitus." *Social Movement Studies* 12, no. 3: 264–279.

Iaccino, Ludovica. 2014. "Saudi Arabian Online Liberal Activist Raif Badawi Sentenced to 1,000 Lashes." *International Business Times UK*, May 8.

ICG (International Crisis Group). 2007. "'Deradicalisation' and Indonesian Prisons." Report 142, November 19. https://www.crisisgroup.org/asia/south-east-asia/indonesia/deradicalisation-and-indonesian-prisons.

Idoumou, R. O. 2012. "Mauritania Mulls Internet Monitoring to Counter Extremism Internet Monitoring." *Magharebia*. July 5.

Ilan, Jonathan, and Sveinung Sandberg. 2019. "How 'Gangsters' become Jihadists: Bourdieu, Criminology and the Crime–Terrorism Nexus." *European Journal of Criminology*, February 15. https://doi.org/10.1177/1477370819828936.

Ingram, Haroro J. 2017. "Learning from ISIS's Virtual Propaganda War for Western Muslims: A Comparison of *Inspire* and *Dabiq*." In *Terrorists' Use of the Internet: Assessment and Response*, edited by Maura Conway, Lee Jarvis, Orla Lehane, Stuart Macdonald, and Lella Nouri, 170–182. Amsterdam: IOS Press.

Innes, Martin. 2006. "Policing Uncertainty: Countering Terror through Community Intelligence and Democratic Policing." *The Annals of the American Academy of Political and Social Science* 605, no. 1: 222–241.

Institute for Strategic Dialogue. 2008. "The Role of Civil Society in Counterradicalisation and De-Radicalisation." A Working Paper of the Europe and Policy Planner's Network on Countering Radicalisation and Polarisation. London: Institute for Strategic Dialogue.

Intelligence and Security Committee. 2006a. *Intelligence and Security Committee Annual Report 2005–2006*. London: Stationery Office.

Intelligence and Security Committee. 2006b. "Report into the London Terrorist Attacks on 7 July 2005." Cm 6785. Norwich: Stationery Office.

Intelligence and Security Committee. 2014. "Report on the Intelligence Relating to the Murder of Fusilier Lee Rigby." HC 795. London: Stationery Office, November 25.

Ip, John. 2011. "The Supreme Court and House of Lords in the War on Terror: *Inter Arma Silent Leges*?" *Michigan State University College of Law Journal of International Law* 19, no. 1: 1–61.

Ip, John. 2013. "The Reform of Counterterrorism Stop and Search after *Gillan v United Kingdom*." *Human Rights Law Review* 13, no. 4: 729–760.

IPAC (Institute for Policy Analysis of Conflict). 2014. "Countering Violent Extremism in Indonesia: Need for a Rethink." Jakarta: IPAC.

Isacson, Zann. 2018. "Combating Terrorism Online: Possible Actors and Their Roles." Lawfare, September 2. https://www.lawfareblog.com/combatting-terrorism-online-possible-actors-and-their-roles.

Islam and Citizenship Education. 2010. "Citizenship Curriculum." http://www.theiceproject.com/training-package-contents.

Jackson, Brian A. 2009. *Considering the Creation of a Domestic Intelligence Agency in the United States: Lessons from the Experiences of Australia, Canada, France, Germany, and the United Kingdom*. Santa Monica, CA: RAND Corporation.

Jackson, Brian A., and Bryce Loidolt. 2013. "Considering Al-Qa'ida's Innovation Doctrine: From Strategic Texts to 'Innovation in Practice.'" *Terrorism and Political Violence* 25, no. 2: 284–310.

Jackson, Richard. 2005. *Writing the War on Terrorism: Language, Politics and Counter-Terrorism*. Manchester: Manchester University Press.
Jackson, Richard, Marie Breen Smyth, and Jeroen Gunning, eds. 2009. *Critical Terrorism Studies: A New Research Agenda*. Abingdon: Routledge.
Jenkins, Brian. 2007a. "Testimony." Hearing before the Subcommittee on Intelligence, Information Sharing, and Terrorism Risk Assessment of the US House of Representatives Committee on Homeland Security: Radicalization, Information Sharing and Community Outreach: Protecting the Homeland from Homegrown Terror. April 5.
Jenkins, Brian. 2007b. "Testimony." Hearing before the Subcommittee on Intelligence, Information Sharing, and Terrorism Risk Assessment of the US House of Representatives Committee on Homeland Security: Jihadist Radicalization and Recruitment. June 14.
Jenkins, Roy. 1967. "Racial Equality in Britain." In *Essays and Speeches by Roy Jenkins*, edited by Anthony Lester, 262–269. London: Collins.
Joes, Anthony James. 2004. *The History and Politics of Counterinsurgency: Resisting Rebellion*. Lexington: University Press of Kentucky.
Jones, B. Todd. 2012. "Countering Violent Extremism through Community-Based Approaches." *Grand Rapids Herald Review*, July 25. https://www.grandrapidsmn.com/opinion/countering-violent-extremism-through-community-based-approaches/article_9b8211a8-d65f-11e1-b565-001a4bcf887a.html.
Jones, J. P. 1979. "Limiting Congressional Denationalization after *Afroyim*." *San Diego Law Review* 17, no. 1: 121–148.
Jones, Seth. 2018. "The Rise of Far-Right Extremism in the United States." Washington, DC: Center for Strategic and International Studies.
Jonietz, Erika. 2003. "Total Information Overload." *MIT Technology Review*, July 1. https://www.technologyreview.com/s/401985/total-information-overload/.
Joppke, Christian. 1999. *Immigration and the Nation State: The United States, Germany, and Great Britain*. Oxford: Oxford University Press.
Joppke, Christian. 2007. "Transformation of Citizenship: Status, Rights, Identity." *Citizenship Studies* 11, no. 1: 37–48.
Joppke, Christian. 2009. "Limits of Integration Policy: Britain and Her Muslims." *Journal of Ethnic and Migration Studies* 35, no. 3: 453–472.
Joppke, Christian. 2010. *Citizenship and Immigration*. Cambridge: Polity.
Jourde, Cédric. 2011. "Mauritania 2010: Between Individual Willpower and Institutional Inertia." *Maghreb Review* 1: 11–15.
Karaman, Natalka. 2011. "Altmire & Dent Sponsor Law to Strip Home-Grown Terrorists of Citizenship." *Politics PA*, October 21. http://www.politicspa.com/altmire-dent-sponsor-law-to-strip-home-grown-terrorists-of-citizenship/28935/.
Karawan, Ibrahim A. 1992. "Monarchs, Mullas, and Marshals: Islamic Regimes?" *Annals of the American Academy of Political and Social Science* 524: 103–119.
Karlsson, Michael. 2012. *9/11 and the Design of Counterterrorism Institutions*. Farnham: Ashgate.
Karst, Kenneth L. 1989. *Belonging to America: Equal Citizenship and the Constitution*. New Haven, CT: Yale University Press.
Kathwari, Farooq, Lynn M. Martin, and Christopher B. Whitney. 2007. "Strengthening America: The Civic and Political Integration of Muslim Americans." Chicago, IL: Chicago Council on Global Affairs.

Katzenstein, Peter J. 1996. *The Culture of National Security: Norms and Identity in World Politics.* New York: Columbia University Press.

Katzenstein, Peter J. 2002. "September 11 in Comparative Perspective: The Antiterrorism Campaigns of Germany and Japan." *Dialogue IO* 1, no. 1: 45–56.

Katzenstein, Peter J. 2003. "Same War, Different Views: Germany, Japan, and Counterterrorism." *International Organization* 57, no. 4: 731–760.

Katzenstein, Peter J. 2006. "Introduction: Alternate Perspectives on National Security." In *The Culture of National Security: Norms and Identity in World Politics*, edited by Peter J. Katzenstein, 1–33. New York: Columbia University Press.

Katzenstein, Peter J., Robert O. Keohane, and Stephen D. Krasner, eds. 1998. "*International Organization* at Fifty: Exploration and Contestation in the Study of World Politics." *International Organization* 52, no. 4: 645–1061.

Kaufmann, Eric P. 2004. *The Rise and Fall of Anglo-America.* Cambridge, MA: Harvard University Press.

Kavanagh, Aileen. 2009. "Judging the Judges under the Human Rights Act: Deference, Disillusionment and the 'War on Terror.'" *Public Law* 2, April: 287–304.

Kelly, Ruth. 2006. "Britain: Our Values, Our Responsibilities." Speech to Muslim Organizations on Working Together to Tackle Extremism. Government House, London, October 11. https://webarchive.nationalarchives.gov.uk/+/http://www.communities.gov.uk/staging/index.asp?id=1503690.

Kennedy, Dominic. 2011. "US Sends 'Radical' Islam Activist to Meet British Muslim Youths." *The Times*, June 8.

Kennedy-Pipe, Caroline, and Colin McInnes. 1997. "The British Army in Northern Ireland 1969–1972: From Policing to Counter-Terror." *Journal of Strategic Studies* 20, no. 2: 1–24.

Kepel, Gilles. 2004. *The War for Muslim Minds: Islam and the West.* Cambridge, MA: Belknap Press of Harvard University Press.

Kilcullen, David J. 2007. "Subversion and Countersubversion in the Campaign against Terrorism in Europe." *Studies in Conflict & Terrorism* 30, no. 8: 647–666.

Kim, Nam-Kook. 2011. "Deliberative Multiculturalism in New Labour's Britain." *Citizenship Studies* 15, no. 1: 125–144.

King, Desmond. 2000. *Making Americans: Immigration, Race, and the Origins of the Diverse Democracy.* Cambridge, MA: Harvard University Press.

King, Peter T. 2011. "Opening Statement." Joint Hearing before the Committee on Homeland Security, US House of Representatives, and the Committee on Homeland Security and Governmental Affairs, US Senate: Homegrown Terrorism: The Threat to Military Communities Inside the United States. December 7.

Kingdom of Saudi Arabia. 2005. "National Campaign against Terrorism and Extremism." March 7. https://www.saudiembassy.net/sites/default/files/terrorism-Embassy-PC-Adel-Mar05-Q.pdf.

Koehler, Daniel. 2019. *Violence and Terrorism from the Far-Right: Policy Options to Counter an Elusive Threat.* The Hague: International Center for Countering Terrorism, February 27.

Kofman, Eleonore. 2005. "Citizenship, Migration and the Reassertion of National Identity." *Citizenship Studies* 9, no. 5: 453–467.

Kohlmann, Evan F. 2008. "'Homegrown' Terrorists: Theory and Cases in the War on Terror's Newest Front." *Annals of the American Academy of Political and Social Science* 618, no. 1: 95–109.

Kohlmann, Evan F., and Laith Alkhouri. 2014. "Profiles of Foreign Fighters in Syria and Iraq." *CTC Sentinel* 7, no. 9: 1–5.

Kratochwil, Friedrich V. 1989. *Rules, Norms, and Actions: Laying the Conceptual Foundations.* Cambridge: Cambridge University Press.

Krause, Keith, and Michael C. Williams. 1997. *Critical Security Studies: Concepts and Cases.* London: UCL Press.

Kukathas, Chandran. 2003. *The Liberal Archipelago: A Theory of Diversity and Freedom.* Oxford: Oxford University Press.

Kundnani, Arun. 2009. "Spooked! How Not to Prevent Violent Extremism." London: Institute of Race Relations.

Kundnani, Arun. 2014. *The Muslims Are Coming! Islamophobia, Extremism, and the Domestic War on Terror.* London: Verso.

Kymlicka, Will. 2001. *Politics in the Vernacular: Nationalism, Multiculturalism and Citizenship.* Oxford: Oxford University Press.

LaFree, Gary, and Laura Dugan. 2009. "Research on Terrorism and Countering Terrorism." *Crime and Justice* 38, no. 1: 413–477.

Laghmari, Mehdi. 2019. "Situating Islamic State's Message: A Social and Theological Genealogy." In *ISIS Propaganda: A Full-Spectrum Extremist Message*, edited by Stephane J. Baele, Katharine A. Boyd, and Travis G. Coan, 250–284. Oxford: Oxford University Press.

Lambert, Robert, and Basia Spalek. 2008. "Muslim Communities, Counter-Terrorism and Counter-Radicalisation: A Critically Reflective Approach to Engagement." *International Journal of Law, Crime and Justice* 36, no. 4: 257–270.

Laqueur, Walter. 1977. "Interpretations of Terrorism: Fact, Fiction and Political Science." *Journal of Contemporary History* 12, no. 1: 1–42.

LeBaron, Richard. 2012. "Public Diplomacy as an Instrument of Counterterrorism: A Progress Report." *MountainRunner.us*, June 21. https://mountainrunner.us/2012/06/public-diplomacy-instrument-counterterrorism/.

Lee, Jeremy. 2016. "27 Bangladeshi Radicals Nabbed in S'pore: 5 Things about Anwar al-Awlaki and His Violent Legacy." *Straits Times*, January 20.

Leheny, David. 2002. "Symbols, Strategies, and Choices for International Relations Scholarship after September 11." *Dialogue IO* 1, no. 1: 57–70.

Lehrke, Jesse Paul, and Rahel Schomaker. 2014. "Mechanisms of Convergence in Domestic Counterterrorism Regulations: American Influence, Domestic Needs, and International Networks." *Studies in Conflict & Terrorism* 37, no. 8: 689–712.

Leiter, Michael. 2010. "Testimony." Hearing before the Committee on Homeland Security and Government Affairs of the US Senate: Nine Years After 9/11: Confronting the Terrorist Threat to the Homeland. September 22.

Lemieux, Anthony F., Jarret M. Brachman, Jason Levitt, and Jay Wood. 2014. "*Inspire* Magazine: A Critical Analysis of Its Significance and Potential Impact through the Lens of the Information, Motivation, and Behavioral Skills Model." *Terrorism and Political Violence* 26, no. 2: 354–371.

Lewis, Charles, and Adam Mayle. 2003. "Justice Dept. Drafts Sweeping Expansion of Anti-Terrorism Act." Washington, DC: Center for Public Integrity, February 7. https://publicintegrity.org/national-security/justice-dept-drafts-sweeping-expansion-of-anti-terrorism-act/.

Lewis, Valerie A., and Ridhi Kashyap. 2013. "Are Muslims a Distinctive Minority? An Empirical Analysis of Religiosity, Social Attitudes, and Islam." *Journal for the Scientific Study of Religion* 52, no. 3: 617–626.

Lia, Brynjar. 2005. *Globalisation and the Future of Terrorism: Patterns and Predictions.* Abingdon: Routledge.

Lia, Brynjar. 2008. *Architect of Global Jihad: The Life of Al-Qaeda Strategist Abu Musab Al-Suri.* London: Hurst.

Lia, Brynjar. 2009. *Architect of Global Jihad: The Life of Al Qaeda Strategist Abu Mus' Ab Al-Suri.* New York: Columbia University Press.

Lia, Brynjar. 2015. "Understanding Jihadi Proto-States." *Perspectives on Terrorism* 9, no. 4: 31–41.

Lieberman, Donna. 2011–2012. "Infringement on Civil Liberties after 9/11." *New York Law School Law Review* 56, no. 3: 1121–1126.

Lieberman, Joe. 2010. "Sens. Lieberman and Brown Introduce Terrorist Expatriate Act." *Joe's Corner*, May 6. http://senatorjoescorner.blogspot.com.au/2010/05/sens-lieberman-and-brown-introduce.html.

Lieven, Anatol. 2012. *America Right or Wrong: An Anatomy of American Nationalism.* Oxford: Oxford University Press.

Lindekilde, Lasse. 2008. "In the Name of the Prophet? Danish Muslim Mobilization during the Muhammad Caricatures Controversy." *Mobilization: An International Quarterly* 13, no. 2: 219–238.

Lindekilde, Lasse. 2012. "Neo-Liberal Governing of 'Radicals': Danish Radicalization Prevention Policies and Potential Latrogenic Effects." *International Journal of Conflict and Violence* 6, no. 1: 109–125.

Lindell, Johan. 2017. "Bringing Field Theory to Social Media, and Vice-Versa: Network-Crawling an Economy of Recognition on Facebook." *Social Media + Society* 3, no. 4: 1–11.

Lipset, Seymour Martin. 1996. *American Exceptionalism: A Double-Edged Sword.* New York: W. W. Norton & Company.

Lister, Michael, and Miguel Otero-Iglesias. 2012. "New Problems, Old Solutions? Explaining Variations in British and Spanish Anti-Terrorism Policy." *Comparative European Politics* 10, no. 5: 564–584.

Lithwick, Dahlia. 2007. "Bad Ideas: The Law Promoting Outstanding Excellence in Fighting Terrorism—and Why You Never Heard About It." *Slate*, November 27. https://slate.com/news-and-politics/2007/11/the-law-promoting-outstanding-excellence-in-fighting-terrorism-and-why-you-never-heard-about-it.html.

Lloyd, Baron Anthony John Leslie. 1996. *Inquiry into Legislation against Terrorism*, Vol. 1. CM 3420. London: Stationery Office.

Lorenzo-Dus, Nuria, Anina Kinzel, and Luke Walker. 2018. "Representing the West and 'Non-Believers' in the Online Jihadist Magazines *Dabiq* and *Inspire*." *Critical Studies on Terrorism* 11, no. 3: 521–536.

Luban, David. 2005. "Eight Fallacies About Liberty and Security." In *Human Rights in the "War on Terror,"* edited by Richard Ashby Wilson, 242–257. Cambridge: Cambridge University Press.

Lungren, Daniel E. 2007. "Statement." Hearing before the Subcommittee on Intelligence, Information Sharing, and Terrorism Risk Assessment of the US House of Representatives Committee on Homeland Security: Radicalization, Information

Sharing and Community Outreach: Protecting the Homeland from Homegrown Terror. April 5.
Lynch, Marc. 2006. "Al-Qaeda's Constructivist Turn." *Praeger Security International* 5, June: 1–26.
Lynch, Marc, Deen Freelon, and Sean Aday. 2014. "Syria's Socially Mediated Civil War." Washington, DC: United States Institute of Peace.
Maher, Shiraz, and Martyn Frampton. 2009. "Choosing Our Friends Wisely: Criteria for Engagement with Muslim Groups." London: Policy Exchange.
Mahood, Samantha, and Halim Rane. 2017. "Islamist Narratives in ISIS Recruitment Propaganda." *Journal of International Communication* 23, no. 1: 15–35.
Malet, David. 2013. *Foreign Fighters: Transnational Identity in Civil Conflicts*. Oxford: Oxford University Press.
Malik, Maleiha. 2009. "Extreme Speech and Liberalism." In *Extreme Speech and Democracy*, edited by Ivan Hare and James Weinstein, 96–120. Oxford: Oxford University Press.
Mandaville, Peter. 2001. *Transnational Muslim Politics: Reimagining the Umma*. Abingdon: Routledge.
Mandaville, Peter. 2009. "Muslim Transnational Identity and State Responses in Europe and the UK after 9/11: Political Community, Ideology and Authority." *Journal of Ethnic and Migration Studies* 35, no. 3: 491–506.
Mandaville, Peter. 2011. "Transnational Muslim Solidarities and Everyday Life (Book Review)." *Nations and Nationalism* 17, no. 1: 7–24.
Mariner, Joanne. 2004. "Patriot II's Attack on Citizenship." CNN, January 22. http://edition.cnn.com/2003/LAW/03/06/findlaw.analysis.mariner.patriotII/.
Mariner, Joanne. 2011. "The NDAA Explained: Part One in a Two-Part Series of Columns on the National Defense Authorization Act." *Verdict*, December 11. https://verdict.justia.com/2011/12/21/the-national-defense-authorization-act-explained.
Mariner, Joanne. 2012a. "The NDAA Explained: Part Two in a Two-Part Series of Columns on the National Defense Authorization Act." *Verdict*, January 2. https://verdict.justia.com/2012/01/02/the-ndaa-explained.
Mariner, Joanne. 2012b. "Chipping Away at the NDAA." *Verdict*, February 29. https://verdict.justia.com/2012/02/29/chipping-away-at-the-ndaa.
Markon, Jerry. 2011a. "Lawsuit Alleges FBI Violated Muslims' Freedom of Religion." *Washington Post*, February 22.
Masbah, Mohammed. 2018. "The Limits of Morocco's Attempt to Comprehensively Counter Violent Extremism." *Middle East Brief* 118, May: 1–8.
Mastroe, Caitlin. 2016. "Evaluating CVE: Understanding the Recent Changes to the United Kingdom's Implementation of *Prevent*." *Perspectives on Terrorism* 10, no. 2: 50–60.
May, Theresa. 2014. House of Commons Debates. Immigration Bill, Column 1025, January 30. https://publications.parliament.uk/pa/cm201314/cmhansrd/cm140130/debtext/140130-0002.htm.
Maylor, Uvanney. 2014. "Promoting British Values Opens Up a Can of Worms for Teachers". *The Guardian*, June 13.
McAuley, James. 2016. "To Curb Radicalism, France Targets Foreign Funding for Mosques." *Washington Post*, August 14.
McCants, Will, and Clinton Watts. 2012. "US Strategy for Countering Violent Extremism: An Assessment." Washington, DC: Foreign Policy Research Institute.

McCants, William. 2015. *The ISIS Apocalypse: The History, Strategy, and Doomsday Vision of the Islamic State*. New York: St. Martin's Press.

McCauley, Clark, and Sophia Moskalenko. 2008. "Mechanisms of Political Radicalization: Pathways toward Terrorism." *Terrorism and Political Violence* 20, no. 3: 415–433.

McCord, Mary B., and Jason M. Blazakis. 2019. "A Road Map for Congress to Address Domestic Terrorism." *Lawfare*, February 27. https://www.lawfareblog.com/road-map-congress-address-domestic-terrorism.

McDonald, Matt. 2009. "Emancipation and Critical Terrorism Studies." In *Critical Terrorism Studies: A New Research Agenda*, edited by Richard Jackson, Marie Breen Smyth, and Jeroen Gunning, 109–124. Abingdon: Routledge.

McGhee, Derek. 2005. *Intolerant Britain? Hate, Citizenship and Difference*. New York: Open University Press.

McGlynn, Catherine, Andrew Mycock, and James W. McAuley, eds. 2011. *Britishness, Identity and Citizenship: The View from Abroad*. Oxford: Peter Lang.

McGovern, Mark. 2013. "Police, Community, Conflict, and Context: Some Thoughts on British Muslim and Irish Comparisons." In *Preventing Ideological Violence: Communities, Police and Case Studies of "Success,"* edited by P. Daniel Silk, Basia Spalek, and Mary O'Rawe, 55–66. New York: Palgrave Macmillan.

Meleagrou-Hitchens, Alexander. 2011. "As American as Apple Pie: How Anwar al-Awlaki Became the Face of Western Jihad." London: International Center for the Study of Radicalisation and Political Violence.

Meleagrou-Hitchens, Alexander, Seamus Hughes, and Bennett Clifford. 2018. "The Travellers: American Jihadists in Syria and Iraq." Washington, DC: Program on Extremism, George Washington University.

Melucci, Alberto. 1989. *Nomads of the Present: Social Movements and Individual Needs in Contemporary Society*. London: Hutchinson Radius.

Mendelsohn, Barak. 2005. "Sovereignty under Attack: The International Society Meets the Al Qaeda Network." *Review of International Studies* 31, no. 1: 45–68.

Mendelsohn, Barak. 2009a. *Combating Jihadism: American Hegemony and Interstate Cooperation in the War on Terrorism*. Chicago, IL: University of Chicago Press.

Mendelsohn, Barak. 2009b. "Bolstering the State: A Different Perspective on the War on the Jihadi Movement." *International Studies Review* 11, no. 4: 663–686.

Mendelsohn, Barak. 2011. "Al-Qaeda's Franchising Strategy." *Survival* 53, no. 3: 28–50.

Mendelsohn, Barak. 2012. "God vs. Westphalia: Radical Islamist Movements and the Battle for Organising the World." *Review of International Studies* 38, no. 3: 589–613.

Mendelsohn, Barak. 2015. *The Al-Qaeda Franchise: The Expansion of Al-Qaeda and Its Consequences*. Oxford: Oxford University Press.

Mendikbud (Ministry of Education and Culture). 2012. "Dokumen Kurikulum 2013" [2013 Curriculum Document]. Jakarta: Indonesian Government Ministry of Education and Culture.

Meyer, Christoph O. 2009. "International Terrorism as a Force of Homogenization? A Constructivist Approach to Understanding Cross-National Threat Perceptions and Responses." *Cambridge Review of International Affairs* 22, no. 4: 647–666.

Michel, Lou, and Dan Herbeck. 2001. *American Terrorist: Timothy McVeigh and the Oklahoma City Bombing*. New York: Regan Books.

Miller, David. 1993. "The Northern Ireland Information Service and the Media." In *Getting the Message: News, Truth and Power*, edited by John Eldridge, 73-101. Abingdon: Routledge.

Millman, Brock. 2000. *Managing Domestic Dissent in First World War Britain*. London: Frank Cass.

MINAB (Mosque and Imams National Advisory Board). 2020. "What Is MINAB?" http://minab.org.uk/about-us/.

Ministry of Foreign Affairs of the People's Republic of China. 2018. "Foreign Ministry Spokesperson Hua Chunying's Regular Press Conference on October 24, 2018." https://www.fmprc.gov.cn/mfa_eng/xwfw_665399/s2510_665401/t1606828.shtml.

Mitzen, Jennifer. 2006. "Ontological Security in World Politics: State Identity and the Security Dilemma." *European Journal of International Relations* 12, no. 3: 341-370.

Modood, Tariq. 1990. "British Asians and Muslims and the Rushdie Affair." *Political Quarterly* 61, no. 2: 143-160.

Modood, Tariq. 2003. "Muslims and the Politics of Difference." *Political Quarterly* 74, no. s1: 100-115.

Moghaddam, Fathali M. 2005. "The Staircase to Terrorism: A Psychological Exploration." *American Psychologist* 60, no. 2: 161-169.

Monger, David. 2012. *Patriotism and Propaganda in First World War Britain: The National War Aims Committee and Civilian Morale*. Liverpool: Liverpool University Press.

Muedini, Fait. 2012. "The Promotion of Sufism in the Politics of Algeria and Morocco." *Islamic Africa* 3, no. 2: 201-226.

Mueller, Robert S, 2010. "Testimony." Hearing before the US Senate Committee on Homeland Security and Governmental Affairs: Nine Years After 9/11: Confronting the Terrorist Threat to the Homeland. September 22.

Muir, Hugh. 2003. "Mosques Launch Protests over 'Terror' Arrests." *The Guardian*, December 13.

Mullins, Sam. 2012. "Iraq versus Lack of Integration: Understanding the Motivations of Contemporary Islamist Terrorists in Western Countries." *Behavioral Sciences of Terrorism and Political Aggression* 4, no. 2: 110-133.

Murphy, Paul L. 1979. *World War I and the Origin of Civil Liberties in the United States*. New York: W. W. Norton.

Murray, Nancy. 2012. "It's Official. There Is a Muslim Exemption to the First Amendment." Boston.com, April 12. http://archive.boston.com/community/blogs/on_liberty/2012/04/its_official_there_is_a_muslim.html.

Musallam, Adnan. 2005. *From Secularism to Jihad: Sayyid Qutb and the Foundations of Radical Islamism*. London: Greenwood Publishing Group.

Mycock, Andrew. 2010. "British Citizenship and the Legacy of Empires." *Parliamentary Affairs* 63, no. 2: 339-355.

Naik, Gautam. 2012. "Four Britons Admit to London Stock Exchange Bomb Plot." *Wall Street Journal*, February 2.

Napolitano, Janet. 2009. "Written Testimony." Hearing before the US Senate Committee on Homeland Security and Governmental Affairs: Eight Years after 9/11: Confronting the Terrorist Threat to the Homeland. September 30.

National Intelligence Council. 2007. "National Intelligence Estimate: The Terrorist Threat to the US Homeland." Washington, DC: National Intelligence Council.

National Security Council. 2002. "The National Security Strategy of the United States of America." Washington, DC: White House.

National Security Council. 2006. "The National Security Strategy of the United States of America." Washington, DC: White House.

NBC News. 2014. "Attorney General Eric Holder Revives Domestic Terror Task Force." June 3. https://www.nbcnews.com/news/us-news/attorney-general-eric-holder-revives-domestic-terror-task-force-n121026.

Neal, Andrew W. 2012a. "Normalization and Legislative Exceptionalism: Counterterrorist Lawmaking and the Changing Times of Security Emergencies." *International Political Sociology* 6, no. 3: 260–276.

Neal, Andrew W. 2012b. "Terrorism, Lawmaking, and Democratic Politics: Legislators as Security Actors." *Terrorism and Political Violence* 24, no. 3: 357–374.

Nelson, Rick, and Ben Bodurian. 2010. "A Growing Terrorist Threat? Assessing 'Homegrown' Extremism in the United States." Washington, DC: Center for Strategic and International Studies.

Netherlands Ministry of Immigration and Integration. 2006. "Policies on Integration and Prevention of Radicalisation in the Netherlands: A Progress Report." The Hague: Netherlands Ministry of Immigration and Integration.

Netherlands Ministry of the Interior and Kingdom Relations. 2007. "Polarisation and Radicalisation Action Plan 2007–2011." The Hague: Netherlands Ministry of the Interior and Kingdom Relations.

Neuman, Gerald L. 1994. "Justifying US Naturalization Policies." *Immigration and Nationality Law Review* 16: 83–124.

Neumann, Peter R. 2009. *Old and New Terrorism: Late Modernity, Globalization and the Transformation of Political Violence*. Cambridge: Polity.

Neumann, Peter R. 2013. "The Trouble with Radicalization." *International Affairs* 89, no. 4: 873–893.

Neumann, Peter R., and Brooke Rogers. 2007. "Recruitment and Mobilisation for the Islamist Militant Movement in Europe." London: King's College London.

Newman, Gerald. 1996. "Nationalism Revisited (Book Review)." *Journal of British Studies* 35, no. 1: 118–127.

Norwegian Ministry of Justice and the Police. 2011. "Collective Security—a Shared Responsibility: Action Plan to Prevent Radicalization and Violent Extremism." Oslo: Norwegian Ministry of Justice and the Police.

Norwegian Ministry of Justice and Public Security. 2010. "Action Plan Against Radicalisation and Violent Extremism." Oslo: Norwegian Ministry of Justice and Public Security.

Obama, Barack. 2011. "Remarks by the President in State of Union Address." https://obamawhitehouse.archives.gov/the-press-office/2011/01/25/remarks-president-state-union-address.

Olesen, Thomas. 2009. "Islamism as Social Movement." Aarhus: Centre for Studies in Islamism and Radicalisation, Aarhus University.

Olesen, Thomas. 2011. "Transnational Injustice Symbols and Communities: The Case of Al-Qaeda and the Guantanamo Bay Detention Camp." *Current Sociology* 59, no. 6: 717–734.

Oleszek, Walter J. 2013. *Congressional Procedures and the Policy Process*. 9th edn. Washington, DC: CQ Press.

Olsen, Matthew G. 2013. "Testimony." Hearing before the US Senate Committee on Homeland Security and Governmental Affairs: The Homeland Threat Landscape and US Response. November 14.

Omelicheva, Mariya Y. 2007. "Combating Terrorism in Central Asia: Explaining Differences in States' Responses to Terror." *Terrorism and Political Violence* 19, no. 3: 369–393.

Omelicheva, Mariya Y. 2009. "Reference Group Perspective on State Behaviour: A Case Study of Estonia's Counterterrorism Policies." *Europe-Asia Studies* 61, no. 3: 483–504.

O'Neill, Sean, and Daniel McGrory. 2006. *The Suicide Factory: Abu Hamza and the Finsbury Park Mosque*. London: Harper Perennial.

Onuf, Nicholas Greenwood. 1989. *World of Our Making: Rules and Rule in Social Theory and International Relations*. Columbia: University of South Carolina Press.

Orgad, Liav. 2010. "Creating New Americans: The Essence of Americanism under the Citizenship Test." *Houston Law Review* 47, no. 5: 1227–1297.

OSCE (Organization for Security and Cooperation in Europe). 2020. "United States Mission: Note Verbale No. 2019/15." June 2. https://www.osce.org/files/f/documents/7/c/453603.pdf.

Pantazis, Christina, and Simon Pemberton. 2009. "From the 'Old' to the 'New' Suspect Community: Examining the Impacts of Recent UK Counter-Terrorist Legislation." *British Journal of Criminology* 49, no. 5: 646–666.

Pantucci, Raffaello. 2011 "A Typology of Lone Wolves: Preliminary Analysis of Lone Islamist Terrorists." London: International Centre for the Study of Radicalisation and Political Violence.

Pape, Robert A. 2005. *Dying to Win: The Strategic Logic of Suicide Terrorism*. New York: Random House.

Parekh, Bhikhu C. 2000. *The Future of Multi-Ethnic Britain: Report of the Commission on the Future of Multi-Ethnic Britain*. London: Profile.

Parker, David, and Jonathan Davis. 2017. "Counter-Radicalisation at the Coalface: Lessons for Europe and Beyond." *RUSI Newsbrief* 37, no. 1: 1–4.

Parker, Lyn. 2017. "Religious Environmental Education? The New School Curriculum in Indonesia." *Environmental Education Research* 23, no. 9: 1249–1272.

Parsons, Victoria. 2016. "Theresa May Deprived 33 Individuals of British Citizenship in 2015." Bureau of Investigative Journalism, June 21. https://www.thebureauinvestigates.com/stories/2016-06-21/citizenship-stripping-new-figures-reveal-theresa-may-has-deprived-33-individuals-of-british-citizenship.

Pasha, Mustapha Kamal. 2019. "Political Theology and Sovereignty: Sayyid Qutb in Our Times." *Journal of International Relations and Development* 22, no. 2: 346–363.

Patel, Faiza. 2011. "Rethinking Radicalization." New York: Brennan Center for Justice, New York University School of Law.

Pearson, Elizabeth. 2018. "Online as the New Frontline: Affect, Gender, and ISIS-Take-Down on Social Media." *Studies in Conflict & Terrorism* 41, no. 11: 850–874.

Perliger, Arie. 2012. "How Democracies Respond to Terrorism: Regime Characteristics, Symbolic Power and Counterterrorism." *Security Studies* 21, no. 3: 490–528.

Perliger, Arie, and Daniel Milton. 2018. "Fighting Together? Understanding Bilateral Cooperation in the Realm of Counterterrorism." *Dynamics of Asymmetric Conflict* 11, no. 3: 199–220.

Peterson, Peter. 2002. "Public Diplomacy and the War on Terrorism." *Foreign Affairs* 81, no. 5: 74–94.

Phillips, Andrew. 2011. *War, Religion and Empire: The Transformation of International Orders*. Cambridge: Cambridge University Press.

Philpott, Daniel. 2001. *Revolutions in Sovereignty: How Ideas Shaped Modern International Relations*. Princeton, NJ: Princeton University Press.

Philpott, Daniel. 2002. "The Challenge of September 11 to Secularism in International Relations." *World Politics* 55, no. 1: 66–95.

Piazza, James A., and James Igoe Walsh. 2010. "Physical Integrity Rights and Terrorism." *PS: Political Science and Politics* 43, no. 3: 411–414.

Pickus, Noah. 2014. "Laissez-Faire and Its Discontents: US Naturalization and Integration Policy in Comparative Perspective." *Citizenship Studies* 18, no. 2: 160–174.

Piette, Diane Carraway, and Jesslyn Radack. 2006. "Piercing the Historical Mists: The People and Events behind the Passage of FISA and the Creation of the Wall." *Stanford Law & Policy Review* 17, no. 2: 437–486.

Pilkington, Andrew. 2008. "From Institutional Racism to Community Cohesion: The Changing Nature of Racial Discourse in Britain." *Sociological Research Online* 13, no. 3: 1–13.

Piscatori, James P. 1986. *Islam in a World of Nation-States*. Cambridge: Cambridge University Press in association with Royal Institute of International Affairs.

Pisoiu, Daniela. 2013. "Coming to Believe 'Truths' about Islamist Radicalization in Europe." *Terrorism and Political Violence* 25, no. 2: 246–263.

Pocock, J. G. A. 1975. *The Machiavellian Moment: Florentine Political Thought and the Atlantic Republican Tradition*. Princeton, NJ: Princeton University Press.

Pocock, J. G. A. 1982. "The Limits and Divisions of British History: In Search of the Unknown Subject." *American Historical Review* 87, no. 2: 311–336.

Pocock, J. G. A. 1992. "History and Sovereignty: The Historiographical Response to Europeanization in Two British Cultures." *Journal of British Studies* 31, no. 4: 358–389.

Polletta, Francesca, and James M. Jasper. 2001. "Collective Identity and Social Movements." *Annual Review of Sociology* 27, no. 1: 283–305.

Precht, Tomas. 2007. "Home Grown Terrorism and Islamist Radicalisation in Europe: From Conversion to Terrorism: An Assessment of the Factors Influencing Violent Islamist Extremism and Suggestions for Counter Radicalisation Measures." Copenhagen: Danish Ministry of Justice.

Preston, William. 1994. *Aliens and Dissenters: Federal Suppression of Radicals, 1903–1933*. Urbana: University of Illinois Press.

Preventing Extremism Together Working Groups. 2005. "Working Together to Prevent Extremism." London: Home Office.

President of the Russian Federation. 2009. "Russia: National Security Strategy to 2020." May 12. https://css.ethz.ch/en/services/digital-library/publications/publication.html/154915.

Ranstorp, Magnus. 2007. *Mapping Terrorism Research: State of the Art, Gaps and Future Direction*. Abingdon: Routledge.

Ranstorp, Magnus. 2010. *Understanding Violent Radicalisation: Terrorist and Jihadist Movements in Europe*. Abingdon: Routledge.

Rascoff, Samuel J. 2010. "The Law of Homegrown (Counter) Terrorism." *Texas Law Review* 88, no. 7: 1715–1749.

Rascoff, Samuel J. 2012. "Establishing Official Islam? The Law and Strategy of Counter-Radicalization." *Stanford Law Review* 64, no. 1: 125–189.

Rasmussen, Nicholas J. 2015. "Testimony." Hearing before the US Senate Select Committee on Intelligence: Current Terrorist Threat to the United States. February 12.

https://www.govinfo.gov/content/pkg/CHRG-114shrg24733/html/CHRG-114shrg24733.htm.

Rees, Wyn Y. N., and Richard J. Aldrich. 2005. "Contending Cultures of Counterterrorism: Transatlantic Divergence or Convergence?" *International Affairs* 81, no. 5: 905–923.

Reid, Edna F., and Hsinchun Chen. 2007. "Mapping the Contemporary Terrorism Research Domain." *International Journal of Human-Computer Studies* 65, no. 1: 42–56.

Reid, Edna O. F. 1997. "Evolution of a Body of Knowledge: An Analysis of Terrorism Research." *Information Processing and Management* 33, no. 1: 91–106.

Reus-Smit, Christian, ed. 2004. *The Politics of International Law.* Cambridge: Cambridge University Press.

Reuters. 2009. "Algeria Fights Insurgency With Sufism." *Al-Arabiya News*, July 8. http://www.alarabiya.net/articles/2009/07/08/78165.html.

Richards, Anthony. 2011. "The Problem with 'Radicalization': The Remit of 'Prevent' and the Need to Refocus on Terrorism in the UK." *International Affairs* 87, no. 1: 143–152.

RICU (Research, Information and Communications Unit). 2007. "Counterterrorism Communications Guidance: Communicating Effectively with Community Audiences." London: Home Office.

Radical Middle Way. 2012. "Radical Middle Way" www.radicalmiddleway.co.uk/page/uk.

Robinson, David. 2008. "Community Cohesion and the Politics of Communitarianism." In *Community Cohesion in Crisis? New Dimensions of Diversity and Difference*, edited by John Flint and David Robinson, 15–34. Bristol: Policy Press.

Romaniuk, Peter. 2010. *Multilateral Counter-Terrorism: The Global Politics of Cooperation and Contestation.* Abingdon: Routledge.

Rose, Richard. 1977. "The United Kingdom as an Intellectual Puzzle." *Politics* 12, no. 2: 21–34.

Ross, Alice, and Patrick Galey. 2013. "Rise in Citizenship-Stripping as Government Cracks down on UK Fighters in Syria." Bureau of Investigative Journalism, December 23. https://www.thebureauinvestigates.com/stories/2013-12-23/rise-in-citizenship-stripping-as-government-cracks-down-on-uk-fighters-in-syria.

Ross, Tim, and Steven Swinford. 2011. "WikiLeaks Cables: US Launched Anti-Extremist Campaign to Reverse UK Radicalisation." *Telegraph*, February 4.

Roy, Olivier. 2006. *Globalized Islam: The Search for a New Ummah.* New York: Columbia University Press.

Rudner, Martin. 2017. "'Electronic Jihad': The Internet as Al Qaeda's Catalyst for Global Terror." *Studies in Conflict & Terrorism* 40, no. 1: 10–23.

Ruggie, John Gerard. 1993. "Territoriality and Beyond: Problematizing Modernity in International Relations." *International Organization* 47, no. 1: 139–174.

Ruggie, John Gerard. 1998. "What Makes the World Hang Together? Neo-Utilitarianism and the Social Constructivist Challenge." *International Organization* 52, no. 4: 855–885.

Russell, Jonathan, and Haras Rafiq. 2016. "Countering Islamist Extremist Narratives: A Strategic Briefing." London: Quilliam, January.

Ryan, Michael W. S. 2013. *Decoding Al-Qaeda's Strategy: The Deep Battle against America.* New York: Columbia University Press.

Sackmann, Rosemarie, Bernhard Peters, and Thomas Faist. 2003. *Identity and Integration: Migrants in Western Europe.* Aldershot: Ashgate.

Sageman, Marc. 2008a. *Leaderless Jihad: Terror Networks in the Twenty-First Century.* Philadelphia: University of Pennsylvania Press.

Sageman, Marc. 2008b. "Does Osama Still Call the Shots? Debating the Containment of al Qaeda's Leadership: The Reality of Grass-Roots Terrorism." *Foreign Affairs* 87, no. 4: 163–166.

Sageman, Marc. 2008c. "The Next Generation of Terror." *Foreign Policy* 165, March–April: 37–42.

Sageman, Marc. 2014. "The Stagnation in Terrorism Research." *Terrorism and Political Violence* 26, no. 4: 1–16.

Sainsbury, Diane. 2012. *Welfare States and Immigrant Rights: The Politics of Inclusion and Exclusion.* Oxford: Oxford University Press.

Samuel, Chris. 2013. "Symbolic Violence and Collective Identity: Pierre Bourdieu and the Ethics of Resistance." *Social Movement Studies* 12, no. 4: 397–413.

Saul, Ben. 2005. "Speaking of Terror: Criminalising Incitement to Violence." *University of New South Wales Law Journal Forum* 11, no. 2: 868–886.

Savage, Charlie. 2013. "Obama Disputes Limits on Detainee Transfers Imposed in Defense Bill." *New York Times*, January 4.

Savage, Charlie, and Carl Hulse. 2010. "Bill Targets Citizenship of Terrorists' Allies." *New York Times*, October 5.

Schanzer, David, Charles Kurzman, and Ebrahim Moosa. 2010. *Anti-Terror Lessons of Muslim-Americans.* Washington, DC: National Institute of Justice.

Schlanger, Margot. 2010. "Testimony." Hearing before the Subcommittee on Intelligence, Information Sharing and Terrorism Risk Assessment, US House of Representatives Committee on Homeland Security: Working with Communities to Disrupt Terror Plots. March 17.

Schmid, Alex P. 2014. "Al-Qaeda's 'Single Narrative' and Attempts to Develop Counter-Narratives: The State of Knowledge." ICCT Research Paper. The Hague: International Centre for Counter-Terrorism, January.

Schmid, Alex P. 2016. "Research on Radicalisation: Topics and Themes." *Perspectives on Terrorism* 10, no. 3: 26–32.

Schmid, Alex P., and Janny De Graaf. 1982. *Violence as Communication: Insurgent Terrorism and the Western News Media.* London: Sage.

Schmid, Alex P., and Albert J. Jongman. 1988. *Political Terrorism: A New Guide to Actors, Authors, Concepts, Data Bases, Theories, and Literature.* Rev., expanded and updated edn. New Brunswick, NJ: Transaction Publishers.

Schmid, Alex P., and Eric Price. 2011. "Selected Literature on Radicalization and De-Radicalization of Terrorists: Monographs, Edited Volumes, Grey Literature and Prime Articles Published since the 1960s." *Crime, Law and Social Change* 55, no. 4: 337–348.

Schneider, Dorothee. 2001. "Naturalization and United States Citizenship in Two Periods of Mass Migration: 1894–1930, 1965–2000." *Journal of American Ethnic History* 21, no. 1: 50–82.

Schuck, Peter H. 1989. "Membership in the Liberal Polity: The Devaluation of American Citizenship." *Georgetown Immigration Law Journal* 3, no. 1: 1–18.

Schuck, Peter H. 1997. "The Re-Evaluation of American Citizenship." *Georgetown Immigration Law Journal* 12, no. 1: 1–34.

Schuck, Peter H. 2006. "Federalism." *Case Western Reserve Journal of International Law* 38, no. 1: 5–12.

Schuck, Peter H. 2007. "Citizenship and Nationality Policy." In *The New Americans: A Guide to Immigration since 1965*, edited by M. Waters and Reed Ueda, 43–55. Cambridge, MA: Harvard University Press.

Schuurman, Bart, Lasse Lindekilde, Stefan Malthaner, Francis O'Connor, Paul Gill, and Noémie Bouhana. 2019. "End of the Lone Wolf: The Typology That Should Not Have Been." *Studies in Conflict & Terrorism* 42, no. 8: 771–778.

Schwartz-Shea, Peregrine. 2015. "Judging Quality: Evaluative Criteria and Epistemic Communities." In *Interpretation and Method: Empirical Research Methods and the Interpretive Turn*, edited by Dvora Yanow and Peregrine Schwartz-Shea, 120–161. Abingdon: Routledge.

Scotland, Patricia (Baroness Scotland of Asthal). 2006. House of Lords Debates. Vol. 677, Column 551. January 17. https://publications.parliament.uk/pa/ld200506/ldhansrd/vo060117/text/60117-04.htm#60117-04_spnew7.

Scott, Peter. 1990. *Knowledge and Nation*. Edinburgh: Edinburgh University Press.

Shapiro, Jeremy, and Daniel Byman. 2006. "Bridging the Transatlantic Counterterrorism Gap." *Washington Quarterly* 29, no. 4: 33–50.

Silke, Andrew. 2004. "The Devil You Know: Continuing Problems with Research on Terrorism." In *Research on Terrorism: Trends, Achievements & Failures*, edited by Andrew Silke, 57–71. Abingdon: Frank Cass.

Simmons, Robert. 2006. "Statement." Hearing before the Subcommittee on Intelligence, Information Sharing, and Terrorism Risk Assessment of the US House of Representatives Committee on Homeland Security: The Homeland Security Implications of Radicalization. September 20.

Simpson, A. W. Brian. 1992. *In the Highest Degree Odious: Detention without Trial in Wartime Britain*. Oxford: Clarendon Press.

Sinnar, Shirin. 2019. "Separate and Unequal: The Law of 'Domestic' and 'International' Terrorism." *Michigan Law Review* 117, no. 7: 1333–1404.

Skinner, Quentin. 1978. *The Foundations of Modern Political Thought. Volume 1: The Renaissance*. Cambridge: Cambridge University Press.

Sky News. 2013. "Police Foil July 7-Sized Attack Every Year." March 21. https://news.sky.com/story/police-foil-july-7-sized-attack-every-year-10451029.

Slootman, Marieke, and Jean Tille. 2006. "Processes of Radicalisation: Why Some Amsterdam Muslims Become Radicals." Amsterdam: Institute for Migration and Ethnic Studies.

Slynn, Lord Gordon of Hadley. 2001. "Judgment, Secretary of State for the Home Department v Rehman UKHL 47." House of Lords.

Smith, Adam. 2013. "American Propaganda Allowed Stateside, Transcript." WYNC Studios, July 19. https://www.wnycstudios.org/podcasts/otm/segments/307767-american-propaganda-allowed-stateside.

Smith, Rogers M. 1993. "Beyond Tocqueville, Myrdal, and Hartz: The Multiple Traditions in America." *American Political Science Review* 87, no. 3: 549–566.

Smith, Rogers M. 1997. *Civic Ideals: Conflicting Visions of Citizenship in US History*. New Haven, CT: Yale University Press.

Smith, Rogers M. 2001. "Citizenship: Political." In *International Encyclopedia of the Social & Behavioral Sciences*, edited by Neil J. Smelser and Paul B. Baltes, 1857–1860. Oxford: Elsevier.

Solahudin. 2013. "Is the 'Far Enemy' off the Agenda for Indonesian Terrorists?" *The Interpreter*, August 20. https://www.lowyinstitute.org/the-interpreter/far-enemy-agenda-indonesian-terrorists.

Soriano, Manuel R. Torres. 2007. "Jihadist Propaganda and Its Audiences: A Change of Course?" *Perspectives on Terrorism* 1, no. 2: 1–3.

Soysal, Yasemin Nuhoğlu. 1994. *Limits of Citizenship: Migrants and Postnational Membership in Europe.* Chicago, IL: University of Chicago Press.

Spaaij, Ramón, and Mark S. Hamm. 2015. "Key Issues and Research Agendas in Lone Wolf Terrorism." *Studies in Conflict & Terrorism* 38, no. 3: 167-178.

Spalek, Basia, and Laura McDonald. 2010. "Terror Crime Prevention: Constructing Muslim Practices and Beliefs as 'Anti-Social' and 'Extreme' through CONTEST 2." *Social Policy and Society* 9, no. 1: 123-132.

Speckhard, Anne, and Ahmet S. Yayla. 2015. "Eyewitness Accounts from Recent Defectors from Islamic State: Why They Joined, What They Saw, Why They Quit." *Perspectives on Terrorism* 9, no. 6: 95-117.

Spencer, Ian R. G. 2002. *British Immigration Policy since 1939: The Making of Multi-Racial Britain.* Abingdon: Routledge.

Spencer, Sarah. 2007. "Immigration." In *Blair's Britain, 1997-2007*, edited by Anthony Seldon, 341-360. Cambridge: Cambridge University Press.

Spencer, Sarah. 2011. *The Migration Debate.* Bristol: Policy Press.

Spruyt, Hendrik. 1994. *The Sovereign State and Its Competitors: An Analysis of Systems Change.* Princeton, NJ: Princeton University Press.

Stampnitzky, Lisa. 2013. *Disciplining Terror: How Experts Invented "Terrorism."* Cambridge: Cambridge University Press.

Starkey, Hugh. 2018. "Fundamental British Values and Citizenship Education: Tensions between National and Global Perspectives." *Geografiska Annaler: Series B, Human Geography* 100, no. 2: 149-162.

Steiker, Carol S. 1998. "Foreword: The Limits of the Preventive State." *Journal of Criminal Law and Criminology* 88, no. 3: 771-808.

Stemmann, Juan Jose Escobar. 2006. "Middle East Salafism's Influence and the Radicalization of Muslim Communities in Europe." *Middle East Review of International Affairs* 10, no. 3: 1-14.

Stenersen, Anne. 2008. "The Internet: A Virtual Training Camp?" *Terrorism and Political Violence* 20, no. 2: 215-233.

Stenersen, Anne. 2013. "'Bomb-Making for Beginners': Inside Al-Qaeda E-Learning Course." *Perspectives on Terrorism* 7, no. 1: 25-37.

Stevens, Tim, and Peter R. Neumann. 2009. "Countering Online Radicalisation A Strategy for Action." London: International Centre for the Study of Radicalisation and Political Violence.

Stone, Geoffrey R. 2004. *Perilous Times: Free Speech in Wartime from the Sedition Act of 1798 to the War on Terrorism.* New York: W. W. Norton and Company.

Stone, Geoffrey R. 2007. *War and Liberty. An American Dilemma 1790 to the Present.* New York: W. W. Norton and Company.

Straw, Jack. 1999. House of Commons Debates. Column 152. December 14. https://hansard.parliament.uk/commons/1999-12-14/debates/b8b65fd0-3cdc-4cc0-9d23-dfce015aa510/TerrorismBill.

Streiff, Daniel. 2006. "Will Islam à la Française Take Hold?" NBCNEWS.com, June 6. http://www.nbcnews.com/id/12812201#.Uog6z6y3TCs.

Stubbs, Richard. 1989. *Hearts and Minds in Guerrilla Warfare: The Malayan Emergency, 1948-1960.* Oxford: Oxford University Press.

Suleiman, Yasir. 2009. *Conextualising Islam in Britain: Exploratory Perspectives.* Cambridge, UK: Prince Alwaleed Bin Talal Centre of Islamic Studies.

Sullivan, Kevin, and William Wan. 2016. "Troubled. Quiet. Macho. Angry. The Volatile Life of the Orlando Shooter." *Washington Post*, 17 June.

Sumpter, Cameron. 2017. "Countering Violent Extremism in Indonesia: Priorities, Practice and the Role of Civil Society." *Journal for Deradicalization* 11, Summer: 112-147.

Tan, Charlene. 2008. "(Re)Imagining the Muslim Identity in Singapore." *Studies in Ethnicity and Nationalism* 8, no. 1: 31-49.

Task Force on New Americans. 2015. "White House Task Force on New Americans: One-Year Progress Report." Washington, DC: White House.

TaxPayers' Alliance. 2009. "Council Spending Uncovered II—No. 5: Preventing Violent Extremism Grants." September 7. https://www.taxpayersalliance.com/council_spending_uncovered_ii_no_5_preventing_violent_extremism_grants_opg_c2sx5hfy8ds1jjnh3nxm3ak.

Tempest, Matthew. 2005. "Clarke Reveals Terror Deportation Rules." *The Guardian*, August 25.

Teotonio, Isabel. 2010. "Terror Trial Ends but Extremism Still Growing." *The Star*, June 24. https://www.thestar.com/news/crime/2010/06/24/terror_trial_ends_but_extremism_still_growing.html.

Thomas, Paul. 2012. *Responding to the Threat of Violent Extremism: Failing to Prevent*. New York: Bloomsbury Academic.

Thornberry, Mac. 2012. "Thornberry and Smith Introduce Bill to Help Counter Threats in Information Age." Press Release, May 15. https://thornberry.house.gov/news/documentsingle.aspx?DocumentID=296108.

Tibi, Bassam. 2007. "The Totalitarianism of Jihadist Islamism and Its Challenge to Europe and to Islam." *Totalitarian Movements and Political Religions* 8, no. 1: 35-54.

Tilly, Charles. 1992. *Coercion, Capital, and European States, AD 990-1992*. Oxford: Blackwell.

Tinnes, Judith. 2015. "Bibliography: Islamic State (Part 1)." *Perspectives on Terrorism* 9, no. 4: 165-212.

Tinnes, Judith. 2016. "Bibliography: Islamic State (Part 2)." *Perspectives on Terrorism* 10, no. 3: 59-98.

Tinnes, Judith. 2017. "Bibliography: Islamic State (Part 3)." *Perspectives on Terrorism* 11, no. 3: 96-149.

Tinnes, Judith. 2018. "Bibliography: Islamic State (IS, ISIS, ISIL, Daesh) (Part 4)." *Perspectives on Terrorism* 12, no. 2: 140-175.

Tizon, Tomas Alex. 2004. "Spy Suspect Was Devoted to God, Guns." *Los Angeles Times* February 23.

Tomkins, Adam. 2002. "Legislating against Terror: The Anti-Terrorism, Crime and Security Act 2001." *Public Law* Summer: 205-220.

Touahri, Sarah. 2008. "New Measures to Reform Religious Sector in Morocco." *Magharebia*, October 3.

Tran, Mark. 2007. "Poll Finds Quarter of British Muslims Believe Government and Security Services Involved in July 7 Bombings." *The Guardian*, June 5.

Travis, Alan. 2002. "Anger at Blunkett 'Whining Maniacs' Attack." *The Guardian*, September 6.

Travis, Alan. 2008. "MI5 Report Challenges Views on Terrorism in Britain." *The Guardian*, August 21.

Travis, Alan. 2012. "MPs Call Communications Data Bill 'Honeypot for Hackers and Criminals.'" *The Guardian*, October 31.

Travis, Alan. 2013a. "Hundreds of Young People Have Received Anti-Radicalisation Support." *The Guardian*, March 26.

Travis, Alan. 2013b. "Theresa May Plans New Powers to Make British Terror Suspects Stateless." *The Guardian*, November 12.

Triadafilopoulos, Triadafilos. 2011. "Illiberal Means to Liberal Ends? Understanding Recent Immigrant Integration Policies in Europe." *Journal of Ethnic and Migration Studies* 37, no. 6: 861–880.

Tumelty, Paul. 2005. "Reassessing the July 21 London Bombings." *Terrorism Monitor* September 14. https://jamestown.org/program/reassessing-the-july-21-london-bombings/.

Tyler, Tom R., Stephen Schulhofer, and Aziz Z. Huq. 2010. "Legitimacy and Deterrence Effects in Counterterrorism Policing: A Study of Muslim Americans." *Law & Society Review* 44, no. 2: 365–402.

Ubayasiri, Kasun. 2019. "Islamic State's Quest for Legitimacy: An Analysis of IS Media Frames in *Dabiq* Magazine." *Media, War & Conflict*, July 10. https://doi.org/10.1177/1750635219860422.

UK Border Agency. 2008. "The Path to Citizenship: Next Steps in Reforming the Immigration System: Government Response to Consultation." London: Stationery Office.

UNGA (United Nations General Assembly). 2006. "The United Nations Global Counter-Terrorism Strategy." A/RES/60/288, September 20.

United States Advisory Commission on Public Diplomacy. 2011. "Staff Report on the Public Meeting of the US Advisory Commission on Public Diplomacy." Washington, DC: United States Advisory Commission on Public Diplomacy, July 12.

United States Government Accountability Office. 2012. "Countering Violent Extremism: Additional Actions Could Strengthen Training Efforts." Report to the Committee on Homeland Security and Governmental Affairs, United States Senate. GAO-13-79. Washington, DC: GAO.

US Department of Homeland Security. 2008. "Fact Sheet: Task Force on New Americans." December 28. https://web.archive.org/web/20110514213514/http://www.uscis.gov/files/article/taskforceFS_18dec2008.pdf.

US Department of Homeland Security. 2010. "Readout of Secretary Napolitano's Meeting with Faith-Based and Community Leaders." Press Release, January 28. https://www.dhs.gov/news/2010/01/28/readout-secretary-napolitanos-meeting-faith-based-and-community-leaders.

US Department of Homeland Security. 2013. "Community Engagement." https://www.dhs.gov/community-engagement.

US Department of Homeland Security. 2016a. "Strategy for Countering Violent Extremism." Washington, DC: US Department of Homeland Security, October 28.

US Department of Homeland Security. 2016b. "What Is CVE?" https://www.dhs.gov/cve/what-is-cve.

US Department of Homeland Security. 2016c. "Department of Homeland Security Office for Civil Rights and Civil Liberties Fiscal Year 2015 Annual Report to Congress." Washington, DC: US Department of Homeland Security, June 10.

US Department of Homeland Security. 2017a. "Countering Violent Extremism Grant Applications (Awarded)." https://www.dhs.gov/publication/cve-grants-awarded.

US Department of Homeland Security. 2017b. "US Department of Homeland Security Office for Civil Rights and Civil Liberties Fiscal Year 2016 Annual Report to Congress." Washington, DC: US Department of Homeland Security, December 16.

US Department of Justice. 2016. "Countering Violent Extremism Force Fact Sheet." January 8. https://www.justice.gov/opa/pr/countering-violent-extremism-task-force-fact-sheet.

US Department of State. 2007a. "EUR Senior Adviser Pandith and S/P Adviser Cohen's Visit to the UK, October 9–14, 2007." Confidential. Wikileaks 07LONDON4045_a, October 25.

US Department of State. 2007b. *US National Strategy for Public Diplomacy and Strategic Communication*. Washington, DC: US Department of State, June.

US Department of State. 2008. "Home Secretary Sells the Counter-Terrorism Bill; HMG Rolls Out Local Counter-Radicalization Programs." Secret. Wikileaks 08LONDON1577_a, June 6.

US Department of State. 2009. "Cable: UK Government Seeks Deeper Counter-Radicalization Coordination." Confidential. Wikileaks 09LONDON1933_a, August 21.

US Department of State. 2010. "Center for Strategic Counterterrorism Communications." https://2009-2017.state.gov/documents/organization/116709.pdf.

US Department of State. 2011. "D&CP—Public Diplomacy." Congressional Budget Justification for Public Diplomacy. https://2009-2017.state.gov/documents/organization/158291.pdf.

US Department of State. 2013. "Country Reports on Terrorism 2012." Washington, DC: US Department of State, May.

US Department of State. 2017. "Country Reports on Terrorism 2016." Washington, DC: US Department of State, July.

US Muslim Engagement Project. 2008. *Changing Course: A New Direction for U.S. Relations with the Muslim World*. Report of the Leadership Group on US–Muslim Engagement. Washington, DC: Search for Common Ground and the Consensus Building Institute.

Van Duyn, Don. 2006. "Testimony." Hearing before the Subcommittee on Intelligence, Information Sharing, and Terrorism Risk Assessment of the US House of Representatives Committee on Homeland Security: The Homeland Security Implications of Radicalization. September 20.

Van Kersbergen, Kees. 2010. "Comparative Politics: Some Points for Discussion." *European Political Science* 9, no. 1: 49–61.

Van Oers, Ricky. 2016. "Justifying Citizenship Tests in the Netherlands and the UK." In *Illiberal Liberal States: Immigration, Citizenship and Integration in the EU*, edited by Elspeth Guild, Kees Groenendijk, and Sergio Carrera, 113–131. Abingdon: Routledge.

Vasilenko, V. I. 2004. "The Concept and Typology of Terrorism." *Statutes & Decisions* 40, no. 5: 46–56.

Veilleux-Lepage, Yannick. 2016. "Paradigmatic Shifts in Jihadism in Cyberspace: The Emerging Role of Unaffiliated Sympathizers in Islamic State's Social Media Strategy." *Contemporary Voices: St Andrews Journal of International Relations* 7, no. 1: 36–51.

Vertigans, Stephen. 2010. "British Muslims and the UK Government's 'War on Terror' Within: Evidence of a Clash of Civilizations or Emergent De-civilizing Processes?" *British Journal of Sociology* 61, no. 1: 26–44.

Vertigans, Stephen. 2013. *The Sociology of Terrorism: People, Places and Processes.* Abingdon: Routledge.

Vertovec, Steven. 2007. "Super-Diversity and Its Implications." *Ethnic and Racial Studies* 30, no. 6: 1024–1054.

Vidino, Lorenzo. 2005. "Training Imams in Europe: Italy Chooses the Wrong Partner." Counterterrorism Blog, May 17. https://www.investigativeproject.org/340/training-imams-in-europe-italy-chooses-the-wrong-partner.

Vidino, Lorenzo. 2009. "Homegrown Jihadist Terrorism in the United States: A New and Occasional Phenomenon?" *Studies in Conflict & Terrorism* 32, no. 1: 1–17.

Vidino, Lorenzo. 2012. "Homegrown Jihadist Terrorism in the United States: A New and Occasional Phenomenon?" In *Terrorism Studies: A Reader*, edited by John Horgan and Kurt Braddock, 469–484. Abingdon: Routledge.

Vidino, Lorenzo, and Seamus Hughes. 2015. "Countering Violent Extremism in America." Washington, DC: Center for Cyber and Homeland Security, George Washington University.

Von Behr, Ines, Anais Reding, Charlie Edwards, and Luke Gribbon. 2013. "Radicalisation in the Digital Era: The Use of the Internet in 15 Cases of Terrorism and Extremism." Santa Monica, CA: RAND Corporation.

Vorspan, Rachel. 2005. "Law and War: Individual Rights, Executive Authority, and Judicial Power in England during World War I." *Vanderbilt Journal of Transnational Law* 38, no. 2: 261–343.

Walker, Clive. 1992. *The Prevention of Terrorism in British Law.* 2nd edn. Manchester: Manchester University Press.

Walker, Clive. 2000. "Briefing on the Terrorism Act 2000." *Terrorism and Political Violence* 12, no. 2: 1–36.

Walker, Clive. 2011. *Terrorism and the Law.* Oxford: Oxford University Press.

*Washington Times.* 2006. "Domestic Terrorists Rising as Danger." September 8.

Wasserman, Robert. 2010. "Guidance for Building Communities of Trust." Washington, DC: US Department of Justice, Office of Community Oriented Policing Services.

Watts, Clint. 2012. "Radicalization in the US beyond Al Qaeda: Treating the Disease of the Disconnection." Philadelphia, PA: Foreign Policy Research Institute.

Weber, Max. 1948. *From Max Weber: Essays in Sociology.* London: Routledge & Kegan Paul.

Weed, Matthew C. 2017. "Global Engagement Center: Background and Issues." CRS Insight, IN10744. Washington, DC: Congressional Research Service.

Weil, Patrick. 2013. *The Sovereign Citizen: Denaturalization and the Origins of the American Republic.* Philadelphia: University of Pennsylvania Press.

Whidden, Michael J. 2001. "Unequal Justice: Arabs in America and United States Antiterrorism Legislation." *Fordham Law Review* 69, no. 6: 2825–2888.

Whitaker, Reg. 2006. "A Faustian Bargain? America and the Dream of Total Information Awareness." In *The New Politics of Surveillance and Visibility*, edited by Kevin D. Haggerty and Richard V. Ericson, 141–170. Toronto: University of Toronto Press.

White House. 2010. "National Security Strategy." May. https://obamawhitehouse.archives.gov/sites/default/files/rss_viewer/national_security_strategy.pdf.

White House. 2011a. "National Strategy for Counterterrorism." June 29. https://obamawhitehouse.archives.gov/blog/2011/06/29/national-strategy-counterterrorism.

White House. 2011b. "Empowering Local Partners to Prevent Violent Extremism in the United States." Washington, DC: Executive Office of the President of the United States, August.

White House. 2011c. "Strategic Implementation Plan for Empowering Local Partners to Prevent Violent Extremism in the United States." Washington, DC: Executive Office of the President of the United States, December.

White House. 2011d. "Executive Order 13584—Developing an Integrated Strategic Counterterrorism Communications Initiative." Washington, DC: Office of the Press Secretary, September 9.

White House. 2011e. "Statement of Administration Policy: S. 1867, National Defense Authorization Act for FY 2012." November 17. https://www.presidency.ucsb.edu/documents/statement-administration-policy-s-1867-national-defense-authorization-act-for-fy-2012.

White House. 2011f. "Statement by the President on HR 1540." December 31. https://obamawhitehouse.archives.gov/the-press-office/2011/12/31/statement-president-hr-1540.

White House. 2015. "Fact Sheet: The White House Summit on Countering Violent Extremism." February 18. https://obamawhitehouse.archives.gov/the-press-office/2015/02/18/fact-sheet-white-house-summit-countering-violent-extremism.

White House. 2016a. "Strategic Implementation Plan for Empowering Local Partners to Prevent Violent Extremism in the United States." Washington, DC: Executive Office of the President of the United States, October.

White House. 2016b. "Executive Order 13721 –Developing an Integrated Global Engagement Center to Support Government-wide Counterterrorism Communications Activities Directed Abroad and Revoking Executive Order 13584." Washington, DC: Office of the Press Secretary, March 14. https://www.govinfo.gov/content/pkg/DCPD-201600149/pdf/DCPD-201600149.pdf.

Whitehead, Tom. 2013. "Syria a 'Game Changer' for UK Terror Threat, Warns Home Office Intelligence Chief." *The Telegraph*, July 3.

Whiteley, Paul, Marianne C. Stewart, David Sanders, and Harold D. Clarke. 2005. "The Issue Agenda and Voting in 2005." *Parliamentary Affairs* 58, no. 4: 802–817.

Wight, Colin. 2009. "Theorising Terrorism: The State, Structure and History." *International Relations* 23, no. 1: 99–106

Wight, Colin. 2015. *Rethinking Terrorism: Terrorism, Violence and the State.* London: Palgrave Macmillan.

Wiktorowicz, Quintan. 2001. "The New Global Threat: Transnational Salafis and Jihad." *Middle East Policy* 8, no. 4: 18–38.

Wiktorowicz, Quintan. 2002. "Islamic Activism and Social Movement Theory: A New Direction for Research." *Mediterranean Politics* 7, no. 3: 187-211.

Wiktorowicz, Quintan. 2004. *Islamic Activism: A Social Movement Theory Approach.* Bloomington: Indiana University Press.

Wiktorowicz, Quintan. 2005. *Radical Islam Rising: Muslim Extremism in the West.* Lanham, MD: Rowman & Littlefield.

Wiktorowicz, Quintan. 2006. "Anatomy of the Salafi Movement." *Studies in Conflict & Terrorism* 29, no. 3: 207–239.

Wiktorowicz, Quintan. 2013. "Working to Counter Online Radicalization to Violence in the United States." White House, February 5. https://obamawhitehouse.archives.gov/blog/2013/02/05/working-counter-online-radicalization-violence-united-states.

Wilkinson, Paul. 2006. *Terrorism versus Democracy: The Liberal State Response*. 2nd edn. Abingdon: Routledge.

Wilkinson, Paul. 2011. *Terrorism versus Democracy: The Liberal State Response*. 3rd edn. Abingdon: Routledge.

Winnett, Robert, Christoper Hope, Steven Swinford, and Holly Watt. 2011. "WikiLeaks: Guantánamo Bay Terrorists Radicalised in London to Attack Western Targets." *The Telegraph*, April 25.

Winnett, Robert, and David Leppard. 2004. "Britain's Secret Plans to Win Muslim Hearts and Minds." *Sunday Times*, May 30.

Winter, Charlie. 2015. *The Virtual "Caliphate": Understanding Islamic State's Propaganda Strategy*. London: Quilliam.

Wintour, Patrick. 2015. "'Snooper's Charter': Four Lords in Bid to Pass Changed Version before Election." *The Guardian*, January 22.

Wintour, Patrick, and Sam Jones. 2013. "Theresa May's Measures to Tackle Radicalisation Come under Fire." *The Guardian*, May 27.

Worley, Claire. 2005. "'It's Not about Race. It's about the Community': New Labour and 'Community Cohesion.'" *Critical Social Policy* 25, no. 4: 483–496.

Wray-Lake, Laura, Amy K. Syvertsen, and Constance A. Flanagan. 2008. "Contested Citizenship and Social Exclusion: Adolescent Arab American Immigrants' Views of the Social Contract." *Applied Development Science* 12, no. 2: 84–92.

Xaykaothao, Doualy. 2016. "Some Young Somalis Voice Skepticism about Federal Anti-Terror Program." MPR News, March 24. https://www.mprnews.org/story/2016/03/24/young-somalis-divided-over-federal-anti-terror-program.

Yost, Peter. 2001. "Sedition Law Used to Hold Suspects." Associated Press, November 8. http://www.freerepublic.com/focus/f-news/566699/posts.

Zedner, Lucia. 2007. "Preventive Justice or Pre-Punishment? The Case of Control Orders." *Current Legal Problems* 60, no. 1: 174–203.

Zedner, Lucia. 2010. "Security, the State, and the Citizen: The Changing Architecture of Crime Control." *New Criminal Law Review* 13, no. 2: 379–403.

Zelin, Aaron Y. 2013. "European Foreign Fighters in Syria." ICSR Insights. London: International Centre for the Study of Radicalisation.

Zelin, Aaron Y. 2015. "Picture or It Didn't Happen: A Snapshot of the Islamic State's Official Media Output." *Perspectives on Terrorism* 9, no. 4: 85–97.

Zhou, Zunyou. 2019. "Chinese Strategy for De-Radicalization." *Terrorism and Political Violence* 31, no. 6: 1187–1209.

Zimmerman, John C. 2004. "Sayyid Qutb's Influence on the 11 September Attacks." *Terrorism and Political Violence* 16, no. 2: 222–252.

Zimmermann, Doron, and William Rosenau, eds. 2009. "The Radicalization of Diasporas and Terrorism." Zurich: ETH Zurich.

Zuckert, Catherine. 2016. "The Saving Minimum? Tocqueville on the Role of Religion in America—Then and Now." *American Political Thought* 5, no. 3: 494–518.

# Statutes Index

*For the benefit of digital users, indexed terms that span two pages (e.g., 52–53) may, on occasion, appear on only one of those pages.*

China
   Counter-Terrorism Law 2016, 56, 213n.26
   Xinjiang Anti-Extremism Regulation 2016, 56

Council of Europe
   Convention on the Prevention of Terrorism, 217–18n.14

European Convention on Human Rights, 87–88, 96, 216–17n.10

Saudi Arabia
   Law Concerning Offenses of Terrorism and its Financing 2014, 60

Singapore
   Internal Security Act, 23

United Kingdom
   Act of Union (Ireland) 1800, 69–70
   Act of Union (Scotland) 1707, 69–70
   Act of Union (Wales) 1535, 69–70
   Act of Union (Wales) 1542, 69–70
   Anti-Terrorism, Crime and Security Act 2001, 86–88
   Borders, Citizenship and Migration Act 2009, 218n.20
   British Nationality Act 1981, 69–70, 95, 99–100
   Charities Act 2006, 220n.21
   Civil Authorities (Special Powers) Act (Northern Ireland) 1922, 77
   Counter-Terrorism Act 2008, 92–93, 188
   Counter-Terrorism and Security Act 2015, 75–76, 93–94, 125–26, 220n.26
   Crime and Disorder Act 1998, 216n.6
   Criminal Justice Act 2003, 94
   Criminal Justice and Immigration Act 2008, 94
   Data Retention and Investigatory Powers Act 2014, 221n.33

Defence of the Realm Act 1914, 76–77
Draft Communications Data Bill 2012, 221n.33
Education (Independent School Standards) Regulations 2014, 75–76
Emergency Powers (Defence) Act of 1939, 76–77
Enhanced Terrorism Prevention and Investigation Measures Bill 2011, 217n.11
Human Rights Act 1998, 83, 87–88, 215n.4
Immigration, Asylum and Nationality Act 2006, 96–99
Immigration Act 1971, 96
Immigration Act 2006, 99–100
Immigration Act 2014, 99–100
Immigration and Nationality Act 1981, 98
Nationality, Immigration and Asylum Act 2002, 73–74, 94–96, 98–100
Northern Ireland (Emergency Provisions) Act 1973, 77, 83
Northern Ireland (Emergency Provisions) Act 1996 (EPA), 83, 215n.2, 215n.4
Prevention of Terrorism Act 2005, 88, 216n.9, 216–17n.10
Prevention of Terrorism (Temporary Provisions) Act 1989 (PTA), 83, 215n.2, 215n.4
Public Order Act 1970, 216n.6
Public Order Act 1986, 216n.6
Race Relations Act 1965, 216n.6
Religious Hatred Act (Northern Ireland) 1970, 216n.6
Terrorism Act 2000, 77, 83–86, 87, 99–100, 118, 206–7n.21, 216n.7
Terrorism Act 2006, 88, 89–92, 96, 98, 215n.3, 215n.4, 217n.13, 218n.15, 218n.16
Terrorism Act 2008, 216n.9
Terrorism Act 2011, 216n.9
Terrorism Prevention and Investigation Measures (TPIMs) Act 2011, 217n.11

## STATUTES INDEX

United Nations
  Convention on the Reduction of Statelessness 1961, 95

United States
  Alien and Seditions Acts 1798, 137, 155, 163, 166
  Alien Registration Act 1940, 137, 164, 223n.1
  Anti-Terrorism and Effective Death Penalty Act 1996, 132–33, 138–39, 206–7n.21, 222n.5, 222n.6, 223n.1, 223n.3, 224n.5
  Asian Exclusion Act 1924, 131
  Authorization for Use of Military Force 2001, 159
  Chinese Exclusion Act 1882, 131
  Civil Rights Act 1964, 131–32
  Communist Control Act 1954, 137
  Constitution
    First Amendment, 137, 140, 148, 149, 154–55
    Fourteenth Amendment, 129, 164
    Fourth Amendment, 149–50
  Countering Violent Extremism Act 2015 (proposed), 227n.13
  Domestic Security Enhancement Act 2002 (proposed), 164–65
  Due Process and Military Detention Amendments Act 2012 (proposed), 225n.23
  Enemy Expatriation Act 2011 (proposed), 144, 163–66
  Espionage Act 1917, 137
  Executive Order 13584 (2011), 185
  Executive Order 13721 (2016), 187
  Foreign Intelligence Surveillance Act (FISA) 1978, 138–39, 149–51, 226n.27
  Foreign Relations Authorization Act 1987, 161
  Freedom of Information Act 1966, 178
  Hart–Celler Act 1965, 130, 131–32
  Homeland Security Act 2002, 158, 223n.2
  Illegal Immigration Reform and Immigrant Responsibility Act 1996, 222n.6
  Immigration Act 1917, 131
  Immigration Act 1924, 131
  Immigration Act 1990, 133–34
  Immigration and Nationality Act 1952, 131, 132–34, 164
  Immigration and Nationality Act 1965, 130, 131–32
  Internal Security Act 1950, 133
  Johnson–Reed Act 1924, 131
  McCarran–Walter Act 1952, 164
  McGovern Amendment 1977, 133–34
  Moynihan–Frank Amendment 1987, 133–34
  National Defense Authorization Act for Fiscal Year 2012, 144, 158–61, 195–96
  National Defense Authorization Act for Fiscal Year 2013, 144, 160–63, 198, 225n.21
  National Defense Authorization Act for Fiscal Year 2014, 160–61, 225n.24
  National Defense Authorization Act for Fiscal Year 2015, 160–61, 225n.24
  National Defense Authorization Act for Fiscal Year 2016, 160–61, 225n.24
  Nationality Act 1940, 133, 137, 164, 165–66
  Naturalization Act 1790, 131
  Naturalization Act 1795, 132–33
  Naturalization Act 1906, 133
  Page Act 1875, 222n.3
  Preventing Radicalism by Exploring and Vetting its Emergence as a National Threat (PREVENT) Act 2007 (proposed), 224n.13
  Sedition Act 1918, 137, 223n.1
  Smith Act 1940, 137, 164, 223n.1
  Smith–Mundt Act 1948, 161–62, 163, 198
  Terrorist Expatriation Act 2011 (proposed), 165, 206–7n.21
  USA PATRIOT (Uniting and Strengthening America by Providing Appropriate Tools Required to Intercept and Obstruct Terrorism) Act 2001, 139–40, 144, 145–51, 163, 164, 165, 206–7n.21, 224n.7, 224n.9, 226n.1
  Violent Radicalization and Homegrown Terrorism Prevention Act 2007 (proposed), 144, 151–58, 206–7n.21, 225n.18, 225n.20
  Voting Rights Act 1965, 131–32
  Walter–McCarran Act 1952, 131, 132–34, 164

# Index

*For the benefit of digital users, indexed terms that span two pages (e.g., 52–53) may, on occasion, appear on only one of those pages.*

Abdullah (Saudi Arabia), 58–59
Abdulmutallab, Umar, 40–41
Abedi, Salman Ramdan, 23
Abrahms, Max, 65–66
Abrams, Norman, 224n.7
Adamson, Fiona B., 14–15, 33–34, 208n.12
Afghanistan
 Al-Qaeda, defeat of, 34–35
 foreign fighter attacks and, 41–42, 141–42
 global Islamic resistance in, 35–36
 Taliban, 94–95
*Ahlan* (Dutch online magazine), 63–64
Ahmed, Bilal Zaheer, 216n.7
Algeria
 integration in, 61–62
 Ministry of Religious Affairs, 61–62
 National Observatory of the Struggle against Religious Extremism, 61–62
 Salafism in, 61
 Sufism in, 61
Ali, Javed, 225n.17
Al-Qaeda
 generally, 1–2, 94–95
 Afghanistan, defeat in, 34–35
 As-Sahaab (media wing), 36, 37–38
 "constructivist turn," 36
 foreign fighter attacks inspired by, 41–42
 "franchise model," 198–99
 globally coordinated attacks, 40–41
 homegrown extremism and, 12, 198–99
 individual jihad, turn to, 34–36
 jihadists inspired by, 23
 lone-actor attacks inspired by, 41
 media management and, 36
 propaganda and, 36
 7/7 London bombings (2005) and, 1, 36, 40–41, 80, 89
 sovereignty, views of, 208n.9
 Sykes-Picot Agreement, on, 31
 transnational communities and, 198–99
 transnational political community and, 14–15

Al-Qaeda in the Arabian Peninsula (AQAP), 38, 80
Al-Qaeda in the Islamic Maghreb (AQIM), 62
al-Shabaab, 23, 80, 180–81
Amnesty International, 228n.22
Anders, Christopher, 165–66
Anderson, Benedict, 4–5
Anderson, Ryan, 127
anti-colonialism, 31
Attlee, Clement, 71
Australia
 homegrown extremism in, 23
 integration in, 51–52
 persuasion in, 64–65
al-Awlaki, Anwar, 23, 37–38, 80, 209n.19, 227n.4

Baele, Stephanie, 39–40
Bahrain, integration in, 62
Belgium, homegrown extremism in, 42
bin Laden, Osama, 31, 34
Bjelopera, Jerome P., 177–78
Blair, Tony, 31, 69, 74, 96, 106–7, 129
Blunkett, David, 94–95, 105
Bosnia, foreign fighter attacks and, 141–42
Boubaker, Amel, 61
Boucek, Christopher, 213n.30
Bourdieu, Pierre, 9, 25–30, 185. *See also* symbolic power
Briggs, Rachel, 205n.17
Brown, Gordon, 74
Bush, George W., 31, 63–64, 135, 161, 168

Cameron, David, 109–10, 121, 122, 125, 126, 217n.11, 221n.33
Canada
 Citizenship and Immigration Canada, 51–52
 counterradicalization in, 7
 homegrown extremism in, 41
 integration in, 51–53
 National Security Policy, 52–53
 persuasion in, 63

Carlile, Lord, 121
Center for Constitutional Rights, 146–47, 155
Chang, Nancy, 146–47
Chechnya, foreign fighter attacks and, 141–42
Chertoff, Michael, 142
China
  Communist Party, 56
  counterradicalization in, 7
  Counter-Terrorism Law 2016, 56, 213n.26
  integration in, 56, 62
  Islamic Associations and Women's Federations, 56
  Ministry of Foreign Affairs, 56
  Xinjiang Anti-Extremism Regulation 2016, 56
Choudry, Roshanna, 38
Ciluffo, Frank, 225n.17
citizenship
  citizenship education, 52, 74–75, 134–35
  citizenship studies, 194–97
  defined, 10–11
  rights–status–identity framework, 194–96
  tightening of, 194–97
  UK, in (See United Kingdom)
Clarke, Charles, 84–85, 86, 89–90, 91, 96–97, 107, 217–18n.14
Clarke, Peter, 78–79
Clinton, Hillary, 226n.28
coercion
  counterterrorism, coercive nature of, 16–17
  persuasion contrasted, 65, 213n.26
  political legitimacy, effect on, 65–67
  reluctance to use, 189–90
Cole, David, 148
Colley, Linda, 214n.2
Community Engagement and Resilience Fund, 7
Connolly, William E., 114
constructivist counterradicalization
  generally, 191, 194
  citizenship studies, 194–97
  transnational communities, 198–99
convergence in counterradicalization, 18–22
  generally, 2–3, 22
  global context generally, 44–46
  integration, 16–17, 22, 188–89 (See also integration)
  liberal political model, 18–19
  persuasion, 16–17, 22, 189 (See also persuasion)
  policy diffusion versus, 44, 46–49
  rule of law, 18–19
Corman, Steven R., 30
Council of Europe. Convention on the Prevention of Terrorism, 217–18n.14

Council on American-Islamic Relations, 228n.22
countering violent extremism (CVE), 15–16.
  See also counterradicalization
counterinsurgency, 204n.11
counterradicalization. See also specific country; specific topic
  "common sense" response, as, 6
  convergence in (See convergence in counterradicalization)
  countering violent extremism (CVE), 15–16
  counterinsurgency versus, 204n.11
  counterterrorism, as form of, 15–16
  defined, 15–18
  deradicalization versus, 16
  different levels of government, at, 45
  divergence in (See divergence in counterradicalization)
  diversity in, 45
  future research, 199
  immigration and, 50–52
  integrationist nature of (See integration)
  interpretivist approach, 1–2, 20–21
  local nature of, 47
  measuring efficacy of, 17, 191–92
  Muslim majority states, in, 56–62
  Muslim minority states, in, 50–56
  narrativist approach, 1–2, 20–21
  persuasive nature of (See persuasion)
  political community and, 6
  scholarly attention on, 7–9
  significance of, 7–10
  social networks and, 17–18
  UK, in (See United Kingdom)
  US, in (See United States)
counterterrorism
  coercive nature of, 16–17
  counterradicalization as form of, 15–16
  multilateralism in, 46
"couriers of systemic challenge," 34–40
Crenshaw, Martha, 3, 8, 24, 167, 203n.6
Crick, Bernard, 74–75
critical terrorism studies (CTS), 9–10, 26–27
Croft, Stuart, 71, 104–5, 214n.2, 215n.13
Crone, Manni, 26–27

*Dabiq* (Islamic State magazine), 38–39, 209n.21
Dalgaard-Nielsen, Anja, 13
Daxecker, Ursula E., 65–66
deductive power, 212–13n.23
definitions
  citizenship, 10–11
  counterradicalization, 15–18
  homegrown extremism, 11–13

INDEX 275

radicalization, 13–15
Della Porta, Donatella, 13
Demant, Froukje, 205n.17
Dempsey, James X., 148
Denmark
   Division for Cohesion and Prevention of Radicalization, 51–52
   homegrown extremism in, 23
   integration in, 51
   National Action Plan on Preventing and Countering Extremism and Radicalisation, 63–64
   persuasion in, 63–65
deradicalization, 16, 212n.18
discourse. *See* persuasion
divergence in counterradicalization, 18–22
   generally, 2–3, 22
   "common sense" and, 20
   EU versus US, 48
   formal versus informal political community, 190–91
   legislative response, 21–22
   political community and, 20–21, 190
   reasons for, 6
   "thin" versus "thick" counterradicalization, 19, 174–75
   US hegemony, effect of, 48–49
Donohue, Laura K., 213n.28

encouragement of terrorism, 89, 90–91, 98, 215n.3, 215n.4
Estonia, counterterrorism in, 47
Ethiopia, integration in, 62
European Commission, integration and, 54
European Convention on Human Rights, 87–88, 96, 216–17n.10
European Court of Human Rights, 195–96
"European Islam," 54, 55
European Union
   counterradicalization in, 48
   Declaration on Combating Terrorism, 46
   Plan of Action on Combating Terrorism, 46
Everson, Michelle, 70–71

Farook, Rizwan, 143
Farr, Charles, 119
far-right extremism
   generally, 204n.10, 211n.10
   integration and, 55–56
   UK, in, 81, 193
   US, in, 138–39, 140, 193
Feinstein, Dianne, 160
fields, 27

Fieschi, Catherine, 205n.17
Foley, Frank, 9, 47–48, 214–15n.12
Fontana, David, 222n.7
foreign fighter attacks, 40, 41–42
Foucault, Michel, 212–13n.23
France
   *Charlie Hebdo* attacks (2015), 54, 211n.12
   counterradicalization in, 47–48
   counterterrorism in, 9
   homegrown extremism in, 42
   incitement to terrorism in, 213n.26
   integration in, 54

Gadahn, Adam, 37–38
Genkin, Michael, 11–12
Germany
   counterradicalization in, 1, 45, 47–48
   Federal Office for Migration and Refugees, 1, 64
   Federal Office for the Protection of the Constitution, 51
   homegrown extremism in, 36
   integration in, 51, 53–54, 55
   Islam Konferenz, 55
   9/11 attacks, response to, 8
   persuasion in, 64
Gersten, David, 154
Gibney, Matthew J., 196
Global Counterterrorism Forum, 7, 49
Global Internet Forum to Counter Terrorism, 187
"global Islamic resistance," 35–36
global jihadi community, 203n.4
globally coordinated attacks, 40–41
Goodall, H.L., Jr., 30
Graham, Lindsey, 158, 159
Gutfraind, Alexander, 11–12
Guy, Francis, 108–9

habitus, 27
*hakimiyyah* (sovereignty), 31
Halverson, Jeffry R., 30
Hansen, Lene, 114
Harman, Jane, 151, 152–53, 154–55, 157–58
Hasan, Nidal Malik, 37–38, 142–43, 227n.4
"hearts and minds," 204n.11
Hedayah, 7
Hegghammer, Thomas, 34, 42, 203n.4
Heller, Thomas, 130
Helmus, Todd C., 229n.29
Hess, Michael L., 65–66
Hoffman, Bruce, 207–8n.8
Holder, Eric, 172

homegrown extremism. *See also specific country*
  Al-Qaeda, influence of, 198–99
  defined, 11–13
  foreign fighter attacks, 40, 41–42
  globally coordinated attacks, 40–41
  immigration and, 205–6n.18
  individual jihad, turn to, 35–36
  jihadi strategies, in, 34–40
  lone-actor attacks, 40, 41, 210n.26
  media management and, 36–38
  political community and, 5–6, 23–24, 198–99
  propaganda and, 34–35, 36, 38–39
  social media and, 38–39
  spectrum of, 40–42
  symbolic power and, 3–4, 9, 24–25
  UK, in (*See* United Kingdom)
  US, in (*See* United States)
Hoover, J. Edgar, 67
Hughes, Seamus, 176
Human Rights Watch, 155, 160
Hurd, Ian, 68

Ilan, Jonathan, 26–27
imagined community, 4–5
immigration
  counterradicalization and, 50–52
  homegrown extremism and, 205–6n.18
  integration and, 50–52
  UK, legislation and, 94–100
  US and
    9/11 attacks and, 131–32
    political community and, 130–32
incitement to terrorism, 85–86, 213n.26, 216n.6
Indonesia
  citizenship and, 197
  Coordination Forum for the Prevention of Terrorism (Forum Koordinasi Pencegahan Terorisme) (FKPT), 57–58
  counterradicalization in, 1, 7, 44, 48, 188–89
  deradicalization in, 16
  Engaging with the Islamic World (EWIW) roadshows in, 109–10
  integration in, 57–58
  National Anti-Terrorism Agency (Badan Nasional Penanggulangan Terorisme) (BNPT), 57–58
  National Terrorism Prevention Program, 58
  post-prison release deradicalization in, 212n.18
*Inspire* (Al-Qaeda magazine), 38–39, 209n.20, 216n.7
integration. *See also specific country*
  generally, 2, 16–17, 22, 49–50

citizenship education, 52, 74–75
far-right extremism and, 55–56
immigration and, 50–52
Islam, focus on, 53–54
Muslim majority states, in, 56–62
Muslim minority states, in, 50–56
separatist movements and, 55–56
International Relations, 4, 7–8, 25, 208n.11
Iraq
  foreign fighter attacks and, 81
  global Islamic resistance in, 35–36
Ireland
  creation of Irish Free State, 69–70
  nationalism in, 77
Islamic Emirate of Afghanistan, 32
Islamic Emirate of Somalia, 32
Islamic State
  generally, 1–2
  al-Hayat (media group), 38–39
  homegrown extremism and, 12
  political community and, 32
  social media and, 38–39
  Sykes-Picot Agreement, on, 31
  territory and, 32
Italy
  homegrown extremism in, 36
  integration in, 54

Jailani, Muhammad Anwar, 23
Japan, response to 9/11 attacks, 8
Al-Jedda, Hilal, 95
Jemaah Islaamiya, 55
Jenkins, Brian, 153–55, 225n.17, 225n.18
Jenkins, Roy, 71–72
Jigsaw (Google subsidiary), 187
"jihadi strategic studies," 34
jihadi strategies
  homegrown extremism in, 34–40
  individual jihad, turn to, 34–36
  "leaderless jihad," 39–40, 42–43
  political community in, 3–4, 5, 12, 30–34
  propaganda and, 34–35, 36, 38–39
  social media and, 38–39
  sovereignty, jihadi views regarding, 32–33, 198–99
  symbolic power in, 30–34
Joppke, Christian, 130, 134, 194–95, 197

Karlsson, Michael, 211n.4
Karst, Kenneth L., 130
Katzenstein, Peter J., 8, 194
Kaufman, Eric P., 221n.1
Kelly, Ruth, 110

Kenya, counterinsurgency in, 204n.11
Klein, Kurt, 229n.29

LaFree, Gary, 13
"leaderless jihad," 39–40, 42–43
legislative response. *See also* Table of Legislation
  divergence in counterradicalization, 21–22
  UK, in (*See* United Kingdom)
  US, in (*See* United States)
Leheny, David, 8, 194
Levin, Carl, 158
Lia, Brynjar, 32, 34
Lieberman, Joseph, 165–66
Lipset, Seymour Martin, 221n.1
Lloyd, Lord, 84, 215n.2, 215–16n.5
Locke, John, 68
lone-actor attacks, 40, 41, 210n.26
Lownsbrough, Hannah, 205n.17
Lungren, Daniel, 152–53
Lynch, Marc, 36

Major, John, 84
Malaysia, counterinsurgency in, 204n.11
Malik, Maleiha, 216n.6
Malik, Tashfeen, 143
Mandaville, Peter, 32–33, 207–8n.8
Al-Masarai, Mohammed, 215–16n.5
Mateen, Omar, 127
Maududi, Abul A'la, 31
Mauritania
  counterradicalization in, 44
  integration in, 62
May, Theresa, 99, 220n.22
McCain, John, 158
McCants, William, 32, 34
McTernan, Oliver, 101–2, 119
McVeigh, Timothy, 138–39
media management, 36–38
Mendelsohn, Barak, 5, 12, 32–33, 49, 198–99, 207n.4, 208n.9, 208n.11
Microsoft, 187
Milliband, David, 109–10
Modood, Tariq, 214–15n.12
Moore, Cerwyn, 215n.13
Morocco
  Casablanca bombings (2003), 60–61
  counterradicalization in, 1
  Higher Council of Ulemas, 60–61
  integration in, 60–61
  Salafism in, 60–61
  Sufism in, 60–61
Muhammad, Abdulhakim Mujahid, 142–43
Muhammad VI (Morocco), 60–61

Muslim Public Affairs Committee, 155
Muslim World League, 7

Napolitano, Janet, 52, 53, 169
narratives, 207n.3
nation-states
  *hakimiyyah* (sovereignty) versus, 31
  political communities, as, 4
Neal, Andrew W., 21, 26–27, 82
Netherlands
  counterradicalization in, 45, 47, 188–89
  homegrown extremism in, 23
  integration in, 51–52, 53–54, 55
  Intelligence Service, 51
  Ministry of Immigration, 51–52
  persuasion in, 63–65
  Polarisation and Radicalisation Action Plan 2007-2011, 51
  ReCora, 51–52
Nigeria, deradicalization in, 16
Nixon, Richard, 149–50, 155
North Atlantic Treaty Organization (NATO), 46
Northern Ireland situation, 66–67
Norway
  counterradicalization in, 44
  incitement to terrorism in, 213n.26
  integration in, 51, 53–54, 55
  Ministry of Justice, 51
  persuasion in, 64–65
  Utoya massacre (2012), 204n.10

Obama, Barack, 7, 63–64, 135–36, 159, 160–61, 168, 170, 176–77, 185, 224n.12
Omand, David, 101–2, 111
Omelicheva, Mariya Y., 9, 47, 194
Organisation for Economic Co-operation and Development (OECD), 46
Organisation of Islamic Cooperation, 7
Osborne, Stuart, 81

Padilla, Jose, 142
Pakistan
  Engaging with the Islamic World (EWIW) roadshows in, 109–10
  foreign fighter attacks and, 142
Pelosi, Nancy, 226n.28
Perliger, Arie, 9, 12–13, 24, 25, 26–27
persuasion, 62–68. *See also specific country*
  generally, 2, 16–17, 22, 44
  coercion contrasted, 65, 213n.26
  counternarratives, 63
  online counterradicalization, 63–64
  political legitimacy and, 65–68

persuasion (*cont.*)
  psychological drivers of radicalization and, 65
  recipients and generators of ideas and values, 64–65
Phillips, Andrew, 203n.3
Piazza, James A., 65–66
Pistole, John, 142
political community
  counterradicalization and, 6
  divergence in counterradicalization and, 20–21, 190
  formal political community, 4, 5–6
  homegrown extremism and, 5–6, 23–24, 198–99
  informal political community, 4, 5–6
  jihadi strategies, in, 3–4, 5, 12, 30–34
  nation-states as, 4
  symbolic power and, 3–4
  territory and, 32
  transnational political community, 14–15
  UK, in (*See* United Kingdom)
  *ummah* as, 30
  US, in (*See* United States)
political legitimacy
  coercion, effect of, 65–67
  consent and, 65, 67–68
  persuasion and, 65–68
Precht, Tomas, 11–12
preventing violent extremism, 15–16. *See also* counterradicalization
productive power, 212–13n.23
propaganda, 34–35, 36, 38–39

al-Qurashi, Ahmad, 35
Qutb, Sayyid, 31, 208n.15

radicalization
  defined, 13–15
  foreign policy grievances and, 205n.17
  transnational political community and, 14–15
RAND Corporation, 153, 225n.15
Rawls, John, 196–97
Reagan, Ronald, 133–34
Redirect Method (online tool), 187
Reichert, David, 224n.13
Reid, Richard, 40–41
Rigby, Lee, 124, 126, 221n.32
Romaniuk, Peter, 49
Rushdie, Salman, 104–5, 214n.4
Russia
  Chechnya, foreign fighter attacks and, 141–42
  counterradicalization in, 7
  integration in, 55–56, 62
  National Security Strategy, 55–56

Ryan, Michael W.S., 34

Sageman, Marc, 26–27, 36–37, 42–43, 210n.24
Salafism, 56–57, 60–61
Sandberg, Sveinung, 26–27
Saudi Arabia
  citizenship and, 197
  counterradicalization in, 1, 17–18, 44, 48, 188–89
  deradicalization in, 16
  Engaging with the Islamic World (EWIW) roadshows in, 109–10
  integration in, 58–60
  Law Concerning Offenses of Terrorism and its Financing 2014, 60
  Ministry of Culture and Information, 59
  Ministry of Islamic Affairs, 59
  "National Solidarity Campaign against Terrorism and Extremism," 59
  persuasion in, 63–64
  post-prison release deradicalization in, 212n.18
  Prevention, Rehabilitation, and Aftercare, 58–59
  Riyadh bombings (2003), 58–59
  Sakinah (religious tranquility) campaign, 59, 63–64
Schmid, Alex P., 29–30, 207–8n.8
Schmitt, Carl, 194–95, 196
Schneider, Dorothee, 134–35
Schuck, Pete H., 128–29, 130
*Sharia*, 30
Shazad, Faisal, 165
Sheinwald, Nigel, 221n.33
"shoe bomber," 40–41
Simmons, Robert, 151–52
Singapore
  counterradicalization in, 17–18
  homegrown extremism in, 23
  integration in, 55
  Internal Security Act, 23
  post-prison release deradicalization in, 212n.18
  Religious Rehabilitation Group, 55
Sinnar, Shirin, 150–51
Slootman, Marieke, 205n.17
Slynn, Lord, 216n.8
Smith, Adam, 162–63
Smith, Rogers M., 127–28, 129, 130
social media, 38–39, 209n.22
social networks, counterradicalization and, 17–18
Somalia, foreign fighter attacks and, 41–42
sovereignty
  *hakimiyyah* versus, 31
  jihadi views regarding, 32–33, 198–99

## INDEX

Spain
  counterradicalization in, 47
  homegrown extremism in, 14, 36
  integration in, 54
  Madrid bombings (2004), 14, 36
  Ministry for Religious Affairs, 54
Stampnitzky, Lisa, 26–27
Stone, Geoffrey R., 222n.8
Straw, Jack, 84–85, 219n.13
Suchman, Mark, 68
Sufism, 60–61
al-Suri, Abu Musab, 34–36
Sweden, persuasion in, 63
Sykes–Picot Agreement (1916), 31
symbolic power
  Bourdieusian approach, 25–30
  fields and, 27
  habitus and, 27
  homegrown extremism and, 3–4, 9, 24–25
  interplay of agency and structure, 26
  jihadi strategies, in, 30–34
  language and, 27–28
  9/11 attacks, of, 24
  political community and, 3–4
  social construction and, 28–30
  symbolic capital, 28–30
  terrorism, of, 24–25
  "thinking tools" of, 25–26
Syria
  foreign fighter attacks and, 42, 81
  social media and, 209n.22

Taliban, 94–95
Task Force on Muslim American Civil and Political Engagement, 226n.2
Tenet, George, 58–59
terrorism
  defined, 24
  encouragement of, 89, 90–91, 98, 215n.3, 215n.4
  incitement to, 85–86, 213n.26, 216n.6
  symbolic power of, 24–25
  waves of, 210n.24
Tillie, Jean, 205n.17
transnational communities, 108–9, 198–99
Triadafilopoulos, Triadafilos, 14–15, 194–95
Truman, Harry, 160
Trump, Donald J., 205–6n.18, 228n.21
Tsarnaev brothers, 41
Turkey, counterradicalization in, 7

United Arab Emirates, counterradicalization in, 7

United Kingdom
  Act of Union (Ireland) 1800, 69–70
  Act of Union (Scotland) 1707, 69–70
  Act of Union (Wales) 1535, 69–70
  Act of Union (Wales) 1542, 69–70
  Advisory Group on Citizenship, 74–75
  Ajegbo Review, 75
  Anti-Terrorism, Crime and Security Act 2001, 86–88
  Belfast Agreement 1998, 215n.2
  Borders, Citizenship and Migration Act 2009, 218n.20
  Brexit, 205–6n.18
  British Council, 103–4
  "British Islam," 17, 114
  British Muslim or Wot? program, 188–89
  British Nationality Act 1981, 69–70, 95, 99–100
  "British values," 73–74, 75–76, 122–23
  Cantle Review, 73, 106
  Channel program, 64, 117–18, 170, 192–93
  Charities Act 2006, 220n.21
  Charity Commission, 220n.21
  citizenship
    citizenship education, 74–75
    citizenship test, 73–74, 95, 218n.17
    deprivation of, 99–100
    establishing citizen–state relationship, 83–86
    legislation and, 94–100
    political community and, 71–76
    removal of, 98–99
  Civil Authorities (Special Powers) Act (Northern Ireland) 1922, 77
  Commission on Integration and Cohesion, 51, 107, 108
  community cohesion, 72–74, 102–3, 104–6
  Community Safety Partnerships, 93
  Congress of Cultural Freedom, 116–17
  Contest policy, 101–2, 107–8, 118, 121–22
  Contextualising Islam in Britain project, 114
  Continuous Professional Development program, 114
  control orders in, 88, 190, 195–96, 216n.9, 216–17nn.10–11
  convergence in counterradicalization (See convergence in counterradicalization)
  Countering Terrorism and Radicalisation Programme, 109–10
  counterradicalization in
    generally, 17–18, 101
    adjustment of policy, 114–21
    centralization of, 192–93

United Kingdom (*cont.*)
    civic capacity and leadership, 113–14
    communications technology, 123–24
    Conservative/Liberal Democrat coalition government, under, 121–26
    criticism of, 118–21
    domestic reaction to, 118–21
    emergence of policy, 110–14
    faith institutions and leaders, 114
    initial policy, 101–6
    local solutions, 113–14
    "muscular liberalism" and, 192–93
    online activities, 124
    prisons, in, 125
    7/7 London bombings (2005), in response to, 106–10
    shared values, 112–13
    shifts in policy, 192–93
    "taken for granted" understandings and, 191–92
    "thickness" of, 3, 19
    universities, in, 75–76, 93–94, 125, 192–93, 196–97
Counter-Terrorism Act 2008, 92–93, 188
Counter-Terrorism and Security Act 2015, 75–76, 93–94, 125–26, 220n.26
counterterrorism in, 9, 188
Counter-Terrorism Internet Referral Unit, 123–24, 220n.26
Crick Report, 74–75
Crime and Disorder Act 1998, 216n.6
Criminal Justice Act 2003, 94
Criminal Justice and Immigration Act 2008, 94
Data Retention and Investigatory Powers Act 2014, 221n.33
Defence of the Realm Act 1914, 76–77
Denham Review, 73
Department for Communities and Local Government (DCLG)
    generally, 21–22
    counterradicalization and, 110–12, 192–93
    creation of, 117–18
    inquiries into Prevent policy, 120
    Prevent policy and, 107–8, 121–22, 220n.20
    Research, Information and Communications Unit (RICU) and, 116
Department for Education, 75–76
detention, 86–88, 94, 217n.13
dissemination of publications, 89, 90, 91–92, 218n.16
divergence in counterradicalization (*See* divergence in counterradicalization)
Draft Communications Data Bill 2012, 221n.33
Education (Independent School Standards) Regulations 2014, 75–76
Emergency Powers (Defence) Act of 1939, 76–77
encouragement of terrorism, 89, 90–91, 98, 215n.3, 215n.4
Engaging with the Islamic World (EWIW), 103–4, 108–9, 220n.20
Enhanced Terrorism Prevention and Investigation Measures Bill 2011, 217n.11
Extremism Task Force, 125
Faith and Social Cohesion Unit, 220n.21
Finsbury Park mosque raid (2003), 78–79
Foreign and Commonwealth Office (FCO)
    counterradicalization and (*See* with this heading, "counterradicalization in")
    Engaging with the Islamic World (EWIW), 103, 220n.20
    Prevent policy and, 108–10
    Research, Information and Communications Unit (RICU) and, 116–17
    roadshows, 109–10, 114
    transnational communities and, 198
    "unacceptable behaviours" and, 97
Foreign Office, 103
Forward Thinking (charity), 114, 119
Good Friday Agreement 1998, 214n.10
homegrown extremism in
    generally, 23
    Al-Qaeda, influence of, 78–81
    emergence of, 79–81
    far-right extremism, 81, 193
    managing, 94–100
    7/7 London bombings (2005), 1, 14, 36, 40–41, 80, 89, 106–10
Home Office
    generally, 21–22, 112
    citizenship test and, 73–74
    Communities Division, 117–18
    Community Cohesion Unit, 73
    counterradicalization and (*See* with this heading, "counterradicalization in")
    homegrown extermism, on, 81, 103
    National Indicator 35, 220n.23
    Preventing Extremism Together Working Groups, 107
    Prevent policy and, 121–22
    Research, Information and Communications Unit (RICU) and, 116–17
    "unacceptable behaviours" and, 97

Human Rights Act 1998, 83, 87–88, 215n.4
Immigration, Asylum and Nationality Act 2006, 96–99
  removal of citizenship, 98–99
  "unacceptable behaviours," 96–97
immigration, legislation and, 94–100
Immigration Act 1971, 96
Immigration Act 2006, 99–100
Immigration Act 2014, 99–100
Immigration and Nationality Act 1981, 98
Immigration Removal Centres, 123–24
incitement to terrorism, 85–86, 213n.26, 216n.6
Independent Community Cohesion Review Team, 73
inflammatory statements, 218n.15
integration in, 54, 55, 71–76, 112–13, 115–16, 125–26, 192–93
"invented nation," as, 69–70
Islam and Citizenship Education (ICE) program, 1, 52, 69, 112–13
Labour Party, 72–73, 94
legislation in (*See also* Table of Statutes)
  generally, 82
  citizenship and, 94–100
  citizenship test, 73–74, 95, 218n.17
  control orders, 88, 216n.9, 216–17nn.10–11, 217n.12
  deprivation of citizenship, 99–100
  detention, 86–88, 94, 217n.13
  dissemination of publications, 89, 90, 91–92, 218n.16
  encouragement of terrorism, 89, 90–91, 98, 215n.3, 215n.4
  establishing citizen–state relationship, 83–86
  expanded definition of terrorism, 83–85, 99–100
  homegrown extremism, managing, 94–100
  immigration and, 94–100
  incitement to terrorism, 85–86, 213n.26, 216n.6
  inflammatory statements, 218n.15
  9/11 attacks, in response to, 86–88
  preventing "citizen terrorism," 89–94
  religious and political motivations, 84–85
  removal of citizenship, 98–99
  7/7 London bombings (2005), in response to, 89
  sunset clauses, 215n.1
  "unacceptable behaviours," 96–97
"life in the UK" test, 73–74, 95, 218n.17
Local and Regional Speakers Bureau, 76–77

Luton Ambassadors for Islam, 69, 114
MI5, 79, 103
Ministerial Review Group on Community Cohesion and Public Order, 73
Ministry of Information/ Home Intelligence Bureau, 76–77
Mosaic Muslim Mentoring Scheme, 118
Mosque and Imams National Advisory Board (MINAB), 115–16
multiculturalism in, 71–72, 191
Muslim Contact Unit, 102
Muslim Council of Britain, 118–19
Muslim Engagement Action Plan (MEAP), 105
National Imams and Advisory Commission, 108
National Institute of Adult Continuing Education, 114
Nationality, Immigration and Asylum Act 2002, 73–74, 94–96, 98–100
National Muslim Women's Advisory Group, 115–16
National Resource Centre for Supplementary Schools, 113
National War Aims Committee, 76–77
"New Labour," 72
Northern Ireland (Emergency Provisions) Act 1973, 77, 83
Northern Ireland (Emergency Provisions) Act 1996 (EPA), 83, 215n.2, 215n.4
Northern Ireland situation, 66–67, 77–78, 83, 102, 189, 215n.2, 216n.6
Office for Security and Counter-Terrorism (OSCT), 21–22, 107–8, 112–13, 114–15, 117–18
Operation Crevice, 79–80
Operation Rhyme, 79–80
Parekh Report, 214n.5
persuasion in, 63–65, 123–24, 125, 193
political community in
  generally, 69
  "Britishness" and, 71–76, 192–93
  "British values," 73–74, 75–76, 122–23
  citizenship and, 71–76
  citizenship education, 74–75
  community cohesion, 72–74, 102–3, 104–6
  empire, effect of, 70
  formal versus informal political community, 69–71
  integration and, 71–76
  "invented nation," as, 69–70
  multiculturalism and, 71–72
  state–citizen relationship, 76–78

United Kingdom (*cont.*)
  violence and, 76–78
  wartime, during, 76–78
Preventing Extremism Together Working
    Groups, 107
Prevention of Terrorism Act 2005, 88, 216n.9,
    216–17n.10
Prevention of Terrorism (Temporary
    Provisions) Act 1989 (PTA), 83,
    215n.2, 215n.4
Prevent policy
  generally, 52–53, 55
  Conservative/Liberal Democrat coalition
    government, under, 121–26
  criticism of, 118–21
  funding of, 219n.15
  initial policy, 102
  inquiries into, 118, 120–21
  Internet controls, 211n.11
  persuasion and, 63
  "Prevent Duty," 75–76, 93–94, 192–
    93, 196–97
  Preventing Violent Extremism Pathfinder
    Fund, 110–11, 114, 219n.16
  "Prevent 1," 103
  Strategy for Delivery, 107–8
  transnational communities and, 108–9
  updating of, 114–15
  websites, 117
Projecting British Islam program, 220n.20
Public Order Act 1970, 216n.6
Public Order Act 1986, 216n.6
Race Relations Act 1965, 216n.6
racial unrest in, 72–74
Radical Middle Way, 55, 103–4, 113–14,
    220n.20
Religious Hatred Act (Northern Ireland)
    1970, 216n.6
Research, Information and Communications
    Unit (RICU), 63–64, 116–17, 123–24,
    220n.26
Terrorism Act 2000, 83–86
  generally, 77, 87, 118, 206–7n.21, 216n.7
  expanded definition of terrorism under,
    83–85, 99–100
  incitement under, 85–86
  religious and political motivations
    under, 84–85
Terrorism Act 2006, 89–92
  generally, 88, 96
  detention, 217n.13
  dissemination of publications, 89, 90, 91–
    92, 218n.16
  encouragement of terrorism, 89, 90–91, 98,
    215n.3, 215n.4
  inflammatory statements, 218n.15
Terrorism Act 2008, 216n.9
Terrorism Act 2011, 216n.9
Terrorism Prevention and Investigation
    Measures, 195–96
Terrorism Prevention and Investigation
    Measures (TPIMs) Act 2011, 217n.11
"unacceptable behaviours," 96–97
unitary state, as, 138, 190
Young Muslim Advisory Group, 115–16
United Nations
  Convention on the Reduction of Statelessness
    1961, 95
  Counter-Terrorism Implementation Task
    Force (CTITF), 48–49, 55–56
  Counter-Terrorism Strategy, 47
  Security Council Resolution 1624, 45–47,
    48–49, 210–11n.3, 217–18n.14
  Working Group on Addressing
    Radicalisation and Extremism that Lead
    to Terrorism, 45–46
United States
  Advisory Commission on Public
    Diplomacy, 162
  Alien and Seditions Acts 1798, 137, 155,
    163, 166
  Alien Registration Act 1940, 137, 164, 223n.1
  American Civil Liberties Union (ACLU),
    155, 165–66, 178, 193
  "American identity," 132–36
  "American values," 128–32
  anti-communism in, 67, 133–34, 137, 148,
    149, 161
  Anti-Terrorism and Effective Death Penalty
    Act 1996
    generally, 222n.5
    expanded list of offenses under, 132–33
    habeas corpus and, 222n.6
    material support under, 223n.3, 224n.5
    Oklahoma City bombing (1995), in
      response to, 138–39, 222n.6, 223n.1
    terrorism as federal crime, 206–7n.21
  Arlington Police Department, 181
  Asian Exclusion Act 1924, 131
  Authorization for Use of Military Force
    2001, 159
  Boston Marathon bombing (2013), 41,
    143, 172
  Bureau of Naturalization, 134–35
  Central Intelligence Agency (CIA), 224n.10
  Chicago Council on Global Affairs, 226n.2

Chinese Exclusion Act 1882, 131
citizenship
 citizenship education, 134–35
 state–citizen relationship, 136–41
Citizenship and Immigration Service, 52
Civil Rights Act 1964, 131–32
cohesive civic community, importance of, 176–78
Commission on Immigration Reform, 134–35
Communist Control Act 1954, 137
Communist Party, 133
community-based measures, 170–71
community engagement, importance of, 178–81
Constitution
 First Amendment, 137, 140, 148, 149, 154–55, 176–77, 178
 Fourteenth Amendment, 129, 164, 174–75
 Fourth Amendment, 149–50
"constitutional patriotism," 22, 128–29
convergence in counterradicalization (*See* convergence in counterradicalization)
Countering Violent Extremism Act 2015 (proposed), 227n.13
countering violent extremism (CVE) in
 generally, 17–18, 167–68
 American Muslims as transnational political community and, 181–84
 cohesive civic community, importance of, 176–78
 community-based measures, 170–71
 community engagement, importance of, 178–81
 Congressional hearings, 168
 Constitutional constraints, 174–75
 defined, 167
 emergence of policy, 170–75
 federal attorneys, role of, 45
 funding of, 171–73, 181
 further research, need for, 175
 initial policy, 168–70
 interventions, 173
 online CVE, 184–87
 private sector, collaboration with, 173
 shifts in policy, 193
 symbolic power and, 185–86
 "taken for granted" understandings and, 190–92
 "thinness" of, 2–3, 19, 174–75
 weaknesses of, 173–74
counterradicalization in (*See* within this heading, "countering violent extremism (CVE) in")

Counterterrorism Communication Center, 228–29n.27
counterterrorism in, 188
Defense Advanced Research Projects Agency Total Information Awareness Program (proposed), 223n.2
Department of Defense, 228–29n.27
Department of Homeland Security (DHS)
 Advisory Council, 169, 173, 227n.6
 civil liberties and, 152
 Community Awareness Briefing (CAB), 180, 184, 228n.20
 Community Resilience Exercise (CREX), 180, 184, 228n.20
 countering violent extremism (CVE) and (*See* within this heading, "countering violent extremism (CVE) in")
 Countering Violent Extremism Working Group, 169
 Extremism and Radicalization Branch, 209n.19
 homegrown extremism, on, 14
 immigration and, 51–52
 integration and, 53–54
 National Task Force on Community Engagement, 169
 Office of Civil Rights and Civil Liberties (OCRCL), 53, 169, 172–73, 174–75, 177–78, 183–84
 Office of Community Partnerships, 172–73, 174, 177–78
 Office of Intelligence and Analysis, 168
 persuasion and, 63
 Task Force on New Americans, 135
Department of Justice, 150–51
 Building Communities of Trust (BCOT) initiative, 168–69, 180–81
 countering violent extremism (CVE) and, 171–73, 174–75
 Domestic Terrorism Executive Committee, 140
 Young Somali–American Advisory Council, 180–81
detention, 159–61
detention in, 159–61, 190
Digital Outreach Team, 63–64
divergence in counterradicalization (*See* divergence in counterradicalization)
Domestic Security Enhancement Act 2002 (proposed), 164–65
Due Process and Military Detention Amendments Act 2012 (proposed), 225n.23

United States (*cont.*)
  Eisenhower Commission, 154
  Enemy Expatriation Act 2011
    (proposed), 163–66
    generally, 144
    denationalization, 163, 165–66
    denaturalization, 163–64
  Espionage Act 1917, 137
  Executive Order 13584 (2011), 185
  Executive Order 13721 (2016), 187
  far-right extremism in, 138–39, 140, 193
  Federal Bureau of Investigation (FBI)
    civil liberties and, 152
    community engagement/multicultural advisory councils, 180–81
    community outreach programs, 168–69
    countering violent extremism (CVE) and, 171, 172–73, 174–75, 183
    CVE Coordination Office, 172
    far-right extremism, on, 138–39
    homegrown extremism, on, 227n.7
    information sharing and, 224n.10
    investigations by, 146
    stigma regarding, 67
    surveillance and, 224n.11
    Terrorist Screening Center, 188
  federal republic, as, 138, 190
  Foreign Intelligence Surveillance Act (FISA) 1978, 138–39, 149–51, 226n.27
  Foreign Relations Authorization Act 1987, 161
  Fort Hood shooting (2009), 37–38, 41, 227n.4
  Freedom of Information Act 1966, 178
  Global Strategic Engagement Center (GSEC), 228–29n.27
  Guantanamo Bay detention facility, 159
  Hart–Celler Act 1965, 130, 131–32
  Heartland Democracy program, 188–89
  homegrown extremism in
    Al-Qaeda, influence of, 141–43
    Boston Marathon bombing (2013), 41, 143, 172
    emergence of, 141–43
    far-right extremism, 138–39, 140, 193
    Fort Hood shooting (2009), 37–38, 41, 227n.4
    Islamic State, influence of, 143
    "Lackawanna Six," 142
    Oklahoma City bombing (1995), 131–32, 138–39, 222n.6, 223n.1
    Orlando nightclub shooting (2016), 127
    San Bernardino shooting (2015), 143
    World Trade Center bombing (1993), 138–39
  Homeland Security Act 2002, 158, 223n.2
  Houston Office of Public Safety and Homeland Security, 181
  Illegal Immigration Reform and Immigrant Responsibility Act 1996, 222n.6
  immigration
    9/11 attacks and, 131–32
    political community and, 130–32
  Immigration Act 1917, 131
  Immigration Act 1924, 131
  Immigration Act 1990, 133–34
  Immigration and Nationality Act 1952, 131, 132–34, 164
  Immigration and Nationality Act 1965, 130, 131–32
  integration in, 51–52, 53–54, 135–36
  Intelligence Reform and Terrorism Prevention Act 2004, 226n.27
  Interagency Working Group to Counter Online Radicalization to Violence, 184–85
  Internal Security Act 1950, 133
  interventions, 173
  Japanese American Citizens League, 160
  Japanese internment in, 67, 160
  Johnson–Reed Act 1924, 131
  Kerner Commission, 154
  "Lackawanna Six," 142
  legislation in (*See also* Table of Statutes)
    generally, 144–45
    detention, 159–61
    dissemination of State Department materials, 161–63
    expanded definition of terrorism, 145–47
    formal political community, boundaries of, 147–51
    material support for terrorism, 149
    "national values" and, 144–45
    non-citizens and, 147–48
    resident non-citizens and, 148
    sunset clauses, 215n.1
    surveillance, 149–51
  material support for terrorism, 149
  McCarran–Walter Act 1952, 164
  McCarthyism, 67, 132–33, 155, 160
  McGovern Amendment 1977, 133–34
  "melting pot" approach to immigration, 191
  Moynihan–Frank Amendment 1987, 133–34
  "multiple traditions," 130
  Muslim Engagement Project, 226n.2
  National Commission on Terrorist Attacks Upon the United States (9/11 Commission), 180

National Counterterrorism Center (NCTC)
　Community Resilience Exercise, 228n.20
　countering violent extremism (CVE) and, 169–70, 171–73, 180, 183
　Global Engagement Group, 53
　homegrown extremism, on, 227n.7
National Defense Authorization Act for Fiscal Year 2012, 158–61
　generally, 144, 161
　detention, 159–61
　due process and, 195–96
National Defense Authorization Act for Fiscal Year 2013, 161–63
　generally, 144, 160–61, 225n.21
　dissemination of State Department materials, 161–63
　transnational communities and, 198
National Defense Authorization Act for Fiscal Year 2014, 160–61, 225n.24
National Defense Authorization Act for Fiscal Year 2015, 160–61, 225n.24
National Defense Authorization Act for Fiscal Year 2016, 160–61, 225n.24
National Intelligence Estimate 2007, 142
Nationality Act 1940, 133, 137, 164, 165–66
National Security Council, 169–70, 184–85
National Security Strategy, 208n.10
National Strategy for Counterterrorism, 170
"national values," 144–45
Nationwide Suspicious Activity Reporting Initiative, 180
naturalization, 132–36
Naturalization Act 1790, 131
Naturalization Act 1795, 132–33
Naturalization Act 1906, 133
Nebraska Emergency Management Agency, 181
New York Police Department, 67, 226–27n.3
9/11 attacks
　immigration and, 131–32
　National Commission on Terrorist Attacks Upon the United States (9/11 Commission), 180
　response to, 141
　symbolic power of, 24
　USA PATRIOT Act in response to, 145
Oklahoma City bombing (1995), 131–32, 138–39, 222n.6, 223n.1
Orlando nightclub shooting (2016), 127
Page Act 1875, 222n.3
persuasion in, 63–64, 193
political community in
　generally, 127–28

"American identity," 132–36
American Muslims as transnational political community, 181–84
"American values," 128–32
citizenship education, 134–35
"constitutional patriotism," 22, 128–29
immigration and, 130–32
informal political community, 128–32
"multiple traditions," 130
naturalization, 132–36
race and, 130–32
state–citizen relationship, 136–41
tests, 134
violence and, 136–41
Preventing Radicalism by Exploring and Vetting its Emergence as a National Threat (PREVENT) Act 2007 (proposed), 224n.13
race, political community and, 130–32
San Bernardino shooting (2015), 143
Sedition Act 1918, 137, 223n.1
Smith Act 1940, 137, 164, 223n.1
Smith–Mundt Act 1948, 161–62, 163, 198
State Department
　generally, 154–55
　Broadcasting Board of Governors, 161
　Bureau of International Information Programs, 182–83, 228–29n.27
　Bureau of Near Eastern Affairs, 183
　Center for Strategic Counterterrorism Communications, 63–64, 154–55, 163, 185–87
　City Pair Program, 183–84
　countering violent extremism (CVE) and, 182–84
　Counterterrorism Country Reports, 45–46, 210n.1
　denaturalization and, 164
　dissemination of State Department materials, 161–63
　Global Engagement Center (GEC), 63–64, 187
　online CVE and, 185, 186, 187
　Public Affairs Section, 228–29n.27
　Transatlantic Initiative, 183–84
　transnational communities and, 198
Strategic Implementation Plan 2011, 171, 173, 176–77, 179, 180, 182
Strategic Implementation Plan 2016, 173, 175, 177, 179, 184
Supreme Court, judicial intervention by, 138
surveillance, 149–51
Terrorism Information and Protection System (proposed), 223n.2

United States (*cont.*)
   Terrorist Expatriation Act 2011 (proposed), 165, 206–7n.21
   Transport Safety Authority, Secure Flight Program, 188
   USA PATRIOT (Uniting and Strengthening America by Providing Appropriate Tools Required to Intercept and Obstruct Terrorism) Act 2001, 145–51
      generally, 144, 145, 163, 164, 165, 206–7n.21, 224n.7
      detention under, 226n.1
      expanded definition of terrorism under, 139–40, 145–47
      formal political community, boundaries of, 147–51
      material support under, 149
      9/11 attacks, in response to, 145
      non-citizens under, 147–48
      reauthorization of, 224n.9
      resident non-citizens under, 148
      surveillance under, 149–51
   US Information Agency, 154–55
   Violent Radicalization and Homegrown Terrorism Prevention Act 2007 (proposed), 151–58
      generally, 144, 206–7n.21, 225n.18, 225n.20
      civil society opposition, 155–56, 158
      Congressional findings, 155–56
      Congressional hearings, 151–55
      homegrown terrorism defined, 157
      ideologically based violence defined, 157
      violent radicalization defined, 157
Voting Rights Act 1965, 131–32
Walter–McCarran Act 1952, 131, 132–34, 164
"war on terror," 190, 208n.10
West Point Military Academy, 140
White House Task Force on New Americans, 135–36
Workers (Communist) Party, 222n.7
World Trade Center bombing (1993), 138–39
*USS Cole*, 36

Vidino, Lorenzo, 176

Walker, Clive, 86, 94
Walsh, James Igoe, 65–66
"war on terror," 190, 208n.10
Weber, Max, 4–5
Welsh School, 9–10
Wight, Colin, 7–8
Wiktorowicz, Quintan, 17, 33–34, 170
Wilkinson, Paul, 84
Winter, Charlie, 32

Yemen
   foreign fighter attacks and, 41–42
   post-prison release deradicalization in, 212n.18

al-Zarqawi, Abu Musab, 36
al-Zawahiri, Ayman, 31, 34–35, 36, 207n.5, 208n.15
Zedner, Lucia, 216–17n.10
Zolberg, Aristide R., 14–15